COURT ROLLS

OF THE

MANOR OF INGOLDMELLS

c ≠

COURT ROLLS

OF THE

MANOR OF INGOLDMELLS, *Eng.*

[= (Manor)]

IN THE

COUNTY OF LINCOLN

TRANSLATED BY

W. O. MASSINGBERD, M.A.

AUTHOR OF

'A HISTORY OF ORMSBY'

o

Printed by
SPOTTISWOODE & CO. LTD., NEW-STREET SQUARE, LONDON
1902

TO

CHARLES FRANCIS MASSINGBERD-MUNDY

LORD OF THE MANOR
OF
INGOLDMELLS-CUM-ADDLETHORPE

PREFACE

HAVING, through the kindness of the lord of the manor, been afforded the opportunity of transcribing and studying at my leisure the court rolls of a Lincolnshire manor, which form an unusually complete series, and seem to me of special interest, I have thought it worth while to print the results in the interests of county history, and I am even ambitious enough to hope that my abstracts may be found to have a still wider historical value. I am conscious that the rolls deserve to be edited by an expert, but, as that is impossible, I trust that the deficiencies of an editor who has done his best will be pardoned. A somewhat longer Introduction and some more notes might have been given, but I have largely exceeded my space already, and have felt that for historical purposes it was better to curtail my own remarks than to diminish the extracts from the rolls.

I cannot mark out on a map the boundaries of the ancient manor of Ingoldmells, and I should certainly get very wrong if I attempted to mark out the boundaries of the modern manor of Ingoldmells-cum-Addlethorpe. I show in the Introduction that the manor extended over part of six parishes, and for the information of those who do not know the county well I must explain that Ingoldmells and Skegness have a coast-line of some six miles a little to the north of the Wash, a narrow strip of land in Skegness separating Winthorpe from the seashore and causing Ingoldmells and Skegness to adjoin on the sea coast side, though Winthorpe comes up to the Roman Bank. Very possibly this strip was considerably wider before the fifteenth century, when we read of lands being 'inundated by the sea.' Addlethorpe adjoins Ingoldmells on the west, Burgh is further inland, and Partney and Great Steeping are on the extreme west of Candleshoe Wapentake, in what is called the Wold Division. The sand hills, or meales, may still be seen, and it is important for their consolidation and maintenance that the thorns and synes which grow upon them should be preserved. As regards the *synes* Mr. Woodruffe Peacock tells me that there are two species of grasses called by this name— *Ammophila arundinacea*, which is properly called ' synes,' and *Elymus arenarius*. There are ' Syne Hills ' at Huttoft and North Somercotes, and a ' Syne Hill House ' at Skegness.

I know that experts prefer to have the original Latin text rather than a more or less imperfect translation, and I quite acknowledge that they have good reasons for their preference, but to give both text and translation was in this case out of the question. I have given what may be considered by scholars a bald translation, as thus experts will, I hope, be able to judge how the original text runs, and for the same reason I have left some paragraphs as they are, though I know quite well that they are not good English. The 194 rolls, of which I give extracts, were found by Mr. Richard Cheales in Ingoldmells Church in 1684, having, according to a statement of Sir Drayner Massingberd, been kept private in the county by the tenants, and never returned into the Duchy Office, because they show the fines to be uncertain, while the rolls in the Duchy Office mention the fines to be 2s. an acre. The rolls then in the Duchy Office are now at the Public Record Office, and are temp. Henry VII., Henry VIII., and Elizabeth. There are also rolls temp. Elizabeth and James I. at Ormsby Hall, and from the time of the purchase of the manor in 1658 there is an unbroken series of rolls in books.

I had hoped to be able to give in an appendix some rather long extracts from the Ministers' Accounts &c. at the Public Record Office relating to the manor of Ingoldmells, but have been obliged to refrain. These accounts of the rents and issues of the manor make clear the customs of the manor concerning the acquisition of land by villeins, and mark the progress of their prosperity. It seems that the old rent paid by villeins for bond land was 4d. per acre, and that on alienation an additional

rent of 8*d.* per acre became payable, and that a rent of 2*d.* per
acre was paid for free land purchased by villeins besides the
fines on surrender and admittance. They also give us some
insight into the economic history of a Lincolnshire manor. The
process of subinfeudation enabled great barons to keep up great
retinues, and ride out to war at the head of goodly companies
of knights and followers, but little did they foresee the enormous
loss to their successors. What would have been the value of
the estates of the Earls of Lincoln had the Domesday estates of
Ivo Tailboys, Hugh Earl of Chester, and Ilbert de Lacy been
kept in hand, instead of being granted out to tenants to be held
by knight service, one hardly dare think, but happily the
danger to the country of such estates was averted, and we have
only to consider the actual facts as they concern one of the
manors which were kept. In 1086 the annual value of the
manor of Ingoldmells was 10*l.*, an increase of 2*l.* upon the value
temp. Edward the Confessor. In 1295 the rents of the free
and bond tenants were 51*l.* 17*s.* 1*d.*, inclusive of 10*l.* of tallage,
but exclusive of fines, perquisites of courts &c. amounting to
18*l.* 11*s.* 8*d.*, and some small rents for the N. and S. warrens, &c.
In 1347 the same rents were 61*l.* 9*s.* 4*d.*, and in 1421–2 they
were 71*l.* 10*s.* 3*d.* So far the customs of the manor with regard
to the new rents for lands purchased by villeins had provided an
increase of revenue. But in 1485, 2*l.* 7*s.* 4*d.* has to be deducted
for lost rents, chiefly *per fluxum maris*, from a total of 72*l.* 6*s.* 8*d.*,
so that there is a slight decrease, and when the manor was sold
in 1628 by Charles I. the reserved rent, which corresponded to
the sum of the freehold and copyhold rents then payable, was
only 73*l.* 17*s.* 2*d.*, and this was reduced in 1665–6 to 65*l.*,
because part of the land chargeable was 'swallowed up by the
sea.' It is therefore clear that at Ingoldmells the tenants
appropriated virtually the whole of the increase in the value of
the land, and one sees how hopeless in the face of growing
expenses it was for lords of manors to keep up their position
unless they could acquire actual possession of the lands over
which they had the lordship. Thus a struggle went on for
years. Many county families disappeared, others by some means
or other purchased the freehold lands, and by a system of leases

acquired the bond lands of their manors, and so got together the large and compact estates which we now see in these days when a manor without copyhold lands is worth nothing.

One word more. It must not be supposed that the Ingoldmells villein is quite a fair example of the villeins of Lincolnshire. He had had his services commuted at an exceptionably early period, and probably had other advantages over his neighbours. The Court Rolls for the manors of Sutton and Bolingbroke seem to show that the other villeins of the Duchy of Lancaster fared tolerably well, though they owed some labour services, and the survey of the Bishop's manor of Stow in 1283, and early Lincolnshire Inquisitions *post mortem* show no great hardships, but the Chronicle of Peterborough, and Spalding Priory surveys in the Cole MSS. show exactions that were decidedly more onerous, and papers found by Mr. Cole, of Doddington, in the Swinderby parish chest show that the Knights of St. John exacted on the death of their bond tenants at Eagle, N. Scarle, and Swinderby, one-third of their goods, and were entitled to a third of the full price paid for any land sold.

W. O. M.

ORMSBY RECTORY: *August* 1902.

INTRODUCTION

History of the Manor

I BEGIN my short account of the manor of Ingoldmells, or, as it is now called, Ingoldmells-cum-Addlethorpe, by transcribing two entries from Domesday Book, which I translate.

'Land of Robert Le Despenser [Robertus Dispensator].

'Manor. In Herdertorp Wiuelac had 3 carucates of land for geld. There is land for 3 ploughs. There Robert has 3 ploughs in demesne, and 32 sokemen with a moiety of this land and 12 villeins with six ploughs. There are there two churches, and 400 acres of meadow. In King Edward's time it was worth 8*l.*, now it is worth 10*l.* There is soke in Guldelsmere.

'Soke. In Partenai, and Stepinge, and Tric, and Burg there were 2½ carucates of land for geld. There is land for as many ploughs. There 5 sokemen and 2 villeins have half a plough, and 30 acres of meadow.'

I suggest that 'Herdertorp' is the same place as 'Arduluetorp,' later 'Ardelthorp,' *i.e.* Addlethorpe. We find 'Hardelthorp' for Addlethorpe in 1205, and again in the 15th century. I suggest further that Ingoldmells and Addlethorpe are described under this name of 'Herdertorp,' or 'Herdetorp,' in Domesday Book, and that the manor of Ingoldmells-cum-Addlethorpe with its soke is described in the above entries. Mr. Eyton in his Lincolnshire Collections tells [1] us that he has no doubt that Guldelsmere may be safely identified with Ingoldmells, and eventually he came to the conclusion that Robert Le Despenser's manor of Ingoldmells is, as a manor, described under the name of Herdertorp.

[1] Addit. MSS. 31929 and 31930.

A comparison of the Domesday description of the soke with the following entry in Testa de Nevill leaves no doubt in my mind of the identification of Guldelsmere with Ingoldmells.

P. 334, Wapentake of Candleshoe :

'Lady Matilda de Lacy holds in Ingoldemoles, and in Schekenesse, and in Steping, and in Burg, and in Partenay 3 carucates less half a bovate.' Here, three places (Steeping, Burgh and Partney) are certainly the same as in D.B., so that it seems fair to conclude that Tric is the same as Skegness and Guldelsmere as Ingoldmells, and this conclusion is much strengthened by a charter I am able to produce, which accounts for the possession of the manor by the Lacy family.

Duchy of Lancaster, Royal Charters, No. 1 :

'William king of England to Robert bishop of Lincoln, Os[bert] sheriff of Lincoln, and his barons and faithful men, French and English, greeting. Know ye that I grant the exchange which Ur[so] Abet[ot] and Robert de Laceio made of Ingolnesmera and of Witchona. Witnesses : Robert bishop of Lincoln, and R. fitz Hamon, at Brigstock.'

Robert Bloet became bishop of Lincoln in 1093, William Rufus died in 1100, so we may date the charter between those years. And we find that Urso de Abitot, the hereditary sheriff of Worcestershire, had become possessed of the manor of Ingoldmells before that date, and had exchanged it with Robert de Lacy. Now we know that Urso was brother to Robert Le Despenser, and his possession of the manor of Ingoldmells can be accounted for, if we conclude that he was his brother's heir. The Marmions succeeded to the rest of Robert Le Despenser's lands in Lincolnshire, and this charter shows why they did not succeed also to his lands in Candleshoe wapentake.

Robert Le Despenser has been supposed to be the same person as Robert Marmion, the father of Roger Marmion of the Lindsey Survey, but the fact that the Beauchamps obtained the larger share of Robert Le Despenser's [1] possessions in Leicestershire and Worcestershire points rather, as Mr. Round suggests, to descent on the part of both the Beauchamps and Marmions through his brother Urso.

When the Lindsey Survey was taken c. 1115 the Lacy lands, having been forfeited, were in the hands of Hugh de la Val

---

[1] Round, *Feudal England*, p. 176.

[de Vallo], who held 4 carucates and 6 bovates in the wapentake of Candleshoe. As Roger Marmion, the successor of Robert Le Despenser at Scrivelsby and other places, held nothing in this wapentake, we have here a confirmation of the views set forth.

To Hugh de la Val succeeded Guy, his son and heir, who, or another Guy, gave [1] to the priory of Spalding the church of Addlethorpe. A Guy de la Val also presented [2] to the church of Skegness. It seems that on the death of Hugh de la Val the Honor of Pontefract was [3] divided, and so in 1166 we find Guy de la Val holding [4] 20 out of the 60 fees of the Honor. In 1205 Roger de Lacy obtained the whole of the land in England which had been Guy's.[5]

This Roger de Lacy was son and heir of John fitz Eustace, constable of Chester, and grandson of Richard fitz Eustace and of Albreda de Lisours his wife. Albreda's mother was Albreda de Lacy, daughter of Robert, who obtained the manor of Ingoldmells by exchange, and sister of Ilbert de Lacy, who died without issue, and of Henry de Lacy, whose son Robert died without issue in 1194.[6] By an agreement in 1194 [7] between Albreda de Lisours and Roger, constable of Chester, her grandson, Roger obtained the lands which had been Robert de Lacy's, while Albreda retained the lands of Robert de Lisours, her father, for life, with remainder to William, her son by her second husband, the ancestor of the Fitzwilliams of Sprotborough.

It was Roger's widow that held the Ingoldmells property c. 1212.[8] His son and heir, John de Lacy, was among the north-country barons [9] who won the Great Charter from King John. He married Margaret, daughter and heir of Robert de Quincy, by Hawise his wife, fourth sister and coheir of Ranulph Blundeville, earl of Chester and Lincoln, and was created earl of Lincoln 23 November, 1232, with remainder to the heirs of his body by Margaret his wife. John de Lacy died in 1240, and his widow married as her second husband, about 6 January, 1243, Walter Marshall,[10] 5th earl of Pembroke, who held the Ingoldmells property in her right.

[1] Cole MS. xliii. f. 425.
[2] Pontefract Chartulary, p. xix.
[3] Cal. to Royal Grants.
[7] Leycester, *Hist. Antiquities*, p. 267.
[9] Stubbs, *Constit. Hist.* i. 580.
[3] Abbrev. Plac. p. 85.
[4] Liber Niger.
[6] Pontefract Chartulary.
[5] Testa de Nevill, pp. 334, 348.
[10] He died 24 Nov. 1245.

Testa de Nevill, p. 329:

'Walter Marescall holds the vill of Ingoldemol, Partenay, Burg, Steping, Skeggnes of the king in chief, of the honor of Pumfrey.'

Edmund de Lacy, son of John and Margaret, married Alesia daughter of the marquis of Saluzzo, but died in 1258[1] before his mother. His son and heir, Henry de Lacy, earl of Lincoln, was lord of Ingoldmells when the earliest court rolls we have were written, and had been[2] found to have free warren in Ingoldmells on his own lands and other people's twenty years in 1276.

Henry de Lacy, 'the closest counsellor of Edward I,'[3] took an eminent part in the affairs of the kingdom during the earlier years of the reign of Edward II. He married Margaret, daughter and coheir of William de Longespee. Their son, Edmund, was drowned in a well in Denbigh Castle in the lifetime of his father, and their daughter Alice became their heir. The earl in 1292 granted[4] his honor of Pontefract, with the manors &c. belonging thereto, to the king, but eventually an entail was made, whereby after the death of Henry and Margaret his wife all their castles, manors &c., including Ingoldmells, were settled on Thomas Plantagenet, earl of Lancaster, and Alice his wife, daughter of the earl of Lincoln, and the heirs of their bodies, with remainder to the heirs of Thomas.

Henry de Lacy died at his mansion house, called Lincoln's Inn, 5 Feb. 1311, whereupon Thomas, earl of Lancaster, and Alice his wife became possessed of the manor of Ingoldmells. It is stated on the rolls[5] that the earl of Lancaster held the manor for life only, and after his death in 16 Edward II we find Ebulo le Strange in possession of the manor in right of Alice his wife.

Alice, countess of Lincoln, died without issue in 1348, when under the above-mentioned entail Henry, earl of Derby and Lancaster, became her heir. It was found by an inquisition taken[6] at Bolingbrok, 15 October A.D. 1348, that Alice held the manor of Ingoldmells, with appurtenances, to herself and

---

[1] 14th Report of Hist. MSS. Commission, p. 207.
[2] Rot. Hund.   [3] *Constit. Hist.* ii. 333.
[4] Cal. of Patent Rolls, 1281-92, p. 511. Ayloffe's Cal., Duchy of Lancaster, vol. i.   [5] P. 94.
[6] Chancery Inq. p.m. 22 Edw. III. 1st nr. no. 34.

Thomas earl of Lancaster, formerly her husband, and the heirs of their bodies, with remainder to the right heirs of Thomas, and that the said manor after the death of Alice belongs to Henry earl of Lancaster, kinsman and heir of the same Thomas formerly earl of Lancaster. It is said in another part of the inquisition that Thomas and Alice died without heirs of their bodies, and that Thomas's brother Henry had a son Henry, who is his heir.

This Henry, earl of Derby and Lancaster, was created earl of Lincoln in 1349, and duke of Lancaster in 1351. He died in 1360, leaving two daughters his heirs, Matilda, who married twice but died without issue, and Blanche, who married John of Gaunt, fourth son of Edward III.

John of Gaunt is mentioned on the rolls as lord of the manor of Ingoldmells in 38 Edward III, and, as is well known, had by Blanche, his wife, an only son, afterwards King Henry IV. On John's death in 1399, Henry of Bolingbroke, his son, obtained his great inheritance, and it became merged in the crown, so that 5 Nov. 1 Henry IV the court held at Ingoldmells is that of 'Henry King of England.'

The manor of Ingoldmells continued to be crown property until ' on or about the 9th day of Sept. 4 Car. I,' when the king [1] sold it by letters patent under the great seal of England and duchy seal to Edward Ditchfield, citizen and salter of London, John Heighlord, citizen and skinner of London, Humphrey Clarke, citizen and dyer of London, and Francis Moss, citizen and scrivener of London, and to their heirs, trustees for the mayor, aldermen, and commoners of the City of London, who in pursuance of several acts of Common Council did grant and convey the said manor to John Stone, Nathaniel Manton, Methuselah Turnor, their heirs and assigns, who by their indenture, enrolled in the Court of Chancery 23 Feb. 1657, being authorised by divers acts of the Common Council made by the mayor, aldermen, and commoners of the City of London, sold the manor to Francis Purley of the Inner Temple, London, gent, he being trustee for Sir Drayner Massingberd, knt, to whom in performance of his trust he did grant and release it 26 April 1658.

Sir Drayner Massingberd's [2] great-grandson, Charles Burrell

---

[1] Bill, Massingberd v. Newcomen, 12 June, 1706, at Ormsby Hall.

[2] See *Hist. of Ormsby* for descent.

Massingberd esq^r, died without male issue in 1835, leaving an
only daughter and heiress, Harriet, wife to Charles Godfrey
Mundy esq^r, whose grandson, Charles Francis Massingberd
Mundy esq^r, is now lord of the manor of Ingoldmells-cum-
Addlethorpe.

The jurisdiction of the manor extended over part of six
parishes, but not over the whole of any of them. Its jurisdiction over the greater part of Ingoldmells and Addlethorpe will
not be denied, though it is curious that Addlethorpe is seldom
mentioned by name on the earlier court rolls. Until the reign
of Queen Elizabeth, the manor is called the manor of Ingoldmells,
and Addlethorpe church is called the West Church of Ingoldmells, or the church of S. Nicholas, while in the Bishops'
Institutions we read of the church of ' Ardelthorp in Ingoldmels '
A.D. 1491, and of ' Ardelthorp alias Westingolmells ' A.D. 1555.
It is clear also that the jurisdiction of the manor extended over
the greater part of Skegness. Courts were often held there,
free and bond lands there held under the manor are frequently
mentioned, the township of Skegness sometimes presented
offences, as well as the township of Ingoldmells, and the banks
and dikes of Skegness were under the jurisdiction of the court
as well as the port and the seashore. I cannot find any mention
of a separate manor of Skegness, except a small one[1] belonging
to the dean and chapter of Lincoln, though some land there was
held of the manor of Croft.

The court rolls show that the jurisdiction of the manor
extended over part of Burgh. The courts were sometimes held
there, there were several freehold and some bond tenants holding
lands there, and the common of Skalflete in Burgh was under
the jurisdiction of the manor of Ingoldmells, and trespasses
there were presented and amerced in the court.

The part of Great Steeping under the jurisdiction of the
manor of Ingoldmells must have been small, but the only case
of hanging mentioned on the rolls was that of two Steeping
women for housebreaking at Steeping : and some freehold lands
at Steeping are mentioned.

The small part of Partney under the jurisdiction of the
manor of Ingoldmells is never mentioned on the rolls, but

---

[1] Escheator's Inq^r, series II. file 556.

I find [1] that the lands there were in the possession of Lord John Bek at a rent of 32^d per annum, and that the earl of Lincoln granted this rent to him before A.D. 1295.

The Manorial Court.

It is with much diffidence that I venture to write anything on this difficult subject, and yet it seems well that I should point out a few facts, referring, however, my readers to such works as Professor Maitland's Introduction to ' Select Pleas in Manorial Courts,' and Professor Vinogradoff's ' Villainage in England ' for more general information.

It may be asked, ' who attended and formed the Court of Ingoldmells? ' I answer, the suitors—the tenants who owed suit. These were both freemen and villeins. The villeins were in the earliest times obliged to attend personally, and were not ' essoined ' or excused.[2] The freemen were at first the freeholders, who for the most part owed suit from three weeks to three weeks, though some may only have owed it twice a year and when specially summoned, but later there were freemen who held customary lands for which they owed suit. The freemen could be essoined, and frequently paid a small fine to be excused suit for a year, a practice which villeins were allowed to adopt also later. The list of fines for respite of suit of court 10 Henry V shows 80 tenants who paid, from which I infer that there were over 100 tenants of the manor, for there were 24 tenants on the two inquisitions, and others must have attended the court for various reasons. I am inclined to think that the free and bond tenants were about equal in number, but in consequence of the rule that no villeins were to be essoined the court, except on special occasions when all tenants were summoned, would be composed of more villeins than freemen. On the other hand the list of tenants sworn on the inquisition 4 Edw. III shows more freemen than villeins. A good way to get an idea of the business done in the manorial court will be to turn to the proceedings of three or four courts at different periods, and see what went on. For example we might take [3]

[1] Duchy of Lancaster, Ministers' Accounts, Bundle 1, no. 1, 23 & 24 Edw. I.
[2] P. 2.   [3] E.g. pp. 22, 54, 216 and 289.

a court temp. Edward I, another temp. Edward II, a third temp. Henry IV, and then lastly a fourth temp. Elizabeth.

It will be found that on the earlier rolls pleas of debt and agreement, conveyancing entries, and police cases, all appear together in such a manner as to lead to the inference that the later legal distinctions between the various courts were then disregarded in practice. And the villeins appear in the same court with the freemen, serve[1] on the same juries, join in the same[2] presentments, and form with the freemen the court which finds the judgments. And so the important question is—' What were the powers of the court of Ingoldmells?' The lord of Ingoldmells certainly had a view of frank pledge, and the right of gallows, he had the assize of bread, and of ale, he had rights of wreck and of taking royal fish[3] at Ingoldmells and Skegness, he had rights of warren and of taking waifs and estrays, besides the ordinary jurisdiction over his free and bond tenants which belonged to every lord of a manor. And his tenants had certain immunities[4] from paying toll, and being summoned to other courts.

As regards the business, at first the largest part of the rolls is taken up with pleas of debt and trespass, but as time goes on the conveyancing entries fill more and more space, and at the view of frank pledge held twice a year the presentments occupy considerable space also. These presentments were made at first by the townships, and sometimes Ingoldmells, Skegness and Burgh presented separately.

In 13 Edw. II[5] 12 jurors presented, and so at times until the end of the reign of Edw. III, though still the townships sometimes presented. In the reign of Rich. II two juries appear to present at the views, one of freemen and the other of villeins, but in the other courts the elected presenters of the manor present. There could have been no serious difficulty here in finding sufficient freemen to present, and serve on the inquisitions, and in the fifteenth century the second jury presented certain offences and the first jury affirmed that what they said was true, but I cannot show that the system of double presentment, and another jury says whether he is guilty or no, went on at Ingoldmells.

The presenters present those who are guilty of any offence or misdemeanour, who transgress the customs and regulations of the manor, who entertain strangers contrary to the earl's peace, who carry off wreck, who break the assizes of bread and ale, who obstruct a drain, injure the highway, or trespass in the warren, and the offender is amerced, or otherwise punished according to the nature of his offence. They also present that a free tenant owes fealty or other services, and that a villein is dead, and his heirs owe a fine for entry, or that he has acquired free land and owes a new rent, or that he has left the manor without licence, or that his daughter has been guilty of immorality. It is not told us who imposes the penalty in these cases, but such an entry as that in 9 Edw. II,[1] which tells of a fine for merchet, 'if the steward will accept this,' does not favour the view that penalties were imposed at the will of the steward, for there could not be any doubt about his acceptance of a fine he had imposed himself.

The proceedings[2] in the cases of felony recorded on these rolls show the prosecutors 'appealing' the felons, who had the right to choose between trial by the court or before the king's judges. If they put themselves on the court it is the court that finds them guilty, or not guilty, and, if found guilty, they may 'therefore be hanged.' But[3] legislation during Edw. III's reign provided that justices of the peace should hear and determine all manner of felonies, and we find no such cases tried in the manor court of Ingoldmells after that time. In civil cases the defendant might put himself upon 'the country,' or 'wage his law.' As a rule he put himself upon the country, whereupon the bailiff was ordered to summon an inquisition, which decided not only questions of fact but points of customary law, and lastly the court[4] found the judgment. If the defendant elected to wage his law, he must do so with care and nicety, or he will 'fail in his law.' There is an interesting instance of successful waging of the law in 7 Henry V,[5] when the prior of Bullington appeared with 12 compurgators in the court, composed as it was of freemen and villeins, and said that he owed nothing to the

---

[1] P. 50.   [2] P. 55.   [3] Statutes of the Realm, i. 301, 364.
[4] Pp. 238, 254 and 256.   [5] P. 238.

a

plaintiff, and was allowed to go away quit, and the plaintiff was
in mercy for an unjust claim. Sometimes substantial debts
were recovered, and the limit of 40ˢ evaded. In 7 Henry IV
a plaintiff[1] recovered 39ˢ in each of 5 pleas of debt, and 18ˢ 4ᵈ
in a 6ᵗʰ plea, or 10ˡ 13ˢ 4ᵈ in all, besides damages. In 2
Henry VI 42ˢ[2] were recovered in a plea of debt, and in
19 Edw. III 105ˢ.[3]

Several entries show the steward exercising considerable
influence and control. The court was sometimes held[4] before
him, though even then the township presented what the custom
of the manor was. We find cases postponed for the coming of
the steward, and others presented for the common council. In
7 Edw. II a woman was[5] put in the pillory by the consideration
of the steward. Sometimes he condones a fine. Occasionally
tenants complained to the lord for lack of justice, and the
steward was directed to administer to the parties such justice
that they have no reasonable cause to complain.[6]

It is, of course, well known that the surrenders and admit-
tances of customary tenants were recorded on manorial court
rolls. On the earlier rolls such entries are comparatively few,
the object of recording the proceedings of the courts not being
to afford the villein written evidence of his title to the land he
occupied, but to serve as a check on the manorial officers, and
show what the amercements, fines, and profits of the manor
were.[7] As time goes on we find these entries increasing in
number and importance, a tenant pays a small fine to be allowed
to search the rolls for evidence of his title, later he calls the
rolls to 'warrant' it, and temp. Edw. IV[8] judges begin to give
copyholders some protection in the king's courts, and the conveyancing entries come to take up half the roll, and eventually in the seventeenth century hardly any other entries appear.

I must not omit to mention that the court of Ingoldmells
was the court of a considerable fief. The lord might, perhaps,
have summoned his Lincolnshire tenants to the court of his
honor at Pontefract, but this would have been most inconvenient
to them, and have caused much discontent, and so he summoned
them to his principal manor in the county of Lincoln; even so
they often made default, but eventually seem to have fallen into

[1] Pp. 213 and 214.   [2] P. 258.   [3] P. 119.
[4] P. 69.   [5] P. 32.   [6] P. 275.
[7] Selden Society, vol. II. xiv.   [8] The date is now said to be doubtful.

the custom of paying a fine for respite of their suit of court for a year, though in 2 Henry VI John Harpyswelle of Toft Newton actually served on the inquisition of freemen.

The officers of the manor besides the steward were :

The grave, or reeve, who was elected by the whole homage, *i.e.* by the villeins, and sworn to serve the lord faithfully.   He had to render a strict account of the receipts from fines, amercements &c.

The graves of the sea dikes, or banks, at Ingoldmells and Skegness, whose duty[1] it was to see that all defects were repaired, and to distrain those who did not repair the portion for which they were answerable, the township deciding what was necessary.

The bailiff, who summoned tenants to come to the courts, and to serve on the inquisitions, and levied distraints &c.   To threaten or beat the bailiff, or make a rescue against him, was a serious offence.

The foreign bailiff, who summoned the foreign or outside tenants, and, I suppose, levied the distraints made upon them, but was not always willing to perform his office.[2]

The constables, the wardens and tasters of ale, and the clerk of the courts.   An 'officer of the court' is also mentioned, 1 Henry VI, as condoning certain damages.   A grave of the meadows is mentioned on the earliest roll.

Some of the dues paid for ships may be explained by a lease,[2] 11 July 1511, to Thomas Totoft of 'the herbage of the meles in Skegnes, with the profits of the warren of rabbits there, and with the spreading of nets to dry upon the soil of the lord the king there, and the custom of ships called Leyre, that is to say for a ship laden with herrings, 100 herrings or the price, for every strange ship carrying its nets upon the soil of the lord the king there to dry as often as it shall ground four-pence for custom.'

The Freeholder

There were, in 1086, 37 sokemen at Ingoldmells, including the soke, as compared with 14 villeins.   In later times the numbers of both increased.   We may divide the free tenants into two classes: (1) those who held lands in Ingoldmells

---

[1] P. 291, 'banks of the sea called ": seadyks,"' p. 220.   [2] P. 106.
[2] Duchy of Lancaster, class xi. vol. 30, f. 7, see p. 150.

or the soke; (2) those who held lands outside, but owed suit at the court.

I. The lords of the manor of South Hiltoft held an independent manor, but still were not included amongst the 'foreign' tenants, as S. Hiltoft was in Ingoldmells. On the earliest roll appears the name of Sir Thomas de Burnham, knight, who held this manor probably in right of Philippa his wife, who seems to have been the same person as Philippa de Hiltoft who presented to the church of Ingoldmells in 1273. Robert de Hiltoft had presented to this church in 1227, and Sir William de Hiltoft presented in 1324, whose daughter and heiress Alice married Sir William de Skipwith, and thus the Skipwiths[1] acquired the manor of Hiltoft. From the Skipwiths it passed to the Balletts, and in 38 Elizabeth 'John Ballett died seised of the manor of South Hiltoft freely held of this manor by the rent of 39^s 8^d yearly, and common suit of court, and Nicholas Ballett is his kinsman and next heir.'[2]

The Gipthorps certainly held lands of the lord of Ingoldmells in Skegness, and probably also in Ingoldmells. Sir Peter de Gipthorp, knight, died seised[3] in 1334 of the manor of Wolmersty in Wrangle, Alexander being his son and heir. In 1369 Robert, son of Peter de Gipthorp, chivaler, secured by a fine[4] lands in Burgh, Ingoldmells and Winthorpe, after his death to Peter, son of Alexander de Gipthorp, knight, and Agnes his wife, and the heirs male of their bodies. But before this in 1346[5] William, son of Sir Alexander de Gipthorp, had succeeded to lands in Skegness, which had belonged to Simon de Thorp, whose daughter he had married. To one branch of the Gipthorps William Manby esq^r succeeded as tenant before 9 Elizabeth, having married Alice, daughter and coheir of Thomas Gipthorp. It seems probable that Alice was sister to William son of Thomas Gipthorp, who died[6] in 1506, leaving a son William, who seems to have died without issue. Sir John Babington, who was tenant in 1492, and Lord Sheffield, who was tenant in 1567, held lands which had been William Gipthorp's.[7]

The Lords de Willoughby succeeded to the Bek lands in

---

[1] See *History of Ormsby*.   [2] Ingoldmells Court Rolls.
[3] Chancery Inq. p. m. 8 Edw. III. 1st n^{rs}. no. 36.
[4] Feet of Fines, Lincoln, 43 Edw. III.   [5] P. 129.
[6] Chancery Inq. p. m. 22 Henry VII. no. 165.

INTRODUCTION xxi

Partney, and also to some lands in Great Steeping, which had long been held by a family of the name of Steping. But part of the lands which had been Robert de Steping's were acquired[1] by John son of Simon son of Petronilla de Halton, to whom succeeded Sir John de Cokrington, chivaler. In 1473 the Lord de Kyme was in possession of lands which had been Gilbert de Cokeryngton's, and later we find the names of Robert Umframvile and Robert Tailboys, knights, amongst the tenants. A family of the name of Kelsey also held lands in Great Steeping, who were succeeded[2] in the fifteenth century by Thomas Ruston. In 1506–7 John More[3] sold the manor of Kelsey Hall and lands in Great Steeping to Sir John Hussey, knight. Edward Wythypoll died in 1582[4] seised of the manor of Kelsey Hall, Paul, son of Paul, his eldest son, being his heir. Mr. Maddison of Partney now owns this manor, which was bought by Sir Ralph Maddison of Sir Francis Williamson.

The following freeholders were summoned to serve on two inquisitions in 1330: William de Waycroft, Robert de Westmels, Robert de Steping, William son of Richard de Hilletoft, William Cadihorn, Robert de Caleflete, and William Marays. Here we have the names of families which held free lands under the manor of Ingoldmells, and, frequently appearing in the courts, must have materially influenced the proceedings.

The absence of any survey of the manor makes it difficult to define the social position of the different freeholders. But I have no doubt that there were several small proprietors whose condition was very little superior to that of some of the villeins. I will name only one family as typical of the rest, that of Akewra. John de Akewra paid relief in 13 Edw. II for tenements in Ingoldmells which had been his father's. In 24 Edw. III John son of Simon de Akewra, a freeman, married a woman who had to pay merchet.[5] In 25 Edw. III John son of Robert de Akewra of Ingoldmells gave 6^d yearly to be in the protection of the lord like a bond tenant.[6]

II. I now come to the 'foreign' tenants, several of whom held lands at a considerable distance from Ingoldmells, and were lords of manors themselves.

In 1086[7] Ilbert de Lacy held only two manors in Lincoln-

[1] P. 105.　[2] Exchequer Q.R. Misc. Bk. vol. iv.　[3] Close Roll.
[4] Chancery Inq. p. m. 24 Eliz. no. 78.　[5] P. 135.
[6] P. 138.　[7] Domesday Book.

shire in chief, but he also held lands of considerable extent under the Bishop of Baieux, which were held [1] in chief c. 1115. Although I cannot give exact dates I can trace an outline of the process of subinfeudation, whereby before the end of the twelfth century more than ten knights' fees were parcelled out. Circa 1115 Hugh de la Val, who held the lands which had been Ilbert de Lacy's, and Robert's, his son, held more than 35 carucates of land in Lindsey. Some of these lands had already been sublet. William son of Haco held of him 1 c. 4 b. in Clee and Thrunscoe [Cle and Tirnesco], Richard son of Losward 6 b. in Toft Newton [Newetuna], and Richard, son of Osbert the sheriff, 1 c. in Elsham [Helesham], while he himself sublet [2] to Costa de Widcala 3 c. 7½ b. in Withcall [Widcala]. And William de Freston held in Cockerington 3 c. ⅜ b. of the same Hugh. In 1166 Jordan Foliot [3] held 3 fees of Guy de la Val, probably in Firsby near Lincoln and Hackthorn, and Richard de Dunham held also of the same Guy, probably the 3rd part of 1 fee in Dunholme. The 4th part of 1 fee in Cleatham had been sublet before the death of Roger de Lacy, having been held [4] of him by Richard de Prestun, as also had been the 4th part of 1 fee in Northorpe, which was held of him by Ralph Bardolf.

I will now give a few short notes concerning the tenants of the fees.

Clee and Itterby, ½ fee. Thomas [5] son of William de Saleby succeeded William son of Haco, and his daughter and heir married, first, Norman de Camera, and, secondly, Brian de Insula. William de Hardredeshull held [6] this half fee c. 1243. The name of his grandson, another William, appears on the earliest court roll. The manor of Clee and Itterby, held of the Duchy of Lancaster by the service of half a knight's fee, formerly of William de Hardredhull, and late of Brian Curteys, was purchased before 1575 by Robert Halton esq[r] of Thomas son and heir of Anthony Curteys.[7]

---

[1] Lindsey Survey.   [2] Testa de Nevill, p. 339.
[3] Liber Niger.   [4] Testa de Nevill, p. 345.
[5] A charter of Thomas, son of William, son of Haco de Salebi, is in the Cathedral Register, no. 890.
[6] Testa de Nevill, p. 317. In 1199 William de Aldredesull gave the king 500 marks for having judgment of the court of the king of the inheritance which he claims against the daughter of Thomas de Saleby, and for having an inquisition

Withcall, 1⅜ fees. Costa or Costentinus de Withcale was succeeded by his son Ranulph, who had 3 sons, William, Henry and Simon.[1] Henry son of William held[2] these fees c. 1243. The Lords de Cantilupe are the earliest tenants of these fees mentioned on the court rolls. To them succeeded the Lords de la Zouch, of whom Eudo had[3] married Milicent, daughter of William, and sister and coheir of George de Cantilupe. In 1376 Ralph de Daubenay is mentioned as tenant. I suppose he and others held lands in Withcall which were of the Cantilupe fee, for in 1428[4] the Lord de la Souch, Patrick Skypwith, John Legburn, clerk, William Daubenay and the abbot of Kirkstead held severally 1 fee in Withkall, formerly John Daubenay's, of the fee of Cantilupe. In 1575[5] two manors at Withcall, formerly of William de Cantilupe and Ralph de Newton, late belonging to the College of Tattershall, and now to Henry Sidney, knight, were held of the Duchy of Lancaster.

Ashby cum Fenby, Hole, Itterby and Brigsley, 1 fee.

A.D. 1210–12 John de Lasceles[6] held 1 fee in Askeby, Brigelega, Wathe, Ravendale, Ellesham, Iterby, Hol, of the Honor of Lascy. In 1301 Philip Fraunke, son and heir of Dominus William Fraunke, was distrained for the relief of one knight's fee. The will of William Fraunk, knight,[7] was proved 5 Jan. 1346, and mentions Alan his son. In 1427–8 William Fraunk, chivaler,[8] held half a fee in Briggele and Wathe, and half a fee in Clee and Utterby, which had been Alan Fraunk's. In 1493 Lady Elizabeth Tunstall, widow, daughter and heir of Sir William Fraunk, knight, and Thomas Tunstall, her son and heir,[9] manumitted by deed Robert Abbot of Itterby in the parish of Clee. Thomas Tunstall died[10] 7 May 1493, and his sister and heir, Elenor or Ellen, married John Ascough. In 1547 Richard Ascough, gent., and others were plaintiffs, and John Ascough, esqr, and others deforciants of the manor of Ashby cum Fenby.[11] Later, Sir Christopher Wray, knight, Chief

[1] Cathedral Charters. [2] Testa de Nevill, p. 305.
[3] Chancery Inq. p. m. 1 Edw. I. no. 16.
[4] Exchequer Q.R. Misc. Bk. vol. iv.
[5] Duchy of Lancaster Records, Bundle P. no. 29.
[6] Liber Ruber, i. 518. [7] Test. Ebor. i. 30.
[8] Lay Subsidy Roll, 138/187. [9] Hist. Com. 14th Report, Grimsby MSS.
[10] Church Notes by G. Holles.
[11] Feet of Fines, Lincoln, Mich. 1 Edw. VI.

Justice of England, was [1] seised of the manor of Ashby and lands in Ashby and Fenby, to the use of himself and Anne his wife for life, remainder to William Wray and Lucy his wife and the heirs of their bodies.

Firsby, Ingham, Hackthorn and Saxby, 2¼ fees.

Jordan Foliot gave to the Templars the church of Firsby before 1185. Jordan Foliot held [2] of the Honor of Lascy 3 knights' fees in Friseby, Aketone, Streton and Yngeham, A.D. 1210–12. Roger de Lacy, who died in 1211, held [3] 1 fee in Friseby and Haketorn of the king in chief, Jordan Foliot held it of him. Robert de Tateshale held 1 fee of the king, Jordan Foliot held it of him. In 1236 Jordan Foliot [4] acknowledged the advowson of the church of Saxeby to be the right of the prior of S. Katherine and his church, as that which he has of the gift of William Foliot, uncle of the said Jordan. Richard son of Jordan Foliot gave [5] to Barlinges land in Risom, and in 1251 Richard quitclaimed to the abbot the manor of Risom. In 1275 [6] Richard Foliot had warren in Friseby. In 13 Edw. II Robert Foliot had [7] not done homage. In 41 Edw. III Michael de la Pole had the tenements of Robert Foliot. In 1401–2 William Tynton had [8] the 2¼ fees, formerly Michael de la Pole's.

Elsham and Ravendale, 1 fee. In 1166 [9] Simon de Lacelles held 2 fees of Guy de la Val. William de Lascelles held in Elsham [10] the third part of one fee of the Constable of Chester, c. 1243. In 1401–2 the abbot of Thornton [8] held 1 fee in Elsham and Ravendale.

Cockerington, 2 fees. Hugh de la Val [11] held 3 c. in Cocrington of the king and two parts of 1 b., in Alvingham 3½ b., in Somercotes 1½ b., and in Salfleteby 3 b., and William de Freston held them of Hugh by the service of 2 knights, and the heirs of the said William still hold. A William de Fristona is mentioned in the Pontefract Chartulary, his father was Robert son of Gerbodo, his son Bertram died in his life time, and his [William's] daughter Alice was his heir. In 1210–12 Guy de Olebec [2] held 2 fees in Cockerington ...

1295 it was found [1] that Alice de Vavasor, deceased, held certain lands in Cockerington of Henry de Lascy, earl of Lincoln, and William Vavasor is her son and heir. In 1342 Henry le Vavasour [2] granted his manor of Cockerington to feoffees, who were sworn to assign it to the abbot and convent of Louth Park. His wife, Constance, afterwards said that he was not of sound mind, and I suggest that a compromise was made, for we find the Vavasours in possession of the manor, and the abbot in possession of certain lands there. In 1401-2 Henry Vavasour and the abbot held the 2 fees. In 1427-8 Henry Vavasor held [3] in Cockeryngton and Salfletby two fees, formerly Henry Vavasor's, whereof the abbot of Louth Park held in alms ¼ f., and the prior of Alvingham, the heirs of John Goderde, the abbot of Louth Park and others held between them ½ f. of the said 2 fees.

Henry Vavasour was seised [4] of the manor of Cockryngton, and 31 July 1510 he enfeoffed certain feoffees for the use and performance of certain articles of agreement upon the marriage of John, his son and heir apparent, and Anne, now John's wife, and sister of Henry Lord le Scrop of Bolton. Henry died 31 October 1515, and John Vavasour esq[r] is his son and heir, and 21 and more. The manor is held of the king as of his honor of Bolingbroke. In 1565-6 Sir William Vavasour, knight, and John Vavasour, his son,[5] sold the manor of Cockerington to Ralph Scrope esq[r]. In 1575 the manor [6] formerly of William Vavasor, knt., and now of Adrian Scroope, held of the Queen as of her Duchy of Lancaster by the service of 2 knights, was in the Queen's hand because of Adrian's minority. Certain lands there formerly belonging to the abbot of Louth Park were held of the duchy, and came into the hands of the late King Henry VIII by reason of the dissolution of the abbey.

Dunholme, ⅓ fee. Roger de Lacy, who died in 1211, held the 4th part of a fee [7] in Dunham, and Nicholas de Aula held it

[1] Lansdowne MS. 207, C. p. 629.
[2] Chronicle of Louth Park Abbey, p. 59.
[3] Exchequer Q.R. Misc. Bk. vol. iv.
[4] Chancery Inq. p. m. 8 Henry VIII. no. 113.
[5] Notes on Visitation of 1634, p. 105. There is an excellent account here by Mrs. Tempest of the Scropes of Cockerington.
[6] Duchy of Lancaster Records, Class xxv. Bundle P. no. 29.
[7] Testa de Nevill, p. 345.

of him. In 1341 the abbot of Kirkstead was a tenant in Dunham, and in 1401–2 the abbot held $\frac{1}{3}$ f. there. A family of the name of Dunham are also mentioned as tenants, and seem to have been succeeded c. 1374 by Robert Gaskryk.

Sturton, and Ingleby-by-Stow, $\frac{1}{2}$ fee. Thomas de Moulton of Frampton held lands at Stretton in 1340. This half fee paid nothing in 1401–2, because John son and heir of Thomas Graye was a minor, and his lands were in the hands of the executors of the lord John, late duke of Lancaster. Matilda, daughter and heir of John de Multon, of Frampton, had married Thomas Gray.[1]

Northorpe, $\frac{1}{4}$ fee. In 1302 John de Hale[2] held the $\frac{1}{4}$ f. in Northorp which Simon de Hale formerly held. Nicholas de Hale was the tenant 4 Edward III, and members of his family until 50 Edward III. In 1401–2 the $\frac{1}{3}$ f. in Northorp, late Nicholas Hale's, paid nothing, because of the minority of Lewis son and heir of Edmund Cornewayle. Lewis Cornwaill being seised[3] of the manors of Thunnak and Laghton, and of lands in Upton, Northorp &c., granted them, 6 May 1405, to feoffees, by the name of Lewis Cornwayle, son and heir of Peter Cornwayle. In 1420–1 Edmund was son and heir of Lewis, and of the age of ten years and more.

Cleatham. $\frac{1}{4}$ fee. In 1303[4] the heir of William Cobbe, who held $\frac{1}{4}$ f. in Cletham, was under age, so his tenements were seized into the hands of the lord. John Cobbe was tenant before 1351, in 1376 William Vaus, and in 1401–2 John Gray.

Toft Newton, $\frac{1}{4}$ fee. In 1210–12 John de Neville held half a knight's fee in Newetone and Sichesle of the honor of Lascy. In 1319–20 Robert, son of Herbert de Saltfletby, did homage for lands in Newton by Toft. In 1422 John Harpyswell was the tenant of lands in Toftnewton, late Robert de Saltfletby's.

The Villein.

The researches of Professors Maitland and Vinogradoff have made it clear that the hardness and harshness of legal theory concerning the villein were mitigated in some places by the

[1] See *Ancestor*, July 1902, for the descent.

[2] Lay Subsidy Roll, Lincoln, $\frac{13.5}{}$.

[3] Chancery Inq. p. m. 8 Henry V. no. 76. It will be seen the documents do not agree as to the name of the father of Lewis. De Banco Roll 579, m. 178 d., calls him 'kinsman and heir of Edmund de Cornevaill.'

[4] P. 23.

'custom of the manor,' and it seems to me reasonable to expect that where, as in Lincolnshire, there were, as far as is known, no *servi* towards whose condition he could be depressed, and many free sokemen, attending the same manor courts, serving on the same inquisitions, and sometimes connected [1] by marriage, and not the least likely to acquiesce in unjust or high-handed proceedings, the villein would be able to preserve some of his ancient freedom. And I cannot but think that the sturdy independence of the Lincolnshire man must also be taken into consideration, and that we can see traces thereof in the bold and on the whole successful assertion of his rights by the Ingoldmells villein. The fact that his lord lived at a distance may also have been in his favour, as it prevented any personal interference with his ancient liberties, and made the lord content with money rents instead of labour services under servile conditions. But the best way to give a fair and impartial account of the condition and status of the Ingoldmells villein will, I think, be to set out his disabilities and advantages.

1. His disabilities were the well-known ones. First I must place his disability to bring an action against his lord in the king's courts. An appeal to these courts by a villein who had been wronged by his lord was of no avail, for they will not [2] interfere between the lord and his villein. It is easy to see how liable to oppression by a bad, unjust, or grasping lord this rule of law rendered the villein, though there were some exceptions to the rule, for a villein may not be slain or maimed at pleasure, and the lord may not seize his wainage. Still in ordinary daily life under a decent lord the villein might live on, as he seems to have done at Ingoldmells, without experiencing any grievous wrong through this want of protection by the king's courts. Secondly I must put the exaction of merchet, a fine the villein had to pay for marrying his daughter. This might in some forms, and on some manors, be a most odious tax. But at Ingoldmells as a rule the payment was not large, and does not seem to have had anything degrading about it

lordship nor take orders without the licence of the court, and his goods and chattels were in strict law considered the property of his lord. But the Ingoldmells villein who held land seems to have had no desire to leave it, and the landless man appears to have gone away[1] to get work, paying a small sum of money (chevagium) as an acknowledgement of the lord's hold over him. And the fact that, during the time the rolls cover, there was no demesne farm at Ingoldmells must have made the villein more free to work where he liked, because the lord did not himself require his labour. The villein who took orders and thereby became free was particularly difficult to deal with. The court might, and did,[2] amerce him heavily, but to obtain the fine was quite another matter. And, as regards the personal goods of the villein, neither the court rolls nor the ministers' accounts lead me to suppose that the lord insisted, as a rule, upon his strict legal rights, so as to seize upon his villein's goods either during his life or at his death.

2. I now come to the advantages of the Ingoldmells villein. He had a house and small farm on a tenure that seems to me surprisingly good and secure. As early as 1291 he held his land by a settled money rent, which, however, could be increased by 8*d.* an acre according to the custom of the manor upon alienation. He held at first 'to him and to his boys.' In 19 Edw. III the form is 'to him and to his heirs for ever,' which seems to bring the lord into danger of losing his villein, so the words 'according to the custom of the manor' are added, and a little later 'in bondage.' We find him claiming bond land as 'his inheritance,' and settling it upon his wife and children. A widow could claim her dower, a third part of her deceased husband's lands for life. A widower held his deceased wife's lands for life by the 'curtesy of England.' A villein could sell or purchase bond lands, and the fines on alienation, though at first uncertain, gradually became a fixed sum of 2*s.* an acre. He could and often did, purchase free land. And in

chattels by will.[1] On the whole it must be admitted that his was no servile tenure in the ordinary as distinguished from the legal sense of the term, but rather 'customary freehold,' although he had lost legal protection in the king's courts.[2]

Another advantage the Ingoldmells villein had was having the 'court of Ingoldmells' close at hand. Here he could recover debts and damages for trespasses, and could enforce agreements. Here he could bring his action for land 'in the nature of an assize mort d'ancestor,' or of 'novel disseisin.' Here land was alienated by 'surrender' and 'admittance,' and leased by licence of the court. Here matters of importance to the community were regulated and decided. Here too offenders against the criminal law were punished. And the judgments delivered were, not those of the lord or his steward, but of the court,[3] composed of villeins as well as freemen. Altogether, however unprotected the villein might be under the common law against his lord, he was by no means dependent upon his mere caprice, but was ruled in accordance with the customs of the manor defined by the tenants themselves. In fact the lord was a constitutional ruler,[4] and the villeins, as well as the freemen, had a real share in the system of self-government which prevailed. It must, too, in those rough and turbulent times, have been a considerable advantage to the villein to be under the protection of a great and powerful lord, such as the earl of Lincoln, or later the duke of Lancaster. I think it will be admitted that the Ingoldmells villein was neither down-trodden, wretched, nor miserable, as by some accounts were villeins elsewhere. The contemporary opinion of his condition comes out clearly when we find a freeman actually proving that his wife was a nief, contrary to the assertion of the defendant that she was a free woman, when all he could gain thereby was four acres of bond land.[5] There is abundant evidence that some villeins were in the fifteenth century becoming well-to-do and prosperous. A glance at the Ministers' Accounts[6] for 1421-2 will show this. There we find William Thory, Simon Bailly, William Skegnes, and others purchasing considerable [nativus] of the lord the king belonging to his manor of Ingoldmells,' is said to have [1] married Alicia, daughter of Sir Robert Sylkeston of East Kirkby, a Lincolnshire knight, and certainly with Richard, his son, acquired in 1392 considerable freehold property at East Kirkby, and elsewhere, which they held in bondage [2] [in bondagio] according to the custom of the manor, paying a rent of 40s. yearly, wards, marriages, reliefs, and escheats to the king being reserved. Robert Gryn died before 3 July 1411, and 7 August 1411, Richard, his son and next heir of blood, was admitted to his inheritance. [3] We find Richard on the inquisition of bond-tenants up to A.D. 1422, but in 1433 his younger son, William, was on the inquisition of freemen, and the eldest son, John, is described in 1437 as ' of Kirkby,' so probably they acquired their freedom before 1433. In 1477 Richard Grenne, son of John, is described [4] in a deed as ' gent.'; but as late as 1492 the Kirkby property was treated as held according to the custom of the manor of Ingoldmells, and Richard Skepper and his wife [5] had to come to the court, and ask to be admitted, and pay a fine of 10l. for entry. Additional evidence of the prosperity of the Ingoldmells villein may be found in the fact that one was willing to give [6] as much as 6l. in 1376 to enter on two acres of arable land, and in 1404 land was worth [7] 3s. 6d. an acre as an annual rent beyond the dues and customs of the lord.

I have been fortunate enough to find amongst the Ingoldmells papers an inventory of the goods of a villein A.D. 1569. He had 2 cows, 15 ewes, 6 other sheep, and 1 pig; indoors he had a feather bed and some other comforts. His goods were valued at 10l. 10s. 8d., perhaps 90l. of our money. But his debts amounted to 6l. 14s., of which 4l. 4s. was for rent, and 2l. 4s. 8d. for money borrowed.

I must now make an attempt to consider the difficult question of what changes can be discerned in the condition of the Ingoldmells villein. It is not to be expected that we should find any sudden changes in the social life of the peasant here, but I think we may perceive some indications of a struggle between the claims of the lord and of his villein, and, though I cannot pretend to fix any but approximate dates, there can be

---

[1] Linc. N⁰ and Q⁰, v. 74, 88.   [3] Ministers' Accts. 1421-2.
[2] P. 223.   [4] Linc. N⁰ and Q⁰, v. 90.
[5] P. 283.   [6] P. 175.   [7] P. 208.

no doubt that the villein's condition did gradually but surely improve until at last he became a free copyholder. It seems to me that there are indications of a struggle throughout the reign of Edward III. Sometimes the lord succeeded in enforcing his claim, as when in 1328[1] an attempt was made by the homage to conceal purchases of freehold land by villeins, in order that they might avoid the customary[2] rents and fines. But on the whole the villein seems to have improved his position. From the middle of the fourteenth century the fines on admittance become more certain, and the merchet payments less in amount, and at the end of the century the villein has clearly become more prosperous. And when we get into the fifteenth century his prosperity is undoubtedly increasing, he is allowed contrary to former practice to be essoined, and in 1419 the merchet has become a fine for a marriage licence. I have included some extracts from the rolls of 9 and 10 Elizabeth, as an example of villeinage in a dying condition. Most of the villeins have already been enfranchised, but there is still an attempt made to keep up former claims. In 9 Eliz. the inquisition of *nativi* still appears, the names of 11 villeins are put down, but only 5 seem to have come and been sworn;[3] an effort is also made to draw up an account of the villeins and their progeny. The next year there are 6 names on the inquisition of *nativi*, in 20 Eliz. 2, and henceforward the attempt to form an inquisition of *nativi* is given up, although as late as 2 James I. 3 *nativi* are amerced 3s. 4d. each for default of suit of court.

[1] P. 101.

[2] Free land purchased by a villein was arrented at 2^d an acre, and a fine was due upon each admittance.　　　[3] P. 286.

NOTE. *Page* 164.

For 'prolutus' read 'for clay.' The scribe seems to have written pro lutus, but it would be an offence to dig down for the clay under the sand banks, and thus weaken them, so probably 'pro luto' is the right reading.

INGOLDMELLS COURT ROLLS

COURT of Ingoldemels,[1] held on Wednesday next before the day of All Saints, in the year of Edward, 19 ending and 20 beginning [31 Oct. A.D. 1291].

Alan at Raue (is essoined) of the common (advent) by John son of William the first time. Stephen le Walays by Peter Cook. William Neucomen by Walter de Akewra. William de Wegland by Robert de Langtona. Alice Wybyan by Bernard de Burgh. William de Kelseye by Robert Vest. Peter at Church (ad Ecclesiam) by William son of Lucy. Henry son of Alan by Richard son of Sarah. William de Ryg by Ranulph the bailiff. Robert de Boyland by Walter de Akewra.

William de Hardrycehil, the heirs of Robert de Steping, Defaulters except William de Kelseye, Peter de Steping, and Matilda Vest.

From Matilda Vest for respite of suit of court until the feast of S. Michael vj^d, pledge the bailiff. | vj^d

[2]John Brun was distrained by v sheep for destroying one drain to remake the same drain, and the distraint is replevied until the coming of the steward by Walter Slet.

The township presents that one Alan Viles retained one penny of annual rent unjustly through vi years of a certain place of land which he bought of Alan Romfar of one place which is called Romfar Croft, therefore let him be attached.

Also they present that Agnes daughter of Robert at Dammes is 'cognita,' therefore let the father of the said Agnes find a pledge for the said trespass, pledge Ranulph the bailiff. | sp

---

[1] On the back of the roll is written: 'Taken out of the Parish Church of Ingoldmells on the 24th day of October in the 36th year of King Charles II. by Richard Cheales.'

[2] This is repeated at next Court.

vj^d   Also they present that Beatrice Cat sold bread contrary to the assize, therefore she is in mercy vj^d.

vj^d   Richard son of Roger in mercy for the like.

Mercy xij^d   Also they present that William de Stachou ploughed the way at Stachoubrig, and he was present and acknowledged this, therefore he is in mercy, pledge Ranulph the bailiff.

Mercy vj^d   Also they present that Alan de Wegland raised the hue unjustly upon William de Skell, therefore the said Alan is in mercy, pledges Simon Thori and the bailiff.

Also that one way is said to be under the bank of the sea from the house of Robert de La to the house of Robert Haster, and is obstructed by Robert de le La, pledges Richard son of Sarah and the bailiff.

Also that the wife of Walter son of Hugh sold beer contrary to the assize, therefore she is in mercy. The wife of Guy son of Richard in mercy for the like.

xiij^s iiij^d   From Thomas de Wegland that he be able to marry Clementia Thori, pledges Simon Thori and Alan Plummer. From Alice de Burgh for respite of suit of court until the Feast of S. Michael iij^s, pledges William Neucomen and Alan Church.

Ranulph Tude came into full court, and surrendered to the lord ij acres of land, and Peter son of Ranulph gives to the lord for entry iiij^s, and xvj^d of increase of rent.

First Court.   Sum of money xxv^s viij^d.

Court of Ingoldmels held on Wednesday next after the Feast of S. Edmund the King 20 E. [28 Nov. A.D. 1291].[1]

Alan Romfare is essoined of a plea of trespass by William son of Alan for the first time.

The essoin does not lie because he holds bond land, therefore let him be distrained for default.

xviij^d   From Peter at Church for respite of suit of court until the Feast of S. Michael xviij^d, pledge Simon son of Peter.

Distraint   Simon Purdefys (and two others) were summoned to the court, and did not come, therefore let them be distrained.

Peter at Church (and another) were essoined at the preceding court, and nevertheless now have not come, therefore they are in default, and let them be distrained.

[1] I omit here and afterwards most of the essoins.

Let William de Hardrycehil be distrained for default.

It is presented by the township that Alan Vil retained j^d   Mercy xij^d
of annual rent unjustly through vi years of a certain place of
land which he purchased of Alan Romfar &c., and Alan admitted
and paid the said vj^d to the grave, and pledged the mercy for
the detention, pledges Alan son of Hugh and Walter Cat.

William de Stachon complains of Walter Grin, pledge to   Complaint
prosecute the bailiff, and says that the said Walter unjustly   Mercy vj^d
detains from him xx^d, and Walter came and granted it, therefore he is in mercy, pledge Alan the grave.

Master Henry Peticlrek offered himself against Dominus   Distraint
Gilbert parson of Skegenesse, who is distrained by ij sheep for
many defaults against the said Henry, let them be retained,
and a better distraint be made.

Walter son of Robert, the grave of the meadows, because he   Mercy xij^d
did not prosecute against William de Wegland, he and his
pledges are in mercy, pledge the bailiff.

It is ordered to distrain John son of Roger for default   Distraint
against John Charite and to answer ‘de principali.’

It is presented by the township of Ingoldemels that Alan
Vil purchased of Alan Romfar one place of land in the vill of
Ingoldemels which is called Romfartoft with all its appurtenances,
and it contains ij acres and a half and xviij perches, and because
the aforesaid xviij perches by the report [of the township] when
that land was purchased were in the dike and of no value
he shall give a halfpenny to the lord of new rent.

Meriet complains of Alan at Castle, pledge to prosecute the   Complaint
bailiff, and says that the said Alan unjustly detains from him   Mercy vj^d
xij^d; and it is found by the inquisition that Meriet ought to
have nothing of the xij^d, therefore the said Meriet is in mercy
for his false plaint, pledge the bailiff.

William son of Alysot complains of Thomas Rychald, pledge   Complaint
to prosecute the bailiff, and says that when he put in his house   Mercy vj^d
one lamb, value viij^d, there came the said Thomas and opened
the door of his house and he lost the said lamb. Thomas comes

The wardens say that the wife of Walter son of Hugh (and two others) sold beer contrary to the assize. vj^d (each).

Sum vj^s vij^d ob.

[1] Court of Ingoldmels held on Wednesday next before the Feast of S. Thomas the Apostle, 20 E. [19 Dec. A.D. 1291].

Court —— on Wednesday next after the Feast of S. Hilary, 20 Edw. [16 Jan. A.D. 1291–2].

Complaint — Robert son of William de Wegland complains of Roger de Slotheby, pledges to prosecute Alan de Wegland and Ranulph the bailiff.

Distraint — Master Henry Petyclrek offered himself against Gilbert rector of the church of Skegnes, who does not come, so is distrained by ij sheep, let them be retained and a better distraint be made.

The messuage which Alice de Heye held is taken into the hand of the earl, let it be replevied.

Alan son of Ernys gives to the lord annually for frank pledge vj^d, pledges Walter Bogg and Alan Bogg.

The brewers present the wife of Guy son of Richard for assize of beer broken, and likewise because she did not send for the warden.[2]

[3] Court on Wednesday next after the Feast of the Conversion of S. Paul, 20 Edw. [30 Jan. A.D. 1291–2].

Robert son of Inge versus Robert at Red of a plea of trespass (is essoined) by Alan Romfar the first time.

Master Henry Petyclerk versus Dominus Gilbert parson of Skegenesse of a plea of debt (is essoined) the first time by Alan at Castle.

Robert at Red complainant versus Robert son of Inge of a plea of trespass is (essoined) by William his brother the second time.

Respite — Robert son of William de Wegland offered himself against Roger de Sloeby, who offered himself, and Gilbert de Gremewyke, and it is put into respite until the next court.

Distraint — It is ordered to distrain Dominus Gilbert rector of the

---

[1] Torn.   [2] 4 similar cases.
[3] Short roll written on one side.

church of Skegenesse for default against Master Henry Petyclerk. He is essoined.

It is ordered as before to distrain the heirs of Robert de Steping, except William de Kelseye, Peter de Steping, and Matilda West.

Alan Romfar offered himself against Dominus William the chaplain, who offered himself, and it is presented for the common council, and the said Alan is in mercy, pledges William the chaplain and Ranulph the bailiff. So that is to say that the said Alan release to the said William all actions which he had against the said William from the beginning unto this day. *Mercy vj^d*

It is ordered as before to distrain William Coper (and another) for wreck of the sea carried away. *Distraint*

It is ordered as before to sell the hurdles and all other things found of wreck of the sea.

that there come a good inquisition to the next court concerning the thorns cut near le La.

that the grave retain in the hand of the earl the land which John Fowler held and is dead.

Emma de Dufdyk came in full court and granted to Alan the grave one acre of arable land lying in Ingelfastland from the day of the Purification of the Blessed Mary in 20 Edward until the same Feast of the Purification of the Blessed Mary in one year.

John Pulayn complains of Ralph Gunny, pledge to prosecute Ranulph the bailiff, and Ralph does not come, therefore he is in mercy and let him be distrained to answer ' de principali.' *Complaint Mercy vj^d*

from Walter . . . that he may be removed from his office viz. of warden of the assize, xij^d, pledge Robert Bug. *xij^d*

A messuage which Alan at Castle held of the lord was taken into the hand of the lord, and let it be replevied.

From Henry Tailor to have a lease of one acre of land which he hired of Alan de Horreby from the Feast of S. Martin in the year xx to the same feast vj^d, pledge Ranulph the bailiff. *vj^d*

In an inquisition taken on the oath of Robert Bug, Richard Godard, William de Dufdyk, Walter Puredfis, Alan Aubray, Simon Reyner, Walter Gryn, William Gryn, Ranulph Tude, Robert at Dammes, William de Wegland, Alan de Golewaye, and Alan Aldiet concerning a dike which is called Donedyk which has been destroyed, they say on their oath that Master *Inquisition*

Henry Peticlerk cut the said dike by night. . . . Stephen . . . and others whose names are not known, and they say that never before was it cut . . . , and it is to the prejudice of the earl and the country, therefore it is commanded to the bailiff that the said Henry be distrained.

The wardens say that Walter Bug sold beer contrary to the assize.

Court——on Wednesday, S. Gregory's day, 20 Edward [12 March A.D. 1291–2].

Robert son of Ing against Robert de Red of a plea of trespass (is essoined) the third time by William Gunny.

Mercy vj⁴ Richard Godard complains of Walter son of Alan de Orreby, pledge Ranulph the bailiff, and afterwards the said Richard comes and agrees with the said Walter, and the said Walter is in mercy, pledges Alan Gedde and Robert de Red.

Mercy vj⁴ Ranulph the bailiff offered himself against the said Walter, who offered himself, and at the prayer of the parties they are agreed, and the said Walter is in mercy, pledges Alan Gedde and Robert de Red.

Mercy vj⁴ Alan at Castle offered himself against Matilda wife of William Wycpac, who offered himself, and says that she unjustly detains from him xxvij⁴ from Tuesday next before the Feast of S. Martin in the present year 15 years have past until this day, and yet she unjustly detains to his damage ij⁵, and of this he put himself on an inquisition, and the said Matilda comes and denies the whole, and of this she puts herself on the inquisition, and let the inquisition be taken upon this, and afterwards they are agreed, and the said Matilda is in mercy, (pledges) Robert at Dammes and Alan Albry.

Distraint Master Henry Peticlerk offered himself against Dominus Gilbert rector of the church of Scegenesse, who is distrained by two sheep, let them be retained, and a better distraint be made.

Mercy vj⁴ John Polayn offered himself against Walter son of Alan de Orreby, and says that the said Walter unjustly detains xxxiij⁴ from Tuesday next before Lent in the present year until this day and this unjustly to his damage xij⁴, and the said Walter comes and agrees and puts himself in mercy, pledges William Gunny and Robert at Dammes.

Thomas Richild offered himself against William son of

Elysot who offered himself, and afterwards the plea is put into respite until the next court.

Walter Cat pledges the mercy for a trespass made in the court, pledge the bailiff.

It is presented by the township of Ingoldemels that Alan son of William de Wegland raised the hue justly ‘per vim Thome fratris sui,’ therefore the said Thomas is in mercy, pledges Alan Romfar, and Alan Plommer, and Simon Tori and Alan son of Peter.

Alan at Castle complains of Thomas son of Beatrice, pledge   Complaint
to prosecute Alan Bug, and it is put in respite before the steward.

The same Alan complains of Robert Hatter, pledge to prosecute Alan Buge, and it is put in respite until the coming of the steward.

It is ordered as before to distrain the tenants of Robert de   Distraint
Steping, except William de Kelseye, Peter de Steping, and Matilda West.

The suit between John son of Roger and John Charite is put in respite until the next court.

It is ordered as before to distrain John Ingelberd and William Coper for wreck of the sea carried away.

It is ordered as before to sell the hurdles and all other things found of wreck of the sea.

that there come a good inquisition to the next court concerning thorns cut near le La.

John Fowler held of the lord iiij acres & a half, and is dead, and William his son and heir comes into court and offers himself to do for the lord what he ought to do.

Alice Wybyan held of the lord xv acres of land for xiij^{d} yearly, and is dead, and the land which she held is taken into the hand of the earl, and Simon Boteler who married the daughter and heir of the said Alice (came) and offered himself to satisfy the lord for the said land what he ought to do.

One messuage which Alan at Castle held of the lord is taken into the hand of the earl.

Master Henry Petyclerk is distrained for the dike destroyed   Distraint
by him at Donedyk.

Court of Ingoldemels on Wednesday next after Palm Sunday, 20 Edward [2 April A.D. 1292].

Thomas de Watecroft (is essoined) of the common (advent) by Walter atte Hou, William le Neucomen by Walter de Akewra.

Master Henry Peticlerk offered himself against Gilbert rector of the church of Skegeness, who is distrained by ij sheep, let them be retained and a better distraint be made.

Alan Polain comes in full court and finds pledges, viz. Alan atte Lathe and John Polain, to bring his wife to . . .

A place which is called Milne acre which Agnes Plommer bought of A. Plommer is taken into the hand of the earl and it is ordered that it be measured before the next court.

Thomas Richild offered himself against William son of Alice and at the prayer of the parties they are agreed, and it is put in respite until the next court.[1]

Court of Ingoldmeles on Wednesday next before the Feast of S. Philip and S. James, 20 E. [April 30 A.D. 1292].

Leyrwite vj^d

It is presented that Beatrice wife of Henry Puredfys is 'cognita.'

Heriot vj^d

Alan at Appelgare gives to the lord vj^d to have the messuage which Alan at Castle formerly held, saving the claim of the next heir.

Attorney

Robert at Red put in his place his attorney, Alan at Castle, against Robert son of Inge.

Complaint

William de Nevyle complains of Alan de Wegland, pledges to prosecute Robert de Prestthorp and the bailiff.

Robert son of Lambert held of the lord xj acres of land, and is dead, and the land which he held is taken into the hand of the earl.

Master Henry Peticlerk offered himself against Gilbert rector of the church of Skegenesse, who was distrained by ij sheep and could not be distrained better, therefore the said Henry can recede from the court and complain when he likes by the grant of the court.

Thomas Everard demands against Alan de Castle xiiij^s iiij^d, and Alan admitted the debt in full court that he is indebted to the said Thomas at two terms, viz. at the Feast of S. Michael vij^s ij^d and at Christmas vij^s ij^d, and for this admission the said

---

[1] Bottom of the roll in bad condition.

Alan gave the lord vj^d, pledges Alan Bug, William son of Alice de Duneswra, and they are pledges for the debt.

Alan Polayn came into full court and surrendered into the hand of the lord one acre of land and a half. And <u>Agnes Plummer</u> came and satisfied the lord for having entry on the said land. xij^d. And she renders of new rent xij^d yearly.

Heriot xij^d new rent xij^d

Alan Polayn came into full court and surrendered to the lord iiij acres, j perch, and xiij rods, and it is ordered that it be measured, and—Polayn took the said land and shall give for entry ij^s. And he renders yearly of new rent xxxij^d.

Heriot ij^s new rent ij^s viij^d

Walter de Orreby came into full court, and surrendered to the lord one acre of land except xvj —, and Henry Tailor came and took the said land, and gives the lord for entry vj^d, and renders of new rent vj^d ob. q.

Heriot vj^d new rent vj^d ob. q.

Thomas Richild offered himself against William son of Alice and says that he unjustly beat and ill used him, and of this he put himself on the inquisition, which says that the said William struck the said Thomas and ill used him as he says, therefore the said William is in mercy, pledges Ralph Aldiet, and Alan at Castle, and the damages are taxed at xij^d.

Mercy xij^d

John Fowler held of the lord iiij acres of land and a half, and is dead. And William his son and heir came and offered himself (to do the lord) what he ought to do, and it is found by the inquisition that he is the nearest heir, and he gives the lord for heriot iij^s.

Heriot iij^s

It is presented that the dike round the manor of Ingoldemel is worth vj^d by the year in common years.

The inquisition taken concerning the thorns carried away and concerning the rushes at le La says that . . . , let them be attached if they be found in the fee of the earl.

Inquisition

Peter Cook finds a pledge for a trespass made on the 'dunys' next the sea with his sheep [rest torn].

Mercy vj^d

From the township of Ingoldmels for a false inquisition xl^s.[1]

xl^s

Court of Ingoldemels on Wednesday next before Ascension Day, 20 E. [14 May A.D. 1292].

William Clerk attorney of Dominus Thomas de Brunham (is essoined) of the common (advent) by Andrew de Akewra the first time.

William de Waleby and Roger son of Alan at the prayer of

Mercy xij^d

----

[1] Rest of roll torn.

the parties are agreed of a plea of debt at le La, and the said William is in mercy, pledge Alan at Church.

Complaint   Robert de Gipthorp complains of William de Thoresby, pledge to prosecute [blank].

Seizure   Robert son of Lambert held of the lord xj acres of land, and is dead, and the land is taken into the hand of the lord.

Complaint   Robert de Red offered himself against Robert son of Inge, for that he unjustly detains from him v^s, which he ought to have paid on the Tuesday next after the Feast of S. Hilary in the present year, and as yet he detains them unjustly to his damage ij^s, and afterwards at the prayer of the parties they are agreed, and the said Robert son of Inge is in mercy, pledges Peter Cook and Alan at Church.

sic

Mercy vj^d   It was ordered that Thomas (son of) Rychild be attached to produce John his son, and he has not produced him, therefore he is in mercy.

The wardens say that (they present) the wife of Guy son of Richard for breaking the assize, Walter Bug for the like, Richard son of Roger for the assize of bread, Thomas Meriet for the like.

Mercy vj^d   Ralph son of William offered himself against William son of Richard and says that he unjustly detains from him xxij^d, and William comes and denies and puts himself upon an inquisition, and an inquisition taken upon this says that the said William detains from the said Ralph as he says xxij^d, therefore the said William is in mercy, pledges Ranulph the bailiff and Walter Bug.

xij^d   From Walter Faukes for having his lease of one acre of land which he hired of Agnes Faukes with the consent of Robert her son, who was in her ward, from the Purification in the present year until the end of six years xij^d, pledge the grave.

Court of Ingoldmels on S. Barnabas's day [11th June], 20 E.

Distraint   William de Thoresby was essoined at the preceding court against Robert de Gypthorp, and now has not come, nor sent an essoiner for him, therefore let him be distrained.

Heriot   William atte Owdayl of Ingoldmels is dead, who held of the
xxvj^s viij^d   lord earl in villeinage xxj acres of land, of which xv acres are each at iiij^d and vj acres each at xij^d. John, son and heir of the said William, came and demanded the land. Who gives to the

lord for heriot xxvj^s viij^d, pledges to pay Ralph de Modeland and Ranulph the grave.

Alan Est complains of Peter Cook for that on Ascension Day in the present year he came and fished in the dike of Walter Cat. . . . Peter Cook took him by the neck and threw him against the ground, and called his dog which bit him and drew blood from him, to his damage xiij^s iiij^d, and thereof he produced suit. The said Peter Cook comes and defends the words of court and says that he did not take him by the neck and throw him, but because the house of his neighbour was broken he thought he was a robber, and therefore he put his dog upon him, and this he wishes to be verified (before an inquisition) and Alan likewise. Which says that the said Peter took him by the neck and threw him against the ground, and his dog bit him, and that he knew him who he was, therefore the said Peter is in mercy, pledges Alan the grave and Alan Thorand. *Mercy vj^d*

William Polber complains of Thomas Rychild and <u>Agnes his wife</u> that whereas formerly a strife was raised between them so that . . . in this form that the said Thomas and Agnes ought to have paid 2^s, viz. 12^d in hand and . . . are put in respite if the said Thomas and Agnes his wife shall in any things do him wrong that they shall give the said 12^d . . . Agnes the wife of the said Thomas and slandered the said William saying that he desired to strangle his mother as is known by half the vill, and that he did not place upon him other enormities, and he demanded that it be inquired into and William likewise. (The inquisition) says that he defamed him as he says. Therefore he is convicted of xij^d, and is in mercy, pledge Ralph Aldiet.

Let the land which Robert ad Gotam purchased of William ad Spinas be taken into the hand of the earl.

From Alan the grave for having his lease of two acres of land, which he hired of A. Gedde to the end of six years, and he shall begin at Christmas 20 Edw., and shall give for entry vj^d.

Court of Ingoldemels on Monday next after the Feast of S. Margaret, 20 E. [21 July A.D. 1292].

Ranulph son of Stephen complains of <u>Alice daughter of Agnes Thours</u>, pledge to prosecute the bailiff. The same *Complaint*

Ranulph complains of <u>Ellen daughter of Agnes Thours</u>, pledge to prosecute the bailiff, and they do not come, therefore are in default.

xij⁴   Ranulph son of Stephen offered himself against <u>Alice daughter of Agnes Thours</u>, for that the said Alice undertook for William Wykpac to pay to the same Ranulph xxxij⁴ at the Feast of S. Margaret, and when the day came she paid nothing, but unjustly detained, to his damage xij⁴, and this he desires may be verified, and the said Agnes [sic] comes and says that she never became surety for the said money for the said William, and of this she put herself upon the inquisition, and the inquisition taken upon this says that she undertook as he says, therefore the said Agnes is in mercy, pledge the grave, fine xij⁴.

vj⁴   Walter de Orreby came into full court and acknowledged himself indebted to Alan ad Curiam Aulae vˢ iiij⁴, therefore he is in mercy, pledge the bailiff.   fine vj⁴.

Mercy   John Wynstan and his pledges are in mercy because he did not prosecute against Richard son of Walter, therefore let them be distrained.

xij⁴   From Alan the grave for having a lease of iij acres iij roods xix rodefalles, which he took of Walter de Orreby for a term of xij years, xij⁴, so that the said Alan shall acquit the said (land) against the lord.

The land which Robert at Gote purchased of William ad Spinas is taken into the hand of the lord.

ijˢ   From Gilbert Tori for having a lease of ij acres of land at Hauedik which he took of Alan Romfar for a term of x years, the term beginning at the Feast of S. Margaret, and the same Gilbert shall acquit against the lord all services touching the said land, and he gives the lord ijˢ, pledge the grave.

vj⁴
new rent   From Richard Reyner for having entry upon iij perches of land which he purchased of Alan Chald vj⁴.   And he shall give
vj⁴   of new rent yearly vj⁴.

Peter Heylmer is dead, and he held of the lord iiij acres, value of each acre iiij⁴, and the land is taken into the hand of the lord.   Ranulph son of the said Peter came and demanded the land.

Mercy vj⁴   Peter Cook offered himself against Alan Est, and says against the said Alan, that the said Alan cut his peas . . . to his damage vijˢ, also he says that the said Alan cut his corn value iiij^d. . . . Alan comes and says that he did not, and this he puts upon the inquisition. The inquisition taken says that the said Peter is in mercy.[1]

Sum of the Court vj^s.

Court of Ingoldmeles of Wednesday next after the Feast of the Decollation of S. John, 20 Edw. [3 Sept. A.D. 1292].

Alan Romfar complains of Walter Bogg for that on the Wednesday next after the Assumption of the Blessed Mary last past in a place that is called ' nortcotes,' which the said Walter hires of the said Alan for a term of iij years, he came and wrongfully defamed the wife of the said Alan by calling her robber, and said that she stole his beans in the same place, to his damage half a mark. The said Walter comes and defends (saying) that he did not call her robber, nor did he defame her, and he demanded that this be inquired, and Alan likewise. And these are the inquisition, Robert de Presthorp, Thomas Warner, Peter Cook, William de Stachow, Ralph son of Peter, John Belt, Gilbert Thory, Alan Hawkes, Alan Est, Alan Vyles. *Mercy vj*^d Ralph Haldiet, Walter son of Sarah, who say on their oath that the said Agnes took away none of his beans and in all things is faithful, therefore she is quit, and Walter is in mercy, pledges Robert and Alan Bogg.

Matilda wife of Alan Rumfar complains of Agnes wife of Walter Bogg for that on the Thursday next after the Assumption of the Blessed Mary last past she defamed her by calling her robber for carrying off her beans, to her damage half a mark. The said Agnes comes and defends the whole, and demands that it be inquired into, and Matilda likewise, and these are the inquisition underwritten, who say on their oath that the said Agnes did not call Matilda robber nor defame her. Therefore let the said Agnes go quit, and Matilda is in *Mercy vj*^d mercy, pledges Thomas Lake and Ranulph the bailiff.

Alan son of William de Galwaythe found pledges to make *Mercy vj*^d amends for a trespass made on Walter de Orreby, a villein of the lord earl, William de Galwaythe and William de Doufdyk.

Walter de Orreby complains of Alan son of William de Galwaythe for that on the Friday next before the Feast of

---

[1] Below are entries of a Court held near the Feast of S. Laurence (10 August) torn.

S. Bartholomew last past he took him by the shoulders, and held him firmly until Robert Palmer prevented him, and broke his head, so that blood flowed from his head, to his damage half a mark, and he demands that it be inquired into. The said Alan comes and defends the words of court and the damages, and demands that it be inquired into, and the inquisition taken upon this says that the said Alan did not hold him by the shoulders, nor did he strike him, as he says, therefore the said Mercy vj^d Walter is in mercy, pledges Alan at Grange and Alan at Church.

Attachment William de Galwaythe complains of William de Wra that he entered his house by night, and took thence one greyhound, which he took in the warren. Therefore he is attached, and afterwards the said William found pledge for the mercy, pledges Simon son of Peter and Walter Oreby, and it is put in respite.

Alan at Castle complains of Thomas Herward, and says that he mowed his meadow, value iij^d. The said Thomas denies the whole and demands that it be inquired into. And the inquisition taken upon this says that the said Thomas mowed his meadow with one . . . ,

therefore the said Thomas is in mercy.

Court held on Wednesday next before the day of S. Michael, 20 E. I. [24 Sept. A.D. 1292].

Mercy vj^d Bernard de Burgh pledges the mercy for that he made default in his law waged against Ranulph the bailiff, pledges Simon son of Peter and Walter Brok.

Law John Blaunchard and Alice his wife offered themselves against Bernard de Burgh for that the said Bernard beat his (John's) wife, and they agreed on the Lord's day next before the Feast of S. Michael xix E. in the churchyard of S. Peter of Burgh, that the said Bernard ought to give to the said John x^s for the trespass made on his wife by good arbitration, viz. v^s on the Feast of the Purification of the Blessed Mary xx E., and v^s at Pentecost in the same year, and when the days came he paid nothing but unjustly detained it from him to his damage xl^s, and of this he produced suit. Bernard comes and defends the words of court and says that he never put himself into the arbitration so as to be bound to him in x^s. Upon this he wages his law, pledges Simon son of Peter and Walter Brok.

Gilbert de Nevyle offered himself against Ralph de Wynthorp, he is essoined. Walter Purchase is distrained for default against Thomas son of William. It is ordered as before to distrain William de Thoresby for many defaults against Robert de Gipthorp. **Distraint**

It is presented by the township of Ingoldmel that Walter de Orreby raised the hue justly upon one Robert Palmer, therefore let the said Robert be attached. **Attachment**

From William at Flet for having and holding of the lord one acre and a half of land which he purchased of Robert de la Clay j^d ob. yearly of rent: from Ralph Aldiet (for same) j^d yearly: from Ranulph the bailiff because he has not attached Baldrick Gedde xij^d. **New rent j^d**

John ad Fontem complains of Robert ad Dammes, pledge Ranulph the bailiff, and says that the said Robert ought to have paid him x^s at the Feast of the Apostles Peter and Paul xix E. Robert came and admitted, therefore the said Robert is in mercy, pledges William de Wegland and Alan at Dammes, and he shall pay v^s at the Feast of S. Martin and at Christmas v^s. **Complaint Mercy vj^d**

From Sarah ad Aulam because she held the dike round the hall without warrant for xx years iij^s. **iij^s**

From the same Sarah for the dike round the hall of Ingoldemel. **vj^d**

Sum of this Court vj^s ix^d.
Sum total of all Courts x^{li} xix^s x^{d}q.

Court of Ingoldemel on Wednesday next after the Feast of S. Peter ad Vincula, 21 Edward [5 August A.D. 1293].

Agnes de Waytecroft (is essoined) of the common (advent) by William her son the first time.

The suit between William Lawys and William Lamb is put in respite until the next court so that both parties shall appear without essoins.

Thomas Richild held of the lord v acres of land and rendered for each acre iiij^d, and is dead, and the land is taken into the hand of the lord, and afterwards came John his son and heir and gave to the lord for heriot xx^s, pledges William at Flet and William de Duneswra. **Heriot xx^s**

Thomas son of William is distrained for default against Philip de Waytecroft, the vicar of Burgh is distrained because **Distraint** found in the fee of the earl for a trespass made at Scalflet. Roger Haldan is distrained for trespass made in the warren. Dominus William de Cantilupe for default. It is presented to distrain Rose Tynet because ' cognita.'

Heriot xviij^d

Beatrice Puredfys comes into court and surrenders to the lord j acre of land and xxxij rodefalls to the use of Walter Lamb, and he shall give to the lord for entry xviij^d, and of new

new rent ix^dq.

rent ix^dq., pledges William son of Andrew and Ranulph the bailiff. (She also surrenders) j acre, j rood, and vj rodefalls to

Heriot ij^s

the use of Alan Est, and he gives to the lord for entry ij^s. And

new rent x^dq.

.he shall give of new rent x^dq., pledges William at Flet and the bailiff.

Attach-ment

Alan Kurtays offered himself against Walter son of William Clerk, who has not come, therefore let him be distrained, if found on the fee of the earl, and he is attached by corn growing on iij acres.

Leyrwite vj^d vj^s viij^d Inquisi-tion

From Beatrice Purdefys because ' cognita.'

From William son of Andrew for having an inquisition concerning v acres of land, which Thomas Richild formerly held, vj^s viij^d, pledges Walter Lamb and William at Flete.

Calumnia

Alan Church is accused that he took half a mark from Hugh Polayn, also that he had j boat, and he calls Dominus Thomas de Brunham to warrant.

Fine xij^d

Richard son of Sarah purchased ij acres of land of Walter son of Alan de Frisseby (Firsby), and it is taken into the hand of the lord, and afterwards he made fine for entry xij^d, pledge Alan Church.

Sum of all Courts held this year ix^li xiiij^s iij^dq.

Court of Ingoldemels on Wednesday next before the Feast of S. Luke the Evangelist in the end of the 30th year of King Edward [17 October A.D. 1302].

Fine vj^s viij^d

From Richard le Walays for respite of suit of court until the Feast of Michael half a mark.

Fine xij^d

From Peter de Stepyng for the same xij^d, pledge the grave.

Distraint

Philip ffraunke son and heir of Dominus William ffraunke is distrained for the relief of one knight's fee.

William Lawys is attached by one cow for wreck of the sea carried away, and does not justify himself, therefore let it be retained, and a better distraint be made.

Matilda Gedde and Joan her sister offered themselves against Matilda Inglebritht, who many times has made default, therefore let her be distrained as before.

Matilda Gedde and Joan her sister complain of Matilda Inglebrith that when they were in the peace of the king in the vill of Hoggestorp there came the said Matilda and assaulted them, and beat them, and ill used them, to their damage four shillings, and thereof they produce suit. And Matilda Inglebritht comes and defends force, &c., and demands that it be inquired into, and Matilda and Joan likewise, and they have respite unto the next court. Which comes and says that Matilda Inglebrith struck and ill treated them to the damage of two pence, therefore the said Matilda is in mercy, pledges Thomas Smith and the bailiff. *Inquisition Mercy vjd*

William Taunt is accused of carrying away the ropes of a certain 'Saylyard' which came of wreck of the sea, pledge William son of Alice. *Wreck vjd*

Court of Ingoldmells on Wednesday next after the Feast of S. Martin in the beginning of the 31st year of King Edward [14 November A.D. 1302].

William Lauys found pledges, viz. Peter Cook and Robert Germayn, for himself and for his men for to be before the steward to satisfy the lord for ropes, wreck of the sea carried off. *Respite*

Peter de Burtoft complains of Alan Curtays that he took of the land of the said Peter xxiiij rodefalls in length and in breadth one 'becheus' in one 'fouea' between the land of the said Peter and of Alan, to his damage half a mark, and thereof he produced suit. And the said Alan defended the whole, and demanded that it be inquired into, and the plaintiff likewise. *Complaint*

Therefore comes an inquisition, which says that Alan took of the land of Peter to his damage 1 penny, therefore the said Alan is in mercy, pledge Alan the grave. *Mercy vjd*

William de Kellesey purchased tenements of Matilda West, and has a day at the next court to acknowledge by what services he claims to hold the said tenements of the lord.

Court of Ingoldemeles on Wednesday next after the Feast of S. Clement the Pope, 31 E. [28 November A.D. 1302].

Hugh atte Watcroft (is essoined) of the common (advent) by Alan at Grange.

Attorney Thomas de Ardelthorp, chaplain, put in his place Walter de Akwra junior against William de Presthorp in a plea of debt.

Mercy xij^d Distraint Richard Fuller was attached by one horse, and was replevied by Ranulph de Metheland and John son of Guy, who undertook to produce him in this court, who does not come, therefore his pledges are in mercy, and nevertheless let the said Richard be distrained and his pledges.

Mercy xij^d Matilda and Joan Gedde, sisters, complain of Agnes Inglebrith for that she beat and ill treated the said Matilda and Joan on the day of S. Margaret the Virgin in the vill of Hogestorp to the damage of two shillings, and thereof they produce suit. And the said Agnes came and defended, &c., and says that she never beat them as they say, and demands that it be inquired into, and the said Matilda and Joan likewise. Which says that Agnes beat them to their damage vj^d, therefore the said Agnes is in mercy, pledge Henry Sigworthe.

√strife sp.

Mercy vj^d, Matilda and Joan Gedde, defendants, offered themselves against Agnes Inglebrith, plaintiff, who is not present, therefore she and her pledges are in mercy.

Mercy vj^d Thomas Cat pledges the mercy for the hue, pledge Alan Est.

Mercy xij^d Ranulph Lamb pledges the mercy because he entertained persons against the assize, pledge Robert Germayn.

William Gunny complains of John son of John Plumer of a plea of trespass, pledge to prosecute the grave. Against whom he says that on Tuesday next before the Feast of S. Clement he beat and ill treated him, to his damage xl^s, and thereof he produced suit, and the said John comes and defends the whole, and demands that it be inquired, and the plaintiff likewise. The inquisition comes and says that the said John struck him and **Mercy xviij^d** evilly beat him, to his damage one mark, and the said John is in mercy, pledges William his brother and Walter his brother.

Mercy iij^d Walter Pryur complains of William Chapman of a plea of debt, pledge to prosecute the beadle. They are agreed by licence so that Walter puts himself in mercy, pledge William Chapman.

Increment of new rent j^d Simon Lamb acquired one messuage with the court, of the fee of John de Orreby, and he gives to the lord of new rent.

Respite The inquisition concerning the way of Gilbert Thory is in respite unto the next court.

Court held on Wednesday next before Christmas same year
[19 December A.D. 1302].

Walter son of Stephen and Walter Purdifys are agreed by Mercy vj^d licence in a plea of debt, so that Walter Purdifys puts himself
in mercy, pledge Ralph Aldiet.

William de Akewra, junior, complains of Thomas Biide of a Complaints plea of debt, pledge to prosecute the beadle.

Gilbert, the servant of William de Maressey, complains of
Beatrice, wife of Thomas Bride, that she unjustly detains from
him xv^d of silver, of one agreement between them made to
pasture 5 styrkes from the Feast of the Apostles Philip and
James to the Feast of S. Martin.   And the said Beatrice comes
and defends the whole and demands that it be inquired into,
and the plaintiff likewise.   Which inquisition says that Beatrice Mercy iij^d was bound in xv^d, therefore she is in mercy, pledges Ralph
Cliner and the beadle.

Robert Faukes complains of Alan son of Alan Michel that
he called him 'false robber,' and said to him other enormities,
and imprisoned him in the house of Alan Bug, to his damage Mercy iij^d half a mark, and the defendant came and defends the whole,
and demands that it be inquired into and the plaintiff likewise.
Which inquisition says that the said Alan called him 'false
robber,' as he alleges, to his damage iij^d.   And the said Alan is
in mercy, pledges William del Hauedick.

Richard Fuller pledged the mercy for many defaults for
himself and his pledges, pledges Ranulph de Metland and John Attachment son of Guy, and the said Richard appeared in the court and
receded in despite of court because he was unwilling to answer,
therefore let the said Richard be attached.

Gilbert Thori and his wife in mercy because they did not Mercy xij^d prosecute against Robert Rengot in a plea of trespass, pledge
the beadle.

Sabilla de Westrig gives the lord for leyrwite, pledges Alan Leyrwite vj^d de Wegland and the beadle.

Court of Ingoldmells on Wednesday next after the Feast of
the Epiphany, year as above [9 January A.D. 1302-3].
W.... ... ... f Thomas de Brunham (is assoined)

Increment
xv^d

the house built thereupon, and it is ordered the bailiff that the said land be measured before the next court, and it is measured, so that there is found one acre and a half and xxvij perches, and Alan ad Curiam Aule comes and demands to be admitted to the said tenements, and he gives the lord for entry, pledges Walter de Orreby and Ranulph his brother.

Walter Lamb, plaintiff, offered himself against Alan son of Alan at Church in a plea of debt, who is attached by an instrument 'tele lanose,' and because he does not justify himself therefore let him be distrained better.

Mercy iij^d

Gilbert Thori pledged the mercy because he bought a net (?) [1] of Alan Polber against the injunction of the steward, pledges John de Hudeyl and the beadle.

ij^s

John de Braddefelt comes and gives the lord ij^s of silver for the safety of his goods in the fee of the earl, and he pays the silver.

Attach-
ments

William son of Thomas Bride raised the hue upon Robert atte Skelles, and justly, therefore let the said (Robert) be attached.

Beatrice daughter of Richard de Toft raised the hue upon Robert son of Margaret, and unjustly, therefore let the said Beatrice be attached.

Leyrwite
vj^d
Leyrwite
ij^d

Let Agnes daughter of Alan son of Ralph be attached for leyrwite : Duce de Wegland for the same.

Sum of this roll xxiiij^s.

Court of Ingoldemeles on Wednesday next after the Feast of the Purification of the Blessed Mary, the year as above (31 E. I.) [6 Feb. A.D. 1302–3].

Dominus Robert de Gipthorp (is essoined) of the common (advent) by Peter Cook.

Thomas Bride and William son of William de Akewra are agreed by licence in a plea of debt, so that the said Thomas puts himself in mercy, so that the said William shall have one place of pasture, containing two acres and one rood, from the preceding Feast of the Purification to the Feast of S. Martin next to come, pledges for the mercy Alan de Wegland and William son of Alice.

Complaint

Walter Lamb complains of Alan son of Alan at Church that

<hr>

[1] Heke.

he unjustly detains from him v^s viij^d of his guarantee against Peter Motting, which he paid to him for the same (Alan) at a certain day and place, and the said Alan comes and admits that he was his pledge, but he did not pay for him, and he demands that it be inquired, and the plaintiff likewise : which inquisition says that Walter paid for the same (Alan) v^s viij^u as he says, therefore the said Alan is guilty and in mercy, and because he is attached by an instrument [1] for weaving (?), and because pledges are not found, let him be attached better for the debt and mercy.

Robert at Skelles pledges the mercy for the hue raised justly upon him, pledges for the mercy William de Wegland and William Kopir. *Mercy vj^d*

Beatrice daughter of Richard Toft is attached, as before, because she raised the hue upon Robert son of Margaret, and unjustly, after she pledged the mercy, pledges William Copir and William Lawis. *Mercy yj^d*

Alice daughter of Alan Wyles is attached for leyrwite. *iij^d* *$S\rho$.*

Court of Ingoldemeles on Ash Wednesday at Skegnesse, 31 E. [20 February A.D. 1302-3].

Alan de Castle complains of William atte Flete for that he is indebted to him in vj^d, and one lamb, worth xij^d, of the gift and promise of the said William, which he ought to have paid to him two years past, which are still in arrear to the damage of ij^s, and thereof he produces suit. And William comes and defends force, &c., and says that he is not indebted to him in any money or in any lamb, and demands that it be inquired into, and the plaintiff likewise. Which (inquisition) says that the said William was indebted to him in the said six pence and the said lamb, therefore it is considered that the said William is in mercy. *Mercy vj^d*

William Plomer complains of Walter Kygges that on the Lord's day next before Ash Wednesday he defamed him by calling him 'false man,' and that he killed his hen and carried it away and ate it at the house of Walter de Akewra, and thereof he produces suit. And Walter Plomer comes, and says, and avows his saying, and demands that it be inquired into, and the plaintiff likewise. Which (inquisition) says that William neither carried off nor ate any hen. Therefore it is *Mercy vj^d*

[1] Lanosa.

considered that the said Walter is in mercy, pledges Alan atte Conyngesgate and Robert Germen.

Thomas the chaplain by his attorney offered himself against William de Prestorp, who is distrained by **xx** sheep, and because he does not justify himself let a better (distraint be made).

The inquisition concerning the way of Simon Thory is in respite until the coming of the steward.

Sum of this roll xxj^s iij^d.

Court of Ingoldemels on Wednesday in the second week of Lent, 31 E. [6 March A.D. 1302–3].

Mercy vj^d Alice daughter of Alan Wyles pledges the mercy for ley-cherwite, pledge the same Alan.

Distraint Robert Faukes, plaintiff, offered himself against William de Tofte of a plea of debt, who does not come, therefore let him be distrained.

Mercy xij^d Gilbert Thory, plaintiff, does not prosecute against William son of Robert at Sea [ad mare], therefore he and his pledges to prosecute are in mercy, and the said William is quit without a day.

Distraint Thomas ' the Prest,' plaintiff, offered himself against William de Presthorp, who has made many defaults, and is distrained by **xx** sheep, and does not justify himself, therefore let them be retained and a better distraint be made.

Mercy xi_,^d William Lowis found pledges Robert vj^d Germayn and Peter le keu vj^d for himself and his servants to satisfy the lord for wreck of the sea carried off by them, and he does not come, therefore his pledges are in mercy, and let the said William be attached.

William Cadyhorn, Alan atte Kirke, and Alan atte Rawe pledge the mercy because they have not come upon the inquisition.

Mercy ij^s Damage half a mark It is found by the inquisition, upon which Beatrice wife of Gilbert Thory, plaintiff, and Robert Ringot put themselves, that the said Robert defamed the said Beatrice to her damage half a mark, therefore it is considered that the same Beatrice recover, &c., and the said Robert is in mercy, pledges Ranulph Ringot and Ranulph the beadle.

Mercy vj^d Amia who was the wife of Stephen de Dounedyk pledges the mercy for raising the hue unjustly.

William Cobbe, who held of the lord the fourth part of the fee of one knight by knight service in Cletham, is dead, and his heir under age, therefore it. is ordered that the aforesaid tenements be seized into the hand of the lord.

William son of Agnes who held of the lord five acres and a half of bond land is dead, and upon this comes John the son of the said William, and [1] asks to be accepted to pay heriot for the said land, and he gives to the lord half a mark. *Fine, half a mark*

The jury of the way of Simon Thory in Rygge is in respite until the next court for default of jurors.

The heirs of Philip de Whatecroft, William de Thorp, and William ad Spinas, are distrained for many defaults. *Distraint*

From William son of Stephen atte Hallegarth to have to himself for his whole life the court of the Hall with the building xxˢ, and he shall give to the lord earl iijˢ of new rent besides the ancient rent, pledge the bailiff. *Fine xxˢ New rent iijˢ*

It is presented by the free and bond tenants that Alan atte Church and his wife retain, and entertain divers strangers in their house contrary to the earl's peace, and that they have wounded divers persons, therefore the said Alan is in mercy, pledge Alan Brock. *Mercy ijˢ*

Also they say that William son of Thomas Broune raised the hue justly upon Simon son of Robert, therefore it is ordered that he be attached. *Attachment*

Also they say that a certain boat came as wreck. *Wreck*

From Beatrice Pullayn for licence to marry within the manor iijˢ, pledge the grave. *Merchet iijˢ*

From Margaret Meriet for licence to marry without the manor xviijᵈ, pledges Peter Cook and Alan Faukes. *Merchet xviijᵈ*

Court of Ingoldmels held on Wednesday next before the Feast of S. Mark the Evangelist, 31 Ed. [24 April A.D. 1303].

Hugh Sunyre complains of Walter de Dunedick that he unjustly detains from him xvjᵈ, which he owes him, and the said Walter says that in nothing is he indebted to him, and he demands that it be inquired, and the plaintiff likewise. And it is found by the inquisition that Walter is indebted to him in no money, therefore Hugh is in mercy for a false claim, and Walter is quit. Pledges Alan atte Lathe and Walter Pistor. *Mercy vjᵈ*

[1] Petit acceptari ad dictam terram herietandam.

Attachment

William . . . is accused that he carried off the ropes of a mast that came of wreck, and he cannot deny this, nor does he wish to justify himself, therefore it is ordered that he be attached.

Mercy vj^d

Alan at Church was summoned on the inquisition, and does not come, therefore he is in mercy.

Fine iij^s iiij^d

From Agnes daughter of Walter Bugg to have to herself for the whole life of the same Agnes two acres and a half of land with the buildings, which were Alan Michel's, and one acre of land and one rood lying outside the bank of the sea, which Walter Bugg, her father, resigned to her in court, iij^s iiij^d.

Merchet x^s

From Elena Turs for licence to marry within the manor with five acres of bond land x^s, pledge William Abald.

It is ordered the bailiff to attach Robert Ringot to answer to the earl, or to Sir William de Nony if he shall come first, concerning the things objected against him.

Court of Ingoldemeles on Wednesday the Vigil of the Ascension of our Lord, 31 E. [May 15 A.D. 1303].

Hugh de Whatecroft (is essoined) of the common (advent) by Bernard de Burgh.

Richard the servant of the Lady de Gand found pledges, viz. John son of Guy and Alan ad Fontem, to come before the steward at his next coming for a trespass made in the warren with his greyhounds.

Dominus Philip Frauncke is distrained for many defaults.

Court of Ingoldemeles on Wednesday the morrow of S. Barnabas the Apostle, 31 E. [12 June A.D. 1303].

Law

Robert Cat complains of Alan son of Warin de Dunneswra that he unjustly detains from him fish, value one mark, of a certain agreement between them made that they should be partners and equals in fishing in Ingoldmels and purchasing 'beyt' in Norfolk on Monday the morrow 'quasi modo geniti,' to his damage xx^s, and thereof he produced suit, and the said Alan came and defended the whole and waged his law, pledges for the law Robert Germayn and Walter de Akewra.

Simon Tappard complains of Gilbert Neville of a plea of debt, pledge to prosecute Alan Wytwambe, Dominus Robert comes and demands his court concerning Simon Tappard, and it is ordered to summon the whole court. The judgment of the court is in respite.

William Lawys is accused of wreck of the sea carried off by him and his companions, and he is distrained by one cow, and it is replevied by Peter Cook and Alan Bugge until the next court.

Maria daughter of Guy Gigge complains of William Kuyche that he defamed her by citing her to the chapter before the Dean, and there she lawfully purged herself, to her damage xl⁵, and thereof she produced suit, and William came and defended the whole and demanded that it be inquired, and the plaintiff likewise. It is found by the inquisition that he defamed her to her damage, which is taxed at xˢ, and the said William is in mercy, pledges William de Dunedick and Alan at Grange.

Defam⁰ SP — Mercy ij⁰

From Matilda and Agnes, daughters of Alan Bugge, to have one half-acre of land with one cottage built thereupon for their whole life, or to which of them shall live the longer and shall not be married, which Alan their father resigned to them in court, and they give to the lord for entry, pledges Walter Bugge and Robert Bugge.

Fine xviij⁴

Juetta wife of Alan Bride complains of Beatrice wife of Thomas Bride that the said Beatrice beat and ill used her to her damage ij⁵, and she demands that it be inquired, and the plaintiff against her likewise. The inquisition says that Beatrice beat her to her damage, which is taxed at iij pence, and the said Beatrice puts herself in mercy, pledge Ralph son of Peter.

M. — Mercy vj⁴

Beatrice wife of Thomas Bride raised the hue, and unjustly, therefore she pledges the mercy, pledges Ralph son of Peter and the bailiff.

Mercy iij⁴ M

Agnes Fauner raised the hue, and unjustly, therefore let Agnes be attached.

Attach-ment M

Court of Ingoldemels on Wednesday next after the Translation of S. Thomas the Archbishop, 31 Edw. [10 July A.D. 1303].

As yet it is ordered as at other times to distrain William de Thorp for many defaults.

The tenants of William ad Spinas have been distrained for many defaults by one cow, and do not justify themselves, therefore let it be retained, and a better distraint be made.

Let Dominus Philip Frauncke be distrained for the relief of half the fee of a knight, and for many defaults.

Robert son of Hugh demands against Robert Ringot nine shillings and ten pence, which he owes him for sheep bought and received from him. And Robert says, and well acknowledges that at one time he was bound to him in the said debt, but he says that one Robert Faukes was indebted to him in seven shillings which he assigned to Robert son of Hugh to take, and he confessed this, and this he is prepared to verify, and he says that the said Robert and Robert hired a croft together, and so an agreement was made between them. Afterwards they are agreed by licence, and Robert Ringot acknowledges himself indebted in vj* to be paid on the first of August [ad Gulam Augusti] and the Feast of Michael by equal portions, pledges Peter le Cue and Ranulph Ringot, and Robert Ringot is in mercy.

Mercy vj^d

Gilbert de Nevyle was summoned to answer to William de Boston of a plea that he render to him three shillings and four pence which he owes him, and whereof he says that whereas the same Gilbert bought of the same William one quarter of malt on the day of S. Luke the Evangelist xxx E. in Wynthorp for iij* iiij^d to be paid to the same William on the Lord's day next following, on which day he paid him nothing but detained it, and as yet detains it, whereby he says that he is injured, and thereby has damage to the value of ij*, and thereof he produces suit. And Gilbert comes, and Robert de Gipthorp demanded a court for Gilbert as his tenant, and it is put in respite until the next court, and it is ordered to summon all the free tenants.

William de Presthorp was summoned to answer to Thomas the chaplain of a plea that he render to him xx* which he owes him, and whereof he says that whereas the said William bought of the said Thomas one horse for xl* on the day of S. Dunstan xxix Ed. in Ingoldmels, to be paid to him in the same vill at the Feast of S. Martin and at the Feast of the Apostles Peter and Paul next following by equal portions, of which forty shillings he paid to him xx*, and detained the rest, and as yet detains it, whereby he says that he is injured, and has damage thereby to the value of half a mark, and thereof he produces suit. And William comes and defends force, &c., and says that in no money is he indebted to him, and this he demands may be inquired. And Thomas says that he owes him xx*, as he alleges against him, and this he demands may be inquired, Inquisi-
tion therefore an inquisition comes. They are agreed as in the following roll.

William de Flete junior complains of William Goldyng, Mercy xij^d and says that he unjustly detains from him fifteen shillings and six pence, which he owes him as the pledge of John Rowe of Orreby, and this for one horse which the same John bought from him for 15 shillings and 6 pence. And William Goldyng admits the said debt, pledge Richard Bonde, and the damages are forgiven him.

Alan Polber complains of Agnes wife of Thomas Herward and says that she unjustly carried off the crop of one pit, viz. reeds at Douneswraa, to his damage ij^s, and Agnes says that the said pit where the reeds grow is her own soil, and this she demands to verify. And Alan says that it is his soil, and this Inquisi-
tion he demands may be inquired. And it is ordered that there come a good inquisition, and that they have a view.

Robert Warenner complains of William Louwys and Maria his wife [hominibus R. de Wylughby] of a plea of debt, pledge to prosecute the bailiff, and William and Maria do not come, Distraint therefore let them be distrained.

Peter Cook complains of Alan Est and Gilbert de Presthorp, and says that they unjustly detain from him xxvj^s, which they owe him as the pledges of Walter de Akewraa for one horse, which the same Walter bought of the said Peter for xxvj^s. And Alan and Gilbert well allow the said debt by the said pledge, but say that they have a day until the 1st of August next, and afterwards they concede the money at the next court, pledge one for the other.

Simon Toppard complains of Gilbert de Nevyle of three Mercy xij^d pleas, pledge to prosecute the bailiff. And afterwards they come to an agreement by licence, and Simon puts himself (in mercy), pledges William Bigge and the bailiff.

Beatrice Herward complains of Alan Polber, and says that he beat, and ill used her, and struck her beasts, and detained them, contrary to gage and pledge against the common peace. And Alan says that he did not beat her, nor contrary to gage and pledge detain her beasts, and he demands that it be inquired, and as to the striking of the beasts he says that the said Beatrice drove many beasts over the land of the said Alan as she ought to drive, and disturbing her he took the beasts and not otherwise, and he demands that it be inquired. And it is found by the inquisition that the said Alan is in nothing guilty, therefore Beatrice is in mercy for a false claim, and Alan is without a day.

Mercy xij^d [in margin]

Merchet iij^s [in margin]

From Sarah Swete for licence to marry without the manor iij^s, pledge Ranulph de Medeland and John brother of the said Sarah.

Attach-ment [in margin]

It is presented that Matilda Siggeword and Matilda White and Amicia Whyte (allopantur) are chastised, therefore it is ordered that they be attached.

Mercy vj^d [in margin]

Also they say that Ralph atte Outtedayle raised the hue justly upon Roger Gormond, therefore he is in mercy, pledge William de Wegland.

Exchange vj^d Exchange vj^d [in margin]

From Alan Chalde to have to him and his boys for ever one rood of land in Thyckethorp in perpetual exchange for one rood of land in the same place, which John de Skegenes resigned to him in court, and each of them gives the lord vj^d, pledge one for the other.

Sum of this roll xiiij^s vj^d.

Sum of all the courts of this year xj^{li} vij^s iiij^d ob.q., except a certain boat coming as wreck which is not valued.

Court of Ingoldmels held at Burgh on the Wednesday next before the Feast of S. Michael, 6 E. [27 September A.D. 1312].

Inquisi-tion [in margin]

Walter de Orreby was summoned to answer to William Gonny of a plea wherefore he dug his Ecclesiastical [1] way unjustly where no pit was before that digging, to his damage 2^s, and thereof he produces suit. And the same Walter comes, and defends, &c., and says that in nothing is he guilty, as he alleges against him. And he demands that it be inquired. And the other party likewise. Therefore let an inquisition come.

Mercy vj^d iij^d [in margin]

Damage vj^d [in margin]

Walter Lamb and Beatrice Lamb complain of Joan at Waterlad of a plea of trespass, pledge to prosecute the grave. Afterwards it is found by the inquisition on which the same Joan and Walter Lamb and Beatrice his wife put themselves that the said Joan called the said Beatrice 'meretrix,' and said to her other enormities, in the churchyard of S. Peter of Ingoldemeles,

iij^d

to the damage of the same Beatrice vj^d, therefore the said Joan

[1] Or way to church.

is in mercy, pledge Robert at Waterlad. And (it was found) that the said Joan is not guilty in a certain other plaint against Walter and Beatrice, therefore (they) are in mercy, and the said Joan is quit without a day.

William de Wegland complains of Walter de Orreby of a plea of debt, pledge to prosecute Robert Bogge. And they have a day before the next court before the steward.

Beatrice Lamb, plaintiff, and Beatrice Purdfys in a plea 'Gympil aconnodati' are agreed by licence, and the said Beatrice Lamb puts herself, &c. *Mercy vj⁴*

It was ordered to distrain William de Thorp for suit of court, as appears in the court held on Monday next after the Feast of the Apostles Peter and Paul last, &c., in respite until the next court by the pledge of William Fougler and William Bigge.

It is presented to attach William de Kyme, John Haunsard, and Robert Wilughby for a trespass made in the warren, as appears in the court held on the Saturday next after the Feast of S. Ambrose last, &c. And the same Robert is attached by x sheep, price xiijˢ iiijᵈ, and replevied by the pledge of Peter de Scremby, and they are put in respite until the next court. *Attachment*

It is presented as often to distrain the prior of Ormesby and the prior of Alvyngham for homage, fealty, and other services.

Alan atte Kirke for respite of doing homage until Easter ijˢ, pledge the bailiff, unless the earl shall come before into these parts.

From William Neucomene for same ijˢ, unless, &c., if the steward will accept this. From Alan atte Conyngesgate for same ijˢ.

From Richard Foliot for same vjˢ viijᵈ for homage respited until the Feast of S. Michael, 7 E.

It is ordered to distrain the heir of William de Ryg to show in what manner he claims to hold his tenements in Ingoldemeles of the lord.

From Master Henry Peticlerk for having aid from the lord xxˢ.

Ingoldemeles presents that Thomas Bigge married his two daughters, viz. Cristiana and Eleanor, without the licence of the lord without the manor, therefore he is in mercy. Also for the concealment the township is in mercy. *Mercy ijˢ Mercy vjˢ viijᵈ*

Also it is presented that the same Thomas gave to Eleanor his daughter the moiety of his messuage in Weynflet.

Also that <u>Agnes de Orreby</u> raised the hue justly upon vj^d William son of Alice Wyles, therefore he is in mercy. And nevertheless let him be attached.

Also that <u>Alice daughter of Rose atte Craine</u> raised the hue vj^d unjustly upon William de Donedyk, therefore the said Alice is in mercy, pledge the grave. And because the township did not attach the said Alice it is in mercy xij^d.

Sum of this court liij^s iiij^d.

Court of Ingoldemeles held at Burgh on S. Mark's day, 6 Edward [25 April A.D. 1313].

It is ordered to seize into the hand of the lord all the lands and tenements which Alan Saffron entered upon after the death of Alan atte Kirke, his uncle, in Ingoldemeles. And because the said Alan is a bond tenant of the lord therefore let him be attached, and let the grave answer for the proceeds before the auditors of the account.

(8 essoins of plaints.)

Mercy
ij^s iiij^d

It is found by the inquisition, upon which William Rengot, iij^d xij^d plaintiff, and Thomas de Dufdic, William atte Craine, and xij^d William Cuyhis put themselves, that the said Thomas, William, and William beat, and did damage to the said William Rengot, to his damage xx^s. Therefore it is considered that the said William shall recover the said xx^s. And the said Thomas (and the rest) are in mercy, pledge each for the other.

viij^s from one bovate of land seized into the hand of the lord in Wythcal of the fee of the lord as escheat for the fruits of the same bovate of land in the year 5 and 6.

vj^d vj^d vj^d vj^d
John Pedder, John Typer, Henry Barskyn, and Thomas Mole were attached to answer to the lord for a trespass made in the fee of the lord, and they have a day at the next court, pledges of doing right to the rector of the church of S. Clement each one

for the other.   And now they have not come, therefore they are   Mercy ij⁵
in mercy.

From William son of William son of Peter del Oudayl to   Heriot
have to him and his boys for ever the tenements which he re-   cvjˢ viijᵈ
covered against Ralph de Modeland, Alan de Modeland, Joan
and Sarah daughters of the said Ralph, and John del Oudail, as
appears in the court of Ingoldemeles held on the Saturday next
after the Feast of the Assumption of the Blessed Mary in the
5ᵗʰ year of the reign of King Edward son of King Edward,
together with tenements which Matilda formerly (wife) of
Ranulph the grave held in dower.   And he gives to the lord
for entry cvjˢ viijᵈ, pledges William atte Flete and Ralph
Aldieth.

From William de Hilletoft for duplicate of xiij acres of land   Duplicate
which were his mother's Beatrice ijˢ.   ijˢ

From Walter Chapman for licence to marry Emma his   Merchet
daughter within the manor to Alan Lithfote.   iijˢ iiijᵈ

From Matilda daughter of William Bygge to have to herself   Fine xijᵈ
for her whole life xl feet in length and xxx feet in breadth
in Skegnesse.

The township has respite to inquire of wreck of the sea until
the next court, and of the warren and ways in the same newly
made.

The land which Alan Saffron purchased of Richard atte
Kirke is taken into the hand of the earl.

ijˢ

The township presents that Ralph son of Margery, and   Bakers
vjᵈ   Mercy iijˢ
Thomas de Lincoln sold bread contrary to the assize, therefore
they are in mercy.

iijᵈ   iijᵈ

Agnes de Orreby, Alice Catte.   Tipplers
vjᵈ   ijˢ   xijᵈ

Gilbert Nevyle, Gilbert Thory, Simon Thory, (and 18 others).   Brewsters
The township presents that Robert Faukes, a bond tenant   xiijˢ ixᵈ
of the lord, purchased certain tenements in Holm in Norfolchia,
therefore it is ordered that they be taken into the hand of the
lord, and be rented to the lord.

Also that Peter son of Reginald Safron was ordained without   Attach-
licence, therefore let him be attached.   ment

Also that William son of Margery raised the hue justly upon

Alan son of Alan son of Ralph, therefore the same Alan is in mercy, and nevertheless let him be attached.

It is ordered to attach Walter Lamb to have Beatrice his wife to answer to the lord for goods carried off outside (the manor) contrary to the order.

Fines for homage vˢ From William Neucomen for having his homage respited until Michaelmas xijᵈ, from Peter de Steping, John de Whatecroft, (and 7 others).

Sum of this Court vijˡⁱ vijˢ vjᵈ.

Court of Ingoldemeles held on the Monday next before the Feast of S. Peter ad Vincula, 7 Edward [30 July A.D. 1313].

Essoins (Dns Peter de Gipthorp, William Neucomen, Alan de la Rawe, Joan de Whatecroft, William de Hilletoft, Robert de Boyland.)

Fine vjᵈ From Robert de Westmeles for respite of homage until the Feast of S. Michael vjᵈ.

Mercy vjᵈ It is found by the inquisition upon which William de Donedyk, plaintiff, and Ralph Stotevyle put themselves in a plea of trespass, as appears in the court held on the Wednesday next after the Translation of S. Thomas, that the said Ralph did no trespass upon the said William, therefore it is considered that the said William be in mercy for a false claim, and the said Ralph be quit without a day, pledge the bailiff.

Coram consilio dni Walter Lamb in the absence of Beatrice his wife for the trespass of the same Beatrice was distrained by ij cows and j stirk, worth xxˢ, levied by the lord earl through a composition made by her in the time of H. earl of Lincoln. And the said Walter found pledges, viz. Ralph Aldieth, Alan son of Bride, William son of Alice, Ralph de Modeland. And afterwards by Michael de Meldene at Bolingbrok it was considered that the said Beatrice should be put in the pillory for many trespasses for which she could not be punished by amercements.

Judgment respited The judgment between Robert Warener, plaintiff, and Camilla in a plea of debt is in respite until the next court, (to decide) if a bond tenant ought to be accepted to perfect his law against a bond tenant or (whether the case ought to go) to an inquisition.

Chevage iiijᵈ From Robert ffaukes of Lyndeseye for frankpledge iiijᵈ, pledges William atte fflete and William son of Alice.

Respite The inquisition between the lord earl and John ad Castel concerning his naifty is in respite until the next court unless the council of the lord comes first.

It is found by the inquisition on which John Smith and William Cook put themselves that William Cook made a trespass on the said John to the damage of iij^d. And therefore it is considered that the said John shall recover the said iij^d. And the said William is in mercy, pledges &c.

It is found by the inquisition upon which William Smith, plaintiff, and William Cook put themselves in a plea of trespass that the said William Cook did a trespass on the said William to the damage of vj^d. Therefore it is considered that the said William Smith shall recover the damages which are taxed at vj^d. And the said William Cook is in mercy, pledges &c.

It is found by the inquisition upon which <u>Alice Bride</u>, plaintiff, and <u>William Bride and Agnes his wife</u> put themselves that the said William and Agnes called the said Alice 'false' and 'robber,' saying that the said Agnes (sic) stole . . . and other jewels, to her damage half a mark. Therefore it is considered that the said Alice shall recover the damages which are taxed at half a mark, and the said Agnes is in mercy, pledges William Bride and the bailiff.

From <u>Clementia daughter of Sarah Catte</u> to have to her and her heirs of her body in matrimony begotten the moiety of one messuage and the whole land which William atte fflete junior purchased of Robert ffaukes containing j acre xxxvj falls, which the same William resigned to her before Ranulph the grave, Alan Bogge, bailiff, Ranulph Rengot, William son of Alice, Alan . . . , Walter Chapman, Alan atte Hauedyk, and William son of Walter Catte. And she gives the lord for entry viij^s, pledges &c.

William atte fflete junior, who held of the lord five acres of bond land, is dead. And upon this comes William atte fflete senior, brother of the said William, and next heir, and asks to be accepted to pay heriot for the said land. And he gives the lord for entry xxxiij^s iiij^d, pledges Ranulph the grave and the bailiff.

It is ordered the bailiff to retain in the hand of the lord the fruits of the land of Ralph Cook for a trespass made on Eleanor his wife as is said. Therefore the bailiff is ordered to cause a

D

good inquisition to come to inquire the state between the said Ralph and Eleanor.

Distraint as yet It is ordered to distrain Beatrice Lamb to answer to the lord concerning woollen garments, and wood utensils of Agnes ffraunceis, put in the defence of the lord, and carried off by her, as it is said, and now she does not come, therefore, as often, let her be distrained.

Attach- ment as yet It is ordered to attach Walter Ballok and Richard Seuster for cutting the signal of a ship carried off by them, and to answer to the lord for the trespass.

Attach- ment John son of Milo, plaintiff, offered himself against Gilbert de Whatecroft in a plea of debt, who is attached by j super-tunic, worth iiij^d, and he does not justify himself, so let it be retained and more taken.

Attach- ment as yet It is ordered as before to attach Peter son of Reginald Saffron, who was ordained without the licence of the lord : (and) John Benety for hue raised upon him justly : (and) Thomas Harpour and William Galle for hunting in the warren of the lord.[1]

Mercy vj^d Burgh presents that Thomas son of Hugh de Whatecroft raised the hue justly upon John son of Philip de la Rawe, therefore the said John is in mercy, pledge William Cadi-horn.

Mercy vj^d Ingoldemeles presents that Alan son of Alan raised the hue justly upon &c.

Mercy ij^s Also that Beatrice at Grange, Joan at Waterlad, Matilda daughter of Stephen de Donedyk have been chastised, there-fore they are in mercy.

The township of Ingoldemeles has respite to present divers paths to the sea &c.

New rent ij^s iiij^d John atte Castel, a bond tenant of Ingoldemeles, who pur-chased one messuage iiij acres and iij roods in Hundelby, of which Isabel his wife was jointly enfeoffed of one acre, and three roods of land with . . . situated on half an acre. And because he is enfeoffed of Alan de Hundelby contrary to the form of the statute . . . it is (ordered) that they be levied to the use of the lord for ever, and they are rented at two shillings and iiij^d, and he shall do two (appearances) at the court of

[1] The case of ‘ Gilbert Thory and Beatrix his wife v. Alan de Wegland ’ to be taken ‘ before the steward at the next court.’

Ingoldmeles, viz. at Michaelmas and at the next court after Easter.

Sum of this court lviij^s v^d.

Court of Ingoldemeles held at Burgh on Monday next before Ash Wednesday, 7 E. [18 February A.D. 1313–4].

Dominus Peter de Gipthorp (is essoined) of the common (advent) by Geoffrey son of John.

Alan West of Anderby and Lucia his wife by their attorney, complainants, and Robert Wasteler and Margaret his wife are [agreed] in a plea of debt, and the said Robert and Margaret his wife put themselves in mercy, pledge Robert atte Hauedick.

It is ordered, as often, to attach Thomas le Harpur and William Galle for greyhounds hunting in the warren.

It is ordered to distrain William son of Richard de Hiltoft for homage.

William Plomer pledges the mercy for the hue raised upon him justly, pledge Walter de Orreby.

Little Eudo (and 7 others) all these in mercy for trespass made in the warren of the lord.

(3 persons) distrained for the same.

William ad Spinas, who held of the lord one messuage and one curtilage of free land in Skegnesse, is dead. Upon this come Agnes and Lucy, the sisters and nearest heirs of the said William, and ask to be accepted to (pay) relief for the tenements. And they did fealty. And they acknowledged that they held the said tenements. And they have a day.

From Walter Rasour to be in the frank-pledge of the lord vj^d yearly, pledges Alan son of Simon Litchfot and Alan . . .

From Alan son of Ralph de Modeland to have to him and the heirs issuing of his body one acre of bond land in Ingoldemeles on the west side of the land of the said Ralph de Modeland, which the said Ralph resigned to the said Alan in full court. And he gives the lord for entry vj^s viij^d, pledges Walter de Orreby and Ralph his father. And he gives viij^d of increment. And for this acknowledgment and grant the same Alan granted to the aforesaid Ralph to have and to hold the said acre of land for his whole life.

Marginal notes:
- Mercy iij^d
- Attach-ment
- Distraint
- Mercy vj^d
- Mercy v^s viij^d Distraint
- Fealty
- Respite
- Frank-pledge vj^d
- Fine vj^s viij^d Increment viij^d

Ingoldemelys presents that Thomas Meriet raised the hue justly upon John de Welton, chaplain,

And that Milo de Skegnesse drew blood from Stephen Lake, therefore he is in mercy.

Also that Matilda daughter of William de Wegland, Isabel Thikthorp, and (3 others) have been chastised, therefore they are in mercy.

Inquisition concerning the cutting of Scalflet, and their abettors, where there never was any cutting, by which cutting the township of Ingoldemeles was inundated to the great detriment and disinheritance of the lord earl and his tenants. And who cut the way which is called le Mosegat by which cutting the market place of the lord earl at Weynflet is destroyed.

It is ordered to seize ij acres of land which Simon Cook, a bond-tenant of the lord, demised to John German contrary to the custom of the manor without the licence of the lord.

Also j acre of pasture which Camilla demised to Alan de Hilletoft, a free man, contrary to &c.

It is found by the inquisition that John Vigrous and William son of Mabel made a certain cutting upon Scalflete to the great detriment of the lord and his tenants and the whole community, therefore it is ordered to attach the said John and William. And because it is testified that the said John has nothing in the Bailiwick therefore it is ordered to attach the prior of Bolington to seize the said John, his servant.

Attachment   Also they say that William son of Robert son of Alan Magnus made a certain cutting upon Scalflete, therefore it is ordered that he be attached.

Attachment   Also that by Alan Plant not repairing his dike upon Scalflete the pastures, and meadows of Ingoldemeles, Wynthorp, and Skegnesse are inundated.

Attachment   Also that William Bonde and Walter son of Walter atte Rawe made ij cuttings in le Mosegat, therefore it is ordered that they be attached.

Sum of this roll xxviij⁵ ix^d.

Plaints of the Court held on Monday the Vigil of S. Gregory the Pope, 7 Edward [11 March A.D. 1313-4]. (5)

Plaints of the Court of Ingoldemeles held on Monday next

before the Feast of the Apostles Philip and James, 7 Edw. [29 April A.D. 1314]. (10)

Plaints of the Court held on Monday next after the Feast of the Ascension of our Lord, 7 Edw. [20 May A.D. 1314]. (12)

Plaints of the Court held on Monday next after the Feast of the Translation of S. Thomas the Martyr, 8 Edw. (torn) [8 July A.D. 1314].

Court of Ingoldemeles held on the Monday next before the Feast of the Apostles Philip and James, 7 Edw. [29 April A.D. 1314].

William de Hilletoft (is essoined) of the common (advent) by Walter (torn). Peter de Gypthorp by Walter son of Robert.

It is ordered, as often, to distrain William son of Richard de Hilletoft for homage. To distrain William son of Matilda de Burgh to answer to the lord because he sued Thomas Le Daye, a tenant of the lord, in other courts when he could be sued in the court of the lord.

William son of Mabel pledges the mercy for trespass made upon Scalfled, pledges Simon Boteler and Henry Poleyn. *Mercy xij*^d

It is ordered to distrain John Vigrous, the prior of Boling-ton, and William son of Robert Magnus for divers trespasses upon Scalflet. To attach Walter Bonde and Walter son of Walter atte Rawe for divers trespasses made in le Mosegat, as appears in the court held at Burgh on the Monday before Ash Wednesday. *Attach-ment*

Walter Lamb in mercy for the detention of vij^s v^d against Matilda atte Skelles, pledge William son of Alice. And he undertook to pay the said debt to the said Matilda at the Feast of S. Michael next without further delay. And unless he should do it the lord's bailiff shall cause to be made &c. *Mercy vj*^d

Thomas Meriet acknowledged that he was indebted to Matilda atte Skelles in half a quarter of wheat, worth iij^s, iij bushels of barley, worth iij^s, and j bushel of . . . , worth xij^d, and he is in mercy for the detention. *Mercy vj*^d

William de Toft was attached to answer to Robert son of Margery of a plea of trespass. And wherefore he complains that on the Lord's day next (. . . the Feast) of All Saints last he unjustly caused him to be cited at Stamford by his procuration by the parish chaplain of Ingoldemeles, by which citation he gave to a certain proctor xij^d, and to an advocate ij^s, to the damage of the same Robert &c. (torn). And he produces suit. And the said William comes and defends force &c. And says that he was not summoned, nor did he lose any money by his procuration, as he alleges against him. And he demands that

Inquisition it be inquired, and the other party likewise. Therefore let the inquisition come.

Fine iiij^s From William Auks to have to him and his boys for ever three roods of bond land in Ingoldmeles which Richard his brother resigned to him in full court. And he gives the lord for entry iiij^s, pledge Ralph Aldieth. And for this acknowledgment and resignation he . . . and quit-claims to the said Richard his brother his whole right in three roods of land which he claimed against him.

Mercy xij^d Ingoldmeles presents that Robert Ballok raised the hue unjustly upon Walter Broun. And because the township has not attached the parties, therefore the township is in mercy. And nevertheless let the said Robert be attached.

Also that Guy Rodcol, Gilbert and John, brothers of the same John (sic), Alan son of Alan Mighel are not in chevage, therefore let them be attached.

Also that Robert Knythe is a bond-tenant of the lord, and dwells in Louth without the fee of the lord, therefore it is ordered that all his lands and chattels be seized into the hand of the lord.

Leyrwite ij^s vj^d Also that Isabel Chald (and Inglesia Donedyk ij^s) are chastised, therefore they are in mercy.

Mercy ij^s Also that the fence between Winthorp and Ingoldmeles at Clayclotes is not made by the default of William son of Alice and Walter Lamb, therefore they are in mercy.

Also that William son of Alice cut the way in the same place, and turned the water out of its course, therefore &c.

Mercy vj^d Also that William son of William de Duneswra cut the purse of Thomas Yol with eleven shillings, therefore it is ordered that he be attached.

Also that all damages of dikes and ways of Ingoldemeles be repaired before the first of August. And unless they are they shall give to the lord x^{li}.

ij^s Also that Robert son of Margery and Walter de Brindele~

Also that Simon Thori, (and 10 others), all these are in mercy for forestalling. *vij⁰ vj⁴*

The bakers present that Thomas de Lincoln, Ralph son of Margery, and Matilda wife of Simon son of Gilbert (condoned by the steward) are in mercy for breaking the assize of bread. *ij⁰ vj⁴* ᴍ

The tasters of bread present that Agnes de Orreby, Alice Meriet, (and 3 others) are in mercy because they sold bread contrary to the assize. *Mercy xviij⁴*

The brewsters present that Gilbert Nevill, Walter Grin, (and 18 others), all these are in mercy for breaking the assize of beer.

From Robert Bigge to have to him and his sons for ever one half-acre of bond land in Skegenesse, which William Bigge, father of the said Thomas (sic), resigned to him in full court. And he gives to the lord ij⁰, pledge William atte Flete. And for this acknowledgment and grant the same Robert granted to the same William the said half-acre of land to hold for the term of his life. *Fine*

From Gilbert Thori, Beatrice his wife, and William their son, and the heirs of the said William (to have) three acres and three roods of bond arable and pasture land in Ingoldmeles, which William de Presthorp resigned to them in full court, which Matilda wife of Thomas Meriet holds in dower. And which after the death of the said Matilda ought to revert to the said William de Presthorp shall remain to the said Gilbert, Beatrice, and William, and the heirs of the said William son of the said Gilbert and Beatrice to hold for ever. And they give the lord for entry xx⁰, pledges William atte Flet and Robert atte Hauedyk. ᴍ

From Sarah and Matilda daughters of Thomas de Presthorp to have to them for the term of their lives, and the life of which of them shall live the longer, half an acre of bond land in Ingoldmeles which Thomas, father of the said Sarah and Matilda, resigned to them in full court to hold in the form aforesaid. And they give the lord for entry ij⁰. *Fine ij⁰*

Court of Ingoldmeles held at Burgh on Monday the Feast of the Translation of S. Thomas the Martyr in the beginning of 9 Edward [July 7 A.D. 1315].

William Childe, plaintiff, and Henry vicar of Calceby by

licence are agreed in a plea of agreement, and the said Henry puts himself (in mercy), pledge William Child.

Mercy vj^d

Simon Fairhar, John Bride, and Alan son of Isabel Polayn were attached to answer to Thomas son of Margaret of a plea wherefore on the Lord's day next after the feast of S. Augustin the bishop 8 Edw. II. in the vill of Ingoldmeles they insulted, beat, and ill treated, and did other enormities to him, to the damage of the same Thomas xl^s. And therein he produced suit. And the said Simon, John, and Alan come and defend force &c. and say that they are not guilty, and demand that it be inquired, and the other party likewise. Therefore let an inquisition come. Which says that the said Simon, John, and Alan did the trespass on the said Thomas to the damage of the said Thomas v^s. Therefore it is considered that the said Thomas shall recover the said v^s. And the said Simon, John, and Alan are in mercy, pledges &c.

Inquisition

Mercy xviij^d

As yet distraint

It is presented as often to distrain Peter Safferun who was ordained without the licence of the lord: and Robert Herre, who raised many walls obstructing the common way to the injury and disinheritance of the lord earl and the country.

Mercy vj^d

Ralph Aldieth, plaintiff, offered himself against Alan atte Conigisgate of a plea of debt, who was distrained by one horse and replevied by the pledge of William de Hiltoft and the bailiff. And nevertheless let the said Alan be distrained.

Mercy vj^d

Wreck ix^s v^d

A 'salyard' of a ship, herring nets, one boat, and a panel of a certain ship, which are said to be wreck, are sold for ix^s v^d.

The township of Ingoldemeles is in mercy for the concealment of William son of Walter, bailiff of Ingoldemeles, a bond-tenant of the lord earl of Lancaster dwelling at Huntingdon, and this if Dominus Michael de Meldon will accept it.

c^s

Walter Alewayn came into court and acknowledged himself indebted to Hugh Smyre in xxiij^s iiij^d. And for this he found pledges viz. Simon atte Wallis, Alan atte Dammes, and William son of Alice, to pay to the same Hugh the moiety on the Feast of S. Laurence next and the other moiety on the Feast of S. Michael next, and unless it shall be done he shall cause them (the money) to be made from the lands and chattels of the

Recognitors

said pledges. And the said Walter is in mercy, pledges as above. Mercy vj^d

Walter Polayn (and two more) in mercy because they have not come. Mercy vj^d

It is presented to attach Ralph and John sons of Walter, the bailiff, each to come with four pledges to the next court to answer to the lord. Attach-
ment

The township presents, that Thomas le Daye raised the hue justly upon <u>Agnes le Daye</u>, therefore the said Agnes is in mercy:

that Geoffrey Westerik drew blood from Gilbert Fairhar, therefore the said Geoffrey is in mercy:

that <u>Matilda Tyk</u> has been chastised, therefore she is in mercy vj^d.

From Alan son of Stephen ad Curiam Aule to have <u>Matilda daughter of Alan de Galewayth to wife</u> with six acres and a half of land to themselves and their boys for ever according to the custom of the manor xxvj^s viij^d, pledges William atte Hallegarth and the bailiff. Fine
xxvj^s viij^d

From Henry Dybald to have and to hold iiij selions of arable land from the Purification 8 E. II. to the same feast twenty years next following, which William Redecole demised to him to farm, ij^s, pledge the bailiff.

From Hugh Bond yearly for three acres of land, which he purchased in Weynflet, which are rented to the lord at xij^d. New rent
xij^d

Court of Ingoldmels held at Skegnesse on the Saturday the morrow of the Assumption, 9 Edward [August 16 A.D. 1315].

From <u>Beatrice daughter of William Belte of Skegnesse</u> for licence to marry <u>Alan de Hulseby without the manor,</u> pledge Matilda atte Gote. Merchet
ij^s

It is ordered, as before, to distrain Beatrice to have William her nephew at the next court to answer to the lord: and to John Erwerd of a plea of trespass. Distraint

William Catte perfected his law which he waged against Gilbert Lamb of a plea concerning a horse, therefore the said Gilbert is in mercy, pledge Walter Lamb. And the damages are taxed by the consideration of the court. Afterwards the said William and Gilbert are agreed so that William Catte ought to have his horse with viij^s ix^d. Mercy vj^d

Default
Mercy vj^d Robert Warner and Robert son of Roger are in mercy for tumult.

Merchet
ij^s From William Bigge for licence to marry Margaret his daughter to Robert Kyng without the manor, pledges &c.

It is found by the inquisition, upon which William Bride and Agnes his wife, plaintiffs, and William son of Alice put themselves in a plea of trespass, that the said William called the said Agnes 'meretrix,' to her damage taxed at iij^d.

Mercy vj^d Therefore it is considered that the said William and Agnes shall recover the said damages. And the said William is in mercy.

Inquisi-
tion Let there come an inquisition to inquire concerning the names of those who fished in the fisheries of the lord without the licence of the lord, obstructing the sewers of the community.

> Sum of this roll vij^{li} xv^s j^d.

Court of Inggoldmeles. View held on the Monday next after the Feast of S. Luke the Evangelist in the 9th year of the reign of King Edward son of King Edward [20 October A.D. 1315].

Robert de Westmeles (is essoined) of the common (advent) by Alan atte Conyngesgate.

Fines for
Suit of
Court From Isabel de Wegland for respite of suit of court until the Feast of S. Michael next xij^d, from Peter de Steping for the same xviij^d, from Dominus Richard Waleis for the same vj^s viij^d, from William de Thorp for the same xviij^d, from Robert de Rigg for the same vj^d, from Master William de Burgh for the same xij^d, from Master Alan de Horncastre for the same xl^d, from Simon de Boyland for the same vj^d.

Roger de Stowe, chaplain, was attached to answer to Richard atte Kirk of a plea of agreement. And therein he complains that on the Saturday next before Pentecost in the viijth year of King Edward an agreement was made between them, so that is that whereas the said Richard took xviij sheep for xv^s for a certain yearly rent due to him at the same time the said Roger undertook to resume possession of the said xviij sheep on the octave next following, at which day he did not do so to the damage of the said Richard half a mark. And thereof he produces suit, and the damages are taxed before the
Mercy vj^d steward. And the said Roger comes and fully admits the said

agreement, and admits that he did not resume possession of the said sheep. Therefore it is considered that the said Richard shall recover the said damages. And the said Roger is in mercy. Afterwards they are taxed at ijˢ, pledge William du Mareis.

From Matilda daughter of Alan at Grange for licence to marry William son of Thomas son of Richard without the manor, pledge Alan atte Damnes.   *Merchet vjᵈ*

Ralph son of Margery, plaintiff, offered himself against William de Prestorp of a plea of debt, who was distrained by j horse, worth xvˢ. And it was testified by the bailiff on oath that the said horse was taken by the said William out of the pinfold. Therefore it is ordered that the said William be attached to answer to the lord for the rescue made.   *Attachment*

Thomas de·Lincoln (and 3 others) in mercy for the assize of bread.   *Bakers Mercy iiijˢ*

Gilbert Thory, Simon Thory, Nicholas de Kele (and 13 others) in mercy for the assizes of beer and bread.   *Brewsters Mercy xixˢ iiijᵈ*

Walter Daie (iijᵈ), William in ye groupe (Vavasour iijᵈ), Robert son of Hugh (Vavasour iijᵈ), and Agnes Hacon in mercy for the assize of beer.   *The Brewsters of Kokerington Mercy xijᵈ*

The township presents that John Marcis has injured the king's way to the detriment of the whole community, therefore the said John is in mercy. Also that Agnes Mareis dug the common way next Marais houses, therefore the said Agnes is in mercy. Also that William de Boston dug a certain pit near the house of Walter Rumphar, throwing the land upon his own land, injuring the common way when he ought to have thrown it upon the common way, therefore he is in mercy. Also that Robert Bogge (and 15 others) cut and dug the common ways of the said vill to the injury of the whole community, therefore they are in mercy. Also that through the abetment of William atte Trappe and Simon atte Waterlad, graves of the dikes of the south common of Burgh, many persons cut the defence between Scalflet and the marsh, by which the lands of the tenants of the lord have been inundated, therefore let the said graves be attached. And it is ordered that an inquisition come to inquire concerning the names of the persons who did the said trespass.   *Mercy xiiijˢ vjᵈ*

The township presents that John Bride drew blood from Wymund de Westrig, therefore the said John is in mercy, pledges

Mercy
ij⁕ vjᵈ

&c.; also that Wymund de Westrig drew blood from John Bride, therefore the said Wymund is in mercy &c.; also that Sarah Norman raised the hue justly upon Matilda de Prestorp, therefore the said Matilda is in mercy &c.

Leyrwite
vjᵈ
Chevage
Mercy xxjᵈ

Also that Hawis Sabelyn has been chastised, therefore she is in mercy: also that Ranulph son of Ralph de Modelant (and 2 others) are able to give chevage. Also that John de Swaby, the prior of Bolington, (and 3 others) obstructed a certain watercourse where their beasts ought to be watered by diverting the right watercourse at oxettinggappe, therefore they

Mercy vjᵈ

are in mercy. Also that William de la Rawe (condoned by the steward) and John Oxhird servant of the prior of Bolington cut Scalflet in the north common of Burgh, whereby the lands below the marsh are inundated, therefore they are in mercy. Also

Mercy xijᵈ

that William Magnussone (and 4 others) do not repair nor make the defence between Scalflet and the lands below Burgh, therefore they are in mercy. And nevertheless let the aforesaid be attached to repair and sustain the aforesaid defence.

Attach-
ment

Also that Dominus Philip de Kyme and the commoners of the south common of Burgh have raised a certain bank in the common of Burgh Scalflet to the prejudice and injury of the lord earl and his tenants, therefore let them be distrained. And nevertheless it is ordered that the said bank be thrown

Mercy vjᵈ

down. Also that William Cadihorn, and Hugh son of Roger de Burgh have not repaired, nor sustained a way near hodcroftgate, therefore they are in mercy. And nevertheless it is ordered that they be attached to sustain the said way. Also it is ordered to distrain Richard Calodes to show how he had entry on the fee of the lord.

Mercy vjᵈ

Also that Simon Cook obstructed a certain sewer with 'tainynges' to the prejudice of the whole community, therefore the said Simon is in mercy.

Mercy vjᵈ

The servant of Robert de Boiland is in mercy because he diverts the course of certain water at Boilandland.

Inquisi-
tion

Let an inquisition come to inquire if Alan del Hallegarth raised a certain wall on the soil of the lord or on the land of Walter Polain.

Sum of this roll lxxiiij⁕ vijᵈ.

Court of Ingoldemeles held there on Monday next before the Feast of S. Martin in the winter, 9 Edward son of Edward [10 November A.D. 1315].

Alan Ursel was attached to answer to William Swift and Beatrice his wife of a plea wherefore on the Lord's day next after the 1st of August last in the common way near the house of the said Alan in the vill of Skegnesse he insulted, beat, and ill used the said Beatrice to the damage of the same William and Beatrice. And thereof he produced suit. And the said Alan comes and defends force &c. And says that in nothing is he guilty, and he demands that this be inquired, and the other party likewise. So let an inquisition come. *Inquisition*

William atte Trappe has a day before the steward at the next court to answer to the lord for that many unknown persons by his abetment and consent cut the defence between Scalflet and the marsh so that bond lands and (lands) of tenants of the lord were inundated. So it is ordered that an inquisition come. *Inquisition*

It is ordered, as at other times, to distrain Simon atte Waterlad, the grave of the Suthcommon of Burg, for abetting the cutting of the defence between Scalflet and the marsh. *Distraint*

William Magnussone, Alan Plante, the prior of Bolington, John de Swaby, William Cadihorn do not repair nor make the defence between Scalflet and the lands below Burgh. As at other times it is ordered that they be distrained. It is found by the inquisition that Alan atte Hallegarth raised a certain wall too near the common way. Therefore the said Alan is in mercy. *Distraint*

From William son of Walter Bogge to have and to hold to him and his boys two acres of bond land and xxviij rodfalls, lying between a certain way that is called 'Gateroum' on the east and land of William de Prestorp on the west, which William de Prestorp resigned to him in court. And he gives the lord for fine xvs, pledge Alan Bogge.

The township presents that Matilda daughter of Meriet is chastised, therefore she is in mercy. *Mercy vjd*

They have respite concerning a certain wall unjustly raised at Hallegarth.

Also they present that a way at Redhous is injured by a digging which Walter atte Rede dug near his house. Therefore the said Walter is in mercy. And nevertheless the said way shall be mended. *Mercy ijs Distraint*

It is found by the inquisition upon which John Bride, plaintiff, and Wymund de Westerik in a plea of trespass put themselves that Wimund wounded the said John to his damage vj^d. So it is considered that the said John shall recover the said vj^d. And the said Wimund is in mercy.

Mercy vj^d

It is found by the inquisition upon which Wimund de Westerik, plaintiff, and John Bride in a plea of trespass put themselves, that the said John did the trespass on Wimund to his damage xviij^d. And the said John is in mercy, pledge the bailiff.

Mercy vj^d

ij^s

From Sarah who was the wife of Bernard de Burgh for her homage being respited until the coming of the earl into the country ij^s.

Sum of this court xxv^s ix^d.

Court of Ingoldmels held on Monday the Vigil of S. Katherine the Virgin, 9 Edw. [November 24 A.D. 1315].

It is ordered, as often, to attach Simon atte Waterlad, the grave of the Southcommon of Burgh, for abetment of the digging of the defence between Scalflet and the marsh.

Mercy vj^d

William Cadihorn found pledges, viz. Simon Boteler and the bailiff, to satisfy the lord for that he has not repaired the defence between Scalflet and the marsh.

Distraint still

Let William Magnussone, Alan Plant, and the prior of Bolington be distrained for the aforesaid defence not repaired.

Court of Inggoldemeles held on Monday before the Feast of S. Lucy the Virgin, 9 Edward [8 December A.D. 1315].

Attach-ment

It is ordered, as often, to attach Simon atte Waterlad, the grave of the Suthcommon of Burgh, for abetting the cutting of the defence between Schaleflete and the marsh.

Distraint

William Magnussone, Alan Plante, and the prior of Bolington are distrained for the said defence.

Distraint

It is ordered, as often, to distrain Peter son of William Tector to answer to Matilda who was the wife of Simon de Akewra in a plea of debt, who is distrained by xl^d in the hands of William de Westiby. And he does not justify himself, therefore let (the money) be retained and more &c.

It is found by the inquisition upon which Alan Polber, plaintiff, and Matilda, who was the wife of Ranulph, the bailiff, put themselves in a plea of agreement, that the said Matilda was indebted to the said Alan in vj pair of linen cloths, worth xv^d each, to the damage of the said Alan vj^d. And for the detention she is in mercy, pledges &c. Mercy vj^d

Richard Cobbler was attached to answer to Hawis Picher in a plea wherefore on the Wednesday next before the Feast of S. James the Apostle in the 9th year of King Edward in the vill of Wynthorp he insulted, beat, and ill used her, to the damage of the same Hawis half a mark. And thereof she produces suit. And the said Richard comes and defends force &c. And says that he is not guilty. And of this he puts himself upon his country. Therefore comes an inquisition which says that the said Richard did a trespass to the said Hawis, to her damage, which is taxed at iij^d. Therefore it is considered that the said Hawis shall recover the said iij^d. And the said Richard is in mercy &c. Inquisition Mercy iij^d

Matilda wife of Ranulph the bailiff, Gilbert ffairhar, (and 3 others) are in mercy for obstruction of the common sewers of the whole vill, pledges each for the other. And it is ordered to inquire better. Mercy iij^s vj^d

It is presented that William Lawis obstructed a certain sewer at Lawishous, therefore he is in mercy. Mercy vj^d

Also that Beatrice de Dunedyk married without the licence of the lord, therefore she is in mercy, pledge the bailiff. Mercy iij^d

Also that John Godard, and William son of William de Douneswra are able to give chevage. Chevage vj^d

Court of Ingoldmels held there on the Saturday next after the Feast of the Epiphany, 9 Edward [10 January A.D. 1315-6].

William Copere and Matilda his wife were summoned to answer to Matilda who was the wife of Simon de Akewra of a plea that they render to her xxxj^d ob., which they owe her and unjustly detain, as she says. And wherein she complains that on the Monday next before the Feast of S. Peter ad Vincula 9 Edward the same Matilda Copere bought of the said Matilda de Akewra j quarter of malt for ix^s to pay to her at the next Michaelmas, on which day she paid nothing, but detained it unjustly, to her damage ij^s. And thereof &c. And the said Matilda Copere admits the said xxx^d. And the said Matilda Copere is in mercy, pledge the bailiff. Mercy iij^d

John son of Walter was attached to answer to William Fouler of a plea wherefore on the Saturday the Vigil of

S. Nicholas 9 Edward he took and unjustly imparked his
10 hogs in a certain 'hinham' of William his father, which he
has of his demise between the bank of the sea in Skegnesse and
the dunes, to the damage of the same William c⁸. And thereof
he produced suit. And the said John comes and says that he is
not bound to answer because he says that he took and imparked
the said hogs as it seemed well to him, as grave of the sea

Day banks, as in the common of the said vill. And as the steward
is not present a day is given to the parties at the next court.
Afterwards the same William says that he (John) did not take
the said hogs in the common of Skegnesse, but in le Inham, as
in his several field. And this he demands may be inquired.
And the said John says that (he took the hogs) in the common
and not in his (William's) several field, and this he demands

Inquisi- may be inquired. Therefore comes an inquisition, which says
tion
Mercy iijᵈ that the said John took (the hogs) in the common. Therefore
it is considered that (William) shall take nothing by the complaint, but let him be in mercy. And the said John is quit
without a day.

Mercy   It is presented to attach William Tipir (and 8 others) for
vjˢ **ix**ᵈ trespass made in the warren of the lord, therefore they are
in mercy.

Mercy iijᵈ   Alan Boef acknowledged that he was indebted to Robert
atte Hafdick in xxij⁸ for a certain horse sold to him, to be paid
to him, a moiety at the Feast of the Purification, and the other
moiety at the Feast of the Apostles Philip and James next,
without further delay. And for the detention he is in mercy,
pledge the bailiff.

Mercy ljᵈ   Simon Lamb is in mercy because he has not come to testify
concerning the delivery of a certain distraint made upon Walter
Alewain to answer to Simon atte Wallis in a plea of agreement.
Distraint And nevertheless let the said Simon be distrained.

Gilbert son of Emma was attached to answer to William
Fougler of a plea of agreement. And therein he complains
that on the Monday next before the Feast of S. Ambrose in the
8ᵗʰ year of King Edward son of King Edward it was agreed
between them that the same Gilbert from the said Monday
would neither procure nor cause to be procured any damage or
loss between the said William and a certain Gilbert de Watecroft, for a certain half mark and 'macuela' received from him.

And he says that by the default of the same Gilbert the

same William lost the cropping of one acre worth v⁸ vj^d, which
acre and a half of meadow was demised to the same Gilbert by
the said William.

And he says that the same Gilbert procured the said Gilbert
de Watecroft not to hold the agreements made between the
same William and the said Gilbert, so that the said William has
damage, and is injured to the value of c⁸. And thereof he produces suit. And the said Gilbert comes, and defends &c., and
says &c., that he took no half mark or ' masceuela' from the said
William as he complains against him, and this he defends   Law
against him and his suit, pledge of his law William atte Flet.
And afterwards on the day of law the said Gilbert offered
himself with his law who failed in his law. Therefore it is
considered that the said William . . . the said agreement to-   Mercy iij^d
gether with damages which are taxed at xij^d. And the said
Gilbert is in mercy.

Gilbert son of Emma was summoned to answer to William
Fowler (Auceps) of a plea that he render to him iij⁸ vj^d which
he undertook for William Balderik for a tenth of a fish sold to
the said William on the day of Pentecost last past to be paid to
the same William at the next Michaelmas, on which day Gilbert
paid him nothing, but detained it, and yet unjustly detains it,
to the damage of the same William half a mark, and thereof he
produces &c. And the said Gilbert comes and says that he was
the pledge of the said William Balderik for the said iij⁸ vj^d, but
he says that on the last day of payment of the said money the
same William Fougler assigned another last day, through which
assignment the same Gilbert says he is not bound for the said
iij⁸ vj^d for the said William Balderik. And this he demands   Inquisi-
may be inquired. And the other party says that he never   tion
assigned any day beyond the first day appointed for the payment of the said money. And this he demands may be inquired. Therefore let an inquisition come.

Court of Ingoldemeles held on Saturday next before the
Feast of the Purification, 9 Edward II. [3] January a.d. 1315-6]

plaints, actions, or contracts he had or should have between
Ranulph atte Hallegarth and the same Alan, to Walter son of
Ranulph atte Hallegarth and his heirs for ever for a certain sum
of money which the same Walter gave to him in hand.

Mercy vj^d William Swift and Beatrice his wife, plaintiffs, and Alan
M   Ursel by licence are agreed in a plea of trespass. And the said
Alan put himself (in mercy), pledge William Swift.

It is found by the inquisition upon which Matilda who was
the wife of Simon de Akewra, plaintiff, and Alan Polber put
W   themselves in a plea of debt, that the said Alan is bound to the
said Matilda in x^d. Therefore it is considered that the said
Mercy ij^d Matilda recover the said x^d. And the said Alan is in mercy,
pledge William Copere.

William Fougler was summoned to answer to William son
of Richard de Westemels of a plea that he render to him three
bushels of beans worth iij^s, which he undertook for one Gilbert
de Whatecroft. And therein he complains that on the Lord's
day next before the Feast of S. Ambrose 8 Edward the same
Gilbert bought of the said William son of Richard the said iij
bushels of beans for ij^s to be paid to the same on the Feast of
S. Michael next, which iij bushels the same William Fougler
undertook (to pay for) at the said term, on which day the said
Gilbert paid nothing, nor the same William Fougler, but
detained it. And this they unjustly detain to the damage of
the same William son of Richard half a mark. And thereof he
produces &c. And the said William Fougler comes and defends
force &c. And he says that he is not bound to answer to him,
for that the same William son of Richard granted a day of payment of the said iij bushels beyond the said day assigned for
which he undertook. And William son of Richard says that he
assigned no day to the said Gilbert beyond the said term. And
Law this he defends against him and his suit, pledges for his law
Robert de Westemels, and William atte Trappe, afterwards by
licence they are agreed, and the said William is in mercy.

Condoned Alan Chalde acknowledged that he is indebted to Robert
son of Margaret in iij^s vi^d for beans sold to him. And for the

The township presents that Beatrice daughter of Alan at
Grange is chastised, therefore she is in mercy. Mercy xij^d

Also that William Botheler raised the hue justly upon
Thomas Bolber, therefore the said Thomas is in mercy. Mercy iij^d

Also that Walter Bole raised the hue justly upon Thomas
Bolber, therefore the said Thomas is in mercy. Mercy iij^d

Let Thomas Catte be distrained for the assize of beer. Distraint

It is ordered as at other times to attach William son of
Ralph de Douneswra for 'corbellage.' [1] Attach-
ment as
before

The township presents that the wife of Henry Taillur (and
4 others) are in mercy for bread sold of false weight. Mercy xxj^d

Robert de Orreby (and 3 others) in mercy for trespass made
in the warren of the lord. Mercy xv^d

Alan Plomer, plaintiff, offered himself against Simon the servant of William de Hilletoft [summon him to attach his servant] in
a plea of debt, who does not come, therefore let him be attached. Attach-
ment

Matilda who was the wife of Simon de Akewra was attached
to answer to William Copere and Matilda his wife of a plea
of agreement. And therein they complain that on Wednesday
next after the Nativity of the Blessed Mary 9 E. II. at Ingoldemeles the same Matilda de Akewra sold to the said Matilda
Coper iiij quarters of drag malt for xxxvj^s, price of a quarter
ix^s, to deliver to the said Matilda Coper the said iiij quarters
of malt within the 15 days next following in the said place.
On which day the said Matilda de Akewra delivered to her
only one quarter of malt. And so she detained the said iij
quarters of malt, and as yet unjustly detains them, to the
damage of the same William and Matilda Coper xx^s. And
thereof they produce suit. And the said Matilda Akewra
comes and defends force &c. And she says that if the said
Matilda Coper would have come on the day appointed between
them to ask for the said iij quarters of malt she would have delivered the said iij quarters. And she says that the said
Matilda Coper did not ask for the said iij quarters, as was
agreed between them, through which she has not detained the
said iij quarters of malt, nor does she unjustly detain them, and
this she is ready to verify. And the said William and Matilda
Coper are ready to verify that the said Matilda de Akewra has
detained, and as yet &c. Therefore let an inquisition come. Inquisi-
tion

Sum of this Court xv^s viij^d.

_____
[1] A toll.

E 2

Court of Ingoldmels held on the Saturday next before Ash Wednesday, 9 Edw. [20 February A.D. 1315–6].

Mercy vj^d — *replace* Mercy vj^d

Mercy vj^d William son of Thomas Marescall acknowledged that he was indebted to Matilda who was the wife of Simon de Akewra in iiij^s, and ij^s for damages. And he is in mercy for the detention &c.

Mercy vj^d William Fougler acknowledged that he was indebted to William son of Richard de Westemels in viij^s, to pay iiij^s within 15 days, and iiij^s at Easter next, for beans received from him, and he is in mercy for the detention, pledge the bailiff.

Mercy iij^d It is found by the inquisition upon which William Coper and Matilda his wife of a plea of agreement put themselves that the said Matilda broke the agreement between them made, to the damage of the same William and Matilda xviij^d. Therefore it is considered that the said William and Matilda Coper shall recover the said xviij^d. And the said [1] Matilda is in mercy.

iij^d From Clementia Chelis for acquiring a charter iij^d.

Mercy iij^d It is found by the inquisition upon which Matilda de Akewra, plaintiff, and William Coper and Matilda his wife put themselves in a plea of debt, that the said Matilda Coper is indebted to the said Matilda de Akewra in xviij^d for damages. And therefore it is considered that the said Matilda de Akewra shall recover the said xviij^d with damages, and the said William and Matilda Coper are in mercy.

Mercy vj^d It is found by the inquisition upon which Robert son of Margery, plaintiff, and Robert Lamb in a plea of trespass put themselves, that the said Robert broke his 'hare,' worth xij^d, to the damage of the same Robert son of Margery iiij^d. Therefore it is considered that the said Robert son of Margery shall recover the said xij^d together with damages. And the said Robert Lamb is in mercy, pledge Walter Lamb.

Court of Ingoldmeles held there on the Saturday next after the Feast of S. Gregory the Pope in the 9th year of the king [13 March A.D. 1315–6].

It is found by the inquisition, upon which Simon Cook, plaintiff, and Robert de Cadenay and Alice his wife in a plea of trespass put themselves, that the said Alice took and carried away the vegetables of the same Simon, to his damage j^d. Therefore it is considered that the said Simon recover the

---

[1] Probably Matilda de Akewra.

damages which are taxed at jᵈ. And the said Robert and   Mercy iijᵈ
Alice are in mercy &c.

William Jerman was attached to answer to Richard son of
William de Hiltoft of a plea wherefore on the Saturday next
after the first week in Lent last past in the churchyard of the
Church of S. Peter of Ingoldmel he called the same Richard
'false' and 'robber,' saying that the same Richard had stolen a
horse at Freston and kept that horse in the court of William his
father in Ingoldmels, by which robbery upon him the same
Richard . . . one sack of wool worth xᵘ . . . lost the credit of
the said xᵘ, whereby he was injured, and has damage to the
value of cˢ. And thereof he produces suit. And the said
William comes and defends force and injury, and says that in
nothing is he guilty, and this he is prepared to verify. And
the said Richard is prepared to verify his complaint. Therefore
comes an inquisition, which says that the same William called
the said Richard 'robber' in the form he alleges against him, to
the damage of the same Richard xˢ. Therefore it is considered
that the said Richard shall recover the said xˢ. And the said
William is in mercy, pledge the bailiff.

From Robert Bigge to have to him and his boys for ever one
acre of bond land &c. in Skegnesse, which William Bigge father
of the same Robert resigned to him in court. And he gives the
lord for entry iiijˢ, pledges William Coper and the bailiff.

From William de Thekethorp of Ingoldmels to have to him
and his boys for ever one rood and 15 perches of bond land &c.

From John son of Richard son of Roger Godard to have
&c. one acre of bond land in Ingoldmels &c., which Robert   Fine
son of Roger resigned to him before the grave and the homage   vjˢ viijᵈ
of the vill. And he gives the lord for entry vjˢ viijᵈ, pledge
Richard son of Roger.

Let there come an inquisition between the lord and William   Inquisi-
de Dunnyswra concerning baskets put in the common sewer   tion
against the defence of the lord.

Alan Plomer, plaintiff, and Simon Bercarius in a plea of   Mercy
debt by licence are agreed. And the said Simon puts himself condoned
(in mercy), pledge William lord of Hiltoft.

William Fougler perfected the law which he waged against
Gilbert son of Emma in a plea of debt iijˢ vjᵈ, and in vjˢ viijᵈ
for the damages of the same William, which he demanded
against the said Gilbert, as appears in the court held on the

Monday next before the Feast of S. Lucy the Virgin last.
Therefore it is considered that the said William shall recover
the said iij^s vj^d, and vj^s viij^d for his damages. And the said
Gilbert is in mercy, pledge the bailiff.

Mercy vj^d

Sum of this roll xxj^s viij^d.

Court of Ingoldmels held there on Saturday the Vigil of
Palm Sunday, 9 Edward [3 April A.D. 1316].

William de Dufdick demands xxvj^s viij^d against William de
Presthorp for sheep sold to him, which xxvj^s viij^d he ought to
have paid to him on Christmas Eve last, which he has not yet
paid, but detains, and as yet detains, to his damage xx^s. And
thereof he produced suit. And the said William de Presthorp
comes and defends force &c. And says that in no money is he
indebted to him, and this he demands may be inquired, and the
party against him likewise. Therefore an inquisition comes,
which says that the said William de Presthorp is indebted to
the said William in the said xxvj^s viij^d, together with damages,
which are taxed at xl^d. And the said William de Presthorp is
in mercy.

Inquisi-
tion

Mercy vj^d

William de Dufdick acknowledged that he was indebted
to William de Presthorp in half a bushel of beans. And in
damages which are taxed at vj^d by the court. Therefore it is
considered that the said William de Prestorp shall recover the
said half bushel of beans together with damages. And the said
William de Dufdik is in mercy for the detention.

Mercy iij^d

Demise
ij^s

From William Bride and Agnes his wife to have and to hold
to themselves one place of pasture, containing two acres of land
in Ingoldmels &c. from Christmas 9 Edward II. until the same
feast through six years next following, which Matilda Elmer
demised to them. And she gives the lord for having the term
ij^s, pledges &c., if the demisor live so long.

Fine xl^d
Increment
x^{d}q.

From Henry Dibald, and William his son, and the heirs of
the said William for ever, (to have) one messuage, two selions
of bond land, containing one acre one perch and six rodfalls in
Burgh, which William Redecole resigned to them in court.
And he gives the lord of increment x^{d}q. And for fine xl^d,
pledge the grave.

Thomas Meriet and Matilda his wife came in full court and
granted, remised, and entirely for themselves for ever quitclaimed to Gilbert Thori, Beatrice his wife, and William their

son, and the heirs of the said William, their whole right and claim which they had in three acres and three roods of bond land, arable and pasture, in Ingoldmels, which &c. William de l'restorp resigned (to them): and which the said Matilda wife of the said Thomas Meriet held in dower, as appears in the court held on the Monday before the Feast of the Apostles Philip and James, 7 Edward. And they give the lord yearly of increment ij⁵.

Gilbert son of Eudo, Walter son of William Tipir, Eudo son of Ranulph Godesone, Thomas son of Robert Langeman, and William Slegth found pledges viz. Alan Brok and Little Eudo of standing an inquisition for that they carried off xlvj⁵ viij ᵈ, one purse of ' saye,' one silver seal worth xl ᵈ, one girdle worth ij⁵, which are called 'wreke.' Therefore an inquisition comes which says that they are guilty, therefore they are in mercy.

William Ringot, who held of the lord one messuage and twenty acres of bond land in Ingoldmels, is dead. And upon this comes Ranulph Ringot son of the said William and heir, and asks to pay heriot for the said tenement. And he is admitted. And he gives the lord for heriot (torn).

The townships say that Walter Bole, Ralph Barker found the goods and chattels of Andrew de Hiltoft, therefore let them be attached.

It is ordered to attach Thomas Bobber, Richard Bole of ffreskenay, Ralph Barker of Partenay, Robert Pymak, William Schot, and Simon the servant of John Pedder to answer to the lord for wreck carried off.

Attachment as yet

Peter de Methland and Matilda his wife appeal Peter son of William le Ceker and Thomas his brother of Ingoldmels for that in the night of the Monday before Palm Sunday this year they secretly broke their house, and took one bushel of wheat, and one pig's ham, and carried them off out of their house. And this they are prepared to verify against the said Peter and Thomas, as faithful men against robbers. And the said Peter and Thomas come, and say, that therein they are not guilty. And of this they put themselves for good or evil upon the country. And because they refused to be put for good or evil upon the court they are sent to the Jail at Lincoln Castle. And it is said to the said Peter de Methland and Matilda his wife that they may prosecute if they will.

M

Gayole Linc.

Peter de Methland and Matilda his wife appeal Emma relict

of William Ceker of Ingoldmel that in the night of Monday next before Palm Sunday this year she broke the house of the same Peter and Matilda, and took one bushel of wheat, and one pig's ham, and secretly carried them off. And this they are prepared to verify against the said Emma, as faithful men against a robber. And the said Emma says that she is not guilty therein. And of this she puts herself upon the court for good or evil. Which says that therein she is not guilty. And therefore it is considered that the said Peter and Matilda shall take nothing by their suit, but shall be in mercy for a false appeal, pledges William de Cikethorp and William de Dufdick.

Quit
Mercy iij^d

Increment
xx^d
Fine xij^d

From William son of Stephen atte Hallegarth of Ingolde-meles, a bond tenant of the lord, to have to him and his boys for ever one messuage, and one court, which is called Lascy halle, which messuage and court used to render to the lord v^s yearly, and now are rented beyond the said v^s at xx^d of increment, pledge the grave. And he gives the lord for fine xij^d.

Sum of this roll vj^{li} xv^s xj^dq.

Court of Ingoldemeles held on Saturday next before the Ascension of the Lord, 9 Edward son of Edward [15 May A.D. 1316].

Mercy iij^d

Richard de Lusceby acknowledged that he is indebted to Roger de Stowe, chaplain, in xxvj^s, a loan to be paid from day to day. And for the detention he is in mercy, pledge Roger the chaplain.

Distraint

Roger de Stowe, chaplain, offered himself against Walter son of William de Grenwyk in a plea of debt, who is attached by chattels worth iij^s. And he does not justify himself, so let them be retained.

Mercy iij^d

Richard atte Kirke acknowledged himself indebted to Simon Cook in one bushel of wheat to be paid at Michaelmas. And for the detention he is in mercy, pledge William son of Richard de Hilletoft.

xij^d

From Master Thomas Bekk for searching the rolls concerning a fishing penalty, and an agreement with himself made in full court, as appears in the court held on the Saturday next before the Feast of S. Peter ad Vincula 6 E. II. xij^d.

Alan atte Conynggesgate acknowledged himself indebted to

Robert de Westmeles in xxxij⁸ viij^d, to be paid him on the 1st of August xx⁸, and xij⁸ viij^d at Michaelmas next, without further delay. And for the detention he is in mercy.　Mercy xij^d

It is presented to attach Robert atte Mosgat, bailiff of Candelleseby. to answer to the lord for that he made an attachment in the fee of the lord without the licence of the lord.　Attach-ment as yet

Walter Kygges acknowledged himself indebted to Richard son of William de Hilletoft in xviij^l, and for the detention he is in mercy.　Mercy ij^d

From Alan Est and Agnes his wife to have and to hold to the said Agnes and the boys of the said Agnes for ever one acre and a half and one rood of bond land in North Redeholm, which Alan Wyles father of the said Agnes resigned to her before Ranulph the grave, Alan the bailiff, William atte Flete, and many other bond tenants of the lord. And she gives the lord of increment xiiij^d yearly. And she gives the lord for fine . . . , pledge Ranulph Rengot. And for this grant and resignation the same Alan and Agnes granted the said tenements to the said Alan Wyles to hold for his whole life.　Fine vj⁸ viij^d Increment xiiij^d

M

Thomas son of Alan Hereward, a bond tenant of the lord, who held of the lord one messuage, thirteen acres one rood and six perches of bond land in Inggoldemels, of which three acres and one rood, each acre is (rented) at xij^d, and ten acres of land, each acre at iiij^d, is dead. And upon this came Robert, son and heir of the said Thomas, and asked to be accepted to pay heriot for the said tenements according to the custom of the manor. And he is admitted. And he gives the lord for fine xl⁸, pledge Ralph de Modeland. And the said Robert granted in court that Alice his mother shall have the said tenements wholly until the end of eight years. Days for pay-ment of the fine, Christmas, Purification, and Easter, by equal portion.　Heriot xl⁸

W.

From William atte Hallegarth to have and to hold to him and his boys for ever two acres three roods and thirty perches of bond land in Inggoldemeles, which William de Prestorp resigned to him in court. And he gives the lord for fine half a mark, pledge the grave. In going and returning to the said land through the middle of the land of the said William de Prestorp towards the east (sic).　Fine half a mark

From Richard Bonde, Alice his wife, and John the son of
the said Alice, and the heirs of the said John to have for ever
half an acre and 31 perches of bond land in Inggoldemeles
which Alan Chalde resigned to them in court. And they give
the lord for fine ij⁸, pledge the grave. And he gives the lord
yearly of increment v⁴ ob.

From Henry de Thikkthorp to have to him and his boys for
ever 13½ perches of bond land &c. fine vj⁴. Increment ob.

Distraint

Roger de Stow, chaplain, plaintiff, by his attorney offered
himself against Walter son of William de Grenwik, carpenter,
in a plea of debt, who is attached by one axe and other
chattels, worth iij⁸, and he does not justify himself, therefore
&c.

Attach-
ment
as yet

It is presented as often to attach Thomas Bobber, Richard
Bole of Freskenay, Ralph Barker of Partenay, Robert Pimake,
William Scotte, and Simon the servant of John Pedder to
answer to the lord concerning wreck of the sea carried off.

It is found by the inquisition, upon which Alan Drope,
plaintiff, and William son of Thomas son of J. put themselves
in a plea of debt that the said William was indebted to the
said Alan in v⁸, and vj⁴ for damages. Therefore it is considered

Mercy vj⁴

that the said Alan shall recover the said v⁸ and damages. And
the said William is in mercy.

Attach-
ment

It is presented to attach Gilbert de Watecroft to answer to
Alan atte Rawe in a plea of debt.

Court of Ingoldmels held there on Saturday the Vigil of the
Holy Trinity, 9 Edw. [5 June A.D. 1316].

Attach-
ment
as yet

It is presented to attach Robert atte Mosgat, bailiff of
Candelesby, to answer to the lord for that he made an attachment in the fee of the lord without the licence of the lord.

It is found by the inquisition upon which John son of
William Koke, plaintiff, and Ralph Cook in a plea of agreement put themselves that the said Ralph broke the agreement
between them made concerning a certain place of land sold to
him, to his damage xij⁴. Therefore it is considered that the

Mercy vj⁴

said John shall recover the said xij⁴, and the said Ralph is in
mercy.

Mercy vj⁴

It was found by the inquisition upon which John son of
William Koke, plaintiff, and Ralph Cook in a plea of trespass
put themselves that the said Ralph did the trespass upon him

to the damage of the same John vj^d. Therefore it is considered that the said John shall recover and the said Ralph is in mercy.

Matilda who was the wife of Ralph Elmer was summoned to answer to Hugh son of Emma and Beatrice his wife of a plea that she render to them vij^s iij^d. And therein they complain that on the day of S. Michael the Archangel 9 Edw. in the house of the same Hugh a settling was made, so namely that in all accounts to be computed an allowance is to be allowed, the same Matilda acknowledged that she was indebted to the said Hugh and Beatrice for all debts between them had in the said vij^s iij^d to be paid to the same Hugh and Beatrice in the octave following. On which day she paid nothing, but detained, and as yet unjustly detains, to the damage of the same Hugh and Beatrice v^s. And therein they produce suit. And the said Matilda comes and defends force &c. And she says that in nothing is she indebted to them. And this she defends against them and their suit, pledges of her law Ranulph Ringot and William atte Flete. *Law*

Robert Pymake was attached by j horse, worth xvj^s, to answer to Robert son of Margaret in a plea of debt, and was replevied by the pledge of William Schot, and now he does not come, therefore the said pledge is in mercy, and nevertheless let the said Robert Pymak be distrained. *Mercy ij^d Distraint as yet*

It is ordered, as often, to attach Thomas Bobber, Richard Bole of Freskenay, Ralph Barker of Partenay, Robert Pymake, William Scotte, Simon the servant of John Pedder, to answer to the lord for wreck of the sea carried off. *Attachment as yet*

To attach William de Dunnyswra to answer to the lord for that (he was) in despite of the lord in full court. *Attachment*

Gilbert Lamb and Florentia his sister are in mercy for trespass made in the herbage and corn of William son of Alice, and the damages are taxed by the inquisition at viij^d. *Mercy vj^s*

From William de Cikethorp to have to him and his assigns three roods of pasture in Ingoldmels (for 9 years), which Sarah Chanel demised to him in court, if the demisor live so long. *Demise xij^d*

Fine iiij⁸ From Simon Thori to have and to hold to him and his boys for ever one acre of bond land in Ingoldmels, lying on the west side of land of Alan Rumphar which is called Forland, which Alan Rumphar resigned to him in court. And he gives the

Increment viij⁴ lord for fine. And he gives of increment viij⁴.

It is found by the inquisition upon which Matilda Elmer, plaintiff, and William Bride and Agnes his wife put themselves in a plea of debt, that the said William and Agnes were indebted to the said Matilda in vij˙, and damages, which are taxed at vj⁴. Therefore it is considered that the said Matilda shall

Mercy vj⁴ recover the said vij˙ and damages &c., and the said William and Agnes are in mercy.

Mercy vj⁴ The township presents that Joan Catte raised the hue justly upon William German, therefore the said William is in mercy.

Sum of this roll xij˙ j⁴.

Court of Ingoldmels held on Saturday next after the Feast of S. John Baptist, 9 Edward [26 June A.D. 1316].

Dominus Peter de Gipthorp (is essoined) of the common (advent) by Ranulph son of Robert.

Distraint Let the land which John son of William Fougler sold to William Fougler be taken into the hand of the lord.

It is found by the inquisitions (upon) which Robert atte Hauedik, plaintiff, and William German put themselves in a plea of agreement, that the said William is indebted to the said Robert in one bushel and a half of wheat to be paid on the Feast of S. Michael for the agreement with the said Robert which was broken. Therefore it is considered that the said Robert shall recover the said bushel and a half of wheat.

Mercy iiij⁴ And the said William is in mercy, pledge the bailiff.

Camilla guardian of John son and heir of Alan Meriet, plaintiff, and Robert son of Ralph son of Thomas have a day at

Mercy iiij⁴ the next court in a plea of xvj⁴ and xv⁴, which the same Robert

Inquisition ought to have paid on the Feast of S. Michael last, and on the Feast of S. Botolph last. Wherein an inquisition which says that the said Robert is indebted to the said Camilla in no money as she alleged against him. Therefore the said Camilla is in mercy for a false claim, and the said Robert is quit without a day.

Robert son of Margery, plaintiff, offered himself against

William Lowis in a plea of trespass, who does not come, there-   Attach-
fore let him be attached.   ment

It is presented to attach Robert atte Mosgate, bailiff of   Attach-
Candelsby, to answer to the lord for that he made an   ment
attachment in the fee of the lord without the licence of the
lord.

It is ordered to distrain Robert atte Hauedik to have   M
Robert Wasteler and Margaret his wife at the next court to
answer to William son of Thomas son of John (and 3 others)   Distraint
in a plea of debt.

Richard son of William de Hiltoft, plaintiff, offered himself   As yet
against Thomas del Outdaile in a plea of debt, who does not   distraint
come, therefore let him be distrained.

William de Dunniswra has a day at the next court to
answer to the lord for that he was in despite of the lord in full
court.

Sum of this roll xvij^d.

Plaints of the Court of Inggoldemeles. View held on
Monday next after the Feast of S. Luke the Evangelist, 9
Edw. II. [20 October A.D. 1315].

2 pleas of debt, 3 of trespass, 1 of agreement.

Plaints of the Court held at Ingoldemeles on Monday next
before the Feast of S. Martin in winter, 9 Edward II. [10
November A.D. 1315].

15 pleas of debt, 1 of agreement.

Plaints of the Court of Ingoldmes (sic) held there on
Monday the Vigil of S. Katherine the Virgin, 9 Edward [24
November A.D. 1315].

2 pleas of debt, 2 of trespass.

Plaints of the Court held on Monday next before the Feast
of S. Lucy the Virgin, 9 Edward [8 December A.D. 1315].

3 pleas of debt, 1 of trespass, 1 of agreement.

Plaints of the Court held on Saturday next before the Feast
of S. Hilary, 9 Edward [10 January A.D. 1315-6].

7 pleas of debt, 2 of trespass.

Plaints of the Court of Ingoldmeles held there on the Saturday next before the Feast of the Purification, 9 Edward [31 January A.D. 1315–6].

9 pleas of debt, 6 of trespass, 1 of agreement.

Plaints of the Court held on the Saturday next before the Feast of the day of Ashes (Ash Wednesday), 9 Edward II. [20 February A.D. 1315–6].

4 pleas of debt.

Plaints of the Court held on Saturday next after the Feast of S. Gregory the Pope, 9 Edward [13 March A.D. 1315–6].

11 pleas of debt, 2 of trespass.

Plaints of the Court held on the Saturday the Vigil of Palm Sunday, 9 Edward II. [3 April A.D. 1316].

15 pleas of debt.

Plaints of the Court on Monday the Morrow Quasi modo Geniti, 9 Edward II. [19 April A.D. 1316].

18 pleas of debt, 1 of trespass.

Court of Inggoldmeles held at Kokkehill on the Saturday the morrow of S. George the Martyr, 9 Edward [24 April A.D. 1316].

Eleanor and Rosa, daughters of Robert Sormilk of Inggoldmeles, appeal Matilda, daughter of William Smith of Great Steping, and Agnes, daughter of Simon Rogerman of Great Steping, that on the Monday the morrow Quasi modo geniti 9 Edward II. they broke by night the house of the same Eleanor and Rose at Great Steping, and secretly took, and carried off against the peace of the lord king two carpets worth iij^s, one overcoat worth iij^s, wool and thread worth vj^d, j dish worth vj^d. And this they are prepared to prove against the said Matilda and Agnes as faithful men against robbers. And

Chattels
vj^d
the said Matilda and Agnes say that they are not guilty therein. And of this they put themselves for good or evil upon the court. Which says that they are therein guilty.

Hanged
Therefore they are hanged. The chattels of the felons are valued at vj^d.

Plaints of the Court held on the Saturday next before the Ascension of our Lord, 9 Edw. II. [15 May A.D. 1316].

17 pleas of debt, 1 of trespass.

Plaints of the Court held on the Saturday the Vigil of the Holy Trinity, 9 Edward II. [5 June A.D. 1316].

6 pleas of debt, 2 of trespass.

In tergo.   2 of debt.

Plaints of the Court held on the Saturday next after the Feast of S. John Baptist, 9 Edward II. [24 June A.D. 1316].

4 pleas of debt, 2 of trespass, 1 of agreement, 1 of acquittance of pledge.

Plaints of the Court held on the Monday next before the Feast of S. James the Apostle, 10 Edward II. [19 July A.D. 1316].

5 pleas of debt, 2 of trespass.

Plaints of the Court held on the Monday next before the Nativity of the Blessed Mary, 10 Edward II. [6 September A.D. 1316].

9 pleas of debt, 1 of trespass.

Court of Ingoldemeles held on Monday next before the Feast of S. James the Apostle, 10 Edw. II. [19 July A.D. 1316].

William Typir was summoned to answer to Henry Emmotneve of a plea that he render to him vj⁸, and therein he complains that on the Monday next before the ' Carniprivium ' 6 Edw. at Skegnesse the same Henry sold to the said William six quarters of ' Wilkis,' price of a quarter xviij⁸, to be paid to him at the next Easter, on which day he paid all but vj⁸, which he unjustly detained from him, and still unjustly detains, to the damage of the same Henry xl^d.   And therein he produces suit &c.   And the said William comes and defends force &c. And says that in nothing is he indebted to him.   And this he defends against him and his suit, pledges of his law Alan the Law bailiff and William son of Alice.

From William Fougler of Skegnesse to have and to hold to him and his boys for ever one cottage and twenty rodfalls of

bond land in the same place which William son of John Fougler
Fine xij resigned to him in court. And he gives the lord for entry xij^d,
pledge the bailiff.

Roger son of Brittif of Sloteby was summoned to answer to
Alan Boef of a plea that he render to him xxiiij^s, and therein he
complains that on Thursday next before the 1st of August 8
Edw. II. at Ingoldmels the same Alan at the request of the
same Roger became pledge of Robert son of the said Roger for
xxiiij^s for xx lambs bought by the said Robert of William de
Dunniswra to be paid to the same William at two terms of the
year, viz. at Christmas one moiety, and at the Feast of the
Apostles Philip and James the other moiety. On which day
nothing was paid by the said Robert, and because of his
default the same Alan paid to the said William the said xxiiij^s
to the damage of the same Alan xx^s, &c. And thereof he produces suit &c. And the said Roger comes and defends force
.&c. And says that it was not at his request that the same
Alan became pledge nor security for the said xxiiij^s to the said
William nor paid. And this he defends against him and his
Law suit. And upon this he wages law, pledges of his law Walter
Marais and Gilbert Amy.

From Alan son of Sarah to have and to hold to him and his
Fine xij boys for ever one cottage and the fourth part of one acre of
bond land in Ingoldmels, which Alan atte Hallegarth resigned
to him in court. And he gives the lord for fine, pledge &c.

It is found by the inquisition upon which William de
Dufdik, plaintiff, and Alan atte Dammes put themselves in a
plea of debt that the said Alan is indebted to the said William
in xl^s. Therefore it is considered that the said William recover
Mercy xij the said xl^s, and the said Alan is in mercy, pledge the bailiff.
Mercy vj^d William de Dufdik acknowledged himself indebted to Alan
atte Dammis in xv^s, and for the detention he is in mercy, pledge
the bailiff.

It is found by the inquisition, upon which William Aukis,
plaintiff, and Geoffrey Brittifsone put themselves in a plea of
trespass, that the said William shall take nothing by his com-
Mercy iij plaint, but shall be in mercy, and the said Geoffrey is quit without a day.

From Richard, John, and Beatrice, children of Walter
Pourdefisse, of Ingoldmels, to have and to hold for their whole
life, and to which of them shall live the longer, one toft with

the pits, containing one acre of land on the south part of the
land of the said Walter, which toft Walter Pourdefisse resigned
to them in court. And he gives the lord for entry xl^d,   Fine xl^d
pledge &c.

From William son of <u>William de Wegland and Agnes his</u>   M
<u>wife to</u> have and to hold to them and their boys for ever six
acres and three roods of bond land in Ingoldmels, which
William de Prestorp resigned to them in court, which Matilda,
wife of Thomas Meriet, holds in dower, and which after the
death of the said Matilda ought to revert to the said William,
shall remain to the said William and Agnes and the heirs
of the said William, and he gives to the lord for fine xx^s,   Fine xx^s
pledges &c.

The townships present that <u>Matilda daughter of Alice</u>
<u>Wilis is</u> a common malefactor of beans and other damages, and   SP
is entertained by Alice her mother, therefore the said Alice is   Mercy xij^d
in mercy. And nevertheless let the said Alice be attached to
have the said Matilda her daughter at the next court.

Also they present that Gilbert Lamb is a malefactor of   Mercy
vegetables in the courts of neighbours, therefore he is in   condoned
mercy.   because
he is in
Robert son of Peter de Steping did fealty to the lord, and   Scotland
acknowledged that he held divers tenements in Steping by the   Fealty
service of xxj^d yearly, and suit of court &c. And he gives for
duplication of rent xxj^d.

It is presented as often to distrain Thomas Bolber (and 4   Distraint
others) to answer to the lord for wreck of the sea carried off.

Sum of this roll xxxij^s vij^d.

Court of Ingoldemeles held on the Monday the Vigil of
S. Lawrence, 10 Edw. II. [9 August A.D. 1316].

Little Eudo was attached to answer to Walter de Westemels of a plea wherefore on the Tuesday next before the Feast
of the Apostles Philip and James 5 Edward at Croft he called
the same Walter 'false,' saying that the same Walter plun-
dered lord Philip de Kime of a certain horse, worth xx^s, wherefore the same Walter was attached by a certain horse, of
which horse the same Walter was not able to obtain delivery
until he had paid xxij^s to the bailiffs of the said lord Philip, to
the damage of the said Walter x^s. And thereof he produces

F

suit. And the said Eudo comes and defends force &c., and says that he did not cause him to lose xxij* or any other money, but that by his own default he lost what he did lose, and he says that in nothing is he guilty. And this he demands

Inquisi-
tion may be inquired and the other party likewise, therefore let an inquisition come.

John Coke was attached to answer to Ralph Cook of a plea wherefore &c. Afterwards it is found by the inquisition upon which they put themselves that the said John made trespass

Mercy iij⁴ on the said Ralph to his damage vjᵈ. Therefore it is considered that the said Ralph shall recover the said vjᵈ. And the said John is in mercy, pledge as in the plaint.

Mercy ix⁴   Robert Catte, Thomas Cagoke pledged the mercy for entertaining contrary to the assize.

New rent   From William Fougler, a bond tenant of the lord, who
viij⁴ ob.   purchased iiij acres and the fourth part of one acre of free meadow land, which are rented to the lord at vjᵈ, pledge the bailiff.

It is found by the inquisition upon which Richard son of Rose, plaintiff, and William Aukis put themselves that the said Richard paid ij* to one Roger Brittifson in default of the same William to the damage of the same Richard iijᵈ. Therefore it is considered that the said Richard recover the said ij* and iijᵈ

Mercy iij⁴ for damages. And the said William is in mercy, pledge &c.

Demise ij*   From Robert atte Hauedik for having his term to him and his assigns of a certain place of land, which is called Le Parke, from Christmas 10 E. II. to the same Feast six years after, which he has of the demise of William Aukis, if the demisor live so long, pledge the bailiff.

It is found by the inquisition, upon which William Polber, plaintiff, and Walter Lamb put themselves in a plea of agreement, that the said Walter is bound to the said William to acquit him of damages for one Robert his son, who did not acquit him, to the damage of the same William vjᵈ, whereby the said William entered upon damage to the value of xvjᵈ. Therefore it is considered that the said William shall recover the said xvjᵈ, and damages which are taxed at vjᵈ. And the

Mercy vj⁴ said Walter is in mercy, pledge the grave.

The township presents that Thomas Kigges raised the hue justly upon Richard atte Kirke, therefore the said Richard is in mercy.

Also that William Est entertains Beatrice Bride, Joan Bride, and Agnes Est, therefore the said William is in mercy. And it is presented that the said Beatrice, Joan, and Agnes be attached. Mercy vj^d

Mercy vj^d
Attach-
ment

It is ordered as often to attach Thomas Bobber (and 5 others) to answer to the lord for wreck of the sea carried off.

As yet attach-
ment

Court of Ingoldmels held on Monday next before the Feast of the Nativity of the Blessed Mary, 10 Edw. [6 September A.D. 1316].

Let an inquisition come to inquire if Margaret Wasteler alienated a certain furnace, attached by vj^s without the fee of the lord.

Inquisi-
tion

Hugh son of Lucia was summoned to answer to Robert son of Margaret in a plea that he render to him iij^s, and wherefore he complains that on the Lord's day next after the Feast of S. Lawrence last in the churchyard of S. Peter of Ingoldmeles all agreements between them had and allowances allowed therefore by the consideration of the neighbours it was considered that the same Hugh was bound to the said Robert for all damages done by him to the same Robert in iij^s, which iij^s the same Hugh granted that he was indebted to the said Robert to be paid within the octave next following, on which day he paid nothing, but detained, and still detains, to the damage of the same Robert xl^d, and this he is prepared to verify. And the said Hugh comes, and defends force &c. And says that he is not indebted to the said Robert in the said iij^s, or in any other money for any arbitration between them made. And this he is prepared to verify.

Inquisi-
tion

Henry Emmotneve was summoned to answer to Ernisius Scalpy of a plea that he render to him ij^s. And therein he complains that on the Lord's day in the first week of Lent 7 E. II. at Skegnesse the same Ernisius lent to the said Henry the said ij^s to be paid him at Mid Lent following. On which day he paid him nothing, but detained it, and still detains it, to the damage of the same Ernisius xij^d, and thereof he produced suit. And the said Henry comes, and defends force &c. And says that he lent him no money but was indebted to him in other money. And this he defends against him and his suit, pledge of his law Robert de Westemels.

Law

[1] Alan de Hornecastel was essoined at the last court for the service of the lord king, and now he has not brought the warrant, therefore he is in mercy.

From William son of Thomas Bride to have and to hold to him and his boys for ever one cottage and two acres of bond land in Ingoldmeles &c., which William son of Ralph Elmer resigned to him in court, and which &c. Matilda daughter of Ralph Elmer holds for her life, and which after the death of the said Matilda ought to revert to the said William, shall remain to the said William son of Thomas Bride to hold to him and his boys for ever. And he gives the lord for fine half a mark, pledges &c., and of increment yearly xvj^d.

Fine half a mark. Increment xvj^d

From Henry Polayn for licence to marry Agnes daughter of William Goldif without the manor, pledges &c.

Merchet half a mark

William de Wegland was summoned to answer to William de Prestorp of a plea that he render to him vj^s viij^d. And therein he complains that on the Monday next after the Feast of S. Lawrence 10 E. II. at Ingoldmeles the same William de Wegland granted that he was indebted to the said William de Prestorp in the said vj^s viij^d for land purchased of the same William to be paid before the Feast of the Assumption next following. On which day he paid nothing, but detained, and still detains it unjustly to the damage of the same William de Prestorp xl^d. And thereof he produced suit. And the said William de Wegland says that in no money is he indebted to him as he alleges against him. And this he is prepared to verify, and the said William de Prestorp likewise, therefore let an inquisition come.

Inquisition

As yet of the Court held on Monday next after Ash Wednesday in the 12th year [26 February A.D. 1318–9].

From Beatrice daughter of Emma Clerkesdogter for licence to marry without the manor, pledges &c.

Merchet vj^d

Simon Reyner, a bond tenant of the lord, who held of the lord one messuage, and seven acres and a half, rendering to the lord for each acre iiij^d, and three acres, rendering to the lord yearly for each acre xij^d, is dead. And upon this comes Richard, son of the said Simon, and heir, and asks to be

[1] The essoin of the last court runs thus: Alan de Horncastil, defendant, because he is in the service of the lord king v. Alice atte Kirke in a plea of debt by William Marais.

accepted to pay heriot for the said tenements according to the
custom of the manor.   And he is admitted.   And he gives the
lord for heriot, pledges &c.

Heriot
xlvj⁵ viij^d

The township presents that Clementia wife of Simon Tappart
raised the hue justly upon Walter Pork, therefore the said Walter
is in mercy, pledge Richard Reyner.

Also that Robert Ascyl concealed one ' rothere ' worth . . . ,
therefore (he) is in mercy, pledge &c.

Also that an attachment made upon one Robert atte Dyke
to answer to Ranulph Bragge in a plea of agreement by three
' ares,' 1 ' swaype,' and one sail was arrested by 'Alan Warren,
therefore let the said Alan be attached.

Also that William son of Simon atte Welle drew blood from
Walter atte Hallegarth, therefore the said William is in mercy,
pledge &c.   Also that Walter atte Hallegarth drew blood from
William son of Simon atte Welle, therefore the said Walter is
in mercy, pledge &c.

Court of Ingoldemeles held before William de Wakefeld,
steward, on Wednesday the Feast of S. Benedict, 12 Edw. [21
March A.D. 1318–9].

William de Preesthorp acknowledged that he held detained
in the pasture of the same William from the Feast of the
Apostles Philip and James xii E. to the Feast of S. Michael
following six stirks of the age of one year of the stirks of
Matilda de Cracroft for xij⁵ due to the same Matilda.   And the
said William is in mercy for the unjust detention of the said
money.

Mercy iij^d

From Richard Barebeued of Derby for licence to marry
Alice who was the wife of Thomas Herward, who holds in
dower four acres of land in Ingoldemels v⁵, pledge &c.

Fine v⁵

The township presents that the custom of the manor is that
if any free man begets any [child] by a ' native ' (woman) of the
lord that a ' native ' he ought to remain for ever.   And they say
that William son of Sarah atte Crambes of the same condition
was ordained without the licence of the lord, therefore is in
mercy.

Mercy iij^d

                    Sum of this roll xij⁵ vij^d.

Court of Ingoldemeles held on Wednesday next after the Feast of S. Wulfran, 13 Edw. II. [17 October A.D. 1319].

Fealty Simon le Boteler, who held of the lord of the inheritance of Alice his wife . . . by homage, fealty, and suit of court from three weeks to three weeks, and by the service of xij^d &c., is dead. And upon this comes Alice who was the wife of the same Simon, and asks to be admitted to do fealty, and does it.

Fines of suit of court From Robert de Ryg for respite of suit of court until Michaelmas xij^d, from Robert son of Peter de Steping ij^s, from William Frank xij^d, from Robert le Vavasour x^s, from Peter de Gypthorp ij^s, from William de Thorp ij^s.

^{1} Reygner (and another) in mercy because they came out of Scotland from the lord without warrant.

Defaulters **Mercy** **ij^s ix^d** Alan Sablyn, William Roumfar, Simon Thory, (and 9 others) in mercy, because they have not come.

Merchet **xxvj^s viij^d** From Ralph Lamb for licence to marry Matilda daughter of Walter Catte within the manor xxvj^s viij^d, pledges &c. And he has a day to pay at Christmas.

xij jurors present that Roger atte More holds of the fee of the lord xiij acres j rood, Robert de Boyland holds ij acres of the same fee, William de Boston [distrained by j ox] holds of the same fee x acres, William Chyld holds of the same fee j acre. And William Poleyn, a bond tenant, holds j rood. All these tenements are held of the lord by the service of xviij^d. Therefore let them be distrained for the services being in arrear.

Also that William son of Richard de Hiltoft and Sapientia de Saltfletby hold two parts of xiij acres of free land by the service of two parts of the rent of two shillings yearly, by homage, fealty, and suit of court from three weeks &c. And because the said William and Sapientia have not done homage, therefore let them be distrained.

They have respite about how much Alice Wybyan holds, and by what services &c.

Mercy **ij^s vj^d** Also that by the default of William Cadihorn and Alan son of Hugh son of Roger the king's way is blocked up, and damaged, therefore (they) are in mercy. Also that Thomas Astyn has removed a certain town bridge of the tenants of the lord beyond the common drain at Stertes croft, therefore he is in mercy, and nevertheless it is ordered that the said Thomas

^{1} Vacat quia ex alia parte.

be distrained. Also that Richard atte Kyrke is a man who is against the peace of the lord the king. And he does not desire to justify himself, nor to attach himself to the peace. And because he is a common malefactor of certain trespasses, therefore the constable is ordered that he be attached.

Also it is ordered that all having common in Scalfledd be distrained for pigs digging in the same &c.

Walter le hird, and William de Dunham, foreign bailiffs, are in mercy, because they do not come to perform their offices as of right. *Mercy ijˢ*

The township presents that Robert ffaukes raised the hue unjustly upon William de Burgh, therefore the said Robert is in mercy, pledge the township. *Mercy iijᵈ*

Also that Sibill daughter of William son of Guy is chastised, therefore she is in mercy. *Leyrwyth Mercy xijᵈ*

Also that William son of Alan de Dcunedyk purchased free land, but it is not known how much, therefore let him be distrained. *Distraint*

Also that Richard atte Kyrke drew blood from William Mareys, therefore let the said Richard be attached. *Attachment*

Nicholas de Cantilupe is in mercy for default of suit of court. *Mercy xlᵈ*

The wife of Thomas de Lyncoln is in mercy for assize of bread. *Bakers Mercy vjᵈ*

William Mareys, Richard nephew of the parson of Skegneys, (and 9 others) in mercy for assize of beer. *Brewsters Mercy vˢ iijᵈ*

From Roger atte More for respite of homage until Easter xviijᵈ. *xviijᵈ*

From William Chapman, and Robert Assele, because they have not Richard Reygner with his warrant of his advent from the lord. (A similar case.) *Mercy xijᵈ*

Sum of this roll lxixˢ.

Court of Ingoldemeles held on Wednesday next after the Feast of Leonard, 13 Edw. II. [7 November A.D. 1319].

John Herword acknowledged himself indebted to William atte Flete in ijˢ vjᵈ. And for the detention he is in mercy, pledge the grave. *Mercy xijᵈ*

It is found by the inquisition that John Herword is indebted to William atte Flete in xijᵈ. Therefore it is considered that the said William shall recover the said xijᵈ. And the said John s in mercy, pledge the grave. *Mercy iijᵈ*

Distraint   It is presented as elsewhere to distrain William Childe for homage and other services :

William de Boston by j ox for homage &c. : and William son of Richard de Hiltoft and Sapientia de Salfletby for homage &c. : and all of Burgh having common in the common of Scalflete.

Mercy vj^d   It is found by the inquisition that Ralph son of Margery falsely complained of William Ryngot in a plea of debt, therefore for the false claim he is in mercy.

It is ordered to distrain Thomas Astyn to repair a certain bridge at Stertecroft.

It is found by the inquisition that John Alewayn is indebted to Ralph son of Margery in half a quarter of wheat for the Mercy iiij^d trespass of his beasts made in the corn of the said Ralph. Therefore it is considered that the said Ralph shall recover the said half quarter of wheat, and the said John is in mercy.

It is found by the inquisition that John Alewayn broke the agreement with William Polber concerning the carrying of his hay, to his damage xij^d. And that the said John shall carry the hay of the said William standing in the court of William Mercy iij^d Marays. And the said John is in mercy, pledge the grave.

It is found by the inquisition that Alan atte Hafdick is indebted to William atte Flete in iij^s xj^d, and ij^d for damages, therefore it is considered that the said William shall recover the Mercy vj^d said iij^s xj^d, and ij^d for damages. And the said Alan is in mercy.

It is found by the inquisition that John Alewayn made trespass on William son of Alice by his cattle to his damage ij^s, therefore it is considered that the said William shall recover the Mercy iij^d said ij^s. And the said John is in mercy.

Wreck   One empty cask, one cask half full of honey, which are called wreck. And xxx boards are found of wreck.

Plaints of the Court held at Burgh on Wednesday next after the Feast of S. Clement the Pope, 13 Edw. [28 November A.D. 1319].

[5 pleas of trespass, 2 of debt, 2 of agreement.]

Plaints of the Court held at Ingoldemeles on Wednesday next after the Epiphany of the Lord, 13 Edw. [9 January A.D. 1319-20].

[6 pleas of trespass, 5 of debt.]

Sum of this roll iiij^s vij^d.

Court of Ingoldmeles held at Burgh on Wednesday next after the Feast of S. Clement, 13 Edw. II. [28 November A.D. 1319].

William son of Alan Dufdick, a bond tenant, who purchased free land, but it is unknown how much, has a day at the next court to show the charter by which he is enfeoffed &c. — Respite

It is presented, as often, to attach Richard atte Kirke for blood drawn: to distrain William Childe for homage and other services. William de Boston is distrained by one ox for the homage of tenements of the heirs of Wathecroft &c. It is presented to distrain Sapientia de Salfletby for the same: (and) Thomas Astin to repair a certain bridge at Stertecroft. — Attachment, Distraint

William son of Richard de Hiltoft has a day at the next Court to do to the lord for a tenement, which is held of him, what justice requires. — Respite

It is ordered, as at other times, to attach all the men of Burgh having common in the common of Scalflete. — Attachment

Richard Ranyer and Simon son of Alan son of Ralph are in mercy because they came out of Scotland from the lord without warrant. — Mercy xij

Memorandum of a certain hue raised by William German, as it was said, upon Ralph son of Margery is in respite until the next court. — Respite

Simon son of Petronilla is attached for four stirks found in the warren of the lord, pledge Walter de Westibi 'per eschepium.'

Court of Inggoldemeles held on Wednesday next before the Feast of S. Thomas the Apostle, 13 Edw. II. [19 December A.D. 1319].

Alan atte Halgarth is convicted that he made a trespass on Simon Lamb to the damage of the same Simon xij^d. And for the trespass made the said Alan is in mercy, pledge William atte Halgarth. And the said damages are given to the clerk. — Mercy iij^d, Respite

Ranulph Cobbe is in mercy because he has not come. It is found by the inquisition that William German raised the hue unjustly upon Ralph son of Margery, therefore the said William is in mercy. — Mercy ij^d

Thomas son of Rengot perfected the law which he waged against Thomas Bobber in a plea of debt. Therefore it is considered that the said Thomas Bobber take nothing by his — Mercy ij^d

complaint, but be in mercy. And the said Thomas son of Rengot go thence quit without a day.

Merchet ½ mark From Walter son of Robert for licence to marry Matilda who was the wife of Ranulph atte Halgarth within the manor half a mark, pledge the grave.

New rent From William son of Alan de Dounedyk, a bond tenant of the lord, who purchased j messuage and j half bovate of free land in Welton, containing five acres and a half, and xxj falls and a half, which are rented to the lord at . . . , pledge William de Dounedyk the grave.

Fealty Respite xij^d William de Hiltoft did fealty to the lord, and acknowledged that he held of the lord iiij acres and the third part of one acre of land by homage and fealty. And he gives to the lord for respite of homage until Easter xij^d.

Respite ij^s The Lady de Eresby demands a court and has it From William de Boston for homage to be respited until Easter ij^s. Alan atte Hauedyk, plaintiff, offered himself against Alan son of Robert in a plea of trespass, who is attached by six sheep, and they are replevied by the pledge of Walter Ose until this court. And upon this comes the steward of the Lady de Heresby and demands her court, and it is granted this turn. And they have a day of court.

Attachment William German raised the hue justly upon William Mareschal, and therefore the said William is attached.

Mercy iij^s Walter le Hirde and William de Donham are in mercy, because they do not come to perform their office as is proper.

Sum of this roll xv^s x^d.

Court of Ingoldmeles held there on Wednesday next after the Feast of the Epiphany of our Lord, 13 Edw. II. [9 January A.D. 1319-20].

Memorandum concerning wreck, as in the court held on Wednesday next before the Feast of S. Thomas the Apostle, and to be answered anew.

Heriot iiij^li Richard Goddard, a bond tenant of the lord, who held of the lord one messuage and thirteen acres of bond land in Ingoldmeles, each acre at four pence, is dead. And upon this comes William his son and heir, and asks to be admitted to the said tenements to pay heriot according to the custom of the manor, and he is admitted, and he gives the lord for heriot iiij^li, pledge the grave.

It is found by the inquisition, on which John Alewin, plaintiff, and Ralph son of Margery put themselves in a plea of trespass, that the said Ralph imparked two cows of the same John in the common way unjustly, to the damage of the same John iiij⁹. Therefore it is considered that the said John shall recover the said iiij⁹, and the said Ralph is in mercy, pledge the grave. — Mercy vj⁴

From Robert German to have and to hold to him and his boys issuing of his body one place of land, which is called le Hagh, surrounded with a ditch, which William German resigned to him in court. And he gives to the lord xij⁴, pledge William German. — Fine

The township presents, that the dog of Robert Warrener took one hare, therefore let him answer to the lord for the trespass. — Respite

Also that Matilda Catte is chastised, therefore she is in mercy. Also that William the grave raised the hue justly upon Robert de Orrebi, therefore the said Robert is in mercy, pledge &c. — Mercy vj⁴ / Mercy vj⁴

Sum of this roll iiij¹ⁱ ix⁹ vj⁴.

Court of Ingoldmeles held at Skeggenes on Wednesday next after the Conversion of S. Paul, 13 Edw. II. [30 January A.D. 1319–20].

John Redecol has not come to do suit, therefore he is in mercy. — Default Mercy ij⁴

Hugh Heyr made fine for respite of suit of court until Michaelmas. — Fine vj⁴

Robert atte Gote has a day at the next court to acknowledge relief. — Day

It is ordered, as often, to distrain William Child for homage and other services: and Thomas Astyn to repair a bridge, which is called Stirtescroft brigg: to attach all men having common in Scalflet for trespass made there. — Distraint / Attachment

One cask half full of honey, and xxx boards, valued by the jurors, viij⁹ x⁴. — Wreck

New rent of William son of Alan de Dundyke, a bond tenant, for j messuage, and j half bovate of land in Welton, containing v acres of land and half an acre, and xxj falls and a half, is put in respite to the next court.

Robert Longeman was summoned to answer to Richard de Hiltoft of a plea that he detains from him xviij⁴, and the — Mercy said Robert is not able to deny this, therefore it is considered that the said Richard shall recover the debt, and the said Robert is in mercy, pledge the grave.

Mercy xij^d It is found by the inquisition, upon which Sarah Assell, plaintiff, and Geoffrey de Sloytby put themselves in a plea of debt, that the said Geoffrey is indebted to the said Sarah in j quarter of corn, worth v^s, therefore it is considered that the said Sarah shall recover &c., and damages which are taxed at vj^d, and the said Geoffrey is in mercy, pledge &c.

Mercy vj^s iij^d William Typere of Waynfleet, John Peddere of the same place, Thomas son of Ringot, Stephen son of Juetta, Hernisius Scalpy, and Little Eudo are in mercy for trespass made in the warren with horses carrying fish.

Mercy vj^d The township presents that Richard Parsoneneve drew blood from William atte Dammes, therefore he is in mercy, and because the said Richard has not come, therefore Robert de **iij^d** Westmeles, pledge of the said Richard, is in mercy.

Mercy ij^s vj^d Isabell daughter of Ralph de Houlethorp and Beatrice Bride and Alice Meriet have been chastised, therefore are in mercy.

Mercy iij^d William son of Walter German raised the hue justly upon William le Marescal, therefore the said William is in mercy, pledge &c.

Fine xxvj^s viij^d Alan son of William German, to have and to hold to him and his heirs one messuage and five acres of land, which William German resigned to him after his decease, of land arrented, gives to the lord for a fine xxvj^s viij^d, pledge Alan atte Hauedick. So that the said land, not demised to others, shall remain to the said Alan atte Hauedik for the term of two years.

Court of Ingoldmeles held at Burgh on Wednesday next before the Feast of S. Peter in Cathedra, 13 Edw. II. [20 February A.D. 1319–20].

Relief v^s iij^d Robert atte Got gives to the lord for a relief iij^s iij^d for lands and tenements in Skeknays. Also the same Robert gives to the lord for a relief of tenements in Skeknays ij^s by the pledge of Robert de Westmeles.

Distraint It is ordered, as often, to distrain William Schild for homage and other services: Thomas Austin to repair a certain bridge, **Attach-ment** which is called Stirttescroft brig: and to attach all men having common in Salflet for trespass made in the same.

William son of Alan de Doudych, a bond tenant, acquired to

himself, Joan his wife, and the heirs of their bodies lawfully
begotten, v̇ acres and a half, and xxj falls and a half of land not
arrented, and he gives to the lord of new rent xj^d.

New rent xj^d

Hauwis daughter of William de Dounesgwro for licence to
marry without the manor gives to the lord vj^s viij^d, by the
pledge of John de Loudel.

Merchet vj^s viij^d

John Fryseby in mercy, because he has not (brought) Robert
Foliot, who he undertook should come to the next (court) to
do homage and services. And nevertheless it is ordered to
distrain him as before.

Mercy xij^d Distraint

Nicholas de Cantilupe was attached by the pledge of Walter
the grave to come to the court to do homage and other services,
and he has not come, therefore the said Walter is in mercy,
and nevertheless it is ordered that he be distrained.

Mercy xij^d Distraint

Philip de Tetford was attached by the pledge of Richard
Bonde to do fealty to the lord, and he has not come, therefore
the said Richard is in mercy, and nevertheless let the said
Philip be distrained for fealty &c.

Mercy vj^d

William del Mairys for his homage being respited until
Easter gives to the lord vj^d: Walter del Mairys for the same
vj^d: Alice Boteler for the same &c. xij^d.

Alan Brok,[1] Alan son of Alan of ye Rowe,[1] Peter de Burtoft,
William son of Robert at Sea have not come upon a certain
inquisition, therefore they are in mercy.

Mercy xij^d

Ingoldmeles presents that Isabel daughter of Thomas raised
the hue upon Robert Warren justly, therefore (he) is in mercy.

All presenters of the township of Ingoldmeles have a day at
the next court to present concerning forestallers.

Day

Hugh Brichs, Richard de Benyngton (and 11 others) in
mercy for trespass made in the warren of the lord with their
horses carrying fish.

Mercy iiij^s

It is ordered to distrain William de Caldeflet, Hugh son of
Robert, Sarah Herre, Alice Botiler for homage and services.

Distraint

Sum xxviij^s j^{d}q.

Court of Iggoldmeles held on Wednesday in Easter week,
13 Edw. II. [2 April A.D. 1320].

William Pyncrak offered himself against Walter Westmeles
in a plea of debt, of the unjust detention of xj^s vij^d, Walter

Mercy vj^d

[1] These two were essoined of the common advent, so were probably freemen.

comes into court, and is not able to deny the said debt, therefore it is considered that he recover &c., and damages, which are taxed at vj^d, and the said Walter is in mercy. And it is testified by the bailiff that the said Walter is distrained by j ship and j sail, worth xx^s.

Inquisition   The bailiff is ordered to have a good inquisition at the next court to inquire concerning the fee of the lord in Burgh.

Attachment   It is ordered, as often, to attach Walter de Calflet, for that he drew blood from John Miller.

The parson of Skegnesse has a day at the next court by the pledge of Robert de Calflet concerning services of the lands of William de Caudflet.

Iggoldmeles presents that Thomas de Lincoln raised the hue upon Robert Erward, and justly, therefore &c.: and that Walter de Brindley drew blood from &c. And that the servants of **Distraint** William de ffriskeney took a certain hare in the warren of the lord with greyhounds of the said William de ffriskeney, therefore the bailiff is ordered to distrain the said William to have the said servants at the next court.

Lechwit   Also they present that Agnes daughter of Robert en le Lathe is chastised, therefore the said Agnes is in mercy.

Wreck xij^d   Also that a certain 'merswyn' (porpoise) of wreck of the sea was found, worth xij^d.

Mercy xij^d   It is found by the inquisition, on which Alan Godard put himself against the presentation of the bailiff in a plea of trespass in the warren of the lord with his horses and sheep, that the same Alan is guilty therein. Therefore (he) is in mercy, pledge &c.

Ranulph Thorarld for a certain 'spret' (bowsprit) of wreck of the sea, worth j^d, removed by him.

Peter de Gibthorp has a day at the next court for homage and other services.

Court[1] of Iggoldmeles held at Skegnes on Wednesday next before the Feast of S. George, 13 Edw. II. [16 April A.D. 1320].

Distraint   It is ordered to distrain William de ffriskeney to have his servants to answer to the lord for trespass made in the warren of the lord.

Day   Robert ffoliot has a day at the next court for homage &c.

<hr>

[1] Above, 'Easter View.'   'Leke.'

It is ordered to distrain the parson of Skegnesse for the   Distraint
services of the land of William de Cauldflet.

Thomas Astyn was summoned to answer to John son of   Inquisi-
Petronia in a plea that he render to him v^s by the pledge of   tion
Walter Astyn of Steping, which he owes to him, and &c., to
his damage half a mark. And the said Thomas comes, and
defends force &c., and says that he owes him nothing, and
demands that this be inquired, and the said Walter likewise,
therefore let an inquisition come to the next court.

William de Westmeles has a day at the next court to prove   Day
that that attachment made upon Walter de Westmeles was his
own proper one with the sixth hand,[1] by the pledge of Robert de
Westmeles.

William Swifth in mercy for trespass made in the warren of
the lord for thorns and ' arpis,' pledge Robert atte Gote.

Eleanor Godard gives the lord x^s for licence to marry without   Merchet x^s
the manor, pledges &c.

It is found by the inquisition that Peter de Baumburgh   Distraint
holds of the fee of the lord in Burgh, and made an unjust
distraint upon the tenants of the lord, therefore it is ordered
that he be distrained. It is ordered to distrain Sapientia de
Salfletby and William son of Richard de Hiltoft for homage and
other services, afterwards they made fine for the homage until   Fine xij^d
Michaelmas with xij^d.

Roger of the Mor gives the lord for the same xij^d.   xij^d

Richard son of Alan [2] is put in the frankpledge of the lord,   New rent
and gives to the lord yearly iij^d.   of frank-
  pledge

It is ordered to distrain John de Westmeles for homage and   Distraint
other services. Also the same John is in mercy because he has
not come.

Richard Muriot, to have and to hold to him and his heirs   Fine vj^d
for the whole life of Alice Muriot, his sister, iij rodfalls of land
of the resignation of the said Alice, gives to the lord for fine
vj^d, pledge &c.

John Hardbene of Burgh gives to the lord for respite of   Fine xl^d
homage until Michaelmas for tenements, formerly Robert de la
Chaumber's, xl^d, pledge &c.

Alan Bugge, to have and to hold to him and his heirs for   New rent
ever j toft and iij acres of land in Welton not arrented, gives to   vj^d
the lord of new rent vj^d.

---

[1] Six-handed.   [2] And 9 others.

v⁸
Merchet xij^d
Merchet ij⁸
Matilda Writh for licence to marry without the manor gives the lord v⁸, pledge &c.: Beatrice Wyeth for licence to marry within the manor gives xij^d &c.: Alice Muriot for licence to marry without the manor because she is poor gives ij⁸ &c.

Fine jv^d
Robert Germayn for measuring land formerly William Germayn's gives the lord vj^d.

Iggoldmeles presents that Amia daughter of Richard Priour raised the hue upon Alan atte Welles, and unjustly, therefore (she) is in mercy &c.

Wreck xij^d
Also that ij oars of a certain boat (came) of wreck of the sea worth xij^d, and they are delivered to the grave to answer for the value.

Mercy
Also that Matilda de Lincoln and Alan Bugge baked and sold contrary to the assize, therefore they are in mercy: that Matilda Brok (and 3 others) bought and sold bread contrary to the assize, therefore &c.: also that Gilbert Nevell (and 20 others) brewed and sold contrary to the assize, therefore &c.

Distraint
Also that Robert son of Herbert de Salfletby holds of the lord by foreign service, and is of full age, and owes to the lord for homage for tenements, which he holds of the lord in Neuton next Toft, therefore it is ordered to distrain the said Robert for homage, suit of court, and other services.

Mercy iij^d
William Bugge for default.

Distraint
It is ordered to distrain Richard de Westmeles, and Robert de Steping for homage &c.

Gilbert Thory (and 28 others) have not come to do suit, therefore are in mercy.

Sum of this roll lv⁸ iij^d.

Court of Iggoldmeles held on Wednesday next after the Feast of the Ascension of our Lord, 13 Edw. II. [14 May A.D. 1320].

Mercy v^d
John son of Petronilla, plaintiff, and Thomas Astyn by licence are agreed in a plea of debt, and the said Thomas puts himself in mercy, pledge &c.

Day
The land of William Germayn is measured, and he has a day at the next (court) to certify the steward, and Robert Germayn has the same day to hear.

Plea
John Marrays was attached to answer to William de Dounedik in a plea of trespass, and therein he complains that the said John came on Wednesday next before the Feast of S. Nicholas last, and cut a certain way by divers cuttings, by

which v acres of meadow of the said William were immersed, to his damage xxˢ, and thereof he produces suit. And the said John comes, and defends force &c., and says that he did not cut the said way to his damage, as he puts upon him, and this he demands may be inquired, and the said William likewise, therefore the bailiff is ordered to cause a good inquisition to come.

John de Hakwra did fealty for tenements, which he holds of the lord in Iggoldmeles, after the death of Andrew his father, and he has a day at the next court for homage, relief, and other services.   *Fealty*

William Cobbe is put into the frank-pledge of the lord, and gives to the lord yearly iijᵈ.   *New rent iijᵈ*

Iggoldmeles presents that Matilda wife of Simon son of Ralph raised the hue justly upon William the servant of William de Hiltoft, and Simon servant of William de Rolleston, therefore the said Wm. and Simon are in mercy, pledge the bailiff, and the township has a day at the next court to present concerning blood drawn from the said Simon.

Sum of this roll iijˢ.

Court of Iggoldmeles held on Wednesday next before the Feast of S. Barnabas, 13 Edw. II. [4 June A.D. 1320].

It is ordered to distrain the parson of Skegnesse for the services of the land of William de Cauldflet.   *Distraint*

Robert de Steping did fealty, and gives to the lord for respite of homage until Michaelmas xijᵈ.   *Fine xijᵈ*

It is found by the inquisition, upon which William de Dounedik, plaintiff, and John Marreys put themselves in a plea of trespass, that the said John made trespass on the said William, to his damage xijᵈ. Therefore it is considered that the said William recover the said damages, which are taxed at xijᵈ, and the said John is in mercy, pledge &c.

John de Akwra did fealty, and has a day at the next (court) for homage, relief, and other services, pledge Robert de Akwra.   *Day*

It is found by the inquisition, upon which William de Modland and Robert Thory put themselves in a plea of trespass, that the said Robert beat the said William, to his damage iijˢ. Therefore it is considered that the said William shall recover the damages, which are taxed at iijˢ. And nevertheless the said Robert is in mercy, pledge his father.   *Mercy iiijᵈ*

It is found by the inquisition, upon which Robert Thory and William Modland put themselves in a plea of trespass, that the   *Mercy vjᵈ*

G

said William made trespass on the said Robert, to his damage vj^d. Therefore it is considered that the said Robert shall recover vj^d for damages, and nevertheless the said William is in mercy, pledge William de Hiltoft.

Iggoldmeles presents that William, servant of William de Hiltoft, drew blood from Ranulph de Modland, and because the constables have not attached the parties, therefore they are in mercy. Also Robert Thory drew blood from William Modland,

Mercy
iij^a j^d

therefore (he) is in mercy, pledge &c. Also that William Germayn raised the hue upon Peter Grevell unjustly, therefore the said William is in mercy. Also that Robert Knobbe drew blood from Thomas de Modland, therefore (he) is in mercy, pledge Gilbert Thory. Also the same Thomas raised the hue upon the said Robert Knobbe justly, therefore &c. Also that John of ye Houtdayl raised the hue justly upon Robert Thory, therefore &c.

Sum of this roll vij^s x^d.

Court of Iggoldmeles held on Wednesday the morrow of the Nativity of S. John Baptist, 13 Edw. II. [25 June A.D. 1320].

Mercy

Simon Thori is in mercy because he measured land without licence.

It is found by the inquisition that the land of William Germayn was measured, and nothing more found than when first measured.

Distraint

It is ordered to distrain William son of Richard de Hiltoft for homage.

Fine vj^d

Walter del Marrays made fine for his homage being respited &c.

Mercy iij^d
Fine iij^d

Robert de Akwra in mercy, because he has not (brought) John de Akwra, whom he undertook (&c.). And it is ordered to distrain the same John for homage, relief &c. And afterwards he made fine for the amercement, and for respite of homage until Michaelmas for vj^d.

Mercy

Hugh de Croft, Thomas Drope, Walter de Westmeles, John ffydekyn (and 8 others) in mercy for trespass made, fishing in the warren of the lord.

Merchet ij^s

Beatrice Kegges for licence to marry without the manor gives the lord ij^s, because she is poor.

Mercy

Alan Aubray (and 7 others) have not come to do suit, therefore they are in mercy.

It is ordered to distrain Walter Bernak, John Hardewyn,   Distraint
the prior of Bolington, John de Swaby, William Neucomen,
Henry de Baumburgh for trespass made in Schalflet.

Sum of this roll xij⁸ v^d.

Court of Ingoldmeles held at Skeggeness on Wednesday next
before the Feast of S. Lawrence, 14 Edw. II. [6 August A.D.
1320].

William de Doufuedike, to have and to hold to him and his   New rent
boys le Northwarayn for the term of ten years for vj⁸ viij^d yearly,   xx^d
gives to the lord for entry vj⁸ viij^d. And so there is of incre-   Fine
ment of rent xx^d.   vj⁸ viij⁸

Robert son of Leua, to have and to hold to him and his boys   New rent
le Southwarayn for the term of six years for vj⁸ viij^d yearly,   xx^d
gives to the lord for entry vj⁸ viij^d. And so of increment of   Fine
rent xx^d.   vj⁸ viij⁸

The same Robert to be in the frank-pledge of the lord gives   New rent
to the lord iij^d yearly.   iij⁸

Walter del Marrays, to have and to hold to him and his boys   New rent
for the term of ten years Castesacre for iij⁸ vj^d yearly, gives to   vj⁸
the lord for entry xij^d. And so of increment of rent vj^d.   Fine xij⁸

Roger de Somervill has a day at the great court after   Day
Michaelmas concerning a trespass made in the warren of the
lord by the pledge of William de Hiltoft.

It is ordered (to distrain) the prior of Bolington, and brother   Distraint
Richard de Burgh, his canon, to answer to Simon son of Simon
in a plea of agreement.

William son of Alice in mercy for contempt.   Mercy ij⁸

Robert Jermayn complains of William Jermayn in a plea of   Plea
debt. And therein he complains that he detains from him xvj^d,
which he agreed to pay to him at Easter, on which day he paid
nothing, but detained it, to his damage half a mark, and therein
he produces suit. And the said William says that he owes him
nothing, and he demands that this be inquired, and the said   Inquisi-
Robert likewise, therefore &c.   tion

Ingoldmeles presents that Alan son of Roger obstructed the   Mercy
watercourse in Wynthorp, whereby the lands of the lord and
his bond tenants of Iggoldmeles are immersed, therefore he is
in mercy.

John de Westmeles for homage being respited until Michael-   Fealty
mas xij^d, and he did fealty.   Fine xij⁸

Mercy   William son of Alice (and 5 others) do not agree on a certain inquisition, therefore they are in mercy.

Day   Walter Bernak, John Hardewyn, the prior of Bolington, and others have a day before the council for trespass made in Schalflet.

Cite   It is ordered to cause Walter de Igges, and Beatrice formerly the wife of Master Simon, executors of the same Simon, to answer to Robert son of Margaret in a plea of debt.

Sum of this roll xxxiij⁵ iij⁴.

Court of Iggoldmeles held on Wednesday next after the Feast of the Exaltation of the Holy Cross, 14 Edw. II. [17 September A.D. 1320].

Distraint   It is ordered as often to distrain the prior of Bolington and brother Richard de Burgh, his canon, to answer to Simon son of Simon son of John in a plea of agreement.

Land   William Aucus surrenders j acre of land and a half to the
seized   use of Alan Est &c. by 'exctationem.' Therefore let it be taken into the hand of the lord. And it is ordered that it be retained until the next court.

Ralph son of Margery and Agnes his wife were summoned to answer to William del Clay of a plea wherefore they unjustly detain from him vj⁵, which they owe him for half a quarter of ' Ry flour,' bought from him at the house of the said Agnes in Northolm, on the Vigil of S. Lawrence xi. Edw. II., to be paid on the next Wednesday, on which day they paid nothing, but detained it, to his damage x⁵. And the said Ralph and Agnes defend force &c., and ask judgment whether in this they ought to answer, because they allege that . . . in the house of the said Agnes supposing that she . . . could have because she
Inquisi-   was covered by her husband, and the aforesaid W. comes and
tion   says that she was not covered by her husband on the day aforesaid, and he demands that this be inquired, and the said Ralph and Agnes likewise.

Ralph son of Margery and Agnes his wife were summoned to answer to William atte Clay of Wynthorp of a plea wherefore they unjustly detained from him one quarter of malt, worth vj⁵, which she bought from him in the house of the said Agnes in Northolm in the xj⁴ʰ year, to be paid to the said William on the next Wednesday, on which day she paid nothing, but detained to his damage x⁸. And the said Ralph and Agnes defend force &c.: and they demand judgment whether they ought to answer to such a narration, because in the beginning of the narration he says in the plural they unjustly detain, and in the end he says that she unjustly detains and does not pay speaking in the singular putting the ownership upon the woman when she is covered by her husband, and upon this she demands judgment. And they have a day to hear judgment at the next court. | Judgment

William del Clay, plaintiff, is not present against Ralph son of Margery and Agnes his wife in a plea of debt, therefore he is in mercy. | Mercy iij⁴

Iggoldmeles presents that Magota daughter of Henry raised the hue upon Robert de Akwra justly, and because the constables have not attached the parties therefore they are in mercy.

Sum of this roll ij⁸ v⁴.

Sum of all courts from Michaelmas xiij to Michaelmas xiiij xix¹¹ xviij⁸ viij⁴ q.

Court of Ingolmels held on Wednesday next before the Feast of the Nativity of the Lord, 15 Edw. II. [23 December A.D. 1321].

William Coper and Walter de Brendeleygh have not come to do suit, therefore &c. | Mercy vj⁴

Ingolmels presents that Ralph Est raised the hue justly upon Robert de Leverinton, therefore the said Robert is in mercy, pledge &c.

Sum ij⁸ vij⁴.

Court of Ingoldmeles held on Wednesday next after the Feast of the Epiphany of the Lord, 15 Edw. II. [13 January A.D. 1321-2].

It is considered that William de Dowedik recover from Hugh son of William xiij⁸ for a debt, and xl⁴ for damages, as he narrated against him, because he is in default in perfecting his law. And the said Hugh is in mercy. | Mercy vj⁴

Ingolmeles presents that Ralph son of Margery drew blood from Geoffrey de Westrik, therefore the said Ralph is in mercy: the same Geoffrey drew blood from the same Ralph, therefore he is in mercy, pledge &c.: Also the same Ralph raised the hue | Mercy ij⁸ justly upon the same Geoffrey, therefore the said Geoffrey is in mercy.

Fine xij^d From Ranulph son of Walter Catte to have and to hold to him and his boys for ever one rood of arrented land in Wynthorp, which Walter Lamb resigned to him in court, for fine xij^d.

Mercy xij^d The tenants of the lands of Alice Wybian in mercy, because they have not come to do suit.

Distraint respited Attachment not attached Distraint It is ordered, as before, to distrain Peter de Baumburgh for an unjust distraint made upon the tenants of the lord : to attach Walter de Calflet for blood drawn: to distrain Nicholas de Cantilupe for homage.

Mercy vj^d William son of Alice, and Alan Bef, the sureties of Walter Tailor, in mercy, because he has not come, and nevertheless let **Distraint** them be distrained to produce the said Walter to answer to Ralph son of Margery.

Respite Robert Foliot, and Robert son of Herbert have a day at the next court for homage.

Distraint respited It is ordered, to distrain the parson of Skegneis for homage. Eudo Pouer in mercy for default against Simon Kigis, and the same Simon complains of the said Eudo of a plea wherefore he broke his agreement concerning ij acres of meadow demised to him for a term to the damage of xv^d &c. And the said Eudo comes and defends force &c., and says that he did not break the agreement, and demands that it be inquired, therefore let an inquisition come.

Walter Carpenter was summoned to answer to Alan atte Wall of a plea wherefore he detains from him vj^s iij^d for corn **Law** bought from him, which he ought to have paid at Easter last, to his damage xv^d &c. And the said Walter comes, and defends force &c., and says that he owes him nothing, and of this he puts himself upon the law, pledge for the law &c.

ij^s Alan atte Hauedik gives the lord for searching the rolls ij^s.

Inquisition William son of Rose de Steping was summoned to answer to Walter Imgrem of a plea wherefore he detains from him ix^s, which he owes him for three sheep bought of William Dosome, the servant of the said Walter, which he ought to have paid him at the Feast of Pentecost xiij year, on which day he paid nothing, but detained it, and still detains it, to his damage &c. And the said William comes and defends force &c., and says that in nothing is he indebted to him, and he demands that this be inquired, therein let an inquisition come.

From Robert atte Flete to have and to hold to him and his boys for the term of six years ij acres of pasture, which Simon atte Well demised to him in court, for entry ijˢ.   Fine ijˢ

From Simon atte Well for suit of court until Michaelmas vjᵈ.   vjᵈ

Sum xjˢ.

Court of Ingoldmeles held there on Wednesday next after the Feast of the Holy Trinity, 15 Edward II. [9 June A.D. 1322].

From Maria daughter of William de Douedyk for licence to marry without the manor ijˢ.   Merchet

It is ordered to distrain Sarah Herre, Hugh son of Robert, and William de Caldflete, parceners and coheirs of the lands, which were Alice Wybian's, to do fealty.   Distraint

William Boteler did fealty for the third part of lands which were . . . Wybian's.   Fealty

Robert atte Gote was distrained for fealty, and it is replevied by the pledge of Robert de Westmels, and nevertheless he has not come, therefore the said pledge is in mercy.   Mercy ijᵈ

The township presents that two boards were cast up, therefore let them be valued.   Wreck

Robert Chalde, who held of the lord one messuage, three acres of bond land in Ingoldmeles, is dead. And upon this comes Walter Chalde, brother of the said Robert (and) nearest of blood, and asks to be admitted to the said tenements, and he is admitted. And (he gives) to the lord for heriot ijˢ, pledges &c.   Heriot ijˢ

| Taxers of the Court | William Mareis. Peter de Burtoft. | Alan Bogge Alan Est | bond tenants. |

Robert de Rygg, William Neucomene did fealty.   Fealty

Court of Ingoldmeles held there on Wednesday the Vigil of S. Mary Magdalene, year as above [21 July A.D. 1322].

Hugh son of Robert, William de Caldflete, and Sarah Herre have a day at the next court to show what tenements they hold of the fee of the lord and by what services.   Respite

The township presents that William Fougler of Skegnesse,

a bond tenant of the lord, who held of the lord, is dead, therefore let (his lands) be taken into the hand of the lord.

Sum viij^s ij^d.

Court of the View of Ingoldemeles held on Monday the Vigil of S. George the Martyr, 18 Edw. II. [22 April A.D. 1325].

Distraint It is ordered to distrain Thomas de Moulton, Robert de Salfletby, Richard de Cornewayle for fealty and other services.

Defaulters Mercy iij^s ij^d Nicholas de Cantilupe, Henry Vavasour, John Cobbe of Kirketon were summoned to the court, and have not come, therefore they are in mercy.

Fine xl^d From Agnes Catte to have and to hold to her and her boys for ever the fourth part of one house, and three roods of bond land, which render to the lord ix^d yearly, and three roods of free land, which render to the lord ij^d yearly, which Beatrice Catte surrendered to her in court. And she gives to the lord for fine, pledge &c. And William Est has the said land for the term of his life.

Defaulters Mercy xviij^d Alan Lamb (and 5 others) in mercy for default of suit of court. Ranulph Towres was attached to answer to John Merchant of a plea wherefore on the Saturday next after the Feast of All Saints in Ingoldmeles he insulted him, beat him, and did to him other enormities, to the grave damage of the same John of half a mark, and thereof he produced suit. And the said Ranulph came and admitted the said trespass made on the said John. Therefore it is considered by the court that the said **Mercy iij^d** John recover the said half mark, and the said Ranulph is in mercy, pledge &c.

William Polber and Lucia his wife complain of John son of Guy and Richard Bond, executors of the will of Ranulph de Prestorp, of a plea of debt, pledge to prosecute &c. And therein they complain that whereas in 3 Edw. II. Roger de Cobeldick, then steward of the court of Ingoldemeles, ordered to attach ten shillings to the use of Lord Henry de Lacy for waste, which the said Lucia had made of the goods of the lord, afterwards the said Roger forgave the said Lucia, wherefore the said Ranulph, whose executors the said John and Richard are, was not charged with this in his account, but nevertheless the said Ranulph levied on the said Lucia unjustly, while she was a single woman, to the damage of the same William and Lucia twenty shillings. And thereof they produce suit &c. And the said John and Richard come, and defend

force &c., and say that the said Ranulph, whose executors they
are, levied none of the said ten shillings unjustly on the said
Lucia.   And, if he levied the said ten shillings, he levied them
to the use of the Lord Henry the then lord, and rendered his
account of them.   And this they are prepared to verify &c.
Therefore let an inquisition come.   Which says that the said
Ranulph did not take the said x shillings, nor any portion of the
said ten shillings, from the said Lucia unjustly, as they allege
against them.   Therefore it is considered.

Mercy vj^d

Inquisi-
tion

Court of Ingoldemeles held at Skegnesse on Thursday next
after the Feast of S. Luke and next after the Feast of S. Michael,
19 Edw. II. [24 October A.D. 1325].

From Hugh Eyr for fine of suit of court until Michaelmas
xij^d, from Peter de Gipthorp ij^s, from William ffraunke xviij^d,
from Matilda de Dunneswra, a bond tenant, xij^d, from Master
Thomas Bek xviij^d, from Robert de Steping xij^d, from John
Redcol vj^d, from Alan de Grenwyk vj^d, from William Neucomen
xviij^d, from William de Thorp (he has attorney &c.), from
Richard de Wodhal xij^d.

Fines
xj^s vj^d

Peter de Baunburgh (and 3 others) in mercy [1] because they
have not come.

Defaulters
Mercy iiij^s

It is found by the inquisition, upon which Thomas
Warner, plaintiff, and Alice Warner put themselves, that the
said Thomas depastured the grass of the said Alice, therefore he
is in mercy, pledge &c.

Mercy vj^d

It is found by the inquisition, on which William atte Lathe,
plaintiff, and Robert the bailiff and John his brother put themselves in a plea of trespass, that Robert made trespass on the
said William, to his damage xx^d, therefore the said Robert is in
mercy.   And it is found by the same inquisition that the said
John did damage to the said William to the value of v^s, therefore the said John is in mercy.

Mercy vj^d

Mercy xij^d

William, the servant of Richard Barheued, is attached for
blood drawn from William Michel and is in mercy by the
pledge of Richard Barheued and the beadle, and now he does
not come, therefore the said pledges are in mercy.   And it is
ordered to put him by better pledges &c.

Mercy vj^d

Nicholas de Cauntelu has respite for doing his fealty until
Christmas.

Respite

[1] Walter Lamb is not fined because he has neither land nor chattels.

Mercy ij˙ Henry le Vavasur by his steward at Lincoln undertook to be here at this court to do to the lord his fealty, and to do all other things which pertain to the tenements of the same William (sic) of the fee of the lord, and now he has not come, therefore the said Henry is in mercy. And it is ordered that he be attached by ij mares, let them be retained.

Mercy ½ mark John son of Hugh was attached to answer to the lord for that he filled up the pit between the land of William de Thikethorp and the common way, as was presented by the township in the court held as above, and it was replevied by the pledge of the grave and the beadle, and now he does not **Attach-ment as yet** come, therefore the said pledges are in mercy, and nevertheless let the said John still be attached, and to answer to William de Thikthorp in a plea of trespass.

Mercy vj˙ Robert Thori and William Catte are in mercy, because they undertook to have Alan Lamb at this court, and now he has not come, therefore the said Robert and William are in mercy.

xij˙ For nets dried upon the sands of the lord at le Laa xij^d.

Mercy vj˙ Alan Godard in mercy for trespass made in the warren of the lord, pledge &c.

Day Alan Godard has a day at the next court to show the charter which he has for lands, which he holds of John de Rigg.

Robert Bygg, a bond tenant of the lord, demands against William ffouler x^s for divers contracts between them had. And (William) being present in court granted that he was indebted to the said Robert iiij^s vj^d, and for the detention he is in mercy. And as to the residue he puts himself upon the inquisition as not indebted. And it says that he is indebted to the said Robert in v^s vj^d, therefore it is considered that the said Robert recover the said v^s vj^d, together with damages, which are taxed at vj^d, and the said William is in mercy, pledge the beadle.

Seizure It is ordered to seize into the hand of the lord le Suthe-waren and Catteshaker, which Robert Leueson and Walter Marays hold of the demise of the earl of Lancaster &c.

Mercy vj˙ It is found by the inquisition, upon which William ffouler, plaintiff, and Robert Bygg put themselves in a plea of trespass, that the said Robert is indebted to the said William in divers debts, therefore Robert is in mercy. And as to the plea of **Mercy vj˙** trespass they say that the said Robert made trespass on the said William, therefore he is in mercy, pledge either for the other.

xij jurors present that Hugh, servant of Alan son of Roger, raised the hue justly upon John Smyth, therefore the said John is in mercy ; that the constables did not attach the said John, therefore they are in mercy ; that Roger servant of Walter Carpenter raised the hue justly upon Robert Amy, therefore the said Robert is in mercy ; and that the same Robert drew blood from the same Walter, therefore (he) is in mercy. *Mercy vj* — Mercy vjᵈ, xijᵈ, xlᵈ, xlᵈ

Also that Walter Carpenter drew blood from Robert Amy, therefore let (him) be attached. Attachment

Also that John son of Hugh oppressed William de Thikkethorp, a bond tenant of the lord, unjustly in court Christian by bringing an action about a church way to his damage, therefore the said John is in mercy.

Also that William son of Simon de Aqura drew his sword against William Germayn, and the said William Germayn raised the hue justly upon (him), therefore (he) is in mercy. Mercy iiijᵈ

The tasters of beer present that Ranulph atte More (and 7 others) brewed and sold contrary to the assize, therefore they are in mercy for breaking the assize of beer. Mercy vˢ

The township presents that William son of Alice raised the hue justly upon Hugh Rasur, therefore let the said Hugh be attached.

It is ordered to attach William Elrykes, and John son of Walter to answer to the lord, because they mowed the ' dunes,' and the herbage outside the bank of the sea against the defence of the sea for the salvation of the country. Attachment

Also that Hawys Wage ' typlavit' bread contrary to the assize, therefore she is in mercy. Mercy iijᵈ

Richard de Coucroft was attached to answer to Geoffrey de Walden of a plea wherefore on the Vigil of the Ascension last he struck the same Geoffrey at Burgh in the grange of William Madur, and took from the same Geoffrey iiij gallons of beer, worth vjᵈ, and carried them off, and did to him other enormities to the damage of the same G. xlˢ. And whereby the lord is injured in his beer[1] cˢ. And the said Richard being present in court says that in nothing is he guilty, and puts himself upon an inquisition, therefore let an inquisition come. And the said Richard found pledges of standing the inquisition, Inquisition

[1] So it seems to be.

viz. Alan Plant and William Neucomen of Burgh, and further
to do what is right.

They did
not find
a pledge

Andrew de Ormesby and Matilda his wife complain of
Geoffrey de Walden, bailiff, of a plea of the seizure and detention of one cow, j mare, j foal, j colt, worth xl^s, pledge to
prosecute.

Plaint

William de Thetelthorp complains of Gilbert, abbot of Louth
Park, and William Grabert, of a plea of taking j horse, pledge
to prosecute.

Distraint

It is ordered to distrain Robert de Salfletby for the relief of
the fourth part of one knight's fee: Nicholas de Cantilupe, and
Henry Vavasour for default of suit of court: Richard de Cornwayle for fealty.

Distraint

And, as often, Matilda who was the wife of Simon Leue to
answer to the lord for that she depastured the common of the
lord with her beasts, and to answer to G. de Waldene in a plea
of trespass.

Distraint

William Elrikes is distrained by iiij cows, because he mowed
the brambles outside the sea bank, which is the defence of the
whole community of the vill of Skegnesse, against the custom
used, and they are replevied by the pledge of &c., to be at the
next court to make amends if justice shall require.

Sum, lxv^s iij^d.

Court of Ingoldemeles held on Saturday next after the Feast
of S. Martin, 19 Edw. II. [16 November A.D. 1325].

Mercy iiij^d

John Bonde in mercy, because he has not come.

Thomas Knith is distrained to show how he holds bond land
of the lord, therefore it is ordered to seize it into the hand of
the lord.

It is ordered to distrain Richard son of Ranulph, William
the bailiff, and William atte Lathe to show wherefore their lands
should not be measured and held by equal portion.

Mercy ij^s

It is found by the inquisition that William Elrikes falsely
complained of William atte fflete, Robert son of Hugh, John
Belt in a plea of false presentation, therefore the said William is
in mercy.

Let an inquisition come to inquire if William son of Alice
broke the park of the lord by the distraint made upon him to
answer to Geoffrey de Waldene in a plea of agreement.

John Bride in mercy for trespass made in the warren of the   Mercy xij^d
lord, pledge the beadle.

It is found by the inquisition that John son of William son   Mercy vj^d
of Alice, the domestic servant of the same William, made a
rescue, therefore the said William is in mercy, pledge the
beadle.

It is found by the inquisition that John Bride lied concern-   Mercy vj^d
ing the bailiffs of the lord, therefore he is in mercy.

From William Elrikes for trespass made outside the bank   Mercy ij^s
of the sea between the bank of the sea and the brambles in
mercy.

Roger son of Thomas in mercy because he was summoned   Mercy vj^d
upon the inquisition and has not come.

It is found by the inquisition that William son of Alice   Mercy xij^d
falsely called Geoffrey de Walden 'robber,' therefore the said
William is in mercy (damages xviij^d).

From William de Thikkethorp, a bond tenant of the lord,   New rent
and John son of the same William, who purchased two acres   iiij^d ob. q.
one rood and twenty perches of free land of Alan atte Coningges-
gate, and which ought to be arrented to the lord at four pence
ob. q., therefore let them be seized.

From Robert Lamberd, a bond tenant of the lord, who pur-   New rent
chased two acres one rood and twenty perches of free land of   iiij^d ob. q.
Alan atte Conyngesgate &c. (as in last entry).

From (same), who purchased of (the same) two acres j   New rent
perch and a half of free land, which ought to be arrented to the   iiij^d
lord at iiij^d, therefore it is ordered to seize &c.

Matilda who was the wife of Simon Leue was attached by
hay, worth vj^s, to answer to Peter de Baumborgh in a plea of
trespass. And the same hay that was attached was removed
by Andrew de Ormesby and the same Matilda, therefore it is
ordered that they be attached.

William ffoghler and Robert Bygge of Skegnesse, to have
and to hold the whole pasture which is called South Warrenne
as fully as Robert Leuesone held it of the demise of the lord
Thomas earl of Lancaster, to have and to hold with all easements
and profits from the Saturday next after the Feast of S. Martin
in the 19th year unto the same day ten years fully completed,
by rendering therefore yearly from year to year eleven shillings   Rent xj^s
at the usual terms. And they are pledges for the payment of   yearly
the said (rent), and without destruction or waste being done,

Fine xij^d either for the other and also Alan German. And they give for entry xij^d.

On this day come Alan German and Simon son of Peter Cook and give to the lord for licence to have and to hold all that marsh of the lord with Hauedyk as the said Alan and Simon fully held it of the demise of the lord Thomas earl of Lancaster for a term not yet ended. And because the said lord earl was not able to demise, except for the term of his life, now it was seized into the hand of the lord. And it is demised to them as is aforesaid, to hold from the Saturday next after the feast of S. Martin in the xix. year until the same day 15 years fully completed, by rendering therefore from year to year x^s at the usual terms. And before in the time of the said earl it was demised to them for half a mark yearly. And they give for entry xij^d.

Yearly rent x^s

Fine xij^d

Because William Lamb formerly in court demanded against Alan Lamb, his brother, divers tenements, which the said Alan formerly demised for a term and by licence in court to Robert Thory, and William Catte, as is witnessed in the record of the demise on the rolls. And for the default of the said Alan the said tenements were taken into the hand of the lord. And the said William was not willing to pursue his suit for or make fine for the said lands. Therefore the said tenements are demised to the said Robert and William for the said term fully completed, as is aforesaid, and they give the lord for having the term ij^s, so that they do not take damage by the default of the said Alan in the meantime.

Fine ij^s

Mercy iiij^d William Lamb, plaintiff, does not prosecute against Alan Lamb in a plea of land, therefore William is in mercy, and the said Alan is quit without a day.

It is ordered to seize into the hand of the lord a native messuage, in which Thomas Knith dwells without the licence of the lord, and it is ordered likewise to attach the said Thomas that he be at the next court to show how and in what way he holds the said messuage. The same day is given to Gilbert de Prestorp to show &c.

Day Alan Germen has a day at the next court to show the feoffment, which he has of the marsh &c.

John Cokk is distrained by one cow, worth xij^s, to answer to Ralph Cook in a plea of agreement, and he does not justify himself &c. And by the assent of the steward he has a day &c.

Let an inquisition come [to inquire] what abbots, priors &c. hold tenements of the fee of the lord.   *Inquisition*

It is ordered to attach the prior of Bolington, Robert de Kyme of Burgh, (and 4 others), to answer to G. de Waleden in a plea of trespass.   *As yet attachment*

Nicholas de Cantilupe has a day to do fealty at Christmas.   *Day*
It is ordered to distrain Henry le Vavasour for fealty, suit of court, and other services; Robert de Salfletby for the relief of the fourth part of one knight's fee; and Richard de Cornwayle for fealty &c. It is ordered to distrain Robert Lamberd and William de Thikthorp that they have the charters at the next court by which they purchased free lands &c.   *Distraint*

Sum of this roll xviij^s vj^d ob.[1]

Court of Ingoldmels held at Skegnesse on Friday next before the Feast of the Conversion of S. Paul, 19 Edw. II. [24 January A.D. 1325–6].

William Fougler of Skegness was summoned to answer to Robert son of Leua of the same place of a plea that he render to him vj^s vj^d ob. &c. And therein he complains that on Monday next after the Feast of the Apostles Peter and Paul last at Ingoldmels the same Robert sold to the said William beer, and divers goods, to the value of vj^s vj^d ob. to be paid to the same Robert in the octave next following, on which day he paid nothing, but detained it, and still detains it unjustly, to his damage v^s. And thereof he produced suit. And the said William came, and defended force &c. And says that in no money is he indebted to him, and this he defends against him and his suit.   *Inquisition*

From Thomas Knigte for licence to have and to hold one messuage and one court, which he has of the demise of Gilbert de Presthorp, and William Gunny, for as long as shall please

---

[1] Tied to this roll on a narrow strip of parchment:—' Edward by the grace of God King &c, to the bailiffs of Ebulo le Straunge of Ingoldmeles greeting.

Increment
vj^d them, and he shall give to the lord yearly vj^d at the usual terms, so long as (he) holds the said messuage and court, pledges &c.

The prior of Bolington was attached by ij horses to produce Robert de Kima, his domestic servant, to answer to Geoffrey de Walden in a plea of trespass. And now he has not come, there-
Mercy xij^d
Distraint fore the said pledge is in mercy, and nevertheless let the said prior be distrained.

Robert de Akewra was attached by v quarters of malt, worth xx^s, to answer to Simon Cok in a plea of trespass. Afterwards the said Robert proved the ownership of the said malt. And because the said Simon complained in a plea of debt, and it was
Mercy vj^d found that it was a plea of trespass, therefore the said Simon is in mercy for a false plaint.

Henry le Vavasour has a day at the next court to show that he has discharged himself of suit of court at the court of Ingoldmels.
Distraint It is ordered, as often, to distrain Matilda who was the wife of Simon Leue to answer to the lord, for that she depastured the common of the lord without his licence.
Respite Alan Jerman has a day at the next court to show how he entered on the fee of the lord by purchase.
Fine half
a mark From Ralph Lamb and Matilda his wife to have and to hold to them and their boys for ever three roods and thirty perches of land with appurtenances, lying next land of the same Ralph, which Joan daughter of Alan Bride resigned to them in court, and surrendered. And he gives to the lord for fine half a mark, pledge &c. And for this resignation and surrender the said Ralph and Agnes (sic) granted to the said Alan to hold the said land for (his) whole life.
Mercy xij^d From the whole homage for contempt, and because they do not present the presentments before the steward they are in mercy.
iiij^d
Frank-
pledge From Thomas King to be in the frank-pledge of the lord by the licence of the lord, and he gives yearly by letter of the lord iiij^d, and he did fealty.

Sum of this roll xxv^s xj^d.

Mercy
xviij^d From Alan de la Raw, William de Wayttecroft, William de Hilletoft senior, and William son of Hugh de Rawe summoned upon the inquisition between Geoffrey de Walden plaintiff and Richard de Cowcroft in a plea of trespass, and they do not come, therefore they are in mercy.

Thomas son of Rengot (and 5 others) in mercy, because they contemned the warrant of the lord. — *Mercy xiiij^s ij^d*

It is ordered to retain one mast of the length of 80 feet, which came at Skegnes Laa, as wreck of the sea, and it is ordered that it be appraised at the next court. — *Wreck*

It is ordered to attach all those who make unjust ways beyond the sea bank, unless they have them by the consideration of true men at the next court. — *Attachment*

It is ordered to attach all those who do damage to or pasture the sea bank. — *Attachment*

From Matilda daughter of John Belt for licence to marry without the manor xx^s, pledge &c. — *Merche xx^s*

Sum lxiij^s iiij^d.

Plaints of the Court held on Saturday next after the Purification, 19 Edw. II. [8 February A.D. 1325-6].

(1 plea of agreement and 1 of trespass)

Sum of this roll xxxvij^s v^d.

Plaints of the Court held on Saturday next after the Feast of S. Gregory the Pope, 19 Edw. [15 March A.D. 1325-6].

(3 pleas of debt, 2 of agreement, 1 of trespass.)

Court of Ingoldemels held on Saturday next after the Purification, 19 Edw. II. [8 February A.D. 1325-6].

Geoffrey Walden, plaintiff, does not prosecute against the prior of Bolynton and others in the plaint in a plea of trespass, therefore he and his pledges to prosecute are in mercy. — *Mercy iij^d*

Henry le Vavisour by his steward, Richard de Skupholme, has a day at the next court to show and discharge the said Henry of suit of court at the court of Ingoldemels, or to do suit &c. — *Respite*

Geoffrey de Walden, plaintiff, does not prosecute against Robert de Kyme, (and 4 others), in a plea of trespass, therefore he and his pledges to prosecute are in mercy, and the aforesaid are quit. — *Mercy iij^d*

It is ordered to distrain Alan Germain to show how he entered into free land of the fee of the lord: [and] — *Distraint*

to attach all those who make unjust ways beyond the sea banks, unless &c. — *Attachment*

H

Richard son of Ranulph, William the bailiff, and William
Respite atte Lathe have a day at the next court to show why their land
ought not to be divided between them by equal portion together
with the rent.

Gilbert Fayrehare demands xiiij^d of Robert Herward, which
he owes to him, and unjustly detains, to his damage vj^d, and
thereof he produces suit. And the said Robert, being present
in court, does not deny, therefore it is considered &c., and
Mercy iij^d ordered that Geoffrey recover the said xiiij^d, and damages, and
the said Robert is in mercy.

Attach-
ment   It is ordered, as at other times, to attach all those who do
damage upon the sea bank &c.

Appraise-
ment   It is ordered to retain one mast in length 80 feet, which
came up at Skegnes of wreck of the sea, and it is commanded
that it be appraised at the next court.

It is found by the inquisition, upon which Geoffrey Walden
and Richard de Coucroft put themselves in a plea of trespass,
that the said Richard made no trespass on the said Geoffrey,
therefore it is considered that the said Geoffrey take nothing by
Mercy iij^d his plaint but be in mercy, and the said Richard be quit without a day.

Mercy iij^d William Fouler in mercy for trespass made in the warren
with his sheep.

Robert Herward found pledges, viz. &c., to satisfy Robert
son of Bride for a trespass made on him. Afterwards by licence
they are agreed. And the agreement is such that the said
Robert shall give to the said Robert Bridsone for the said tres-
Mercy xij^d pass half a mark. And the said Robert Herward is in mercy.

Attach-
ment   It is ordered to attach William Fouler to answer to Robert
Leueson in a plea of trespass.

Richard Graymagh is attached by his sheep taken in the
brambles of the lord for trespass made there, by the pledge &c.,
Mercy xij^d and now he has not come, therefore the said pledge is in mercy,
and nevertheless let the said Richard be attached.

Fisherman   It is ordered to seize the whole tenement, which Matilda Big
held until the full age of Robert Big, her son, and to show why
she held it for xviij years beyond his age.

Custody
of
charters   William son of Alan son of Richard and Beatrice his wife
found pledges, viz. &c., for the safe custody of six charters and
fines, which belong to Robert Thori by reason of the reversion

of land after the death of the said Beatrice, and to show to the lord the said charters.

The township presents that a barrel, in which were contained xxiiij 'pisces meluelles,' was found at Kokhille, and appraised at xl^d. And the grave expended j^d in salt, and vj^d to those who found them. Let them be kept safe. Wreck xl^d

Margaret atte Dammes comes in full court, who holds of the lord j messuage, nine acres, and one perch of land of her inheritance, and grants the said tenements with all their appurtenances by the licence of court after her decease to be the right of John son of Walter son of Lucia and of William son of Robert Bug, to have and to hold for their whole lives, or (the life) of either of them, by the services &c. And they give the lord for fine xlvj^s viij^d. And after their decease the said tenements &c. shall remain to Henry son of Walter son of Lucia, as the right heir of the said Margaret, and his heirs, according to the custom of the manor, saving the right of every one for ever. Fine xlvj^s viij^d

From Robert atte Hafdyk, to have and to hold to him and his assigns two acres of pasture from the Purification xx. Edw. II. unto the same feast four years after, which Gilbert Catte demised to him for a term, if the demisor shall so long live. And he gives the lord for having the term, pledge the grave. Demise xl^d

Sum of this roll lxix^s.

Ingoldemels. Court there on Wednesday next before the Feast of S. Peter in Cathedra in the first year of Edward III. [17 February A.D. 1327-8].

From Robert son of Leua for contempt made in full court before the steward, for that he slandered William Fuler in a plea &c. Mercy iij^d

William Fougler was attached to answer to Robert son of Leua of a plea of debt, and therein he complains that he unjustly detains from him vj^s ix^d ob. for timber, iron nails, and divers other things sold to him, viz. on Monday in Whitsun week 19 Edw. II., which he ought to have paid at once, and has not yet paid, but detains, to the damage of the said Robert v^s, and thereof he produces suit. And the said William comes and defends the words of court, and says that in no money is he indebted to him, and upon this he wages his law, pledge of his law Robert Bigge. And upon this comes the said William, and Law

H 2

admits that he is indebted to the same Robert in six shillings, nine pence, and ob. Therefore it is considered that the said Robert shall recover the said vj^s ix^d ob., and damages vj^d. Therefore the said William is in mercy to find a pledge for the debt

Mercy vj^d at the next court, or to pay &c. And afterwards he has a day for payment at Easter and Whitsuntide by equal portions.

Respite   The distraint made upon the abbot of Kirksted is put in respite unto the next court, pledges &c., viz. for an amercement of the court at the next court after Michaelmas, unless the said abbot, or his attorney, produce a letter of the lord, or his steward, which ought to acquit him of the said amercement.

Distraint   It is ordered, as often, to distrain Thomas de Multon of Framton, and Richard de Cornwayl for fealty and other services.

Distraint Mercy xij^d From Peter de Giptorp for default of suit of court, and it is ordered to distrain the said Peter.

Distraint   It is ordered, as often, to distrain William Galle, and Thomas Perers, for that they hunted hares in the warren of the lord, as was presented at the third preceding court: to distrain Walter de Akewra to show how he has entry on the fee of the lord.

Order   It is ordered to retain in the hand of the lord the whole of the land, which Walter Godard and Agnes his mother (hold), which contains iij acres, for that they demised the said land to the rector of the church of S. Nicholas of Ingoldmeles, and his proctor, without the licence of the court &c.

Distraint   It is ordered to distrain the rector of the said church for many trespasses made on the lord, as appears in the preceding court: (also) because he entered on bond land of the lord without the licence of the court. Whereas the homage at the preceding court had respite concerning a wall raised by the same rector, now at this court comes the said homage, and says

Mercy iij^d that the said rector raised the said wall on the bond land of the lord by the length of v feet and the breadth of j foot and a half, therefore the said rector is in mercy.

Fine ij^s From William Gunny to have to him and his assigns one acre of land and one cottage, which Henry de Maroum demised to him from Michaelmas last until the end of three years &c. And he gives to the lord &c. ij^s.

Respite   To this court came Alan son of Alan Goderik and Matilda his wife, bond tenants of the lord, and produced a certain writing, by which they purchased a place of land, which is called Nortcroft cum Roppeles, of John de Rig, viz. to the same Alan and Matilda for their whole lives, and (the life) of which of them shall live the longer. And because it is not known whether free land thus purchased by any bond tenant ought to be arrented to the lord, therefore concerning the arrenting nothing at present &c. And therefore respite.

It is ordered to distrain as often Richard Cobbler for that he carried off one 'hares' of wreck of the lord. *Distraint*

It is ordered to distrain Robert Foliot, Nicholas Cantelupe, Henry Vavasour, John Cobbe of Cletham, Robert de Saltfletby, for default of suit of court. *Distraint*

To inquire concerning a certain distraint made upon Rose Botheler, and which the same Rose took, and carried off without the delivery of the bailiff.

Sum ix^s xj^d.

Ingoldmels. Court held there on Monday next after the Feast of S. Gregory the Pope [1] [14 March A.D. 1327–8].

From the foreign bailiff, because he has not come to certify the court as to what he has done concerning his precepts &c. *Mercy xviij^d*

The distraint taken upon the abbot of Kyrkestede is put in respite until the court next after Easter, as appears in the court next preceding, pledges &c.

It is ordered, as often, to distrain William Galle and Thomas Perers, [he is not guilty as it is found], for that they hunted hares in the warren of the lord, as it was presented in the fourth preceding court. *Order*

It is ordered, as often, to retain in the hand of the lord the whole of the land, which Walter Godard and Agnes his mother hold of the villeinage of the lord, which contains iij acres of land, for that they demised the said land to the rector of the church of S. Nicholas of Ingoldmels and his proctor without the licence of the court. (And) to distrain the s^d rector for many trespasses &c., as appears in the 2nd preceding court: (and) because he has entered upon the bond land of the lord without the licence of the court &c. *Order*

Alan son of Richard Godard of Ingoldmels and Matilda his wife, bond tenants, purchased of John son of William de Ryg of Welton one place, a messuage with twelve acres of land with appurtenances in Ingoldmels, for the term of their lives, by a *Fine xl^d*

[1] The date of this roll is torn off, but it is clearly 1 E. III.

certain writing indented, rendering yearly to the said John
&c. And upon this the lord seizes it by reason of their naifty.
And the said Alan and Matilda give to the lord for licence to
hold it at will, as is aforesaid.

Order   It is ordered, as often, to distrain Richard Cobbler, because
he carried off one 'are' come of wreck.

Order   It is ordered, as often, to retain one mast come of wreck,
which was appraised at j mark in the Michaelmas court.

Arrenta-   William son of Thomas son of John, a bond tenant of the
tion of   lord, purchased one acre and a half, and j rood, and xj perches
free land
new rent   of free land of one Robert de Driby, and now at this court the
iij^d ob. q. said land is arrented to the lord.

New rent   Robert and William Huswyf of Ingoldmels, bond tenants of
vij^d   the lord, purchased three acres and a half of meadow of one
William Wulfhou of Germethorp in the same vill of Germethorp,
and now &c.

Mercy vj^d   The jurors present that a certain stranger, whose name they
know not, raised the hue justly upon &c.

Mercy ij^s   From the presenters for concealment of the said hue in
mercy &c.

Respite   Also they present that William son of Alan, a bond tenant,
and Beatrice his wife purchased one messuage with sixteen
acres of free land of one John de Ryg for the term of their
lives by a certain writing &c. And they found a pledge, viz.
Order   Robert Thory, to show the charter at the next court &c.

Nothing   Also that Alan atte Welle, a freeman, purchased one
because he messuage two acres of bond land of one Alan Polayn, and
made fine
before   therefore he made fine before.

Also that the men of lord Roger Pedewardyn unjustly took
distraint in the fee of the lord upon Peter de Bangburgh at
Burgh, and insulted the said Peter, and drew blood from him
Distraint with arrows, therefore the said men are in mercy, and it is
ordered to distrain them.

Mercy xij^d Also that Alan Boef is a forestaller of fish, therefore he is in
mercy: and that ij maids of Robert Grown made a trespass in
Mercy iij^d le mels, therefore they are in mercy.

It is ordered to retain one anchor and j cord, which came of
wreck, as was presented as appears in the preceding court.

xiij^s vij^d Thomas son of Ryngot, John Pedder, (and 9 others) did
damage in le mels, therefore are in mercy.

Also they present that Agnes Taylour (and 16 others) are

brewsters, and have not sent for the tasters of beer, therefore they are in mercy. *(Mercy iiij˙ iiij˙)*

From Richard de Schalflet, to have and to hold for his whole life one rood of bond land, pasture lying in Ingoldmels, which William his brother rendered to him in court. And he gives the lord for a fine. *(Fine ij˙)*

From Robert atte Hauedyk, to have &c. to him and his assigns two acres and three roods of bond land lying &c., which William Germayn demised to him in court (for 3 years) &c. *(Term. iij˙)*

Afterwards came Walter Godard, and made fine to the lord to recover the land, which was seized into the hand of the lord, as appears above, by the pledges of &c. *(Fine ij˙)*

It is ordered to distrain Alan de Dunneswra, chaplain, because he vexed Robert Assil and Beatrice his wife in a court Christian for a matter not touching a testament or will. *(Order)*

It is ordered to pull down a wall unjustly raised by the rector of the church of S. Nicholas of Ingoldmels upon bond land of the lord by the length of five feet and breadth of one foot and a half, as was found by the scrutiny of the homage in the next preceding court, and also to distrain the said rector for the said trespass. *(Order)*

From Thomas Harfot because he treated with contempt the bailiffs of the lord, when they demanded from him an amercement of the lord, therefore he is in mercy. *(Mercy vj˙)*

From Robert son of Marier, because he made an unjust path from his house beyond le mels, therefore he is in mercy. *(Mercy vj˙)*

Sum xl˙ ix^d ob. q.

Court of Ingoldmels held on Wednesday next after the Feast of S. Lucy the Virgin in the second year of King Edward the third from the conquest [21 December A.D. 1328].

William Cadyhorn was summoned to answer to William Budde in a plea that he render to him iij˙ vij^d, which he owes to him, and unjustly detains. And therein he complains that on the day of S. Martin in the xviij^th year of King Edward, the father of King Edward that now is, the same William Cadyhorn hired a cow of the said William Budde, to hold from the said Feast to the same Feast one year completed, for a certain sum of money, for which he was to satisfy him by the said iij˙ vij^d, which he ought to have paid on the Feast of S. Martin next, on which day he did not pay, but as yet unjustly detains, to the damage of the said Wm. Bud xij^d, and thereof he produces suit. And the said Wm. Cadyhorn comes, and defends force &c., and says that in no money is he indebted to him, as he puts upon him, and he demands that it be inquired, therefore let an inquisition come. And the other likewise.

Respite The inquisition between Robert Thory, plaintiff, and William at Sea is put in respite until the next court for default of jurors.

It is ordered to attach Geoffrey vicar of the church of S. Leonard of Cokrington to answer to John son of John son of Hugh in a plea of trespass.

Respite William Lambert, a bond tenant of the lord, purchased free land in Toynton, and it is put in respite until the next court.

Robert atte Gote, and Peter de Baumburgh in mercy, because they have not come upon the inquisition.

       Sum of this court vj^s v^d.

Court of Ingoldmels held on Wednesday next after the Epiphany in the 2nd year of King Edward [11 January A.D. 1328-9].

Attach- Ralph Tydy was attached by j net, worth xviij^d, to answer
ment to the lord, because he took and carried off a chest found upon the shore of the sea, therefore let it be retained, and more taken.

Distraint It is ordered, as often, to distrain all the tenants of the lands of Waytecroft to show how they hold &c., and for default of suit of court, except Joan who was the wife of Philip de Teford.

New rent Wm. Lambert, a bond tenant of the lord, purchased one
ob. rood of free land in Toynton and is arrented of new (rent) at
Mercy xl^d ob. yearly. And because the homage of Ingoldmels did not present the said purchase for enquiry, therefore it is in mercy for the concealment.

Respite They have respite concerning a certain 'hare' found by Robert son of Walter until the next court.

It is ordered to seize into the hand of the lord x acres of land, formerly Matilda de Dunswra's, until &c.: and

Attach- to attach Wm. son of Alan son of Richard, a bond tenant
ment of the lord.

They present that one log found upon the sands of the lord &c., and sold.

Alan Goderik, junior, who is in the recognizance of the lord iij^d, purchased three acres of free land, which ought to be arrented to the lord vj^d yearly, therefore the said recognizance is——. New rent vj^d yearly

Beatrice daughter of Gilbert de Prestorp gives to the lord for licence to marry without the manor v^s, pledge Gilbert de Prestorp. Merchet v^s

From the homage of Ingoldmels in mercy for the conceal-ment of blood drawn between Wm. son of Alice and John Sormilk. Mercy vj^s viij^d

Alice daughter of John Smith gives to the lord for licence to marry within the manor ij^s, pledge &c. Merchet ij^s

From Robert atte Flete and Joan his wife to have and to hold two acres of bond land for the term of their lives, and two acres of free land lying in Botheby to them and their boys for ever, which Alan Bug resigned to them and surrendered in court, and they give to the lord xij^d at the instance of Robert de Malbirthorp. Fine xij^d

From Joan daughter of Alan Bug for licence to marry within the manor xij^d. Merchet xij^d

Sum xxv^s vj^d ob.
Sum of this roll xxxj^s xj^d ob.

Court of Ingoldemels held on Wednesday next after the Feast of S. Swithin, 4 Edward III. [4 July A.D. 1330].

It is ordered, as often, to distrain John son of Simon son of Petronilla de Halton for fealty, and other services in arrear, for tenements of Robert de Steping. (Also) all the tenants of lands which were Peter de Baumburgh's for (same). Distraint

As yet let the rolls be searched between William Baylif, claimant, Ralph Baylif, Robert Baylif, and John Baylif con-cerning one acre and a half of pasture for the term of their lives, if it be more or less &c. Respite

Robert Kyng was summoned to answer to Robert Leueson in a plea that he render to him ij^s x^d, which he owes him, and unjustly detains. And therein he complains that on the Monday next after the Purification last past the same Robert Leueson sold to the said Robert Kyng bread and beer for the said ij^s x^d, to be paid on the Saturday following, on which day he paid nothing, but detained it, and still unjustly detains it, to his damage ij⁵, and thereof he produces suit. And the said Robert Kyng comes, and defends force &c., and says that in no money is he indebted to him, as he narrates against him, and he demands that it be inquired. Therefore let an inquisition come.

Robert Kyng was summoned to answer to Walter Bygge in a plea that the same Robert hired the said Walter to stand in his service from Michaelmas iii. Edw. to the next Easter for xvjᵈ, to be paid at Easter aforesaid, on which day he paid nothing, but detained it, to his damage xijᵈ, and thereof &c.

Inquisition And the said Robert says that he is not indebted, and demands that it be inquired, therefore let an inquisition come.

Distraint It is ordered, as often, to distrain the prior of Alvyngham for fealty, and other services in arrear, for tenements in Cokrington and Alvyngham : (and) the prior of S. Katherine of Lincoln for (same) for tenˢ in Toft Neuton : and the prior of Bolington for (same) for tenˢ in Akthorne and Engham : (and) the prioress of Henyngs for (same) for tenˢ in Stretton next Stow : (and) Richard de Cornwayle for (same).

Order It is ordered to seize into the hand of the lord two parts of one messuage, and one rood of land, which Alan Lamb, a bond tenant of the lord, formerly held.

William Marays was summoned to answer to John son of Walter Alwayn of Ardelthorp in a plea that he render to him xxˢ, which he owes him. And therein he complains that on the Thursday after Easter in the xᵗʰ year of King Edward, father of King Edward that now is, the same John lent to the said William the said xxˢ, to be paid on the following day, on which day he paid nothing, but detained it, and as yet unjustly detains it, to his damage xˢ, and thereof &c. And the said William comes, and defends force &c., and says that in no money is he indebted to him, as he narrated against him,

Inquisition and he demands that it be inquired, therefore let an inquisition come.

Mercy vjᵈ From the foreign bailiff of Ingoldmels in mercy, because he has not come.

Order It is ordered to attach Alan Bridson to answer to the lord, because he entertained contrary to the assize.

Sum of this court iijˢ vjᵈ.

Court of Ingoldemeles held on Friday next after the Feast of
S. James, year as above [27 July A.D. 1330].

It is ordered to attach Robert Ketelberne for forestalling, to
answer to the lord.

Attach-
ment

Guy Salter was attached to answer to William de Burgh in
a plea of trespass [to the damage of ij⁸. And the said Guy is in
mercy.], and therein he complains that on the Saturday after the
Feast of the Translation of S. Thomas last at Cokhill he insulted,
beat, and ill treated him, and did to him other enormities to his
damage xx⁸, and thereof &c. And the said Guy comes and
defends force &c., and says that he is not guilty, and demands
that it be inquired, therefore let an inquisition come.

It is found by the inquisition that Alan atte Halgarth
slandered William de Doufdyk with malicious words, and called
him 'false,' and 'robber,' and says that he killed his daughter,
to his damage taxed at vj⁸ viij⁴, therefore it is considered that
he recover &c., and the said Alan is in mercy.

It is
ordered
to levy
Mercy ij⁴

Also they present that Robert Ketelberne is a forestaller,
therefore he is in mercy.

Mercy vj⁴

From the foreign bailiff in mercy, because he has not come
to do his office.

Mercy iij⁴

Memᵈ j leyrwit is concealed by the township, viz. the
daughter of William de Doufdyk.

It is ordered that an inquisition come to inquire concerning
a demise of land made to Wᵐ de Weglant by Richard Bond, if
it be made to the prejudice of the fine of the lord.[1]

Order

Sum of this court vij⁸.

Sum of this roll x⁸ vij⁴.

View of the Court of Ingoldemels held on Wednesday
before the Feast of S. Luke the Evangelist, 4 Edw. III.
[17 October A.D. 1330].

They present that Richard son of Rose (and another) are in
mercy for tippling of bread: Richard Barehefed for the assize of
beer: Simon son of Ralph (and 4 others) for tippling of beer:
Robert Byg and (3 others) for the assize cf beer: Simon Nidde
for tippling of bread: Juliana Nevyl for tippling of beer &c.

Mercy v⁴
The
brewsters
& tipplers
of bread
& beer
Mercy
iiij⁸ j⁴

[1] Annexed to this roll on a small piece of parchment are the names of those
on an inquisition, among whom are six villeins.

Defaulters   Dom⁸ Peter de Gipthorp [after he came], Hugh Heyre,
Mercy   Robert ffolyot, Nicholas de Cantilupe, Thomas de Multon of
vˢ ijᵈ   fframton, Robert de Salfletby, Nicholas de Hale, John Cob, and
(21 others) in mercy for default of suit of court.

Fines   From Robert atte Gote for respite of suit of court until
Michaelmas (xviijᵈ), from William Neucomyn (xijᵈ), from
Alexander de Gipthorp (ijˢ), (and 16 others).

     They present William Foular (and 7 others) for trespass
Mercy ixᵈ   made on the brambles upon the meles, therefore they are in
mercy.

New rent   Also they present that Agnes who was the wife of Alan atte
vjᵈ yearly   Halgarth, who held of the lord three acres one rood thirteen
perches of free land, is dead. And upon this come Alice and
Joan, daughters and heirs of the said Agnes, and are arrented
for the said land, to have and to hold to them and their boys
according to the custom of the manor, and they give to the
Fine xviijᵈ   lord of new rent vjᵈ yearly, and for fine for entry xviijᵈ.

     From Agnes daughter of Alan Est, a bond tenant of the
lord, to have and to hold to her and her boys for ever one acre
Fine vjˢ   and one rood of land, lying in Ingoldemels &c., which Alan Est
resigned to her and surrendered in court, and she gives to the
lord for fine vjˢ, and the said Agnes granted all the land to the
said Alan Est for the term of his life &c.

Fine iiijᵈ   For nets put and dried upon les meles iiijᵈ.

     From Master Thomas Bek (and 2 others) for respite of suit
of court until Michaelmas.

                      Sum of this court xxxvˢ iiijᵈ.

     Court of Ingoldemels held on Wednesday next after the
Feast of All Saints, year as within [7 November A.D. 1330].

Demise of   From Alice Chapman, to have and to hold to her and her
land vjᵈ   assigns one place of pasture &c., from the feast of S. Martin
4 Edw. III. to the end of two years, which Simon Pourdefisch
demised to her for the said term, and she gives to the lord to
have the term.

     It is ordered to seize into the hand of the lord all the lands
and tenements, which are called ' Agnuslant,' and the grave is
ordered to answer for the proceeds : also all the lands and tenˢ
which are ··ˡˡ ᵈ ʹᴰ· · ··ˢ····ᵗ· ·ˡ· ·· · · ·

Court of Ingoldemels held on Wednesday next before the
Feast of S. Andrew the Apostle, 4 Edw. III. [28 November A.D.
1330].

It is ordered, as often, to distrain John son of Simon de | Distraint
Halton for fealty, and other services in arrear.

They present that Sarah Catte, who held of the lord in
bondage one messuage and eight acres of bond land, is dead,
and upon this comes Robert son and heir of the said Sarah, as
next heir, and asks to be accepted to pay heriot for the said | Heriot l[s]
land, to have and to hold to him and his boys for ever according
to the custom of the manor, and he gives the lord for heriot l[s],
pledge the grave.

Ralph Meriet in mercy for trespass made in the warren of | Mercy vj[d]
the lord.

William ffraunk, Robert Herword, and William Germayn | Mercy
in mercy for default of suit of court. | xvij[d]

From Clementia Catte (who) gives to the lord for the new | New rent
rent of three acres of bond land &c. | ij[s] yearly

Sum of this court lv[s] xj[d].

Court of Ingoldemels held on the Wednesday next before the
Feast of S. Thomas the Apostle, year as above [19 December A.D.
1330].

They present that John son of William son of Alice drew | Mercy vj[d]
blood from &c.

That Clementia Catte has removed her chattels out of the | Mercy ij[d]
fee of the lord without licence, therefore she is in mercy, and it | Attach-
is ordered that she be attached to answer to the lord. | ment

That Thomas son of Ringot with iij horses, Richard Gray- | Mercy
magh with ij horses, William de Braytoft with j horse, (and 6 | vj[s] iiij[d]
others) are in mercy for trespass made upon les meles which are
called Kedyhers.

Also that Alan Bakehous (and 4 others) are in mercy for | Mercy
trespass made in the warren of the lord, and Guy Russell with | ij[s] ix[d]
his sheep and William ffoular (and another) with ij calves, all
these in mercy in the warren of the lord.

Robert son of Hugh (and 5 others) in mercy because they | Mercy vj[d]
did not agree upon the inquisition between &c.

From Isabel daughter of John Pullayn, (who) gives to the | Merchet
lord for licence to marry within the manor &c. | xiij[d] iiij[d]

Sum of this court xxix[s] vij[d].

Court of Ingoldemels held on Tuesday next after the Epiphany, year as within [8 January A.D. 1330–1].

Does not prosecute Robert del Outdayle was summoned to answer to Robert Marays in a plea of debt, and therein he complains that on Monday next before Michaelmas 1 E. III. the said Robert del Outdayle hired the plough of Robert Marays to plough his land for a certain sum of money, for which he was to make satisfaction worth vj^d, to be paid on the Lord's day following, on which day he paid nothing, but detained it, and as yet unjustly detains it, to the damage of xij^d, and thereof he produced suit. And the said Robert del Outdayle comes, and defends force &c., and says **Inquisition** that he is not indebted to him, and he demands that this be inquired, therefore let an inquisition come.

He takes nothing Robert Kyng was attached to answer to William Foular in a plea of trespass, and therein he complains that whereas the said William had one place of land with dikes the same Robert threw down his dikes and went beyond his land contrary to his will and that of his family, and depastured his corn, and herbage, and trod them down with pigs and cattle and beasts, continually for three years elapsed before the complaint was raised, to his damage xx^s, and thereof he &c., and the said **Inquisition** Robert puts himself upon the country, therefore let an inquisition come.

Mercy iij^d Also they present that Simon atte Skelles cut thorns on les meles, therefore he is in mercy.

Sum of this roll iiij^{li} ix^s ij^d.

View of the Court of Ingoldemels held there on Monday next before the Feast of S. Luke the Evangelist, 15 Edw. III. [15 October A.D. 1341].

Default Henry le Vavasour knt., William ffraunke knt., Robert ffolyot, tenants of the lands of Dom^a Thomas de Multon at Stretton, Robert de Saltfletby, John de Hale, the abbot of Kirkested in Dunham, Walter le Hird, the prior of Bolington, William de Hiltoft, Alexander de Gipthorp knt., Simon de **Mercy xij^s vj^d** Thorp, John son of Alan de la Rawe, John son of Simon son of Petronilla de Halton, Hugh son of Lucy, John de Thikthorp jun^r, Alice Dybald, Gilbert Plomer, and Margaret Kemp in mercy, because they have not come to this court.

Mercy viij^s iiij^d The brewsters present that Ralph Meriet baked bread and sold it contrary to the assize, therefore he is in mercy. Also

that Richard Kyggs (and 19 others) are in mercy for the assize
of beer.   Also that Beatrice daughter of Alice Herwerd (and
4 others) are in mercy for tippling of beer.

Tipplers
of beer
Mercy xj^d

They present that Richard son of Robert de Grenwyk drew
blood from Richard Galeway, therefore he is in mercy, pledge &c.
Also that the said Richard Galeway raised the hue justly upon
the said Richard son of Robert, therefore he is in mercy, pledge
&c.   Also that Ralph de Burton dug land in Scalflet of the
common, therefore he is in mercy.

Mercy vj^d

Mercy xij^d

William Ryngot held of the lady on the day he died
23 perches of land with a cottage, (and) is dead.   Upon this
comes John son and heir of the said William and asks to be
accepted to pay heriot for the said land, and he is accepted,
and he gives the lord for heriot.

Heriot iij^e

It is presented to attach Alan Priour to answer to the lady
for one hare taken without licence.   And to measure the whole
land which Alan son of Ranulph Ryngot purchased of Walter
de Akewra for new rent until &c.

Attach-
ment

Sum xxix^s x^d.

Court of Ingoldemels held there on Monday next before the
Feast of S. Martin [5 November A.D. 1341].

William Neucomyn (is essoined) of the common advent
by &c.

William atte Brig demands against Robert Catte four acres
and one rood of land, which he paid heriot for in the time of
Lord Ebulo Lestrange, to carry the profits thereof wheresoever
(he liked), as the right of Clementia his wife.   And the said
Robert Catte says that the said William is a freeman, and was
a freeman at the time of the heriot, and that it is not the
custom of the bondmen that any freeman shall carry corn
growing on bond land outside the lordship.   He says also that
the said Clementia his wife is free because a bastard, and is not
able to claim any right in bond land.   And the said William
says that the said Clementia is a bondwoman, and he demands
that this be inquired, therefore let an inquisition come.   It
is found by the oath of Alan Pullayn, William de Doufdyk,
William atte Halgarth, Alan Germayn, Simon Pourdfisch,
Robert Lambhird, William Bug, Simon Cook, William de
Scalflet, John Withson, Ralph son of Thomas, and Richard
Reigner, who say on their oath that the manner and custom of

the manor of Ingoldemels was, and before was accustomed to
be that any bastard man or woman could acquire to themselves
lands and tenements of the bond tenants of the manor of
Ingoldemels, like the rest of the bondmen, and were considered
as bondmen, except for the time of ten years next past. They
say also that at the time when Clementia, wife of the said
William atte Brig, acquired to herself the said tenements all
bastards were accepted, like the rest of the bondmen. They say
also that Rannlph Ryngot had the whole of the crops of the said
Judgment four acres and one rood of land for procurement to the use of
respited Robert Catte through one entire year.

Therefore they have respite until the next court to hear
judgment. Therefore it is considered that the said William
shall recover the said land with all appurtenances according to
Mercy ij^d the custom of the manor. And the said Robert is in mercy.
Mercy vj^d John de Westmels in mercy for trespass in les meles with
his sheep.

Sum of this court x^d vj^d.

Sum total of this roll xl^s iiij^d whereof on the part of the
foreign bailiff ix^s iiij^d.

Court of Ingoldemels held there on Monday next before the
Feast of S. Thomas the Apostle, 15 Edw. III. [17 December A.D.
1341].

Fine viij^s From Juliana who was the wife of John son of Guy, and
from Simon son of the same Juliana, to have and to hold to
them, and the heirs of the said Simon for ever, one acre and a
half of land, which is called Westcroft &c., which John son of
Alan resigned and surrendered in court. And she gives to the
lady &c. From John son of John son of Guy, to have and to
Fine vj^s hold to him, and his heirs for ever, one acre and one rood and
four perches of land &c., which John son of Alan resigned and
surrendered in court, after the death of Amia mother of the said
John. And he gives the lady for fine.

Robert Prestsone was attached to answer to Thomas Marays
in a plea of trespass. And therein he complains that on the
Lord's day next after the Feast of S. Barnabas the Apostle last
past he insulted, beat, and ill used him to the damage of xl^s.
And therein &c. And the said Robert comes and says that he
Inquisi- is not guilty, and he demands that this be inquired, therefore
tion let an inquisition come.

Court of Ingoldemels held there on Wednesday in Easter week, 17 Edw. III. [16 April A.D. 1343].

It is ordered to attach William son of Alan to answer to William Thory and Maria his wife in a plea of trespass.

They present that Matilda Russel (and 7 others) are in mercy for the assize of bread. | Mercy xxij^d

Also that Robert Leueson, Richard Parsonnef, (and 13 others) are in mercy for the assize of beer. | Mercy v^s iiij^d

Also that Robert May of Skegnes (and three others) are in mercy for tippling of beer. | Mercy viij^d

From Alan Germayn, to have and to hold to him, and his assigns, one acre of land on the north part of the Etings, for the term of the life of William son of Walter Germayn &c., which William son of Walter Germayn resigned to him, and surrendered in court for the term of the life of the same William, and he gives to the lady for having the term.

From Matilda daughter of John del Outdayle for licence to marry within the manor.

From Simon Germayn to have and to hold to him and his heirs for ever 15 perches of land, which William son of Clementia resigned to him.

Court of Ingoldmels held there on Wednesday next after the Feast of S. John ante Portam Latinam [7 May A.D. 1343].

It is found by the inquisition that William Bernak, the prior of Bolington [attach], and Margery Swabi are in mercy for trespass made in Scalflet with their pigs.

Also that John Boef is a forestaller of fish, therefore he is in mercy.

That j tree was found of wreck of the sea. And it is ordered that it be valued before the next court.

From Eleanor daughter of John Redecole for licence to marry without the manor, pledge &c.

They present that Robert son of Simon de Akewra (and 3 others) are in mercy because they refused to make the bridge at Alan Pullan's. | Mercy viij^d

From Beatrice daughter of William atte Halgarth for licence to marry within the manor, pledge her father. | Merchet ij^s

From Robert Thory, to have and to hold to him, and his heirs, one acre and a half of pasture land &c., from Christmas last to the end of six years, which Hugh son of Lucy and | Demise iij^d

I

114 INGOLDMELLS COURT ROLLS

Beatrice his wife demised to him for the said term. And the said Hugh will warrant to the said Robert until the end of the said six years by all his lands and tenements. And he gives to the lady for having the term.

From John Ringot, to have and to hold to him, and his heirs for ever, two acres and a half of land at Skegnes, called Gerardland, lying next land of Dom⁸ John de Welugby on the one part, and land of Robert Germayn on the other, which Beatrice daughter of Ranulph Ringot resigned to him, and surrendered in court. And he gives the lady for fine.

Fine x⁸

From Alan Ringot and Beatrice his wife, to have &c. to them, and their heirs for ever, two acres and a half and one rood and twenty perches of land &c., which Beatrice daughter of Ranulph Ringot resigned to them and surrendered in court &c.

Fine x⁸

From (Beatrice) daughter of Ranulph Ringot for licence to marry without the manor &c.

Merchet x⁸

Thomas Sharp demands against Thomas Ringson xij⁸, which he ought to have paid him on Monday next after the Feast of S. Michael in the year x for divers 'marchandize,' to the damage of half a mark. And therein &c. And the said Thomas comes, and defends force &c., and says that in no money is he indebted to him, and he demands that this be inquired. Therefore let an inquisition come.

Mercy ix⁸
Mercy vj⁴

Richard Parsonnef (and 3 others) are in mercy for trespass in the warren. John Dobson is in mercy for trespass in les meles. Walter Godard (and another) in mercy for (same).

Sum xlij⁸ j⁴.
Sum of this roll lviij⁸.

Court of Ingoldmels held there on Monday next before the Feast of S. Margaret, 18 Edw. III. [19 July A.D. 1344].

It is ordered, as often, to distrain the heirs of Dom⁸ Henry le Vavasour for fealty and relief.

It is ordered that an inquisition come between Robert Aldyet and Robert de Akewra of a plea of trespass, for that the said Robert de Akewra sold to Robert Aldyet the fourth part of one boat for xxiij⁸ in the xvj[th] year, so that the said Robert Aldiet (go) in the said boat with ij men until &c.

Robert son of Walter complains of Robert son of Simon de Akewra in a plea of trespass. And therein he complains

that on the Wednesday next after the Feast of the Nativity of
S. John Baptist last past he defamed him, and called him
'false,' and 'robber,' and says that he stole ij brass pots and put
them in the ground, to the damage of xl⁵. And thereof &c. And
the said Robert son of Simon says that he is not guilty, and
demands that this be inquired, therefore let an inquisition
come.

Inquisition

From John Ringot to have &c. to him and his assigns
1ʳᵈ 27ᴾ of land &c. for 10 years, which William son of Robert
son of Margaret demised to him &c.

Demise xij⁴

Sum xlvij⁵ j⁴.

Court of Ingoldmels held there on Wednesday next after
the Feast of S. Lawrence, the 18ᵗʰ year [August 25 A.D. 1344].
From ¹ Joan and Sarah, daughters of William atte Halgarth,
to have and to hold to them for their whole lives one place of
land with a cottage, containing one acre and xx perches &c.,
which William atte Halgarth resigned to them and surrendered
before the grave and the homage.

Fine ij⁵

Sum xiiij⁵ vj⁴.
Sum total of this roll lxj⁵ vij⁴.

View of the Court of Ingoldemels held there on Wednesday
next after the Feast of S. Michael the Archangel, 19 Edw. III.
[5 October A.D. 1345].
² It is ordered to distrain the heirs of Domˢ Henry le
Vavasour for relief and fealty for ij fees of knights in
Cokrington.

Distraint

William ffraunke knt., Thomas de Multon of fframpton,
Robert de Saltfletby, Joan who was the wife of James de
Wodstoke, John de Hale, John Cob of Cletham, Walter le Hird,
and John de Gunby in mercy, because they have not come.
And nevertheless it is ordered to distrain them for divers
services in arrear.   Robert de Grenefeld for the same.

Defaulters foreign Mercy vjˢ vj⁴

John son of Alan de la Rawe, Robert de Steping, William
dᵃ Goteshalf, Ralph de Kelesey, William Taunt, John dᵃ

Bug, William ffoular, and William son of Simon Thory are in mercy because they have not come.

Mercy ij*
Order

It is presented that the bridge between William Bug and William Cardinaus is broken to the damage of the lady, therefore the whole township is in mercy. And nevertheless it is ordered that it be repaired before the next court.

Mercy
xj* v^d

Also they present that Ralph Meriet (and 5 others) are in mercy for the assize of bread. That Richard Kyggis (and 14 others) brewed and sold beer contrary to the assize, therefore they are in mercy. Also that John son of Alan (and 2 others) are in mercy because they had no signs for selling beer. Also that all the brewsters did not send for the tasters of beer. Also that Beatrice Harefot (and 7 others) are in mercy for tippling beer.

Respite

They have respite until the next court to inquire concerning the tenements of William Baxster.

Fine vj^d

From John son of Alan de la Rawe for respite of suit of court until Michaelmas.

Fine x*

From William, Ranulph, John, and Alan, sons of Robert atte fflete, to have &c. for their whole lives, or the life of whichsoever shall live the longer, two acres and a half of land, which is called Chesterlant, and one acre and a half of free land arrented, which is called Clayplat, which Robert atte fflete resigned to them, and surrendered in the presence of John the grave, Elias Warner, Alan Germayn, Roger Bug, Ralph Meriet, Ralph son of Margaret, and others of the homage, after the death of Matilda atte fflet, viz. Chesterlant. And they give the lady for fine x*, pledges &c.

Fine iij*

From Alice daughter of Robert atte fflet, to have &c. for the term of her life one acre of land lying in Castellant &c., which Robert atte fflet resigned to her, and surrendered in the presence of John the grave and xij of the homage. And after the death of the said Alice the whole of the said land shall remain to the right heirs of the said Robert. And she gives to the lady for fine, pledges &c.

Heriot
cvj* viij^d

Robert atte fflete, a bond tenant of the lady, who held of the lady on the day he died twenty acres and thirty-one perches of land with a messuage, is dead. And upon this comes Robert, son and heir of the said Robert, and asks to be accepted to pay heriot for the said land, doing all the services due and accustomed according to the custom of the manor, and he is accepted. And·

he gives to the lady &c., pledges &c., to be paid at Christmas, at Easter, at S. Botulph's.

Robert Germayn, a bond tenant of the lady, came in full court, and took of the lady one place of land of the waste at Skegnes with a house built thereupon, which William de Clederhowe, a hermit of the lady, held of the lady, to have &c. for his whole life &c., rendering yearly v⁸ &c., and he shall sustain the said house at his own proper cost. New rent v⁸ yearly at S. Botulph's and Michaelmas

It is ordered that Alan Germayn (and 4 others) be in mercy for trespass in les meles with their beasts. Mercy x⁴

They present that William son of Ralph Swete is not in chevage, therefore he is in mercy &c. Chevage ij⁴

Gilbert Cawks (and 11 others) in mercy, because they have not come. Mercy xij⁴

From William son of William Neucomyn for respite of suit of court until Michaelmas. Fine vj⁴

From Agnes daughter of William de Wegelant, to have and to hold to her and her heirs for ever two acres of pasture land, lying next land of William de Hiltoft on the one side, and land of William Cardinaus on the other, which Alan son of William de Wegelant resigned to her, and surrendered after the death of Agnes who was the wife of William de Wegelant. And she gives the lady for fine v⁸, pledge Robert Thory. Fine v⁸

Alan son of William de Wegelant came in full court, and surrendered into the hand of the lady to the use of W(illiam) Pullayn, and his heirs, two parts of one place of pasture land, which is called Ettyngs, containing three acres and four perches of land, which the aforesaid William holds for the term of nineteen years, to have and to hold to the said William and his heirs for ever &c. And the said land is arrented at a new rent of ij⁸ yearly. Fine x⁸ Increment of rent ij⁸ yearly

Court of Ingoldmels held there on Wednesday next before the Feast of S. Sim(on and S. Jude), same year [26 October A.D. 1345].

From Isabel daughter of William Plomer for licence to marry within the manor, pledge &c. Merchet ij⁸

From William Pullayn, to have &c. to him and his heirs for ever one acre and a half of land, which Agnes Pullayn mother of the said Wᵐ resigned to him, and surrendered in court. And for this resignation and surrender the same William granted for Fine vj⁸ viij⁴ him and his heirs the whole of the said land to the said Agnes for (her) whole life. And he gives &c.

Fine vjˢ viijᵈ Alan son of William de Wegelant came in full court, and surrendered into the hand of the lady to the use of William Pullayn the third part of one place of land, which is called Ettyngs, containing 1½ᵃ 3ᵖ, after the death of Agnes de Wegelant. And upon this came the sᵈ Wᵐ, and took the said land, with all its appurtenances, to have and to hold to him and his heirs doing all services due and accustomed according to the custom of the manor. And he gives &c.

Fine vjˢ viijᵈ Alan son of Wᵐ de Wegelant came in full court, and surrendered into the hand of the lady to the use of Wᵐ Pullayn two acres of land on the south side of le Ettyngs &c. after the term of 15 years. And upon this came the sᵈ Wᵐ and took the whole of the said land &c. And he gives to the lady for increment of rent yearly xvjᵈ.

Increment of rent xvjᵈ yearly

Attachment It is ordered to attach John de Westmels to answer to the lady for divers trespasses.

Plaint Wᵐ Pullayn complains of John Lomberd in a plea of debt. And therein he complains that the same John unjustly detains vˡⁱ and vˢ, which he ought to have paid to him on S. Peter's day last past, as the pledge of Alan son of Wᵐ de Weglant &c., on which day he paid nothing, but detained &c., to the damage of the said Wᵐ &c. And the said John comes and says that he was not pledge, and demands that this be inquired, therefore let an inquisition come.

Inquisition

Plaint Inquisition John Lomberd complains of Agnes de Weglant of a plea of pledge, pledge to prosecute the bailiff.

Sum total of this roll xˡⁱ xxijᵈq.

Court of Ingoldemels held there on Wednesday next after the Feast of S. Martin in winter, 19 Edw. III. [16 November A.D. 1345].

Attachment It is ordered to attach William son of Ralph, and John son of Robert atte Welle, to answer to the lady for a certain attachment broken &c.

Mercy ijᵈ Alan son of William de Wegelant in mercy, because he has not come.

Mercy iijᵈ It is found by the inquisition that John Lomberd is indebted to William Pullayn in cvˢ, as the pledge of Alan son of William de Wegelant, therefore it is considered that he recover the said cv*, and the said John is in mercy.

It is found by the inquisition that Agnes de Wegelant is indebted to John Lomberd in cv*, as the pledge of Alan son of William de Wegelant, therefore it is considered that he recover the said cv*, and the said Agnes is in mercy.

Mercy iij*

Agnes de Wegelant complains of Alan son of Wm de Wegelant of a plea of surety, pledge to prosecute &c., and it is ordered to distrain the said Alan to answer to the said Agnes concerning the pledge.

Distraint

Also they present that Richard Galeway sold to Walter Galeway ij acres of land, therefore it is ordered to seize it until &c.

Robert son of Walter in mercy because he has not (produced) John de Westmels. And nevertheless it is ordered to distrain him to answer to the lady for thorns carried away at les meles &c.

Mercy ij*

Robert May came in full court and took of Robert son of Robert atte fflete by the licence of the lady 5 acres of land &c. for 5 years &c.

Demise vj* viij*

From William Ringot, to have &c. to him and his heirs for ever half an acre of land &c., which William son of Robert Magotson resigned to him, and surrendered in court &c.

Fine xl*

Sum xvj* xj^d.

Court of Ingoldmels (date torn).

From Ralph Chitte, to have &c. to him and his assigns ½ acre with cottage &c. for 10 years &c., which John Carter and Isolda his wife demised to him &c. And he gives to the lady for having the term. And he is to render to the said John and Isolda iiij* yearly.

Demise xij*

Agnes who was the wife of William de Wegelant, plaintiff, does not prosecute against Alan son of Wm de Wegelant in a plea of trespass, therefore she and her pledges to prosecute are in mercy.

Mercy ij*

From Wm Pullayn, to have &c. to him and his heirs for ever 1½ acres 12 perches of land, lying at ffletwong &c., which Alan son of Wm de Wegelant resigned to him, and surrendered in court after the term of 12 years. And to have &c. 3^r xvij^p at Pennystykes &c. And the said land is arrented at the increased rent of xix^d ob. yearly.

Fine vj* viij* and not more because the said land pays an increased rent

Sum of this court xxj* ob.
Sum of this roll xxxvij* xj^d ob.

Court of Ingoldemels held at Burgh on Wednesday the Feast of the Holy Innecents, 19 Edw. III. [28 December A.D. 1345].

Thomas Marys junr. was attached to answer to Beatrice Smith of a plea wherefore on the Lord's day next after the Feast of S. Martin last past in Ingoldemels he insulted, beat, and ill used her to the damage of xl⁸. And thereof &c. And the said Thomas comes, and defends force &c., and says that he is not

Inquisi-
tion
guilty, and demands that this be inquired, therefore let an inquisition come.

Attach-
ment
It is ordered to attach Wᵐ son of Ralph, and John son of Robert atte Welle to answer to the lady for that they removed xl stone of hemp attached by her bailiff.

Mercy iijᵈ
It is found by the inquisition that Walter Galeway beat Richard Galeway to the damage of xijᵈ, therefore it is considered that he recover, and the sᵈ Walter is in mercy:

Mercy iijᵈ
That Richard Galeway made trespass on Walter Galeway to the damage of ij⁸, therefore it is considered that he recover, and the said Richard is in mercy.

Mercy iiijᵈ
Also they present that Robert Leueson made trespass in les meles with his sheep, therefore he is in mercy.

Alan son of Wᵐ de Wegelant came in full court, and sur-rendered into the hand of the lady to the use of Wᵐ Pullayn 1ᵃ 27ᵖ of land with a house built thereupon, lying next land of Wᵐ Surmilk on the one side, and land of Robert de Gipthorp

Fine iiijˢ
on the other. And thereupon came the sᵈ Wᵐ and took the whole of the said land to have &c. to him and his heirs for ever, doing all services due and accustomed according to the custom of the manor. And he gives to the lady for fine iiijˢ. And 23ᵖ

Increment
of rent
1ᵈq. yearly
are arrented at the new rent of 1ᵈq., and not more because 1ᵃ 4ᵖ were arrented in the time of the lord Henry de Lascy earl of Lincoln.

Fine ijˢ
Increment
of rent
vᵈ yearly
From Wᵐ Pullayn, to have &c. to him and his heirs for ever ½ acre and 20ᵖ, which Alan son of Wᵐ de Wegelant resigned to him, and surrendered in court after the term of 15 years &c.

Sum xjˢ iijᵈq.

Court of Ingoldmels held there on Wednesday next after the Feast of S. Hilary, 19 Edw. [18 January A.D. 1345-6].

trespass on Beatrice Smith, to the damage of xij^d. Therefore it is considered that she recover, and the said Thomas is in mercy.

It is ordered to attach W^m son of Ralph, and John son of Robert atte Welle, to answer to the lady, for that they removed, and unjustly took against the will of the bailiff of the lady xx stone of hemp attached by the bailiff. | Attachment

Also they present that John son of John atte Dammes demised to Wm Goshawk ij acres and a half for j year &c.

Also that Alan Germayn and Matilda de Burgh are in mercy for trespass in les meles. | Mercy iiij^d

Matilda daughter of Wm Coke came in full court, and demised to farm to Margery Blaunchard 5 acres in Burgh &c. for 3 years. Sum vj^s ix^d. Sum of this roll xviij^sq. | Demise vj^d

Court of Ingoldemels held on Wednesday next after the Purification of the Blessed Mary, 20 Edw. III. [8 February A.D. 1345–6].

Walter atte Waterlade and Beatrice his wife acknowledge themselves indebted to John Ringot in j bushel of beans, therefore it is considered that he recover, and Walter and Beatrice are in mercy. And as regards iiij^d he says that he owes him nothing. The inquisition says that the said Walter and Beatrice are indebted to John Ringot in iiij^d with damages j^d, and the s^d Walter is in mercy. | Mercy ij^d Mercy ij^d

From Alan Pullayn and Robert (his) son, to have &c. to them and their heirs for ever 2^a 14^p &c., which Ralph Maggeson and Walter atte Waterlade and Beatrice resigned to them and surrendered in court &c. | Fine xiiij^s iiij^d

From Agnes, Matilda, and Beatrice, daughters of Alan de Modelant, to have &c. for their whole lives, or to which of them shall live the longer, 1½ acres 14 perches &c., which Alan de Modelant resigned to them and surrendered in the presence of John son of Guy, the grave, and 12 of the homage &c. | Fine v^s

It is ordered to attach the township of Ingoldmels to repair the bridge between Wm Bug &c. | Attachment

Sum of this court xv^s.

Court of Ingoldmels held at Burgh on Wednesday next after the Feast of S. Matthias the Apostle in the 20th year [1 March A.D. 1345–6].

It is ordered to distrain the tenants of Simon de Thorp for fealty : (and) the heir of Walter de Akewra for fealty and relief. | Distraint

Distraint It is ordered to distrain W^m son of Robert Magotson to answer to the lady, for that he beat, and threatened her bailiff.

Merchet xij^d From Maria Whitewombe for licence to marry without the manor &c.

Sum of this court vij^s.

Court of Ingoldmels held there on Wednesday next before the Feast of the Annunciation, 20 Edw. [22 March A.D. 1345–6].

W^m son of Ralph was attached to answer to Wm Bug of a plea of trespass. And therein he complains that on Monday next before the Feast of S. Lawrence in year xviij he trod down a place of beans, worth iiij^s, with his horses, to the damage of x^s. And therein &c. And the s^d W^m comes, and defends

Inquisition force &c., and says that he is not guilty, and demands that this be inquired, therefore let an inquisition come.

Mercy vj^d W^m son of Ralph and John son of Robert atte Welle put themselves in mercy against the lady, pledge &c.

Wm Polber [1] found pledges for the peace against John Ringot, and Thomas son of Ranulph, viz. &c., under the pain of xl^s. And the same John and Thomas found pledges for the peace against the same W^m, viz. &c.

Distraint It is ordered to distrain the heir of Dom^s Henry le Vavasour for fealty and relief.

Mercy iiij^s ix^d They present that Roger Thory, Wm de Braytoft, (and 12 others) are in mercy for trespass made in les meles called Baytars.

Sum of this court ix^s viij^d.
Sum of this roll xxxj^s viij^d.

Court of Ingoldemels held there on Wednesday next before Easter, 20 Edw. III. [12 April A.D. 1346].

Distraint It is ordered to distrain the heirs of Wm de Hiltoft for fealty and relief.

Peter Warner came in full court, and surrendered into the hand of the lady 2½ acres of land with a cottage &c., lying between land of Wm Pullayn and land of Robert Cheles, to the use of W^m and Margaret, (his) children, to have &c. to (them)

Fine viij^s and their heirs for ever, doing all services due and accustomed

[1] He had been amerced vj^d twice for drawing blood from Thomas, and twice for same in case of John Ringot.

according to the custom of the manor. (Peter and Emma his wife to hold for life.)

They present that j mast of one boat was found of wreck, therefore the grave is ordered to answer. Wreck

Alan de Wegelant came &c., and surrendered &c. 1 place of land with a house (19ᴾ) to use of Wᵐ Pullayn &c. And the sᵈ land is arrented at the new rent of jᵈ yearly. Fine
xviijᵈ
New rent
jᵈ

Wᵐ Catte (and 5 others) are in mercy for trespass made in les meles. Mercy xijᵈ

It is ordered to attach John Carter to answer to the lady for trespass made, and thorns carried off and removed in les meles. Attach-
ment

Sum xjˢ jᵈ.

Court of Ingoldmels held there on Wednesday the Feast of the Invention of the Holy Cross, 20 Edw. [3 May A.D. 1346].

They present that Wᵐ de Westeby made trespass in les meles with his sheep, therefore it is ordered to attach him to answer to the lady. Mercy vjᵈ
Attach-
ment

Also that John de Essyngton, a bond tenant of the lady, has not come, and has j toft in Welton next Hamby.

Also that Wᵐ Lambert, a bond tenant of the lady, dwells in Toynton, and holds land there, therefore it is directed to seize it.

Also that Henry de Essyngton, a bond tenant of the lady, purchased land in Partenay, therefore it is ordered to seize it.

Also that Alice wife of Richard Barehefd received of Alan Barehefd and Wᵐ his brother j stone of wool of wreck. Also that Isabel Barehefd j quarter, (and 19 others different quantities,) all these they found of wreck of the sea, therefore it is ordered to attach them to answer to the lady (also 2 more for same).

Also they present that Katherine wife of Simon Catte (and 9 others) are in mercy for the assize of bread. Also that Richard Kyggis (and 15 others) brewed and sold beer contrary to the assize, therefore they are in mercy. Also that Robert son of Walter (and 10 others) are tipplers of beer contrary to the assize, therefore they are in mercy. Mercy
vjˢ xᵈ

Agnes daughter of Alan Brideson, a bond tenant of the lady, who held on the day she died 3ᵃ 3ʳ with a house, is dead. And thereupon come Beatrice, Eugenia, Maria, Agnes, and Heriot
xiijˢ iiijᵈ

Matilda, daughters and heirs of the said Agnes, and ask to be accepted to pay heriot for the said land, and they are accepted, doing all services due and accustomed according to the custom of the manor &c.

Distraint   It is ordered to distrain all tenants of lands, which are held by foreign service, to do homage &c.

Mercy ix^d   They present that Maria daughter of Alan Brideson and Isabel Bray are in mercy for wool found of wreck of the sea.

Merchet xij^e   From Robert son of Wm de Calflet for licence to have to wife Agnes widow of Walter Pullayn &c.

After Michael-mas for nets put next the sea to farm   Richard Parsonnef came in full court for licence to put nets in Le La next the sea for his profit from the Feast of Pentecost next for one whole (year). And he gives the lady ij^s this year to be paid at Michaelmas xij^d and Easter xij^d.

Distraint   From Elias Warner for j mast of wreck of the sea sold xviij^d.

John de Westmels, Richard Parsonnef, Wm de Burtoft, John Hayre, John Cadyhorne, Robert ffrauncays, Henry de Kele, Robert Peteclerk, Robert de Grymeslant, Wm Blakoft, Walter Brok, and Thomas son of Evorard, presenters of the articles, because they have not presented that Dom^s Simon de Akwra purchased of Walter de Akewra land, and Margaret daughter of Walter de Akewra purchased of the said Walter her father divers tenements. And because the said jurors have not presented this, therefore the said jurors are in mercy.

It is ordered to distrain all free tenants against the next court for homage.

Sum of this roll l^s vj^d.

Court of Ingoldmels held there on Wednesday the Vigil of the Ascension, 20 Edw. [24 May A.D. 1346].

After he came   Wm de Scalflet in mercy, because he has not come.

Mercy condoned   Wm Pullayn in mercy for contempt.

Order to seize   It is ordered to seize into the hand of the lady the land, which Wm Bakester held of the lady in Welton on the day he died.

Mercy ix^d   Also they present that W^m son of John [took] j lb. of wool. Robert Kyng and Hugh ffidkyn are in mercy for wreck of the sea.

Order to seize   It is ordered to seize into the hand of the lady all the land which Roger Bug held of the lady &c. They present that

certain broken boats came as wreck of the sea, therefore it is
ordered to seize them into the hand of the lady &c.

Thomas Marays was attached to answer to Robert Smith of
a plea that on Monday next after the Feast of S. Botulph in
the 16th year he took, and carried off against his will ij staffs,
worth xd, to the damage of xijd. And thereof &c. And the
sd Thomas comes, and defends force &c., and says that he is
not guilty, and demands that this be inquired, therefore let   Inquisi-
an inquisition come.   tion

Robert Smith was attached to answer to Thomas Marays
and Margaret his wife of a plea of trespass, and therein they
complain that on the Tuesday next after the Feast of the
Apostles Peter and Paul last past the same Robert called the
said Margaret 'false' and 'robber,' to the grave damage of
¼ mark. And the sd Robert comes, and says that he is not
guilty, and demands that this be inquired, therefore let an   Inquisi-
inquisition come.   tion

It is ordered to distrain all tenants of lands which are held   Distraint
by foreign service for homage.

It is ordered to seize into the hand of the lady all the land   Order
which Henry de Eshington holds in Partenaye.

It is ordered to distrain John de Eshington for divers   Distraint
services as a bond tenant of the lady.

                                        Sum iiijˢ xjd.

Court of Ingoldmels held there on Wednesday next after the
Feast of S. Barnabas the Apostle, 20 Edw. [14 June A.D. 1346].

It is ordered to distrain Walter son of Wm de Hiltoft for   Distraint
fealty and relief: and the heirs of Simon de Thorp for fealty,
and of Walter de Akewra for fealty and relief.

It is ordered to attach Robert son of Simon de Akewra to   Attach-
answer to the lady for that he had j ewe with ij lambs straying. ment

It is ordered to distrain Wm son of Robert de Calflet for   Distraint
fealty for a cottage, which he purchased of Wm Pusse.

They present that certain boats were found in the sea by   Orders
John son of Emma as wreck of the sea, therefore it is ordered
to retain them in the hand of the lady.

As yet it is ordered to retain in the hand of the lady 1 boat
of wreck of the sea as appears in the preceding court.

Alan de Wegelant came in full court, and surrendered into
the hand of the lady, to the use of Agnes who was the wife of

Fine
vj⁵ viij⁴

Wm de Wegelant 1½ᵃ 3ᵖ of land with a house built thereupon
&c., and one half acre of land &c.   And upon this came the s^d
Agnes, and took of the lady the s^d land, with all appurtenances,
to have &c. to her and her heirs or assigns for ever, doing all
services due and accustomed according to the custom of the
manor.   And she gives the lady for fine ½^m.   And one half

New rent
yearly iiij⁴

acre is arrented anew iiij^d yearly, and not more because 1½ᵃ 3ᵖ
of land were arrented in the time of lord Henry de Lascy &c.

Mercy vj⁴

Richard de Brinkill went backwards and forwards with his
carrying carts in les meles, doing damage, and was attached by
the pledge of Wm de Westiby.   And because the s^d Richard has
not come, therefore the s^d pledge is in mercy.

Mercy
ij⁵ viij⁴

Wm de Westeby is in mercy for trespass made in les meles
with his sheep, (12 others) in mercy for the same.

Sum of this roll xvj⁵ v⁴.

Court of Ingoldmels held there on Wednesday next after the
Feast of the Apostles Peter and Paul, 20 Edw. III. [5 July A.D.
1346].

Mercy ij⁴

Thomas Raven in mercy for a false claim against Alice atte
Halgarth, and W^m her son, executors of the will of W^m de
Halgarth, in a plea of debt.

Gilbert Smith was attached to answer to Thomas Marays of
a plea wherefore on the Lord's day next before Christmas last
he insulted, beat, and ill treated him to the damage of x⁵.
And thereof &c.   And the s^d Gilbert comes and defends force

Inquisi-
tion

&c., and says that he is not guilty thereof, and demands that
this be inquired, therefore let an inquisition come.

Fealty

Margaret daughter of Walter de Akewra did fealty to
the lady for iiij acres of land.

Attach-
ment

It is ordered to attach John de Essyngton for chevage.

Mercy ij⁴

Thomas Marays and Margaret his wife are in mercy for a
false claim against Robert Smith in a plea of trespass.

Mercy ij⁴

It is found by the inquisition that Thomas Marays made
trespass on Robert Smith to the damage of v^d, therefore it is
considered that he recover the said v^d, and the said Thomas is
in mercy.

Roger Bug, who held of the lady on the day he died
3½ acres with a messuage, whereof there was in reversion 2½ᵃ,
is dead, and upon this comes Robert, (his) son and heir, and

asks to be accepted to pay heriot for the said land, doing all services due and accustomed according to the custom of the manor, and he is accepted. And he gives &c. Heriot
vj⁸ viij^d

W^m son of Robert de Calflet did fealty to the lady for one messuage and one place of land, and he has a day at the next court to acknowledge &c. services &c. Fealty

Agnes who was the wife of Thomas son of Ralph demands against Ralph son of Thomas iij roods of land in the name of dower, and she has respite until the next court. Respite

From Alan son of Wm de Methelant to have for the term of his life 1½ᵃ 2ᵖ of land &c., which Wm de Methelant resigned to him and surrendered in the presence of the grave and others of the homage &c. Fine
vj⁸ viij^d

From Beatrice daughter of William de Methelant to have for life 1ᵃ 1ʳ 24ᵖ of land, which Wm de M. &c. Fine v^s

Walter son of Wm de Hiltoft and Agnes his wife did fealty to the lady for vij acres of land, and acknowledged the services, viz. vij^d a year, and one advent at the great court next after Michaelmas. Fealty

From Alan Pullayn for a certain boat found of wreck of the sea xl⁸ [sold by the council of the lady]. Wreck xl⁸

They present that John Carter (and two others) are in mercy for trespass made in les meles. Mercy xvj^d

The distress made upon Robert son of Simon de Akewra is in respite until the next court concerning ij sheep straying.

From Alice daughter of Wm de Wegelant for licence to marry within the manor with Alan son of Ranulph Ringot &c. Merchet
vj⁸ viij^d

Sum of this court lxxj⁸ ij^d.

Court of Ingoldmels held there on the Wednesday next after the Feast of S. James the Apostle, 20 Edw. III. [26 July A.D. 1346].

Ralph son of Thomas gives the lady for having an inquisition concerning the right to iij roods of land and the custom of the manor &c., it is ordered to summon Simon son of Thomas son of Ralph against the next court to answer &c. concerning the s^d 3 roods of land. xl^d
Summons

Wm de Methelant, who held of the lady on the day he died one messuage and 16½ᵃ of land &c., is dead. And upon this comes Richard, son and heir of the said W^m, and asks &c. Heriot
cvj⁸ viij^d

vj^d

Mercy ij^d
Fine xij^d
Increment
of rent
ob.q.
yearly
Mercy iiij^d
Demise vj^d

Robert son of Roger Bug gives to the lady for scrutiny of the rolls concerning 1 rood of land which John Bug holds, and it is ordered to summon the said John against the next court.

Wm de Westeby is in mercy for trespass in les meles.

From Wm Pullayn to have &c. 17^p of land with a house, which Alan de Wegelant resigned to him, and surrendered in court &c.

They present that John Ringot (and 3 others) are in mercy for trespass in les meles with their pigs.

From Robert Thory, to have &c. to him and his assigns 3^a 25^p of land with a house &c. for 9 years, which Robert atte Halgarth demised to him &c.

Sum cxij^s iij^d ob. q. also xl^d.

Court of Ingoldmels held there on Wednesday the morrow of the Assumption, 20 Edw. [16 August A.D. 1346].

Seizure

It is ordered to seize into the hand of the lady all the land which W^m son of Robert Magotson demised without licence.

It is ordered to seize into the hand of the lady one place of pasture &c. in Hoggestorp, which is called Bungidayle, which Agnes daughter of Richard son of Ranulph of Ingoldemels, a bond tenant of the lady, purchased of Robert son of Philip de Halbertoft.

Merchet
xl^d

From Beatrice daughter of Alan Brideson for licence to marry within the manor &c.

Court of Ingoldmels held there on Wednesday next before the Feast of the Nativity of the Blessed Mary, 20 Edw. [6 September A.D. 1346].

Order

It is ordered to seize into the hand of the lady all the land, which John Curtays holds in bondage, until &c., viz. xv acres.

As yet it is ordered to seize &c. one place of pasture in Hoggestorp, which is called Bungydayle, which Agnes daughter of Richard son of Ranulph of Ingoldemels, a bond tenant of the lady, purchased of &c.

Agnes atte Howe, a free woman, held on the day she died one messuage, and 14 acres of land, and one perch of free land, (and) is dead. And John Belt, a bond tenant of the lady, son and heir of the said Agnes, entered on the said land and tenement, therefore it is ordered to seize them into the hand of the lady until &c. And the s^d land is arrented anew at ij^s iiij^l ob. yearly, and he did fealty.

New rent
ij^s iiij^d ob.
yearly

From Alice daughter of Thom⁵ Herwerd for licence to marry without the manor &c. | Merchet iij⁵

Alan Germayn (and 2 others) in mercy for trespass in les meles. | Mercy vj⁴

Sum viij⁵ j⁴ ob.
Sum of this roll vj^ll ix⁵ q.

Court of Ingoldemels held there on Wednesday next before the Feast of S. Michael, 20 Edw. [27 September A.D. 1346].

Wm de Prestorp demands against Wm Herwerd x⁵, which he owes to him, and unjustly detains &c. And the s⁴ Wm Herwerd admits ij⁵ v⁴, and is in mercy. And as to the vij⁵ vij⁴ he says that he owes him nothing, and he demands that this be inquired. The inquisition says that the s⁴ Wm Herwerd is indebted to the s⁴ Wm de Prestorp vij⁵ vij⁴, with damages iij⁴, and the s⁴ Wm Herwerd is in mercy. | Mercy ij⁴ / Mercy ij⁴

As yet, it is ordered to retain in the hand of the lady all the land which John Curtays holds of the lady in bondage &c. | Order

W^m son of Dom⁵ Alexander de Gipthorp did fealty to the lady for lands and tenements, which were Simon de Thorp's in Skegnes. | Fealty

Agnes daughter of Richard son of Ranulph of Ingoldemels, a bond tenant of the lady, purchased of Robt son of Philip de Albertoft one place of pasture with appurtenances in Hoggistorp, which is called Bungydayle, containing 4 acres and j rood of free land. And the said land is arrented to the lady anew at viij⁴ ob., and she did fealty to the lady. | New rent viij⁴ ob. yearly

Henry de Kele is distrained by iij cows for homage and other services in arrear &c. | Respite

From Alan Gunny for licence to marry Eleanor widow of Wm de Methelant &c. | Merchet x⁵

Eugenia del Hill in mercy for trespass in les meles. | Mercy ij⁴

Sum of this court xvj⁵ j⁴ ob.

View of the Court of Ingoldemels held there on Wednesday the Feast of S. Luke the Evangelist, 20 Edw. III. [18 October A.D. 1346].

Dom⁵ W^m ffraunk knt, Thomas de Multon of fframpton knt, Robert de Saltfletby, Joan widow of James de Wodstok, John de Hale, John Cob of Cletham, Walter le Hird, John de Gunby, | Default of the foreign tenants

K

and Richard son of Wm de Dunham, were summoned for suit of court, and now they have not come, therefore they are in mercy, and nevertheless it is ordered to distrain them for homage, and suit of court, and other services in arrear.

John de Burtoft, chaplain, came in full court and did fealty to the lady for j messuage and xv acres of land with appurtenances in Ingoldemels, and acknowledged the services, viz. xv^d yearly, and suit of court.

Mercy xj^d   Wm de Godshalf, Agnes de Akewra (and 4 others) in mercy for default of suit of court.

Mercy xl^d   From Master Thomas Beek in mercy for default of suit of court, and nevertheless it is ordered to distrain him &c.

Mercy xx^d   They present that John de Tointon dug the soil in the common way, and there carried it, therefore he is in mercy: also that the same John raised a certain new wall in the common way, to the injury &c., therefore he is in mercy, and it is ordered to throw it down: also that the same John (and 2 others) obstructed the common way with clays, to the injury &c., and it is ordered to open it: also that Agnes widow of Walter Reddcok dug the soil of the waste in Scalflet, therefore &c.: also that John and Wm Ringot obstructed the common sewer, therefore &c.: also that W^m son of Robert Magotson holds bond land, and the houses of the same W^m are ruinous, therefore it is directed to seize them for waste until &c.

Mercy vij^s j^d   Also that John Germayn (and 3 others) are in mercy for the assize of bread: also that Robert Leueson (and 15 others) are in mercy for the assize of beer.

Respite   John de Cokrington has respite until the next court concerning his services for tenements which were John son of Simon de Halton's.

Order to seize   It is ordered to seize into the hand of the lady all the land which John Curtays holds in bondage.

Chevage yearly iiij^d   Philip son of Wm Bakester, and Richard son of Wm Bakester give the lady yearly for chevage, pledge &c.

They present that j oak was found upon the sand of wreck of the sea, therefore let it be retained &c.

Demise of the court of the port to the use   Elias Warner came in full court before the steward, and took of the lady the court of the port, and the whole of the profits of the plaints and amercements of the said court, from the morrow

Court of Ingoldmeles held there on Wednesday next after the Feast of All Saints. 20 Edw. [8 November A.D. 1346].

It is ordered to seize &c. all the land which W^m son of Robert Magotson holds for waste made. *Order*

W^m son of Henry Pullayn of Burgh was elected by the whole homage to the office of grave, and afterwards the said W^m came at Bolingbrok, and made fine to the lady for being released from his office for the whole life of the lady Countess, pledge Robert Thory. *Fine xl^s*

From W^m, Simon, and Thomas, sons of Alan Gunny, to have &c. for the term of their lives 2^a 3rd 25^p of land &c., which Alan Gunny resigned to them, and surrendered in court &c. *Fine v^s*

From Beatrice, Matilda, and Joan daughters of Wm Gunny to have &c. for life 1rd 25^p &c. *Fine xx^d*

Sum of this court lj^s v^d.
Sum total of this roll iiij^{li} iij^s iij^d.

Ingoldmels. Court held there on Wednesday next before the Feast of the Conversion of S. Paul in the 20th year [24 January A.D. 1346–7].

Wm de Hiltoft (is essoined) of the common advent by Robert de Westmels: Symon de Boyland by Richard de Hiltoft. *Essoins*

Walter Mareys was attached to answer to W^m son of Alan in a plea of debt, and therein he says that on the Lord's day next before the Feast of S. Peter in Chains in the 20th year the same W^m lent to the same Walter xviij^s of silver, to be re-paid on the Feast of S. Martin next following in the same year, on which day he paid nothing, but detained it, and still detains it, to the damage of $\frac{1}{2}$ mark, and thereof he produces suit. And the same Walter comes, and defends force &c., and says that in no money is he (indebted) to him. and he demands that this be inquired, and the s^d W^m likewise. *Inquisition*

W^m son of Alan demands against Walter Mareys xij^d, as a pledge &c., who comes, and admits &c., therefore it is considered that he recover the said xij^d, and the s^d Walter is in mercy. *Mercy vj^d*

From Robert de Acwra, who was summoned to come upon the inquisition [1] between &c., and is not willing to take the oath, nor to be on the inquisition, therefore he is in mercy, and it is ordered to distrain him against the next court. *Mercy iij^d*

[1] Put in respite until the next court.

x 2

It is ordered, as often, to summon Richard de Benyngton, and Wm de Brayton for forestalling, as appears in the third preceding court.

Fealty

On this day comes Ralph son of Matilda de Kelsey, and does fealty to the lord for tenements, which he purchased of John de Kelsey, his father, in Great Steping, to Ralph and Joan his wife and the heirs of their bodies.

lj^a

From Peter de Gybthorp for default of suit of court, and it is ordered to distrain him.

Order

It is ordered, as often, to attach Wm Galle and Thomas Perers, for that they hunted in the warren of the lord, as was presented in the next preceding court.

Order

It is ordered as at other times to attach Walter de Acwra to show how he entered into the fee of the lord, as appears in the next preceding court.

Mercy lij^d

John son of W^m comes, and puts himself in mercy for forestalling, and for this that he broke the park of the lord concerning a boat attached for divers trespasses &c.

Mercy lij^d

It is found by the inquisition that Symon son of Geoffrey impleaded Robert Germayn in court Christian to the damage of xviij^d, therefore it is considered that he recover the said xviij^d, and the s^d Symon is in mercy.

Merchet ij^a

From Rose daughter of Wm Coper for licence to marry Thomas Warner, a bond tenant of the lord, pledges &c.

vj^d

From (torn) because he disagreed with his fellows in a verdict before the steward.

It is found by the inquisition that John Godard, and Alan son of John Polayn, either made trespass on the other, to the damage taxed on either part of vj^d, therefore it is considered that either of them recover from the other vj^d, and either of them is in mercy.

The jurors present that the rector of the church of S. Nicholas of Ingoldmels by himself and his (men) dug, and caused to be carried away to his house (some) of the land of Walter Godard, a bond tenant of the lord, and thereof he made walls, therefore the s^d rector is in mercy, and it is ordered to distrain him; also he dug &c. (some) bond land of the lord, which Agnes Godard holds of the lord in dower, and thereof he made walls, therefore he is in mercy &c. Also the said rector filled a certain dike of the bond land of the lord, which Walter Godard holds.

Also they present that the s^d rector and Robert his proctor hold all the said land without the licence of the court, therefore they are in mercy. Mercy respited

From Walter Godard, and Agnes his mother, in mercy because they demised the s^d tenements without the licence of the court: and it is ordered to seize the said land into the hand of the lord, and to answer for the explees. Mercy iij^d Explees

Also they present that Henry de Marum demised one acre of bond land to one Wm Gunny for the term of 3 years without the licence of the court, therefore they are in mercy, and it is ordered to seize the s^d land &c. Mercy xij^d

Also they present that Alan Godard, a bond tenant of the lord, purchased one place of free land of John de Ryg for the term of his life, and built there a house without the licence of the court, therefore he is in mercy, and it is ordered to distrain him. Mercy ij^s

Also that a certain anchor and ij ropes came of wreck of the sea, which it is ordered to value.

Robert Bygge, a fisherman, and other fishermen upon the sea in their boats were accused of this, that they came, and drew out their boats upon the sands next Ingoldmels, and there rested the said boats and there put to open sale to divers men the fish they had caught in the sea, and therefore give to the lord no profit for the said easement, who say that neither they nor any other fishermen from time immemorial have given or paid anything for the said easement, and they demand that this be inquired. The inquisition sworn upon this says that fishermen resting there upon the sands have not been accustomed to give to the lord anything for having the easement with their boats upon the sands, but have come at their will, and gone away quit, from the beginning of this lordship until now, &c. Therefore it is considered that as to this they shall go away quit &c. Plaint

Also they present that Alan Germayn (and 2 others) made trespass in le mels &c. Mercy ix^d

It is ordered to distrain Richard Cobbler for that he took and carried off j 'hare,' of the length of xvj feet, of wreck of the lord. Order

From Robert le Warner, to have and to hold one acre and one rood of free land for the term of v years, which W^m son of Clement demised to him by the licence of the court &c. Fine ij^s

Licence | It is granted to Agnes atte Hafdyk to dwell upon the tenement of Roger her son of the fee of Orby, holding tenements for the term of her life, and she found pledges (4) that she justify herself with all her goods and chattels against the lord and his bailiffs, to do for him all she ought to do during the time she dwells there at the will of the lord.

Sum xxiij[•] j^d.

Sum of this roll xxiij[•] j^d.

Court of Ingoldemels held there on the Saturday next before Palm Sunday, 24 Edw. III. [20 March A.D. 1349–50].

Respite | William de Wegelant demands against Alan Germayn 1 acre and 1 rood of land of his inheritance after the death of Isabella Lake. In respite to the next court.

Distraint | It is ordered, as often, to distrain William de Teford for fealty.

They present that Agnes daughter of Alan Brideson is 'deflorata.' And she gives the lord for leyrwit &c.

Fine iij[•] | John de Tointon came in full court, and made fine for 1½ acres of land, which he holds by the courtesy of England after the death of Sarah his wife, to have &c. for his whole life, doing all the services &c. according to the custom of the manor &c.

Fine iij[•] | Stephen Croudsone came &c. (as above) after the death of Cristiana his wife.

Order | It is ordered to seize &c. 17 acres of land, which were Ranulph's son of Wm de Prestorp, until &c.: also 5 acres which were Matilda Taylour's in Wynthorp.

Respite | Margaret daughter of Gilbert son of Thomas de Saltflethaven demands against John Cardinaus and Joan his wife 3½ acres of his right after the death of Agnes Mighill. In respite to the next court.

Merchet xij^d | From Simon Smith for licence to have to wife Agnes daughter of Alan Brideson &c.

Sum x[•] vij^d.

Court of Ingoldemels held there on the Saturday next after the Octave of Easter in the 24th year [10 April A.D. 1350].

Mercy vij^d | The heirs of Robert Peteclerk in mercy for default of suit of court, the heirs of John Redecole and of John atte See in mercy for the same.

It is ordered to seize &c. the whole of the land which Walter   Order
de Steping held in bondage.

Alan son of Guy (and 4 others) in mercy for default of suit   Mercy xij⁴
of court.

Robert son of Alan Germayn came &c. and took of the lord   Entry viij⁴
iij acres of land [free land arrented of the fee of Wyl.] after the
death of William son of Alan Germayn, to have &c. to him and
his heirs, doing all services due and accustomed &c.

From Wᵐ atte Enges, to have &c. to him and his assigns   Demise ij⁴
5 acres of land in Burgh &c. for 6 years, which Margaret Coge
demised to him &c.

From John son of Guy, to have to him and his heirs for ever   Entry
2½ acres of land &c., which Alice widow of Alan Ryngot resigned   vj⁴ viij
to him, and surrendered in court &c.

Alice widow of Alan Ryngot came in full court, and sur-   Entry
rendered the whole of her right to Simon son of John son of   xxvj⁴ viij⁴
Guy in 13 acres of land with a messuage, to have &c. for the
whole life of the said Alice, doing all services &c. And after
the death of the said Alice the whole of the said land shall
remain to John Ryngot and his heirs, doing &c.

From Alice widow of Alan Ryngot for licence to marry John   Merchet
son of Simon de Akewra a free man &c.   xiij⁴ iiij⁴

From John son of Alan Gunny, to have &c. to him and his   Entry ij⁴
heirs for ever ½ an acre of land &c., which Matilda daughter of
Gilbert de Prestorp resigned to him, and surrendered in court.

Matilda daughter of Gilbert de Prestorp came in full court,   Entry xxx⁴
and took of the lord 1 messuage and 13 acres of land of her
inheritance after the death of Ranulph son of Wᵐ de Prestorp,
to have &c. to her and her heirs, doing all services &c.

They present that Richard Ermegard is a common male-   Mercy iij⁴
factor against the peace of the lord the king, therefore he is in
mercy, and nevertheless it is ordered to attach him.

It is ordered to distrain Richard de la Rawe for fealty and   Fealty
other services in arrear: (also) the heirs of John Hayre for
fealty and suit of court.

Stephen Ponrdfisch released, and quitclaimed the whole of   Quitclaim

xxij year for the debt of Alice his mother, on which day he paid
nothing, but &c. to the damage of xl^{li}, and thereof he produces
suit.   And the said William comes, and defends force &c. and
says he owes him nothing, and begs that this be inquired.

Chattels
of a
fugitive
vj^s

John of North Walsham is a fugitive for robbery, and the
chattels of the same John are valued at vj^s, also it is ordered
that the township answer &c.

.   Sum cxiiij^s iiij^d.

View of Frankpledge of Ingoldemels held there on the
Saturday next before the Feast of S. Luke the Evangelist,
25 Edw. III. [15 October A.D. 1351].

Essoins

Richard de la Rawe (is essoined) of the common (advent) by
William de Waytecroft, Edmund Chaumberlayn, and Alice who
was the wife of Dom^s Alexander de Gipthorp by Robert son of
Walter, and William Neucomyn by William Marays.

Distraint

It is ordered to distrain Dom^s Henry le Vavasour, Robert
ffolyot, Dom^s John de Multon, chivaler, the prior of Bolyngton,
Robert de Saltfletby, the heir of Nicholas de Hale of Northorp,
the heir of John Cob of Cletham, John de Gunby, John de
Dunham, and the abbot of Kirkestede for fealty, and other
services in arrear, and for homage.

Default
Mercy
ij^s ix^d

The heir of Simon le Boteler, John de Burtoft, Robert de
Steping, the heir of Robert Peteclerk, Ralph de Kelesey, the
heir of Alan atte See (and two more) are in mercy for default of
suit of court &c.   And Dom^s John de Crokrington, chivaler, is
in mercy for the same.

Mercy xvj^d

Robert son of Alan Gryn, Alan atte Halgarth (and 5 more)
are in mercy, because they have not come.

Distraint

It is ordered to distrain William son of Dom^s Alexander de
Gipthorp for fealty &c.

It is ordered to seize into the hand of the lord one toft,
formerly John Day's, in Welton, for the minority of the son and
heir of the said John.

New rent
yearly

It is presented that Richard de Hiltoft held 7½ acres of land
freely [of the fee of Candelsby], (and) is dead.   And Robert son
of Robert atte Hafdyk, a bond tenant of the lord, is the next
heir in blood of the said Richard, therefore the said land is
arrented at the new yearly rent of xv^d.

Also they present that Alan Germayn, a bond tenant of the
lord, purchased of Dom^s Simon de Akewra one place of land,

which is called Cauntland, of the fee of the lord duke, containing half an acre, with one ' mershe,' to have &c. to him and his heirs. And the s^d land is arrented at the new &c.

Also they present that the house of Richard Godard is fallen   Mercy vj^d
into ruins, (also) the house of Robert Taylor, therefore it is ordered to seize.

Also they present that j panel of a boat was found of   Wreck iij^d
wreck of the sea, worth iij^d, and it is ordered that the grave answer.

They present that William Carter, Dyne Boucher, are in   Mercy x^d
mercy for trespass made in les meles with pigs, and that Julia Kyng cut synes in les meles, therefore she is in mercy.

From Agnes Reigner for having an inquisition concerning   xij^d
her land to be divided between her and Robert Rayner xij^d.

Eudo Pylat took of the lord a cottage in Welton until the   Entry vj^d
full age of the heir of John Day, to have &c. to him and his assigns, doing all service &c.

Sum xviij^s.

Court of Ingoldemels held there on the Saturday next after the Feast of the Apostles Simon and Jude, year 25 [29 October A.D. 1351].

They present that Alan de Wegelant is in mercy, because   Mercy iij^d
he sold beer . . .

Simon Swete surrendered &c. the reversion of 6½ acres of   Entry x^d
land with a messuage to the use of Alan Cob after the death of Maria who was the wife of William Swete, to have &c. to him and his heirs &c. doing all services &c.

John Godard demands against Richard de Scalflet six acres   Respite as yet
of land with a messuage of his inheritance after the death of Hauwis his mother &c.

From John son of Robert Maggeson, and Margaret his wife,   Entry iiij^s
to have &c. to him and his heirs for ever 2½ acres of land, lying next the land of Dom^s Philip de Somervyle on the one side, and land of the lord de Wilughby on the other, which Alan Pullayn resigned to him and surrendered in court &c.

Sum xx^s iiij^d.

Court of Ingoldemels held there on the Saturday next after the Feast of S. Hugh, year 25 [19 November A.D. 1351].

From Matilda who was the wife of William de Wegelant for   Merchet ij^s
licence to marry without the manor &c.

Merchet ij⁰	From Ralph de Croft for licence to have to wife Joan daughter of Matilda de Westrig &c.
Mercy ix⁴	John de Cokrington, chivaler, Walter son of Richard de Hiltoft, Robert Peteclerk, and the wife of William Blaykster are in mercy for default of suit of court.
Entry ij⁰ New rent yearly xvj⁴	From Alan and Richard de Wegelant to have &c. for the term of the life of Matilda daughter of William de Wegelant two acres of land, which the said Matilda resigned to them &c.
Entry ij⁰	Alan Cob surrendered into the hand of the lord the reversion of two acres of land after the death of William de Barlings to the use of Alan son of Alan Pullayn, to have &c. to him and his heirs &c.

Sum xij⁰ vj⁴.

Court of Ingoldemels held on the Saturday next before the Feast of S. Lucy the Virgin, year 25 [10 December A.D. 1351].

Mercy ij⁴	John Godard in mercy for a false claim against Richard de Scalflet in a plea of land.
Attachment	It is ordered to attach Hugh ffidkyn [by ½ a boat worth xv⁰] to answer to the lord for that he beat the bailiff of the lord.

Sum v⁰ vj⁴, the whole for perquisites.

Court of Ingoldemels held there on the Saturday next before the Feast of the Circumcision of the Lord, year 25 [31 December A.D. 1351].

Demise iij⁰	From Agnes who was the wife of Roger Thory, to have &c. to her and her assigns 4 acres with a messuage for the term of the life of William son of Robert son of Hugh &c., which the s⁴ Wᵐ. demised to her &c.
Frankpledge of the lord	John son of Robert de Akewra of Ingoldemels gives to the lord yearly vj⁴ to be in the protection of the lord, as a bond tenant of the lord, pledge Robert son of Walter.

Sum ix⁰ ix⁴.

Court of Ingoldemels held there on the Saturday next after the Feast of SS. Fabian and Sebastian [21 January A.D. 1351-2].

Chevage	From William son of Robert Magotsone, (who) gives to the

From Joan d. of William de Prestorp for licence to marry   Merchet xij^d
without the manor.

From Alan son of Alan Pullayn, to have &c. to him and his   Entry v^s
heirs for ever 2 acres and 1 rood of free land arrented, which is
called Baronlant, and 1 acre of land formerly Alan de Dunswra's
next the common Waterlade on the north, and 1 toft called
Pourdfish, which the s^d Alan Pullavn resigned to him, and
surrendered in court &c. And for this resignation the s^d Alan
Pullayn, father of the same Alan, shall have the said land for
his whole life &c.

Sum vij^s viij^d.

Court of Ingoldemels held there on the Saturday next after
the Feast of S. Matthias the Apostle, 26 Edw. III. [3 March
A.D. 1351–2].

William Neucomyn in mercy for default, and nevertheless it   Mercy vj^d
is ordered to distrain him to answer to Joan Blaykester of   Distraint
Burgh in a plea of trespass.

From John Godard, to have &c. 4 acres with cottage for   Demise
4 years, which Alan son of Alan Godard demised to him &c.   iij^s

From Richard Club (who) gives to the lord to be in (his)   Frank-
protection ij^d yearly &c.   pledge yearly

From Isabel Plomer for licence to marry without the manor.   Merchet xij^d

Sum viij^s ij^d.

Court of Ingoldemels held there on the Saturday next before
the Annunciation, 26 Edw. [24 March A.D. 1352].

Joan Blaykester of Burgh, plaintiff, offered herself against   Respite
William Neucomyn in a plea of debt, in respite.

William de Waytecroft in mercy, because he does not pro-   Mercy j^d
secute against Richard the servant of Richard de la Rawe in a
plea of trespass.

Alan Pullayn of Ingoldemels and Joan his wife and Alan   New rent
son of the same Alan purchased of Dom^s Peter de Scremby,   yearly
chivaler, 3½ acres of free land by charter, to have and to hold to
them, and the heirs of the said Alan and Alan, doing to the
chief lords of the fee the services thence due and accustomed.
And the said land is arrented anew at vij^d yearly.

It is ordered to summon all tenants against the next court,   Summon
and that there come an inquisition to inquire concerning the
articles.

Sum iij^s j^d.

Court of Ingoldmels held there on the Friday in Easter week, 26 Edw. III. [13 April A.D. 1352].

Entry x⁸ From John son of Robert, to have &c. to him and his assigns 3 acres and 14 perches of land &c., which Richard son of Robert atte Hafdyk resigned to him and surrendered in the presence of the steward, and others of the homage, after the death of Beatrice daughter of Robert atte Hafdyk &c.

Mercy iij⁴ William Neucomyn puts himself in mercy against Joan Blaykester in a plea of trespass &c.

Mercy ij⁸ order The jurors present that a certain bridge, which is called Cadyhornebrig, is obstructed [in default of the township of Burgh] to the damage &c., therefore (the township) is in mercy, and it is ordered that it be mended.

Mercy ½ mark order Also that the bridges of Ingoldemels are broken in default of repair by the tenants of Ingoldemels, therefore they are in mercy, and it is ordered that they repair them by the next court.

Order That John son of W^m son of Thomas, who held of the lord 2 acres of land with appurtenances, (is dead). And Alan de Wegelant put in his claim against the next court, therefore it is ordered to seize.

Mercy ij⁴ Alan de Wegelant in mercy because he has not come.

Damages vj⁸ viij⁴ Order to seize Also that Beatrice Bug made waste of a certain messuage, formerly Richard Godard's, to the damage of ½ a mark, therefore it is ordered to seize &c.

Mercy viij⁸ v⁴ Also that John son of Robert baked bread, and sold it contrary to the assize: that Agnes wife of Roger Thory (and 6 others) are in mercy for the assize of beer: also Richard atte Halgarth (and 2 others) for tippling beer.

Graves of the Dikes John Withsone, W^m atte Halgarth, Simon Smith, Robert son of Walter, and Alan Pullayn were elected to the office of graves of the dikes, and made oath to serve faithfully.

Entry¹ xl⁸ Beatrice Pullayn took of the lord the marriage of Agnes daughter of John Lambert of Ingoldemels, together with the lands and tenements of the said Agnes, to the use of her son, and she gives to the lord for the marriage [as well for the entry of the land as for] xl⁸, pledge Alan Pullayn.

Sum lxxvij⁸.

¹ The scribe first entered this as a merchet, but corrected this to an entry (ingressus).

Court of Iugoldemels held there on the Friday next after the Invention of the Holy Cross, 26 Edw. III. [4 May A.D. 1352].

Alan de Wegelant & Agnes his wife came in full court, and took of the lord 2 acres of land &c. of the inheritance of Agnes wife of the said Alan after the death of John son of W^m son of Thomas, brother of the s^d Agnes, to have &c. to them and their heirs, doing all services &c. | Entry viij^a

Alan de Wegelant came before the steward and took the guardianship of W^m son of Richard Godard until the full age of the s^d W^m with 1 messuage and xvii acres of land &c., to have &c. until the full age of the s^d W^m, together with all his lands and tenements, doing all services due and accustomed according to the custom of the manor, and the s^d Alan found pledges (4 named) to answer to the said W^m when he shall come to his full age concerning the proceeds of the lands and tenements to be calculated beyond the sustentation of the s^d William &c. | Entry liij^a iiij^d

Sum lxiij^s v^d.

Court of Ingoldmels held there on the Friday next before the Feast of Pentecost, 26 Edw. III. [25 May A.D. 1352].

Richard son of Richard de Wrangle for the ward of 1 horse and ij oxen, pledge &c. | Mercy xij^d

From W^m atte Halgarth in mercy for contempt of court. | Mercy iij^d

They present that Wm Astyn opened le Gote, so that the lands and tenements of tenants of the lord were submerged, therefore he is in mercy. | Mercy xl^d

Also that W^m atte Skelles destroyed the common way to the injury &c., therefore he is in mercy, and it is ordered that it be amended. | Mercy xij^d

Sum lj^s.

Court of Ingoldemels held there on the Friday next after the Feast of S. Barnabas the Apostle, 26th year [15 June A.D. 1352].

They present that Wm Godard demised 1 acre and 1 rood of land to W^m son of Richard son of Ranulph and Agnes his wife in exchange without licence, therefore they are in mercy, and it is ordered to seize until &c. | Mercy xij^d

Order

Alan atte Halgarth sen^r was attached to answer to John de

Tointon of a plea of trespass, and therein he complains that on the Monday next after the Feast of the Apostles Philip and James last he insulted, beat, and ill treated him, to his damage xl⁸, and thereof &c. And the s⁴ Alan comes, and defends

Inquisi-
tion force &c., and says that he is not guilty, and he demands that this be inquired, therefore let an inquisition come.

Richard son of Robert atte Hafdyk was attached to answer to John Kellok of a plea wherefore he beat, and ill treated the wife of the said John, to the damage of xl⁸, and thereof &c.

Inquisi-
tion And the s⁴ Rich⁴ says that he is not guilty, and demands that this be inquired.

Simon Smyth and Agnes his wife surrendered in the presence of John Ryngot, Wᵐ de Skegnes, Wᵐ del Outdayle, Thomas Smyth, Wᵐ de Modelant, and others of the homage, 3 acres of land with a cottage. And upon this came Simon Smyth and Agnes his wife and took of the lord the whole of the said land

Entry xl⁴ to hold &c. for the term of their lives, and to the heirs and assigns of the s⁴ Agnes, doing &c.

Demise ij⁸ Margaret widow of Walter Handsone surrendered into the hand of the lord the 3ʳᵈ part of 3½ acres of land to the use of Alan Pullayn of Burgh, to have &c. for the term of the life of the s⁴ Margaret the 3ʳᵈ part of (same), which (she) held in the name of dower &c.

Order It is ordered to seize into the hand of the lord ten acres of land with a messuage, which Alan Germayn claims as his right &c.

Sum viij⁸ iiij⁴.

Court of Ingoldemels held on the Saturday the Feast of the Commemoration of S. Paul, 26 Edw. [30 June A.D. 1352].

Mercy ij⁴ Richard son of Robert atte Hafdyk put himself in mercy against John Kellok in a plea of trespass.

Mercy ij⁴ It is found by the inquisition that Alan atte Halgarth senʳ made trespass on John de Tointon to the damage of iij⁴, and the s⁴ Alan is in mercy.

Entry vj⁴ Wᵐ Coper surrendered to the use of John son of Robert and Beatrice his wife and their heirs a place of land with a house thereupon, viz. 40 feet in length and breadth, to have &c.

Entry
iij⁸ iiij⁴ Alan Germayn came in full court, and surrendered 2 acres of land, pasture and arable &c., to the use of Matilda widow

of Robert son of Hugh, to have &c. to her and her heirs
&c.

Alan Germayn &c. surrendered 3½ acres of land &c., and
upon this came the sᵈ Alan and Margaret his wife, and took of
the lord the whole of the sᵈ land for the term of their lives, or
to whichsoever of them shall live the longer, and after (their)
death the sᵈ land shall remain to the right heirs of the said
Alan &c.

Entry iij·

Sum xjˢ iijᵈ.

Court of Ingoldemels held there on the Friday next after
the Feast of S. James the Apostle, 26 Edw. III. [27 July
A.D. 1352].

Wᵐ son of Richard son of Ranulph came &c., and surrendered 3 roods and 27 perches of land, with a messuage &c.,
to the use of Wᵐ son of Richard son of Ranulph until the term
of the life of Agnes his wife &c.

Entry iij·

Richard son of Robert son of Hugh surrendered to the use
of Alan Pullayn, and of Alan the son of the same Alan, 4 acres
of land, called Marchallant, to have &c.

Entry vj·

They present that John Dobson (and 8 others) are in mercy
for trespass made upon les meles with their pigs.

Mercy
xxijᵈ

Sum xvˢ vjᵈ.

Court of Ingoldemels held there on the Friday next after
the Feast of the Assumption of the Blessed Mary, 26 Edw.
[17 August A.D. 1352].

Sum xjᵈ.

Court of Ingoldemels held there on the Friday next before
the Nativity of S. Mary, 26ᵗʰ year [7 September A.D. 1352].

Walter atte Kirke in mercy for trespass made on the banks.

Mercy vjᵈ

Sum ijˢ xjᵈ.

Court of Ingoldmels held there on the Friday next before
the Feast of S. Michael, 26ᵗʰ year [28th September A.D. 1352].

It is ordered to distrain Robert Perers for fealty, and other
services in arrear.

Distraint

From Joan d. of John son of Wᵐ for licence to marry
within the manor &c.

Merchet
ij·

Summon   It is ordered to summon all tenants against the next court.

Matilda daughter of Gilbert de Prestorp surrendered into the hand of the lord, in the presence of Alan Pullayn, Wm Cardinaus, Alan Cob, Simon Lamb, Walter Galway, and others of the homage, 10 acres of land with a messuage &c., to have &c. to her and her heirs.

Entry xl^s   (Also) 10 acres with a messuage to the use of Simon son of Guy, to have &c. to him and his assigns for ever. And the s^d Matilda binds herself and her heirs to warrant the s^d land to Simon his heirs and assigns in the presence of (same names) and others of the homage &c.

Sum xlv^s vj^d.

Court of Ingoldemels held there on the Saturday next before the Feast of the Nativity of the Blessed Mary, year 29 [5 September A.D. 1355].

Mercy vj^d   Wm Neucomyn, and Hugh Lancaster in mercy, because they have not come.

Sum xxiij^d.

Court of Ingoldemels held on the Saturday next before the Feast of S. Michael, 29 Edw. III. [26 September A.D. 1355].

Inquisi-   From John son of Ryngot for licence to have an inquisition
tion xij^d   between him and Robert son of Walter.

Sum iiij^s ij^d.

View of Frankpledge of Ingoldemels held there on the Saturday next before the Feast of S. Luke the Evangelist, 29 Edw. III. [17 October A.D. 1355].

Mercy ix^d   William Neucomyn, and Thomas Eborard in mercy, because they have not come upon the inquisition of the articles.

Foreign   Henry le Vavasour, Robert ffolyot of ffrisby, the heir of
tenants   Nicholas de Hale in Northorp, the heir of John Cob in Cletham,
Mercy iij^s   the abbot of Kirkested, and John de Dunham in mercy, because
Distrain   they have not come, and nevertheless it is ordered to distrain them for homage.

Mercy   The jurors present that Alan de Wegelant (and six others)
iij^s xj^d   are in mercy for the assize of beer, also because they have not sent for the tipplers of beer.

Default   William de Gipthorp, Dom^s John de Cokrington, the heir of

John de Westmels, Edmund Chaumberleyn, Peter atte See, and (10 others) are in mercy for default of suit of court.

From v boats for nets drying this year.

Sum xxj⁸ v^d.

For nets drying v⁸

Court of Ingoldemels held there on the Saturday next before the Feast of S. Martin, year 29 [7 November A.D. 1355].

John de Wyhom defendant against Robert de Gipthorp in a plea of debt by Robert ffraunceys.   Essoins

Robert de Gipthorp in mercy, because he does not prosecute against John de Wyhom in a plea of debt.   Mercy iij^d

Robert de Gipthorp complains of John de Wyhom in a plea of debt, pledge &c., therefore it is ordered to summon.   Plaint Summons

From Dom⁸ John de Cokrington, chivaler, for respite of suit of court until Michaelmas: from Wᵐ Boteler for the same.   Fine xij^d Fine iij^d

It is ordered to attach Alan Ward for chevage.   Attachment

From Joan d. of Ranulph Est for licence to marry Thomas of York.   Merchet xij^d

It is ordered that there come an inquisition between Agnes de Hiltoft, plaintiff, and William atte Halgarth, concerning sheep killed with a dog in the year 26.   Order

It is ordered to attach Robert de Gipthorp to answer to Robert atte fflete in a plea of trespass.   Attachment

Sum vij⁸ ij^d.

Court of Ingoldemels held there on the Saturday next before the Feast of S. Andrew the Apostle, year 29 [28 November A.D. 1355].

John de Wyhom puts himself in mercy against Robert de Gipthorp in a plea of debt.   Mercy ij^d

Robert de Gipthorp puts himself in mercy against Robert atte fflete in a plea of trespass.   Mercy ij^d

It is found by the inquisition that Wᵐ atte Halgarth made trespass on Agnes de Hiltoft to the damage of xij^d, and the s^d Wᵐ is in mercy.   Mercy iij^d

Richard Kyng of Skegnes made fine to the lord for having respite until Michaelmas concerning a presentment.   Fine xij^d

Dynne Boucher for trespass made in les meles with his horses.   Mercy xij^d

Wᵐ del Outdayle was elected to the office of grave by the whole homage, and made oath to serve the lord faithfully.   Election of grave

Sum v⁸ j^d.

L

Court of Ingoldemels held there on the Saturday next before the Feast of S. Thomas the Apostle, year 29 [19 December A.D. 1355].

Mercy vj⁴   William son of Dom⁵ Alexander de Gipthorp in mercy, because he has not come.

Sum ij⁵ vij⁴.

Court of Ingoldemels held there on the Saturday next before the Feast of the Purification in the beginning of the 30ᵗʰ year of Edw. III. [30 January A.D. 1355–6].

Mercy iij⁴   It is found by the inquisition that William Harefot has timber, worth xvˢ, of the chattels of Robert Thory to the use of Ralph son of Thomas, therefore the sᵈ Wᵐ is in mercy.

Mercy vj⁴   Also they present that the bridge between Robert son of Robert atte Hafdyk and the Lady de Hiltoft is broken, therefore they are in mercy.

Merchet viij⁵   From Alice daughter of Robert atte Halgarth for licence to marry Wᵐ de Thikthorp with vij acres.

Sum xij⁵ j⁴.

Court of Ingoldemels held there on the Saturday next before the Feast of S. Peter in Cathedra, 30 Edw. III. [20 February A.D. 1355–6].

Mercy vj⁴   Lady Alice widow of Dom⁵ Alexander de Gipthorp in mercy for default of suit of court, therefore it is ordered to distrain.

Mercy iiij⁴   It is found by the inquisition that Walter de Hiltoft, and Wᵐ de Medelant made trespass on Wᵐ de Stakhou, to the damage of viij⁴ &c.

Sum vˢ iiij⁴.

Court of Ingoldemels held there on the Saturday the Feast of S. Gregory the Pope, year 30 [12 March A.D. 1355–6].

Mercy he offered himself

Distraint   Wᵐ son of Dom⁵ Alexander de Gipthorp in mercy for default of suit of court, and nevertheless it is ordered to distrain him for homage.

Attach- ment   They present that Wᵐ Skynnerd (was) in the warren of the lord with his dog, and took j hare, therefore &c.

Distraint   It is ordered to distrain Robert ffoular to answer to the lord concerning j charter of Maria Belt.

Fine iij⁴   From Walter son of John de Westmels for respite of suit of court until Michaelmas.

Sum ij⁵ ij⁴.

Court of Ingoldemels held there on the Saturday next before the Feast of S. Ambrose, year 30 [2 April A.D. 1356].

Alan de Wegelant (and 5 others) in mercy for selling beer by discs not marked. | Mercy xij^d

Richard de Scalflet in mercy, because he has not come upon the inquisition. | Mercy ij^d

Sum iiij^s.

| Graves of the dikes and sewers. | W^m del Outdayle.
W^m atte Halgarth.
Simon Smith.
Roger Astyn.
William Marays.
Alan atte Welle. | Sworn. |

Court of Ingoldemels held there on the Saturday next after the Feast of S. John of Beverley, 30 Edw. [14 May A.D. 1356].

Lady Alice de Gipthorp (is essoined) of the common (advent) by Richd de Westmels. | Essoins

The jurors present that Wm de Cokrington, Simon of ye Enges (and 2 others) damaged the common way with their ploughs, to the damage of the lord and the community, therefore they are in mercy, and nevertheless it is ordered that this be amended before the next court &c. | Mercy ij^s

Also that John de Croft (and 2 others) occupied the common of Scalflet with sheep : also that the prior of Bolington made trespass with his pigs in Scalflet &c. | Mercy iij^s vj^d

Hugh de Lancastr' purchased of Wm de Akewra 3 acres of free land of the fee of the lord, and did fealty to the lord, and acknowledged the service of vj^d yearly, and suit of court. | Fealty

Also they present that Alan de Wegelant (and 14 others) are in mercy for the assize of beer. | Mercy v^s iij^d

Also that Richard the servant of Robert de Gipthorp raised the hue justly upon John Haldeyn, therefore &c. | Mercy ij^d

Also that the cellarer of Markeby took j hare with a dog, therefore it is ordered &c. | Order

Also that Dynne Boucher (and 5 others) are in mercy for forestalling fish, and that (he and another) made trespass in the warren of the lord with his cattle. | Mercy iiij^s iiij^d

Alan de Wegelant holds the tenements of William Goder, and the houses are in ruins, therefore he is in mercy. and he has | Mercy iiij^d

L 2

Order	a day at the next court under a penalty to repair the houses of the same W^m.
Mercy ij^d	Walter Galeway for waste made upon the houses of Alan atte Walles &c., and it is ordered to repair &c.
Mercy iij^d	Also they present that Wm Galt occupied the common of Scalflet with the sheep of John Croft without licence.
Fine xij^d	W^m atte Halgarth exchanged with Alan Pullayn ij acres of land for ij acres and iij roods, therefore they are in mercy. And because it was not presented by the township, therefore it is in mercy for the concealment, afterwards Alan Pullayn came, and made fine.
Fine ij^s	Alan Pullayn surrendered 2 acres and 3 roods of land formerly W^m atte Halgarth's to the use of Alan son of Alan Pullayn, to have &c. for the term of the life of the s^d W^m atte Halgarth &c.
Fine ij^s	Alan Pullayn surrendered 1 acre and 3 roods and 25 perches of land of the vill, which W^m atte Halgarth holds for the term of his life, to the use of Alan son of Alan Pullayn, to have &c. to him and his heirs after the death of the said W^m.
xl^d	Joan who was the wife of Wm Harefot took of the lord all the lands and tenements, which were Robert Thory's, until the full age of Alan son and heir of Robert Thory, and to answer for the profits and debts, as Wm Harefot formerly held, pledges &c., and she gives to the lord for having the licence.

Sum xxv^s iij^d.

Court of Ingoldemels held there on the Saturday next after the Ascension, 30 Edw. [4 June A.D. 1356].[1]

Court of Ingoldemels held on the Saturday next after the Feast of S. John Baptist, year 30 [25 June A.D. 1356].

Court of Ingoldemels held there on the Saturday next after the Feast of the Translation of S. Thomas, year 30 [9 July A.D. 1356].

iij^d	Margery ffouler for ward of one horse.
Mercy ij^d	W^m son of Thomas in mercy for excess.
Mercy they offered themselves	Wm de Prestorp and Simon son of Guy in mercy for contempt of court [because they have not come].

[1] This roll is torn.

John Surmilk surrendered 1 rood of land &c. to the use of John Gunny, to have &c. to him and his heirs, in exchange for 1 rood w^h John Gunny surrendered to the use of John Surmilk &c.

Entry vj^d

Thomas Ward demised to farm to Simon Germayn ½ an acre of arable land, lying next the land of Simon Germayn of the one part, and land of the Lady of Hiltoft on the other &c., for 8 years.

Demise vj^d

Sum ij^s viij^d.

Court of Ingoldemels held there on the Saturday next before the Feast of S. Lawrence, year 30 [6 August A.D. 1356].

From Matilda daughter of John Plomer for licence to marry John Bray &c.

Merchet xiij^s iiij^d

Sum xv^s iiij^d.

Court of Ingoldemels held there on the Saturday next before the Beheading of S. John Baptist, year 30 [27 August A.D. 1356].

Walter son of Richard de Hiltoft, and John son of Guy are in mercy, because they have not come.

Mercy iiij^d

Sum ij^s.

Court of Ingoldmels held there on the Saturday next after the Exaltation of the Holy Cross, year 30 [17 September A.D. 1356].

The jurors present that John Dobsone purchased of W^m son of Thomas Magotsone 5 acres of arable land with a cottage of the fee of the lord of Eresby, therefore it is ordered to seize until &c.

Order

W^m of ye More was attached to answer to Agnes daughter of John de Brandelsby of a plea why on the Lord's day before Carniprivium in Burgh he insulted, beat, wounded, and ill treated her, and tore her clothes to the damage of xl^s, and thereof &c. And the s^d W^m comes and defends force &c., and says that he is not guilty thereof, and demands that this be inquired, therefore let an inquisition come.

Plea

Inquisition

Walter de Hiltoft because he did not agree with the inquisition between the parties.

Mercy iij^d

Siouge y
lands by uge

Entry
xiij⁵ iiij⁴

Matilda daughter of John Doufsone surrendered to Alan Pullayn of Ingoldemels the moiety of 15 acres of land arable and pasture with a messuage in Ingoldemels and Skegnes, and upon this came the sᵈ Alan, and took the sᵈ land to hold &c. to him and his heirs &c.

Merchet
vj⁵ viij⁴

From Matilda d. of John Doufsone for licence to marry without the manor &c.

Sum xxj⁵ vᵈ.

As yet of the Court of Ingoldemels held on the Saturday next after the Feast of S. Hugh, year 30 [19 November A.D. 1356].

Distraint

From Lady Joan de Cantilupe in mercy for default of suit of court, and let her be distrained for fealty.

The jurors present that Richard Alaunkrayne chased j hare out of the warren, and took it out of the warren.

New yearly rent

Gilbert Meriet of Ingoldemels and Wᵐ his son purchased of Wᵐ de Akewra one acre and one rood of free land by charter arrented, and the said land is arrented anew at ijᵈ yearly &c.

viij⁵ iiij⁴

From v boats for drying nets, viz. each c herrings by custom, viz. from Walter de Burgh, John son of Leua, John Mileson, John de Holme, and John Dobson.

Wᵐ Vavasour, Lady Joan de Cantilou, and the abbot of Louth Park in mercy for default of suit of court.

Sum xiiij⁵ ixᵈ.

Court of Ingoldemels held on Saturday next before the Feast of the Circumcision, year 30 [24 December A.D. 1356].

Order

It is ordered to seize into the hand of the lord 9½ acres of land, which Alan son of Wᵐ Thory [holds], because he is foolish [stultus].

Order

It is ordered to seize into the hand of the lord all the land which Ralph de Kelesey held of the lord on the day he died &c.

Sum xj⁵ vᵈ.

Court of Ingoldemels held there on the Saturday the Feast of S. Botolph, year 31 [17 June A.D. 1357].

It is ordered to seize as in dors

Robert Taunt, who held of the lord on the day he died 5 acres of free land arrented, and bond, is dead, and upon this comes Ranulph, son and heir of the said Robert, and asks to be accepted to pay heriot for the said land, and he is accepted, to have and to hold to him and his heirs. And he gives to the lord for entry.

Hugh Goderik demands of Alan son of Ralph Magsone ij^s vj^d, w^h he ought to have paid him on Monday after Michaelmas year 28 for beer sold to him, on which day &c. And the said Alan comes and defends force &c., and says that he is not indebted anything &c. Inquisition

They present that Alan de Wegelant (and 10 others) are in mercy for selling a gallon of beer at 1½^d, and because they sold by measures not sealed. Mercy iij^s j^d

Maria who was the wife of Alan de Burgh, plaintiff, offered herself against W^m son of Richard Randsone of a plea of land according to the nature of ——, and the said W^m has not come, therefore it is ordered to seize &c. Law Order to seize

It is ordered to seize into the hand of the lord vij selions of land, which Simon Ward of Hoggestorp demised to farm to Walter son of Henry de Hoggestorp, and one place of meadow surrounded by a ditch in Tiptoft, which Eudo Miry of Cumburworth demised to (the same) &c. And William de Modelant, a bond tenant of the lord, had the said land of the gift of the said Walter, and upon this came Richard Grayf, and seized the said land unjustly &c. Order to seize

Sum vj^s ix^d.

Court of Ingoldemels held there on the Saturday next after the Translation of S. Thomas the Martyr, year 31 [8 July A.D. 1357].

It is ordered to attach Wm Beryng of Croft to answer to W^m son of Philip de Westmels in a plea of agreement. Attachment

Ranulph son and heir of Robert Taunt took of the lord 5 acres of free land arrented, and bond, after the death of the said Robert, to have and to hold to him and his heirs, doing all services due and accustomed according to the custom of the manor, and he gives the lord for entry &c. Entry xiij^s iiij

Sum xviij^s vij^d.

Court of Ingoldemels held there on the Saturday next after the Feast of S. James, year 31 [29 July A.D. 1357].

John Smith was attached to answer to Alan del Outdayle of a plea wherefore on the Thursday next after the Feast of the

Inquisi-
tion

Nativity of S. John Baptist last past he insulted, beat, and ill treated him, to the damage of **xx**ˢ, and therein &c., and the said John comes, and defends force &c., and says that therein he is not guilty, and asks that this be inquired.

Court of Ingoldemels held there on the Saturday next after the Feast of the Assumption, 31 Edw. III. [19 August A.D. 1357].

Merchet
vjˢ viijᵈ

From Robert atte Waterlade for licence to have to wife Margaret Cage, pledge &c.

Entry
xxvjˢ viijᵈ

Wᵐ de Wegelant, who held of the lord on the day he died 1 messuage 9 acres and 3 roods of land, and the reversion of 1 acre which Isabel daughter of the said Wᵐ holds for life, is dead, and upon this came John, son and heir of the said Wᵐ, and took the whole of the said land, to hold &c. to him and his heirs according to the custom of the manor, and he gives &c.

Inquisi-
tion

John son of Alan complains of Domˢ Robert the chaplain of a plea wherefore on the day of S. Margaret last past he entered his close against his will, and removed Julia daughter of the said John out of his service, to the damage of xlˢ, and therein &c. And the said Robert comes, and defends force &c., and says that he is not guilty, and asks that this be inquired.

For drying
nets
ijˢ iiijᵈ

From John Mileson (and 6 others) in mercy for drying nets near the sea.

Sum xlˢ xjᵈ.

As yet of the Court held on the Friday next before the Feast of S. Michael, year 31 [22 September A.D. 1357].

Ingoldemels. View of Frankpledge held there on the Saturday next after the Feast of S. Michael, 33 Edw. III. [5 October A.D. 1359].

Mercy vjᵈ

Wᵐ Neucomyn, John de Calflet, and Simon Germayn in mercy, because they have not come upon the inquisition of the articles.

Mercy iijᵈ

Alan atte Skelles in mercy for default, and nevertheless it is ordered to distrain him to answer to John Milner in a plea of trespass.

Distraint

It is ordered to distrain Robert son of Walter de Skegnes to answer to James Maltwate of ffriyng and Emma his wife, executors of the will of John son of Thomas de Skegnes, in a plea of detention of chattels.

Walter son of Wm de Hiltoft in mercy, because he has not come on the inquisition. Mercy vj^d

Also they present that Walter son of Wm Baxster is not in the chevage of the lord, wherefore let him come, therefore he is in mercy. Mercy iij^d

It is ordered to seize the whole of the land which Wm Harefot formerly held &c. Order to seize

Also they present that John Haldeyn (and 11 others) are in mercy for the assize of beer: also that John son of Robert (and another) are in mercy for tippling beer. Mercy v^s viij^d

Joan widow of Alan Aldyet demised to farm to Wm de Modelant, and Gilbert Miriet 5 acres of pasture land for (4 years) &c. Demise ij^s

It is found by the inquisition that Walter Engrayne, and Alan de Wegelant broke their agreement with John Haldeyn &c. Mercy vj^d

For j horse, of waif, sold ij^s. Wayf ij^s

It is ordered to attach Alan Thoraud to answer to the lord for j horse, of waif, removed, afterwards sold. Wayf iiij^s

W^m le Vavasour, Robert ffolyet, Lady Joan de Cantilupe, Robert de Saltfletby, Nicholas de Hale, and John de Gresby in mercy, because they have not come.

Lady Alice de Gipthorp, Wm de Gipthorp, John de Cokrington, chivaler, Edmund Chaumberlayn, W^m son of Walter de Akewra, Richard de Wegelant, W^m son of Ranulph, Wm Godard, and John de Tointon in mercy, because they have not come. Mercy ij^s ix^d

John son of Robert Aldyet and Beatrice his wife surrendered in full court 3 acres of pasture land &c. to the use of Alan Pullayn and Joan his wife and W^m son of the same Alan &c. Entry xl^d

Sum xxxj^s vj^d.

Court of Ingoldemels held there on the Saturday next before the Feast of the Apostles S. Simon and S. Jude.

Court of Ingoldemels held there on the Saturday after the Feast of S. Martin, year 33 [16 November A.D. 1359].

Mercy vj^d
They present that Alice Graymagh, and Hugh ffidkyn are in mercy for trespass in les meles with their pigs.

Mercy iij^d
Also that Wm Neucomyn drew blood from Margaret servant of Philip Pynder, therefore let him be in mercy: also

Mercy vj^d
that the s^d Margaret raised the hue justly upon the s^d W^m, therefore let him be in mercy.

Demise xij^d
Alan Pullayn of Burgh demised to farm to Wm Gryn 1 rood of land &c. for the term of the life of the said Alan &c.

ij^s
From ij boats with customary herrings, pledge the bailiff.

Sum v^s vij^d.

Court of Ingoldemels held there on the Saturday next after the Feast of S. Nicholas the Bishop, 33 Edward [7 December A.D. 1359].

Mercy vj^d
Philip Pynder in mercy because he did not prosecute against Wm Neucomyn in a plea of trespass.

Merchet xviij^d
From Matilda d. of Wm Germayn for licence to marry Thomas Cole &c.

Mercy iij^d
They present that John fferur raised the hue justly upon Alan Thory, therefore (Alan) is in mercy &c.

Order that there come
It is ordered that there come an inquisition to inquire concerning blood drawn from John Becheres by W. de Elshem.

Mercy vj^d
Richard Kyng has not come to present, therefore he is in mercy.

Demise of le Gote
John Gunny, Wm Marays, W^m atte Halgarth, and John Ryngot came in full court and took of the lord the fishery of the eels 'del gote' of Ingoldemels, to have &c. for the term of their lives, rendering to the lord yearly v^s &c.

Sum vij^s x^d.

Court of Ingoldemels held there on the Saturday next after the Feast of S. Hilary, year 33 [18 January A.D. 1359-60].

Mercy iij^d
A. It is found by the inquisition that Wm de Elshem drew
is ordered from John Becheres, therefore he is in mercy.
trespass. because this was not presented at the last court, there-

Distraint
It is ordered jurors are in mercy for the concealment.
to answer to James

Sum v^s ij^d.

Court of Ingoldemels held there on the Saturday next after the Feast of the Purification, 34 Edw. [8 February A.D. 1359–60].

They present that Dom⁸ Wᵐ de Slotheby took j hare in the warren of the lord with the dog of the parson of the church of Candelsby, and this is presented by Simon Lamb, therefore it is ordered to attach. **Attachment**

From Lady Alice de Gipthorp in mercy for default. **Mercy vjᵈ**

Beatrice, daughter of Ranulph Ryngot, wife of Richard de Westeby, took of the lord 6 acres of land with a messuage, which were Matilda Ryngot's, to have &c. to her and her heirs, doing all services &c. **Entry vjˢ viijᵈ**

Ryngot etc.

Sum ixˢ vᵈ.

Ingoldemels. View of Frankpledge held there on the Saturday next after the Feast of S. Michael, 38 Edw. III. [5 October A.D. 1364].

They present that Wᵐ son of Ranulph is a taster of beer, therefore he is in mercy because he has not come. **Mercy iijᵈ**

Also that Alan de Wegelant (and 7 others) are in mercy for the assize of beer: that (3 persons) are tipplers of beer contrary to the assize &c. **Mercy iijˢ** **Mercy ixᵈ**

The heir of Ralph de Kelesey, John de Cokrington, Edmund de Grynnslant, Domˢ Wᵐ de Gipthorp, Lady Alice de Gipthorp, Thomas de Rig, Dynne Boucher, and Matilda de Kelesey, are in mercy, because they have not come, and Robert de Boylant for the same. **Default** **Mercy iijˢ jᵈ**

They present that the bridge called Whelebrig is broken down, in default of repair by the prior of Bolington, to the damage of the community, therefore the sᵈ prior is in mercy, and it is ordered that it be repaired before the next court. **Mercy xlᵈ** **Order**

Also they present that the prior of Bolington has obstructed the common sewer, wʰ is called Whelebrig, to the injury of the community, therefore he is in mercy, and it is ordered that it be repaired. **Mercy xlᵈ** **Order**

It is ordered to distrain Peter de Cokrington, and Robert de Cokrington for fealty for tenements of Domˢ John de Cokrington. **Distraint**

Simon Swete for chevage, pledge &c. **Chevage**

From Walter de Westmels and (3 others) for respite of suit of court. **Fine xiijᵈ**

Mercy iij^d They present that Dynne Bocher made trespass with his horses and beasts, therefore &c.

Mercy ix^s ij^d The jurors present that Robert Germayn (and 12 others) are in mercy, because they have not repaired the banks next the sea, and it is ordered that they be repaired before the next court.

Default ix^s ij^d W^m le Vavasour, the tenants of the lands of Robert ffolyot, the heirs of Dom^s Nicholas de Cantilupe, Robert de Saltfletby, the heirs of Nicholas de Hale, John de Gresby, and John de Dunham, and the prior of Bolington are in mercy for default of suit of court.

Robert Germayn is elected to the office of grave of Ingoldemels, and made oath to serve faithfully.

Sum xxvj^s iij^d.

Ingoldemels. Court held there on the Saturday next before the Feast of the Apostles Simon and Jude, 38 Edw. III. [26 October A.D. 1364].

Merchet ij^s From Matilda daughter of Ranulph Marays for licence to marry &c.

Sum x^s vj^d.

Ingoldemels. Court held there on the Saturday next after the Feast of S. Martin, year 38 [16 November A.D. 1364].

Mercy iij^d Wm Kemp in mercy, because he went to the inquisition without licence.

Duplicate ij^s vj^d Thomas son of Wm Marays did fealty to the lord for tenements after the death of the said William, and he gives to the lord for duplicate of the farm ij^s vj^d.[1]

Sum x^s x^d.

Ingoldemels. Court held at Skegnes on the Saturday next after the Feast of S. Nicholas, year 38 [7 December A.D. 1364].

Attachment It is ordered to attach Dynne Boucher to answer to the lord because he broke the attachment.

Custom ij^s viij^d For the custom of iiij boats of herrings.

Demise xij^d Alan Thory demised to farm to Robert ffoular one cottage in Skegnes, with garden, and two parts of an acre of land &c., for the term of 40 years, paying to the s^d Alan vij^s yearly &c., and the said Robert shall sustain the said house at his own cost &c.

[1] ' It is found by the jurors ' in a case of bloodshed.

The tenants of lands of Robert May, because they have not   Mercy xij^d
repaired the banks of the sea, are in mercy, and it is ordered   Order
that they be repaired &c.

Ingoldemels.   Court held at Burgh on Saturday next after
the Feast of S. Hilary, 38 Edward III. [18 January A.D. 1364–5].

Dynne Boucher (and 8 others) are in mercy for trespass   Mercy
made with their beasts and pigs.   xviij^d

Ranulph Bug surrendered one acre with a house &c. to the   Entry ij^o
use of Robert Meriet, to have and to hold to him and his heirs
for ever.

It is found by the inquisition that Wm de Prestorp and   Mercy iij^d
Joan his wife made waste of the tenement of Alan Thory to the
damage of xij^d, therefore it is considered that it be repaired,   Order
and the s^d W^m and Joan are in mercy.

Ralph son of Thomas de Skegnes in mercy for default, and   Mercy xij^d
it is ordered to distrain him to answer to Robert ffoular in a plea
of debt.

John de Stikeford in mercy for trespass made in the warren   Mercy iij^d
of the lord &c.

Sum ix^s.

LANCASTER.

COURT OF THE LORD JOHN DUKE OF LANCASTER

Ingoldemels. Court held at Burgh on the Saturday next after the Purification in the beginning of the 39th year of Edw. III. [8 February A.D. 1364-5].

Mercy iij^d — Ralph son of Thomas de Skegnes acknowledges himself indebted to Robert ffoular in xj^s ij^d, with damages iiij^d &c.

John Nevill demands against Richard de More xx^d, which he ought to have paid him on the Monday next after the Feast of S. Martin in the xxxijnd year, for ploughing land with his Inquisi- plough, to the damage of xl^d, and therein &c., and the said tion Richard comes, and says that he is not indebted to him anything, and he demands that this be inquired.

They present that Matilda daughter of Ralph son of Peter made a trespass in les meles.

Sum ij^s xj^d.

Court held at Burgh on the Saturday next after the Feast of Matthias the Apostle, 39 Edward [1 March A.D. 1364-5].

Respite — Thomas of York and Joan his wife offered themselves against Hauwis Est of Ingoldemels in a plea of land &c. In respite until the next court.

Sum ij^s iiij^d.

Court of the lord John Duke of Lancaster held at Skegnes on the Saturday next before the Annunciation, 39 Edw. [22 March A.D. 1364-5].

Summons — It is ordered to summon Hauwis Est of Ingoldmels to answer to Thomas of York and Joan his wife in a plea of land.

Mercy iij^d — Richard de More is indebted to John Nevill in xx^d, and damages vj^d &c.

From Matilda daughter of John de Thikthorp for licence to marry John Pullayn.

Merchet vj⁸ viij⁴

Sum xj⁸.

Ingoldemels. Court of the lord Duke of Lancaster held at Burgh on the Friday next after the Feast of the Apostles Philip and James, 39 Edw. III. [2 May A.D. 1365].

It is ordered to summon the prior of Bolington to answer to John de Broghton in a plea of debt. — Summons

Hauwis Est of Ingoldmels defendant v. Thomas of York and Joan his wife in a plea of land (is essoined) by &c. — Essoin

They present that Agnes Taunt [Hiltoft], Dynne Boucher (and 11 others) are in mercy for the assize of beer. — Mercy iiij⁸ iij⁴

Also that Wᵐ son of Alice (and 7 others) are in mercy, because they have not sent after the tasters of beer. — Mercy xvj⁴

Also that Wᵐ son of Roger made rescue. — Mercy ij⁸

It is ordered to distrain Peter de Cokrington for fealty for tenements of John de Cokrington. — Distraint

They present that the prior of Bolington was accustomed to repair the bridge, which is called Whelebrig, and it is fallen, to the damage of the lord and the community, and it is ordered that it be repaired before the next court. — Mercy ij⁸ / Order

It is ordered to distrain Domᵘ Dionisius, parson of the church of Skegnes, and Domᵘ Dionisius the chaplain, and Domᵘ Robert de Hiltoft for fealty for tenements which were Dynne Boucher's. — Order

Dynne Boucher in mercy because he has not repaired the banks of the c acres in Ingoldmels, and he has respite until the next court for other things. — Mercy iiij⁴ / Respite

It is found by the oath of (12), who say on their oath that Philippa de Hiltoft was seised in a certain place of pasture, containing 1 acre and 1 rood of land, called Capeltoft, and gave it to Matilda atte fflet, and the heirs issuing of her body, which same Matilda took to her husband Ralph de Wra, which same Ralph (had) of the sᵈ Matilda two daughters Joan and Beatrice, and the sᵈ Ralph and Matilda gave the said place to the sᵈ Joan, and the heirs issuing of her body, which same Joan died without heir of her body, and so the sᵈ place went back to the said Beatrice, which same Beatrice took to her husband Wᵐ de Wegelant, a bond tenant of the lord, and the said Wᵐ begot of the said Beatrice (a son), called Wᵐ de

Wegelant, a bond tenant of the lord as was his father, in which time of the son the place was arrented at ij^d ob., which W^m begot Isabella of Alice his wife, which same Isabella died without heir, after whose decease Margaret lady of Hiltoft, and Agnes her daughter, and Wm de Skipwith, knt., as of the right of his wife, entered upon the said place, claiming it to be their inheritance by the form of the gift aforesaid.

Sum xv^s vij^d.

Ingoldemels. Court held there on the Saturday next after the Ascension, year 39 [24 May A.D. 1365].

Mercy xij^d They present that Alan Pullain (and 3 others) are in mercy, because they have not repaired the banks of the sea of the c acres.

Entry xvj^s John Thory surrendered 7½ acres of land &c. to the use of Alan brother of the said John, to have &c. to him and his heirs for ever &c.

Merchet ij^s From Inglesia daughter of John de Doufdyk for licence to marry Alan the servant of Gilbert Smith, pledge &c.

Entry xviij^d Wm Pourdfisch surrendered one acre of land, lying in two places, to the use of John Gryn, to have &c. to him and his heirs, doing &c.

Sum xxij^s ix^d.

Ingoldemels. Court of the lord Duke of Lancaster held there on the Saturday next after the Feast of Corpus Christi, 39 Edw. III. [14 June A.D. 1365].

Essoin   The prior of Bolington defendant v. John de Broghton in a plea of debt (is essoined) by Richard the clerk.

Entry xl^d Wm Cardinaus surrendered 2 acres of land with a grange &c. to the use of Agnes who was the wife of Roger Thory, to have &c. to her and her heirs for the term of the life of Alice daughter of Robert Magotsone.

demised to Alice daughter of Robert

3 roods of land, which Hauwise Est holds, to have &c. to themselves and the heirs of the said Hauwise, doing all services due and accustomed.

From Maria Baillif for licence to marry Robert son of | Merchet
Richard Siklyng &c. | xl*

Simon son of Guy (and two others) in mercy, because they | Mercy ix
did not go with the grave for the business of the lord.

Walter son of Hugh atte Waterlade in mercy for selling | Mercy vj⁴
beer contrary to the assize.

Sum l* ix⁴.

Court of the lord John Duke of Lancaster held there on the Saturday next before the Feast of the Translation of S. Thomas, 39 Edw. III. [5 July A.D. 1365].

It is ordered to distrain Beatrice who was the wife of | Distraint
Richard Kyngson for services in arrear.

Sum v* vij⁴.

Ingoldemels. Court of the lord John Duke of Lancaster held on the Saturday next after the Feast of S. James the Apostle, 39 Edw. III. [26 July A.D. 1365].

Eleanor Perers in mercy because she did not prosecute | Mercy iij⁴
against John Stikford in a plea of debt.

Alice daughter of Roger Knight demands v. Ranulph Bug
one acre and one rood of land &c.

It is ordered that an inquisition come between Alan | Inquisi-
Pullayn of Burgh, plaintiff, and Wᵐ Peteclerk in a plea of | tion
trespass, for that he trod down his herbage with his beasts for
three years.

Sum v* iiij⁴.

Court of the lord John Duke of Lancaster held there on the Saturday next after the Feast of the Assumption, 39 Edw. III. [16 August A.D. 1365].

Ingoldemèls. Court of the lord John Duke of Lancaster held at Skegnes on the Saturday next before the Feast of the Nativity of the Blessed Mary, year 39 [6 September A.D. 1365].

Mercy iij^d Wm Peteclerk put himself in mercy v. Alan Pullayn of Burgh in a plea of trespass.

Mercy vj^d It is found by the inquisition that Alan Thory is indebted to W^m son of Alice in xiij^s for one cow, and damages iiij^d &c.

Entry ij^s Alan Ingrain and Beatrice his wife surrendered half an acre of land, with a cottage, in the presence of the grave, and others of the homage, to the use of W^m atte Dammes, to have &c. to him and his heirs.

Exchange Entry iij^s Alan Pullayn surrendered 4 acres of pasture, w^h are called Hellesares, to the use of John Pullayn, to have &c. to him and his heirs by exchange: John Pullayn surrendered 4 acres of pasture of the fee of Percy, w^h are called Clerkeslant, to the use of Alan Pullayn and Agnes daughter of the said Alan, to have &c. to them & the heirs and assigns of the said Agnes.

Sum vij^s xj^d.

Court of the lord Duke of Lancaster held there on the Saturday next before the Feast of S. Michael, 39 Edw. III. [27 September A.D. 1365].

Summons It is ordered to summon Dom^s W^m parson of the church of S. Peter of Ingoldemels to answer to John son of Matilda, chaplain of Ingoldemels, in a plea of agreement.

Sum xviij^d.

Sum of all courts from Saturday next after the Purification vij^{li} xix^s j^d.

Ingoldemels. View of Frankpledge of the lord Duke of Lancaster held there on the Friday next after the Feast of S. Michael, 41 Edw. III. [2 October A.D. 1367].

Distraint [1] The jurors present that Agnes daughter of Robert son of John purchased of Gilbert Smith ij acres of land of the fee of the lord in Skegnes, therefore it is ordered to distrain.

Mercy j^s x^d They present that Robert ffoular, Agnes Taunt [Hiltoft], (and 8 others) are in mercy for the assize of beer.

[1] Sixteen persons pay fines for respite of suit of court until Michaelmas (Dom^s Wm de Gipthorp, Lady Alice de Gipthorp).

Also that Walter son of Thomas, and Wm de Kyme are forestallers of herrings and fish. Mercy iiij·

It is ordered to seize into the hand of the lord the whole of the land with the messuage, which Richard Kyng holds, for waste made upon the bondage of the lord on the part of his wife. Order to seize

John Catte, W^m son of Robert Magotson, Alan son of John de Wegelant, Gilbert Plomer, Wm Baxster, W^m son of Wm de Orreby, and W^m son of Roger Thory in mercy for chevage, because they have not come. Mercy xx^d

Also that Robert son of W^m son of Walter broke the fold by reason of an attachment. Mercy ij·

W^m le Vavasour, Michael de Pole for tenements of Robert ffolyot, John de Multon, the heir of Nicholas de Cantilupe, Robert de Saltfletby, Nicholas de Hale, John de Gresby, John de Dunham, the heir of Wm de Dunham, and John de Gunby are in mercy for default of suit of court, and it is ordered to distrain, and the prior of Bolington for the same. Default of foreign tenants Mercy xiiij· viij^d Distraint

It is ordered to seize &c. 4 perches of land, which Wm Whitewomb held on the day he died. Order to seize

Wm Peteclerk, Matilda de Kelesey, Richard of ye more, Wm Pourdfisch, John son of Wm Bug, and John de Burton in mercy for default of suit of court. Mercy xvij^d

Wm Godard was elected to the office of grave, and made oath to serve faithfully, pledge, the whole homage. Grave

Ralph son of Thomas, Robert ffouler, and Simon Smith were elected to the office of tasters of beer. Tasters of beer

Sum xxxix^s iiij^d.

Court of the lord Duke of Lancaster held there on the Saturday next before the Feast of the Apostles Simon and Jude, 41 Edw. III. [23 October A.D. 1367].

From Beatrice Godard for licence to marry W^m atte Dammes &c. Merchet

Beatrice Godard demised to farm to Wm Randsone 3 roods ... land for 6 years &c. Demise vj^d

Ingoldmels.   View of Frankpledge held there on the Friday the Feast of the Translation of S. Hugh, 48 Edw. III. [7 October A.D. 1374].

Ingold-
mels
Mercy
ij⁵ xjᵈ

The tasters of beer present that Beatrice Ingraney baked bread contrary to the assize, therefore she is in mercy, also that Alan de Wegeland (and 5 others) brewed, and sold beer contrary to the assize, therefore &c., also that Beatrice Polber (and another) are tipplers of beer contrary to the assize &c.

Mercy
ij⁵ vjᵈ

Skegnes presents that Robert ffoular, junʳ, (and 4 others) brewed, and sold beer contrary to the assize &c., and that Roger Kyger (and 3 others) are in mercy because they cut 'le sines' in ' le mels.'

Pledge

John Godard found pledges of the peace, viz. (2), towards Gilbert Plomer and towards the people of the lord the king under the penalty of cˢ.

Foreign
tenants
Mercy
vij⁵ jᵈ

Michael de Pole, the heir of Domˢ Nicholas de Cantilupe, Thomas de Stepyng, Thomas Waus, Robert de Gaskryk are in mercy, because they have not come.

Chevage
vjᵈ

From Robert and John Bygge, because they have not come, in mercy.

Mercy xijᵈ

They present that Wᵐ son of Thomas (and another) trod down the soil of the lord with their carts, therefore they are in mercy.

Increment

The jurors present that Wᵐ Brydson, a bond tenant of the lord, alienated 2½ acres of land to Agnes his daughter to have &c. to her and her heirs in bondage for ever according to the custom of the manor, rendering therefore yearly to the lord xxᵈ beyond the accustomed rent: also that Alice daughter of Emma, Isabel daughter of Alan de Slotheby, Amicia niece of John son

Order to
come

of Amicia, and (others) dug 'prolutus' excessively, therefore they are in mercy, and it is ordered that they come.

Election
of grave

Also they elect John Thori grave, and he is sworn, also John Kyng, Alan Godard, Thomas de Tointon, Walter son of

Mercy
iiij⁵ ijᵈ

Wᵐ, the heir of Richard atte Hauedyke, Simon Magoson, John son of Robert atte fflete, Alan Polayn of Borugh, bond tenants, have not come, therefore are in mercy: also John de Kelsey, Matilda de Kelsey, Wᵐ Peteclerk, Wᵐ de Watecroft, John de Burton, John Hayer, John atte Rode, John son of Sarah, John de Gunby, free tenants of the lord, have not come, therefore are in mercy.

Sum of this court xvij⁵ iiijᵈ.
Also of increase of rent yearly xxᵈ.

Court of the lord Duke of Lancaster held on the Saturday
next after the Feast of S. Luke the Evangelist, year as above
[21 October A.D. 1374].

A day is given between Richard Keng, plaintiff, and W^m   *Respite*
Bernak in a plea of trespass &c.

John de Braytoft (and two others) in mercy for default, and   *Mercy vj^d Distraint*
it is ordered to distrain them to answer to Richard Keng in a
plea of trespass : John de Braytoft in mercy for default, and it   *Mercy ij^d Distraint*
is ordered to distrain him to answer to (same) in a plea of debt.

A day is given to Ranulph Raper and his fellow jurors   *Inquisition Respite*
(between Agnes Thory, plaintiff, and Alan Ingrayne and
Beatrice his wife, defendants, for that the same Alan and his
wife owe to the said Agnes xix^d ob. for one quadrant of gold
received in the name of one penny &c.) under the penalty to
each of them of half a mark if they do not return their verdict
at the next court.

From Margaret Ragcot for licence to marry Robert de   *Merchet v^s*
Manthorp &c.

Sum of this court vij^s v^d.

Court of the lord Duke of Lancaster held there on the
Feast of S. Martin the Bishop, 48 Edw. III. [11 November
A.D. 1374].

John Buntyng complains of John Kemp for that the said   *Inquisition*
John came into his close, and carried off iij trees, to the value
of xl^s, to the damage of the said John xl^d, and the said John
defends force, and strength, and says that he did not do as he
complains, and upon this he asks that it be inquired.

Agnes Thory plaintiff v. Alan Ingraney and Beatrice his   *Mercy ij^d*
wife is in mercy for her unjust complaint.

Alan Thory came into court, and surrendered &c. ij acres of   *Entry iij^s iiij^d*
land &c. to the use of John Coke, to have &c. to him and his
heirs (for 20 years), and the s^d Alan shall defend the s^d land
in all services due and accustomed, except the taxation of the
lord the king, and the church of Ingoldemels &c.

John Thori, the grave, accounts that he has paid for the
repair of the bank of the sea xiij^s iiij^d by the view of the
steward, the bailiff, and other tenants of the lord.

Sum of this court vj^s j^d.

Court of the lord Duke of Lancaster held on the Friday next after the Feast of the Epiphany, 48 Edw. III. [12 January A.D. 1374-5].

[1] Sum of this court iijˢ xjᵈ.

Court of (same) held on the Saturday next after the Purification, 49 Edw. III. [3 February A.D. 1374-5].

Mercy vjᵈ   John de Braytoft (and two others) put themselves in mercy against Richard Kyng in a plea of trespass : (as also) does John
Mercy ljᵈ   against (the same) in a plea of debt.
Inquisition   It is ordered that there come an inquisition between Agnes Baxster, plaintiff, and Simon Lamb, defendant, in a plea of trespass, for that he beat, and badly wounded her on the Saturday next before the (torn), year xlviii.

Also between Simon Lamb, plaintiff, and Agnes Baxster, defendant, in a plea of trespass for that she beat his daughter within his close.

Ingoldmels presents that Agnes Baxster raised the hue on Simon Lamb justly, therefore the said Simon is in mercy : also &c. upon Alice daughter of Simon Lamb justly: also that the said Alice drew blood from Agnes Baxster : also that Matilda wife of Wᵐ Coper raised the hue on Joan Smith justly, also they have respite concerning blood shed.   Skegnes nothing.

Sum ijˢ xjᵈ.

Court held on the Friday next after the Feast of S. Peter in Cathedra, year as above [23 February A.D. 1374-5].

Inquisition,   It is ordered that there come an inquisition between Simon Lamb, plaintiff, and Robert son of Helwys, defendant, in a plea of trespass, for that he burnt his house on the Lord's day, the vigil of Xᵐᵃˢ Day last, and xix sheep gathered within.
Mercy ijᵈ   John Dobson in mercy for default, and it is ordered to distrain him to answer to Henry son of Geoffrey in a plea of trespass, for that he trod down his herbage with his beasts.

Ingoldmels presents that Agnes Baxster drew blood from Alice daughter of Simon Lamb : also that Robert German demised to farm ij acres of arable land to John Cook for x years, and the sᶜ John did not make fine to the lord for the said land, therefore he is in mercy, and upon this came John

[1] Ingoldmels presents 2 cases of hue and 1 of bloodshed.

Thori and Ralph Bugg, bond tenants of the lord, and asked to
be accepted (to hold) the said land for the said term of x years, Fine xvilj^d
and upon this Robert German demised to (them) ij acres &c.,
rendering the first year nothing, the 2nd year ½ mark, and each
following year x^s &c., and he gives the lord for fine.

 Robert German &c. demises to Ralph Bugg one acre of Fine vj^d
pasture land in Kokesthoft &c. for the term of ix years paying
yearly vij^s &c., and the s^d Robert shall defend the s^d land in all
things &c.

Sum iij^s.

 Court held on the Friday next after the Feast of S. Gregory
the Pope, year as within [16 March A.D. 1374-5].

 It is ordered that there come vj [jurors] between Simon
Lamb, plaintiff, and Robert son of Helwys in a plea of agreement.

 A day of love is given between Agnes Baxster, plaintiff, Non
and Simon Lamb in a plea of trespass: also between Simon sequitur
Lamb, plaintiff, and Agnes Baxster in a plea of trespass. Love

 It is found by the inquisition that John Dobson made Non sequitur Mercy ij^d
trespass on Henry son of Geoffrey to the damage of xviij^d,
therefore it is ordered that the s^d Henry recover the s^d money,
and the s^d John is in mercy.[1]

Sum of this court v^s.

 Court held on the Friday in the first week of the Passion of
our Lord, year as above [6 April A.D. 1375].

 Agnes Baxster does not prosecute v. Simon Lamb, sen^r, in Mercy
a plea of trespass, therefore is in mercy.

 Simon Lamb does not prosecute v. Agnes Baxster &c.

 Henry Boucher, plaintiff, offered himself v. Robert ffoular
in a plea of agreement, for that the s^d Robert compounded with
the s^d Henry concerning a certain annual rent of xl fish
during the life of the s^d Henry, and of this to give security to
the s^d Henry, and he did not do it, damage &c.

 Simon Lamb does not prosecute v. Robert son of Helwys, Mercy vj^d
therefore is in mercy.

 Alan Thori complains of Henry son of Geoffrey in a plea of Plaint
trespass, for that they were partners with ploughs to plough

---

[1] Ingoldmels presents 1 case of bloodshed: Skegnes that 5 persons cut les
synes in les mels to the damage and peril of the country, mercy ij^s vj^d.

their lands, and in the absence of the said Alan the s^d Henry
fled from his oxen in the plough (so) that they are on the point
of loss by which the said Alan could not plough the land to the
damage of xx^s.   And the said Henry says that he is not guilty,
as he complains, and he asks that it be inquired &c.

Demise of custom and portmotes The lord demised to Alan de Scalflete and John de Lynne
a certain custom in Skegenes, called Spredage, together with
the portmotes there, to have and to hold from Michaelmas next,
with all profits to the said custom, and portmotes belonging,
until the end of 3 years, paying therefore yearly to the lord
15^s &c.

Ingoldmels presents nothing : Skegnes nothing.

Sum of this court xvij^d.

Court of the lord Duke of Lancaster held on the Friday in
Easter week, 49 Edw. [27 April A.D. 1375].

[1] *Fines for suit of court*

From Wm de Whatecroft vj^d, Lady Alice de Gibthorp vj^d,
Wm de Gibthorp chivaler vj^d, Elizabeth Vavasour ij^s, John de
Cokerington chivaler vj^d, Thomas de Rygg xij^d, John de Gunby
viij^d, and (10 others).

Sum ix^s viij^d.

Ingoldmels. Court of the lord Duke of Lancaster held
there on the Friday next before the Feast of S. Dunstan, 49
Edw. [18 May A.D. 1375].

Pledge of the peace Alan Thori found pledges for the peace towards John
Polayn and the people of the lord the king, viz. (2), under the
penalty of c^s.

Mercy ij^d It is found by the inquisition that Henry son of Geoffrey
did not make any trespass upon Alan Thori, therefore the s^d
Alan is in mercy for a false complaint.

Mercy ij^d It is found by the inquisition that Henry son of Geoffrey
made trespass on Alan Thori to the damage of ij^d &c.

ij^d The presenters present that Beatrice Ingraney cut the sines
in 'les mels,' therefore she is in mercy. Skegnes (presents)
nothing.

Demise xij^d John Gunny demised to Robert Thori by the licence of

[1] On a separate roll.

the court 1 acre and ¼ rood of land called Stakhow &c. for 4 years &c.

John Granne and Matilda his wife come into court, and surrender &c. 2½ acres of land, called Stakhow, with all profits and appurtenances &c., which are of the right of the s⁴ Matilda, to the use of Robert Thori, to have &c. to him and his heirs in bondage for ever, doing &c. | *Entry v*

Alayn Polayn and Joan his wife come &c., and surrender 4 acres of land, wʰ are of the right of the s⁴ Joan, which formerly were Wᵐ de Acrwra's, to the use of John Polayn to have &c. | *Entry viij*

Alan Polayn comes into court, and surrenders 2½ acres of pasture, which he purchased of Wᵐ Cardinax &c., to the use of Joan wife of the said Alan, to have &c. | *Entry vjˢ viijᵈ*

John Alaynson comes &c., and surrenders 1 messuage and 2 acres of pasture &c. to the use of Wᵐ (his) son, after the decease of the said John and Alice his wife, to have &c. | *Entry vˢ*

William Herward &c. surrenders 3 acres of land in Ingoldmels abutting upon the sea shore towards the east, together with the profit adjacent of the waste of the sea, and other their appurtenances, to the use of Wᵐ atte Houtdayle, to have &c., so that the s⁴ Wᵐ Herward shall have &c. the s⁴ 3 acres with the appurtenances for his whole life, and after his decease (it) shall remain to the s⁴ Wᵐ Houtdayle, to have &c. | *Fine vjˢ viijᵈ*

Wᵐ Herward by the licence of court granted to Wᵐ atte Outdayle the reversion of 1 messuage and 2 acres of arable land in Ingoldmels abutting upon the sea shore, to have &c. after the death of Agnes Goddard &c. | *Fine iijˢ iiijᵈ*

Alan Skalflet and John son of Wᵐ Gunny came &c., and surrendered 3 acres in Stakhow, which (they) had of the feoffment of the lord for the whole life of Wᵐ Gunny by the forfeiture of the same Wᵐ, to the use of John de Acrwra, and Robert Thory, to have &c. during the life of the said Wᵐ Gunny &c. | *Fine ijˢ*

Sum of this court xxxixˢ viijᵈ.

Court held there on the Friday next after the Ascension, 49 Edw. [1 June A.D. 1375].

John Thori, plaintiff, v. Robert Kyggs made faith that he owes him iijˢ viijᵈ, therefore it is considered by the steward that | *Mercy ijᵈ* the s^d John shall recover the s^d debt, and the said Robert is in mercy, and it is ordered to levy.

Scrutiny xij^d John Waug and Joan his wife give to the lord xij^d for scrutiny of the rolls for Alan Brideson, sen^r, and Agnes his wife, in the time of the king the father, or in the 1st or 2nd time (*sic*) of the king that now is &c.

Fine x^s Wm de Hengs of Burgh, who held of the lord in bondage xiij acres of land in Burgh, is dead, and upon this came Simon his son and heir, and took of the lord the s^d land, to hold in bondage, and he gives of fine.

The presenters present that Wm Peticlerk and Agnes Baxster cut the sines upon les meles, therefore are in mercy.

Sum of this court xij^s iiij^d.

Court held on the Saturday next after the Feast of the Apostles Peter and Paul, year as above [30 June A.D. 1375].

Fealty John Kellok comes into court, and claims to hold of the lord two places of pasture in Wynethorp and Ingoldmels, to hold for the term of the life of Margaret, who was the wife of Walter de Westmels, and for the term of ten years of the said Margaret, which pastures the said John has of the demise of Wm de Kyme of Skegnesse, and John de Calflet of Burgh, and the said John Kelloc shall do to the chief lords the services therefore due and accustomed according to the form of the indenture made between them, and he did fealty.

Sum viij^d.

Ingoldmels. Court of the lord Duke of Lancaster held there on the Friday the Feast of S. Margaret the Virgin, year 49 [July 20 A.D. 1375].

Inquisition It is ordered that an inquisition come between John Ryngot, plaintiff, and John Koce, defendant, in a plea of trespass, for that he devastated his herbage with his beasts &c.

Pledges Robert Wyte found pledges of the peace towards Margaret de Stokhow, viz. &c., under a penalty of c^s.

Fine vj^d Alan Polayn comes &c., and surrenders &c. the moiety of xx perches of land &c. to the use of Gilbert Meriot &c.

Fine xij^d Alan Polayn &c. surrenders 3 roods &c. to the use of Robert Thori &c.

Sum iij^s.

Court held on the Saturday next after the Feast of S. Lawrence, year as above [11 August A.D. 1375].

Ranulph Bugg (and another) in mercy for a tumult in court. Mercy iiij^d

Wm de Waytecroft, John de Burtoft in mercy, because Mercy vj^d they have not come upon the inquisition.

It is ordered that an inquisition come between John att Inquisi-Hauedyk, plaintiff, and John de Wyum, defendant, in a plea of tion agreement, for that he sold him one healthy pig, and it was not healthy, but sick, to his damage xl^d, and the s^d John Wyum says that he did not break his agreement with him, and upon this he asks that it be inquired.

It is ordered that an inquisition come between Robert att Inquisi-fflete, plaintiff, and John Kaglok, defendant, in a plea of tion trespass, for that he mowed his reeds.

Alan Thori &c. demised to Walter Meriot 4 acres of Fine xviij^d pasture land, lying between land of Wm de Skipwyth on the west, to have &c. for 3 years &c. And the said Alan shall defend the s^d land in all things.

Sum iiij^s iij^d.

Court held on the Friday next after the Feast of the Decollation of S. John [31 August A.D. 1375].

Wm de Whaytecroft and John de Burton in mercy, because Mercy vj^d they have not come on the inquisition.

From Alan de Schalflet because he speared [eels] Mercy xij^d [fuscellavit] in the common sewer against the defence of the lord &c.

Sum iij^s vij^d.

Ingoldmels. Court of the lord Duke of Lancaster held at Skegnes on the Friday the Feast of S. Matthew the Apostle, 49 Edw. III. [21 September A.D. 1375].

Also the jurors present that Robert de Hilletoft, John de Mercies Hilletoft (and 28 others) speared (eels) in the common sewers viij^s vij^d against the custom in the time of drought, to the grave damage of the whole community, therefore they are in mercy.

Sum of this court xij^s ix^d.

Sum total of xviij courts held this year vij^{li} xij^s xj^d, whereof for fines for suit of court released ix^s viij^d, for entries lix^s iiij^d, and of wreck of sea nothing this year. Also of increment of rent xx^d.

Ingoldmels. Court of the lord Duke of Lancaster held on the Friday next after the Epiphany, 49 Edw. III. [11 January A.D. 1375–6].

William de Modland, who held of the lord ij acres of arable land in bondage in Ingoldmels, a bastard, died seised without heir of his body, therefore the s^d land is seized into the hand of the lord as escheat, and because the moiety of the s^d land was seized before the death of the said W^m, Matilda his wife came into court, and took the other moiety, to hold until the Feast of Michaelmas next, and she shall give to the lord ij^s viij^d beyond services and customs, and beyond the dower belonging to her.

It is ordered to seize into the hand of the lord iiij acres of pasture called Howhettings in Skegnes, which Henry Boucher demised to the parson of the church of Skegnes without the licence of the lord.

Sum vj. v^d.

Court of ₁the lord Duke of Lancaster held on the Friday next after the Feast of the Conversion of S. Paul in the beginning of the 50th year of Edw. III. [1 February A.D. 1375–6].

Fine v^s   Alan Cobbe surrendered ij acres of pasture &c. to the use of Simon Cobbe &c.

Ingoldmels. Court of the lord Duke of Lancaster held there on the Friday next after the Feast of S. Augustine Bishop of the English, 50 Edw. III. [30 May A.D. 1376].

Fine xx^s   W^m son of Alan Thori, kinsman and heir of Robert Thori, came into court, and made fine for v acres of land and pasture &c., which Beatrice, who was the wife of Hugh Loutlou, held for the term of her life, who is now deceased, and the reversion of which after (her) death belonged to the s^d W^m &c.

Plaint   Margery Mire complains of Robert son of John Thori in a plea of land, pledges &c., and she protests that she is willing to prosecute in the nature of mort ancestor.

The presenters present nothing.

Sum xx^s vj^d.

Court of the lord Duke of Lancaster held on the Friday
next after the Feast of S. John Baptist, year as above [27 June
A.D. 1376].

John de Dufdyk found pledges of the peace towards
Gibert Plomer, viz. (2), under the penalty of cˢ.

John Thori, a bond tenant of the lord, who held of the
lord viij— — died seised, and upon this came Robert,
son and heir of the said John, and took the said land of the
lord, to hold in bondage, and he gives the lord for fine, and it
is granted that if the sᵈ Robert, who is under age, shall die
within a year from the present day that then Beatrice, (his)
mother, shall have the said tenements until she shall have
levied costs, and her reasonable expenses.

Ralph son of Thomas, and his fellows present, that
concerning those 3 acres of land, which Simon Smyth, now
deceased, held for the term of his life, that the reversion of
2 acres with the edifices belongs to Agnes daughter of Wᵐ son
of Thomas Brydson, kinswoman and heir of Agnes, who was
the wife of the said Simon, who died without heir of her body,
which same Agnes, wife of Simon, was daughter of Alan
Brydson, brother of the said Thomas Brydson: and they say
that the reversion of the 3ʳᵈ acre belongs to Alice Stotevile,
and to Wᵐ and Isabel, children of the sᵈ Alice, as of their
purchase, as appears in the rolls of the court of that year,
and upon this came Agnes daughter of Wᵐ and did fealty to
the lord, and also (made) fine &c.

Sum xlvˢ iijᵈ.

Court of the lord Duke of Lancaster held on the Friday
next after the Feast of S. Swithin, year as above [18 July
A.D. 1376].

It is found by the inquisition that no tenant in bondage
is bound to answer in any plaint until he comes to the age of
xv years, and such was the custom within this lordship for
xv years, and more, therefore respite without a day.

John son of Simon (and others) complain of Beatrice

*Pledge of
the peace*

xxxˢ

*Fine
vjˢ viijᵈ*

Plaint

Ingoldmels. View of Frankpledge of the lord Duke of Lancaster held at Skegnes on the Monday the Feast of S. Edward the Confessor, 50 Edw. III. [13 October A.D. 1376].

Respite   All parties, plaintiffs and defendants, have a day at the next court in the same state that they now are.

Foreign tenants
Mercy
xij⁺ vij⁴   Elizabeth Vavasour, Michael de Pole, the heirs of Nicholas de Cantilupe, Ralph Daubeney, the heirs of Robert de Saltfletby, Thomas de Stepyng, Thomas Vaus of Cletham, Robert Gascryk, Wᵐ de Hale ought to come and have not come, therefore are in mercy : Wᵐ ffrank chivaler also.

Chevagii   Simon Catte, John Bygge, John son of Alan Smyth, chevagii, have not come, therefore &c.

New rent
iij⁺   Wᵐ atte Outdaile, a bond tenant of the lord, purchased 4½ acres of land to have after the death of Simon Smyth now deceased, and therefore the sᵈ land is arrented anew, and each acre will render viijᵈ yearly.

New rent
iij⁺ iiij⁴   Wᵐ Thori purchased v acres of bond land to have after the death of Beatrice wife of Hugh, which same Beatrice is now dead, and the sᵈ land is in the hand of Wᵐ son of Alan Thori, kinsman and heir of the sᵈ Robert (*sic*), therefore the sᵈ land is arrented anew &c.

Ingoldmels and Skegnes present that Simon ffydkyn baked bread contrary to the assize : also that (he and 5 others) brewed
Mercy
iiij⁺ xjᵈ   and sold beer contrary to the assize &c. : also that John de Lynne is a tippler of beer contrary to the assize : also that Walter Tewet (and another) baked bread contrary to the assize: also that (he and 7 others) tippled beer contrary to the
Distraint   assize &c. : also they say that Robert att Hallegarth has entered the fee of the lord, and has not done fealty, therefore it is ordered to distrain him, also John son of Richard Hadyk likewise &c.

Election of grave   Also they elect Robert Kyggs, or Walter son of Wᵐ, to the office of grave, and the sᵈ Wᵐ (*sic*) is sworn.

The great inquisition presents that John de Kyme entered
Fealty   the fee of the lord for ij places, and did fealty, and it is ordered
Distraint   to distrain him for homage : also John de Stykeford likewise &c. : also they say that Wᵐ Tolymund, Wᵐ vicar of Croft, Simon the chaplain of the chapel of S. Elene entered the fee of the lord through John de Cokeryngton, chivaler, and it is ordered to distrain them for fealty, and to do services.

Entry vjˡˡ   Wᵐ atte Outdaile, a bond tenant of the lord, came into

court and took of the lord two acres of bond arable land in
Ingoldmels, which came into the hand of the lord, as escheat,
after the death of Wm de Modland, a bastard, who died seised
without heir of his body, to have and to hold to the same
W^m att Outdaile and his heirs in bondage, doing the services
and customs therefrom due, saving to Matilda who was the wife
of Wm de Modeland, her dower according to the custom of the
manor, and the s^d W^m att Outdaile gives to the lord of fine vj^{li},
whereof he shall pay one moiety at the feast of S. Martin next,
and the other moiety at the feast of S. Botulph next, pledges for
the fine &c., and he did fealty.

Be it remembered that on Wednesday last at Skegnes
before Dom^s Thomas de Hungerford, knt., chief steward of the
lord Duke of Lancaster, Simon Symeon, steward of the honor
of Bolyngbrok, Dom^s Thomas de Mapelton, auditor, John de
Stafford, receiver, Wm de Spaigne, feudary of the s^d lord, and
John de Hagh, locum tenens of the s^d Simon, and others of the
council of the lord, it was found by an inquisition of free men
and of bond, that Henry Boucher, who held of the lord one place
with appurtenances in les South Mels in Skegnes in bondage by
the court rolls, that the s^d Henry alienated the s^d place with
appurtenances by charter to Richard Kyng to hold to him and
his heirs for ever in fee simple, whereby the s^d Dom^s Thomas by
the advice of the s^d council seized the said place with appurtenances into the hand of the lord as forfeited. And afterwards
the s^d Henry came before Dom^s Thomas and others of the
council of the lord at Bolyngbrok, and made fine to the lord,
as appears in the rolls of the s^d Dom^s Thomas. And it is
granted by the s^d Dom^s Thomas, and the council, and also by
this court, that the same Henry shall have back the said place
by the metes and bounds by ij inquisitions, viz. one of free
men, and the other of bond tenants, made at this court, with
free ingress and egress, viz. by that way which leads from the
rectory of Skegnes, to have and to hold to the s^d Henry and his
heirs in bondage according to the custom of the manor, paying
therefore yearly to the lord and his heirs iij^s iiij^d at the Feasts of
S. Botulph and S. Michael by equal portions for all services.

Agnes daughter of Ranulph Raper of Ingoldmels, a bond
woman of the lord, has licence to marry John Ward &c. — Merchet vj^s viij^d

Henry Bocher comes into court, and renders into the hand
of the lord 22 acres of land and pasture, with a certain cottage, — Fine xiij^s iiij^d

with appurtenances, in Skegnes, which the same Henry had of
the demise of Richard Keng, to the use of the same Richard, to
have &c. for the whole life of the same Richard of the lord in
bondage according to the custom of the manor, under, however,
such condition, that if the s⁴ Richard does not pay to the s⁴
Henry 9 marks on May 1, or within the next 15 days, that
then it shall be fully allowed to the s⁴ Henry to re-enter upon
a certain place of pasture of the said tenements, called
Howettyngs, and hold it of the lord in bondage notwithstanding
this demise &c.

Fine
vj⁴ viij⁴ Henry Boucher comes &c. and renders &c. one place ——,
with edifices and appurtenances, which he held of the lord in
bondage to the use of Dionisius parson of (the church of)
Skegnes, and the lord delivered and granted the s⁴ tenement to
hold to him and his heirs of the lord in bondage according to
the custom of the manor by the services therefore due &c.

Sum viij^{li} v^s.
Also of new rent as above vj^s viij^d.

Court of the lord Duke of Lancaster held on the Friday the
Vigil of All Saints, year as below [31 October A.D. 1376].

Respite A day is given between John de Hiltoft, plaintiff, and John
Kelloc, defendant, in a plea of agreement.

The presenters present that there is nothing this day.

Sum of this court xviij^d.

Court of (same) held on the Friday next after the Feast of
S. Edmund the King, year as above [21 November A.D. 1376].
The presenters present that there is nothing yet.

Sum of this court x^d.

Court &c. held . . . S. Andrew the Apostle [30 November
A.D. 1376].

Day A day is given between John de Hiltoft, plaintiff, and
John Kellock, defendant, in a plea of agreement.

Sum ij^s j^d.

Ingoldmels. Court of the lord Duke of Lancaster held on the Friday after the Epiphany, 50 Edw. III. [9 January A.D. 1376-7].

John Kellok in mercy for default, and it is ordered to distrain him to answer to John de Hiltoft in a plea of agreement.[1]

Mercy

Sum xxij^d.

Ingoldmeles. Court of the lord Duke of Lancaster held on the Friday next after the Feast of S. Juliana the Virgin, 51 Edw. III [20 February A.D. 1376-7].

Henry Jeffraysone and Mary his wife surrendered &c. ½ acre pasture to the use of Robert Jerman (who took it).

Fine xviij^d

Robert Jerman, a bond tenant of the lord, rendered into the hand of the lord iij acres of land and pasture &c. to the use of Wm Seriaund of Otoft for the term of viij years, and after the end of the said years the s^d tenements shall remain to John and Matilda, children of the s^d Robert Jerman, to hold for their whole lives of the lord in bondage, and after the death of John and Matilda the s^d tenements shall remain to the right heirs of the s^d Robert &c.

Entry
Fine x^s

Robert Jerman by the licence of the court granted that ij acres in Ingoldmeles with a house situated thereupon, which Peter Jerman held for life in bondage of the inheritance of the s^d Robert, after the death of the said Peter shall remain to John and Matilda, children of the s^d Robert, &c.

Fine v^s

Robert Jerman surrendered &c. vj acres and j rood of land and pasture in Ingoldmeles and Wynthorp to the use of Agnes, Alice, and Joan, daughters of the s^d Robert, to hold &c. for their whole lives, and after their death the s^d tenements shall remain to the right heirs of the s^d Robert to hold &c.

Fine xviij^s

Robert Jerman rendered &c. j acre and j rood of pasture in Ingoldmels to the use of Robert son of the s^d Robert, a bastard, to hold in bondage for his whole life, (remainder to Robert's right heirs).

Fine iiij^s

Robert Jerman died seised of xl acres of land and pasture, lying in divers places in Ingoldmels, with a messuage situated thereupon, and thereupon came W^m son and heir of the s^d Robert, and took the s^d tenements, to hold of the lord in bondage for ever, saving to Helen widow of the s^d Robert her dower therefrom, &c.

Fine vj^{li}
xiij^s iiij^d

---

[1] A case respited for default of jurors.

N

Fine viij^d Robert Jerman rendered &c. xxix perches of land with a cottage situated thereupon in Ingoldmels to the use of Henry Jeffraysone and Mary his wife (who took to hold to Henry and the heirs of Mary &c.).

Sum viij^{ll} xvij^s xj^d.

Court of the lord Duke of Lancaster held on the Friday next after the Feast of S. Gregory, 51 Edw. III. [13 March A.D. 1376–7].

Fine vj^s viij^d Gilbert Plomer and Elena his wife surrendered &c. 1 messuage, 4½ acres and 1 rood of land and pasture in Ingoldmels, in a place called Balyland, to the use of John Godard &c., and the s^d land shall give an increased rent after the death of John de Laxton.

Ingoldmeles. Court of the lord Duke of Lancaster held there on Friday next after the Feast of S. Botulph, year as above [19 June A.D. 1377].

Mercy xij^d From Robert Kygges, a bond tenant of the lord, because he impleaded Simon ffydkyn, a tenant of the lord in bondage (native), outside the lord's court.

Fine xiij^s iiij^d Alan Polayn renders into the hand of the lord iiij acres of land and meadow, except 10 perches, lying together in Ingoldmeles &c., and the lord granted, and delivered the said tenements to the said Alan, to hold in bondage for (his) whole life, and after (his) decease the said tenements shall remain to the said Robert Hewsone, to hold of the lord in bondage according to the custom of the manor, by the services and customs therefore due for ever. And the said Robert gives to the lord for a fine xiij^s iiij^d.

Fine vj^s viij^d Alan Polayn renders into the hand of the lord ij acres of pasture in Ingoldmeles, butting on land formerly Robert German's &c., and the lord granted, and delivered the s^d pasture to the said Alan, to hold in bondage for (his) whole life, and after the decease of the said Alan the said pasture shall remain to Robert Kygges, to hold in bondage for his whole life, and after (his) decease shall remain to Alan son of the same Robert, to hold &c.

Rent xl^s Dionisius, parson of the church of Skegneys, came before Thomas de Hungerford, chief steward of the lord, and others of the council of the lord, and took of the lord the pasture and

herbage of the meles in Skegneys, to have from next
Michaelmas until the end of xij years with free ingress and
regress, rendering to the lord yearly and to his heirs xl˙ at the
usual terms, saving to the lord &c. the warren, the thorns
growing there, and other profits in the same place.

The same Dionisius came before the same steward, and [Fine x˙]
council, and took of the lord the reasonable chase and hunting
of rabbits in the said place of the meles, to have for (same time),
(rendering) therefore yearly to the lord and his heirs x˙.

Sum xxiij˙ vj^d.
Also of ferm as above l˙.

Court of the lord Duke of Lancaster held on Friday next
after the Feast of the Translation of S. Thomas in the first year
of Richard II. [10 July A.D. 1377].

John Smyth jun^r in mercy for default. And it is ordered [Distraint
to distrain him to answer to John Kempe and Amye his wife in Mercy ij^d]
a plea of debt, for that they hired him to serve on a ship upon
the sea, and afterwards they are agreed &c.

Sum xij˙ ij^d.

Ingoldmeles. Court of the lord Duke of Lancaster held
there on Friday next after the Feast of S. James, 1 Richard
[31 July A.D. 1377].

It is ordered that an inquisition come between Robert [Inquisi-
Rayner, plaintiff, and Amya formerly the servant of John   tion]
Rayner, in a plea of debt: he demands ij˙ for a certain house
let to her, which she ought to have paid on the Feast of S.
Botulph, 49 Edw. III. The defendant denies it, and let it be
inquired into.

Sum ij˙ j^d.

Ingoldmeles. Court of the Duke of Lancaster held there on
Friday next after the Feast of the Assumption &c., year as above
[21 August A.D. 1377].

Amia formerly the servant of John Rayner puts herself in [Mercy ij^d]
mercy against Robert Rayner in a plea of debt.

Henry Bocher comes into court, and surrenders into the hand [Fine xij^d]
of the lord viij acres of pasture land, with le Mersche, called Belt-
land, and with its other appurtenances in 'Skegnes, to the use of
John son of Simon de Akewra, to have and to hold to him and his

N 2

heirs and his assigns from the Purification next to the term of 40
years, rendering therefore yearly to the said Henry and his heirs
ij marks of silver &c., and the said Henry shall defend at his own
proper costs the said land against the sea, and against the lord
of the fee, and he gives to the lord for having the term.

**Recog-
nizance**

Ranulph Bugg came into court, and acknowledged that he
owed John son of Simon de Akewra xx marks sterling to be
paid to (him) and his executors within the space and term of v
years, each year iiij marks, viz. from the Feast of S. Michael last
to the term of the said v years fully completed, at the terms of
S. Botulph and S. Michael, and if the said payments shall be in
arrear at any term during the existing term it shall be fully
allowable to the said John to distrain on all the lands of the said
Ranulph, and retain the distraint until the said payment with
arrears be fully satisfied.

Great Court of the lord Duke of Lancaster held at Ingoldmeles on Wednesday after the Feast of S. Dionisius, 10 Rich.
II. [10 October A.D. 1386].

Respite.

All parties, plaintiffs and defendants, have a day at the next
court in the same state in which they now are.

**Mercy
iiij⁸ iiij ͩ**

The free jurors present that Gilbert Watkynson of Skegnes
(and another) are common forestallers of fish to the great damage
of the lord and his tenants: also that William Milner and
Róbert German went out of the vill of Ingoldmeles to the vill of
Swaby for excessive salary to the great damage of the lord and
the whole community.

**Entry on
land
xxvjˢ viijͩ**

The bond tenants present that Robert Polber in the presence
of the grave and others of the homage, viz. Robert Hewson,
Simon German, John Taunt, William Mason, Robert son of
William, Ranulph Bug, Alan son of John Hawitson, Alan son
of John Dobeson, Simon Lamb junʳ, Gilbert Lamb, Walter and
John Mereot, and John Cardywax, surrendered into the hand of
the lord xij acres of land and pasturage in Ingoldmeles to the use
of John Polray and William Dodik, to hold to them and their
executors (for 12 years), and after the said term the said tenements shall remain to Joan late the wife of the said Robert
Polber, and to William and Alice, children of the same Robert
born before marriage and to the heirs of the said William and
Alice, (to hold) of the lord in bondage for ever.

Mercy iiij ͩ

Also they present that John Taunt, and Alice the wife of

William Milner went out of the vill of Ingoldmeles for excessive gain; also that John Gryn senior of Thorp who held of the lord one acre of pasture in Thorp next Waynflet . . . , therefore it is ordered to seize the said land &c.

Also they elect John Smyth to the office of grave, and he is sworn. *Election of grave*

John Ryngot surrendered &c. one acre of land in Ingold-mels to the use of Beatrice his daughter, and the said land gives to the lord of increment of rent viij^d. *Increment of rent viij^d*

From John Cokeryngton vj^d, John German iij^d, William de Kyme iiij^d, John de Gunby iiij^d, Peter de Gipthorp vj^d, Alan Tothoth iij^d, Thomas de Ryg xij^d, (and 31 others). *Fines for suit xj^s iij^d*

Elizabeth Vavasour, Michael de Pole, Ralph Daubenay, Robert Gascrik, Thomas de Stepyng, the heirs of Nicholas de Cauntelew. *Foreign [tenants] vj^s*

Sum lj^s ix^d.

Court of the lord Duke of Lancaster held on Wednesday the Vigil of All Saints, year as within [31 October A.D. 1386].

It is ordered to summon William de Kyme to answer to Thomas de Alford in a plea of debt. *Summons*

William de Kyme put himself in mercy against John de Gunby in a plea of debt. *Mercy ij^d*

Thomas de Toynton, and Eudo Kaa and Agnes (his) wife, she being diligently examined, came into court, and released all their right &c. in 3 roods of pasture in Ingoldmels to the use of Simon Lamb, jun^r, &c. *Entry on land xij^d*

Alan Cobbe in the presence of the grave, and others of the homage, surrendered 7 perches of pasture in Ingoldmels to the use of John his son, to hold of the lord in bondage for the whole life of the same John, and after (his) decease the said land shall remain to Joan (his) sister, and the heirs of her body lawfully begotten, and if she shall die without (such) heirs then to the right heirs of Alan &c. *Entry vj^d*

Alan Cobbe surrendered one cottage in Ingoldmels, which contains in length j perch and a half and xiiij feet in breadth by the ell [per ulnam], to the use of John, his son, to have after the death of William Swete, to hold (as before). *Entry iiij^d*

John Gryn surrendered 1½ roods and iij perches of land in Ingoldmels to the use of William Couper to have &c. in bondage for ever. *Entry viij^d*

Entry iiij⁕   John Polayn surrendered one acre of land in Ingoldmels to the use of Robert de Orby &c.

Entry viij⁕   John Ryngot, who held of the lord two acres of pasture with the houses situated thereupon in Burgh &c., is dead, and thereupon came Richard Stevenson and Matilda his wife, Robert Heuson and Beatrice his wife, daughters and heirs of the said John, and asked to be admitted to the said land, and are admitted.

Sum xvj⁕.

Ingoldmeles. Court of the lord Duke of Lancaster held there on the Friday the Conversion of S. Paul, 10 Rich. II. [25 January A.D. 1386–7].

Demise viij⁴   William Cobbe came into court, and demised to Robert Priour, chaplain, 3 acres of land and pasture in Ingoldmels in a place called Southettyngs (for 7 years). And the same Robert shall perform all charges meanwhile.

Demise ij⁕   Henry Geffryson and Mary his wife &c. demised to William Horn 3 acres of pasture in Ingoldmels (for 10 years).

Sum iij⁕ vj⁴.

Court of (same) held at Burgh on Wednesday the Morrow of S. Valentine, year as above [February 15 A.D. 1386–7].

Entry xl⁴   John de Lyn and Agnes his wife &c. surrendered one place of land, called les meles of Skegnes, with the houses situated thereon, in which the said John lately dwelt, to the use of Simon ffidkyn, to hold to him and his heirs in bondage for ever &c.

Entry xviij⁴   William son of Simon German, who held of the lord iij roods and xx perches of land in Ingoldmels, is dead, and thereupon comes Simon German, brother of the said William, and asks to be admitted to the said land, as next heir of blood, and he is admitted &c.

Sum iiij⁕ x⁴.

Ingoldmeles. Court of the (same) held there on the Wednesday next before the Feast of S. Gregory the Pope, 10 Rich. II. [6 March A.D. 1386–7].

Sum xxij⁴.

Court of the lord Duke of Lancaster held there[1] next after Feast of the Annunciation (25 March), 10 Rich. II. [A.D. 1387].

Sum xij^d.

View of Frankpledge of (same) held on Wednesday next after the Feast of SS. Tiburtius and Valerian, year as above [17 April A.D. 1387].

The bond tenants present that John Modeland and (3 others) baked bread, and sold it contrary to the assize.   *Mercy ij^s vj^d*

Also that Ranulph son of Ranulph Raper, John son of John Aldyat, and John son of William Kempe are of the age to be in chevage, therefore &c.   *Chevage ix^d*

Sum iiij^s.
Also of chevage ix^d a year.

Court of (same) held on Friday next after the Feast of the Apostles Philip and James, year as above [3 May A.D. 1387].

William Mason came into court, and demised to William Horn one place of land, containing 5 roods (for xx years) &c.   *Entry xl^d*

Simon and Hugh Cobbe found pledges for the peace, and good conduct, towards Alan atte Hadik, and the people of the lord the king, viz. &c., under the pain of c^s.   *Pain*

Richard Lytster, who held of the lord in bondage x acres of pasture in Ingoldmels, called Togland, by the law of England after the death of Beatrice his wife, is dead, and upon this comes John Kyngeson, son and heir of the said Beatrice, and asks to be accepted for the said land, and is admitted &c.   *Entry xxx^s*

Richard Stevenson and Mary his wife, she being diligently examined, surrender &c. one acre of land in Burgh &c., to the use of Alan Polayn of Burgh &c.   *Entry ij^s vj^d*

Sum xxxvj^s ij^d.

Court of (same) held on Wednesday in Whitsun week, 10 Rich. II. [29 May A.D. 1387].

The presenters present that Gilbert Lamb drew blood from Robert Kigges, therefore &c., and that Robert Kigges raised the hue on the said Gilbert &c.   *Mercy v^d*

Alan Polayn of Burgh surrendered one acre of land in Burgh &c. to the use of John (torn) and the heirs of his body, (remainder) to Agnes daughter of the said Alan.   *Entry ij^s vj^d*

Sum iiij^s j^d.

[1] Day omitted.

Court of (same) held on Wednesday next after the Feast of S. Botulph, year as below [19 June A.D. 1387].

Mercy ij^d   Robert Thory in mercy, because he has not come to answer to Alan Thory in a plea of debt.

Sum xvj^d.

Court of (same) held on the Saturday next after the Feast of the Translation of S. Thomas, year as below [July 13 A.D. 1387].

Mercy ij^d   Robert Thory put himself in mercy against Alan Thory in 3 plaints of debt.

Fine xl^d   Robert Gryn rendered into the hand of the lord one place of pasture in Little Stepyng (4 acres), to the use of Robert de Maltby and Margery his wife, and the heirs of the same Margery, in bondage, in exchange for iiij acres j rood of pasture in Ingoldmels, called Knyghtland, under such condition, that, if the said Robert Gryn his heirs or assigns shall in any way be expelled from the said place of pasture, called Knyghtland, by the said Margery or her heirs, then the said Robert Gryn and his heirs shall have again the said place called 'coupastour.'

Demise   Henry Geffryson and Mary his wife demised to William
xl^d   Horn iij acres of pasture in Ingoldmels for ix years &c.

Sum vij^s x^d.

Court of (same) held on Wednesday the Morrow of S. Peter ad Vincula, 11 Rich. II. [31 July A.D. 1387].

New rent   William Thory, a bond tenant of the lord, and Emma his
viij^d   wife acquired of Simon Rede of Waynflet 4 acres of free land in Waynflet, and the said land is arrented by the lord at viij^d, viz. each acre at ij^d.

Entry viij^s   John Smyth and Matilda his wife demised to Robert son of the said John xj acres of land and pasture with a messuage in Ingoldmeles, to have after the death of the said John for xx years, under the condition, that the same Robert shall pay in the first x years, each year ij marks in works of charity for the soul of the said Matilda, by the view and ordinance of the parson of the church of Ingoldmeles, who for the time shall be. and if the said Robert shall die during the life of the said John Smyth that then William Godard and William atte Outdayl, jun^r, shall have the said land for the whole of the said

term, so that they pay, and make the true value of the said
land each year in works of charity for the said soul by the view
and ordinance abovesaid.

John Smyth and Matilda his wife surrendered j acre of
pasture with messuage &c., and the lord rendered the said land
to the said John and Matilda for the term of their lives,
(remainder) to Alice and Matilda for life, and to right heirs of
the said Matilda.

Entry xij^d

Sum ix^s vj^d.

Also of new rent viij^d yearly.

Court of (same) held on Wednesday next before the Feast
of the Beheading of S. John Baptist, year as above [28 August
A.D. 1387].

It is ordered to attach Robert de Gipthorp, and Matilda his
wife, to answer to Robert Kigges in a plea of debt.

*Attach-
ment*

Joan Brok, [libera tenens native] a free woman, holding
bond land, has licence to marry William Osmound, and gives to
the lord for licence xl^d.

*Merchet
xl^d*

Sum iij^s vj^d.

Court of (same) held on Wednesday next after the Feast of
the Exaltation of the Holy Cross, 11 Rich. II. [18 September
A.D. 1387].

Agnes Cardywax gives to the lord vj^d, Thomas Marays iiij^d
for searching the rolls.

*Searching
the rolls
x^d*

Sum xvj^d

Great Court of the lord Duke of Lancaster held at Ingoldmels on Tuesday next after the Feast of S. Dionisius, 12 Rich.
II. [13 October A.D. 1388].

The inquisition of bond tenants presents that (3 persons)
baked and sold bread, and (3 persons) brewed and sold beer
contrary to the assizes &c.

From Hugh de Lancaster (6^d), Thomas de Ryg (12^d),
John German (and 25 others 3^d).

*Fines for
suit of
court*

The inquisition of free [tenants] presents that Alan Souter,
Matilda Souter, William Ingraine, and Thomas de Tointon,
went out of the lordship of this manor last autumn to take
excessive salaries, therefore each is in mercy.

*Mercy
vij^s x^d*

Sum xviij^s x^d.

Court of (same) held on Wednesday next after the Feast of All Saints, year as above [4 November A.D. 1388].

Sum xx^d.

Court of (same) held on Wednesday the Feast of S. Katherine the Virgin, year as above [25 November A.D. 1388].

The presenters present that Geoffrey de Holbetch drew blood from Robert Webster &c.

Sum xvj^d.

Court of (same) held on Friday next after the Feast of S. Clementia, year as above [11 December A.D. 1388].

Sum viij^d.

Court of (same) held at Burgh on Friday next after the Feast of the Epiphany, year as above [8 January A.D. 1388–9].

Mercy iij^s iiij^d   The presenters present that Alice de Scalflet, Alan atte Lathe, John Clarys went out of the vill of Ingoldmels last autumn for excessive gain, therefore each is in mercy.

Sum iij^s x^d.

Court of (same) held at Burgh on Friday next after the Feast of the Conversion of S. Paul, year as above [29 January A.D. 1388–9].

New rent iij^d   Alan de Scalflet, a bond tenant of the lord, purchased ij acres of meadow with appurtenances in Mumby of Eudo de Lystoft, lying between land of Thomas de Westmels on the south, and of John Rust on the north, and the said ij acres are arrented to the lord at iij^d &c.

Mercy ix^s viij^d   Elizabeth Vavasour, Robert Gascryk, Robert de Salfletby, Nicholas de Cauntelew, the abbot of Louth Park, and Gilbert atte Hall ought to come, and have not come, therefore each is in mercy.

Sum x^s vj^d and new rent iij^d.

Court of (same) held on Friday next after the Feast of S. Juliana, year as above [19 February A.D. 1388–9].

Demise iij^d   John Cardyvax demised to Alan de Scalflet ij acres of pasture in Ingoldmels (for xj years). And the said John shall perform and defend all charges incumbent on the said land during the above said term &c.

Sum iij^s iiij^d.

Court of the (same) held on the Friday the Feast of S. Gregory, year as above [12 March A.D. 1388-9].

William de Modeland surrendered all his right in xj acres Entry xx^a of land and pasture with one messuage in Ingoldmels at Modeland—to have after the term of xx years next after the death of John Smyth, who holds the said land for the term of his life of the grant of Matilda formerly his wife, which tenements after the death of the said John ought to remain to the use of Robert, son of the same John, of the grant of the said Matilda for the term of the said xx years, the reversion then of all the said tenements belonging to the said William de Modeland, kinsman and next heir of the blood of the said Matilda, as is certified in court by the whole homage of the bondage of Ingoldmels—to the use of Alan Thory, rendering each year to the said William, or his executors, during the term of xx years, xx^s &c., and if the said payment of xx^s be not paid &c. at the said term, or within xiiij days, then it shall be fully lawful to the said William, or his executors, to distrain, and carry away the distraints on all the lands and tenements of the said Alan in Ingoldmels, and retain the distraints until payment of the xx^s and arrears be fully satisfied, and the said William gives to the lord for fine xx^s.

William de Modeland surrendered all his right in 1 acre of Entry xl^d land with a cottage in Ingoldmels, which ought to descend to him after the death of John Smyth, and Alice and Matilda, daughters of John de Modeland, and which they ought to hold for the term of their lives of the grant and delivery of a certain Matilda de Modeland, the reversion thereof belonging to the said William de Modeland, kinsman and heir of the said Matilda, to the use of Alan Thory, to have and to hold to him and his heirs of the lord according to the custom of the manor for ever &c.

William de Modeland surrendered 2½ acres of land and Entry xl^d pasture in Ingoldmels and v perches, between land of Walter de Hiltoft on the east, and land of John Smyth on the west, to the use of Alan Thory, to have after the death of John and Robert Smyth, who hold the said tenements for their lives, the reversion thereof belonging to the said William de Modeland, kinsman and heir of one Matilda de Modeland, of whose grant and delivery the said John and Robert hold the said land for the term of their lives, and after the death of the same John and Robert the s⁴ land shall remain to the said Alan Thory, to have &c.

Entry ij⁸ — Alan Jakson Dobson (*sic*) surrendered the reversion of viij acres land and pasture in Ingoldmels, which ought to descend to him after the death of Margaret his mother, to the use of William de Westeby, to have the said reversion, when it shall happen, to the said William and his heirs of the lord in bondage according to the custom of the manor for ever &c.

Entry iiij⁸ — William Kemp came into court and surrendered one acre of land called Sundirland in Ingoldmels to the use of John Cardyvax, to have &c.

New rent j⁴q. — William de Skegnes, a bond tenant of the lord, acquired by charter, as is presented, of Robert son of Richard de Hiltoft one place of pasture in Ingoldmels, which contains half an acre and xx perches &c., and the said land is arrented to the lord at the new rent of j⁴q.

Sum xxxiij⁸ ij⁴.

Great Court of the lord Duke of Lancaster held on Wednesday in Easter week, 12 Rich. II. [21 April A.D. 1389].

Mercy iiij⁸ iiij⁴ — The jurors present that William German (and 10 others) cut sines on the meles upon the soil of the lord, and carried them away thence without the licence of the lord, therefore &c.; also that John Modeland (and 3 others) baked bread, and brewed beer, and sold contrary to the assizes, therefore they are in mercy; also that Robert atte Bakhouss and John Couper brewed and sold beer contrary to the assize, therefore &c.

Entry xl⁴ — John Bray and Alice his wife &c. surrendered 2½ acres in Ingoldmels, with one cottage, called Barowland, to the use of John son of William Cook, to hold &c.

Entry xl⁴ — John son of William Cook surrendered 2½ acres with cottage in Ingoldmels, called Chelesland, to the use of John Bray and Alice his wife, to hold to them and the heirs of the same Alice of the lord in bondage according to the custom of the manor for ever.

New chevage vj⁴ — It is presented by the inquisition that John son of Alan Godard, and John Coper are of the age of xv years and more, therefore they are in chevage.

Entry vj⁸ — Walter Mereot and Robert Hewson surrendered two acres of pasture in Ingoldmels, at Modeland, to the use of John Polayn, to hold &c.

Sum xvij⁸ iiij⁴.
Also of new chevage vj⁴.

Court of the (same) held on Wednesday next before the Feast   Entry
of S John ante Portam Latinam, year as above [5 May A.D. 1389].   xvij⁸ iiij⁴

Henry Geffryson came into court, and surrendered 4 acres
in Ingoldmels at Rig, called Arwardland, to the use of William
de Skegnes, to hold &c.

Sum xvij iiij^d.

Court of (same) held on Friday next after the Feast of S.
Petronill, year as above [4 June A.D. 1389].

William Clymson surrendered 1½ acres in Ingoldmels at   Entry iij⁸
Modeland to the use of Robert Thory and Alice daughter of
Ralph to hold &c.

William Mason came into court, and by licence of the court Demise ij⁸
demised to Simon German one place of pasture in Ingoldmels,
called Rumfortoft, to hold from Christmas after the end of 4
years next following after the present date, for a certain sum of
money in hand paid, and the said William and his heirs shall
support all the burdens and services incumbent upon the said
tenement during the said terms, and if the said Simon his heirs
or assigns within the said term of xx years shall be disturbed or
be impleaded by any, so that he cannot hold the said tenements
peaceably, then it shall be fully lawful for the said Simon, his
heirs, or assigns, to enter upon 4 acres of pasture with messuage
in Ingoldmels between land of John de Skipwith on the south,
and land of Joan German on the north, and take distraints
therefrom, and retain them, until all the said agreements are
satisfied, and fully restored.

Sum v⁸ ij^d.

Court of (same) held 30th June, year as below (13 Rich. II.
A.D. 1389).

Sum viij^d.

Court &c. held on Wednesday next after the Feast of S.
Thomas the Martyr, year as below [14 July A.D. 1389].

It is found by the inquisition that Beatrice Cheles made Mercy ij⁴
trespass upon Adam Thory to the damage of ij^d, therefore &c.

Sum ix^d.

Court of (same) held on Wednesday next after the Feast of
S. Peter ad Vincula, year as below [4 August A.D. 1389].

Sum xij^d.

Court &c. held on Wednesday next after the Feast of S. Bartholomew, year as below [25 August A.D. 1389].

Sum xiij^d.

Court of (same) held on Tuesday next before the Feast of S. Matthew the Apostle, year as below [14 September A.D. 1389].

Sum xj^d.

Ingoldmels. Court of the lord Duke of Lancaster held there on Thursday next after the Feast of S. Luke the Evangelist, 15 Rich. II. [19 October A.D. 1391].

Mercy v^s v^d The free jurors present that John Burgh (and 5 others) baked bread, and brewed beer, and sold contrary to the assize, &c. ; also that Alan Kemp (and 2 others) are tipplers of beer contrary to the assize &c.

The bond tenants present that John Pynkes entered into the fee, and has not done fealty, therefore let him be distrained &c.

Election of grave Also they elect John Everard to the office of grave this year, and he is sworn.

Merchet vj^s viij^d Agnes daughter of Simon Withson, a bond woman of the lord, has licence to marry Richard de Wele, a free man.

Demise xviij^d Margaret, who was the wife of John Dobson, demised 10 acres with a cottage in Ingoldmels to William Modland &c.

Fines for suit of court x^s From John Gunby (iiij^d), Thomas de Boyland (vj^d), John German (iiij^d), Ranulph Withson (iiij^d) (and 27 others).

Foreign [tenants] Mercy xv^s vj^d Henry Vavasour, Ralph Daubenay, Robert Salfletby, Robert Gascrik, the abbot of Louth Park, the prior of Bolyngton, John Grayne, the Lord de la Souch ought to come, and have not, therefore are in mercy.

Sum xxxix^s j^d.

Court of (the same) held 9 November, year as above [A.D. 1391].

Demise xl^d William Mason demised 4 acres in Ingoldmels for 10 years to Simon German &c.

Entry x^d William de Kelsay of ffrisby surrendered 10 perches of land in Ingoldmels, called Stakhawland, to the use of Robert Thory, to hold to him and his heirs of the lord in bondage for ever.

Sum vij^s ij^d.

Court of (same) held 13 December, 15 Rich. II. [A.D. 1391].

It is ordered that there come an inquisition between Thomas   Inquisi-
Westacre, plaintiff, and John son of Philip Baxter, defendant of a   tion
plea of debt, and he demands xxiiij* of rent for a certain farm &c.

It is ordered to summon Robert de Gipthorp to answer   Summons
to William Jonkynson of Waynflet of a plea of debt.

Sum vij^d.

Court of (same) held on Thursday the Feast of S. Thomas
the Apostle, year as above [21 December A.D. 1391].

Joan who was the wife of Alan Polayn died seised of 18 acres   Entry
in Ingoldmels in bondage with 2 messuages &c., and thereupon   xviij*
Simon Lamb, sen^r, kinsman and one of the heirs of the said
Joan, asks to be admitted to the portion of the inheritance
belonging to him, viz. to 6 acres &c.

Thomas de Toynton and Eudo Kaa and Agnes (his wife) &c.   Entry vj^d
surrendered the whole claim which they had in ½ acre to the use
of John atte Hadik, to hold &c.

Alan atte Lathe surrendered a cottage in Ardelthorp, and   Entry
5 acres of land and pasture, lying between land of the rectory   xvj* viij^d
of Ardelthorp on the north and land of John Godard on the south,
to the use of Thomas Ward of Tetford, to hold to him and his
heirs of the lord in bondage according to the custom of the
manor for ever &c.

Sum xxxvj* vj^d.

Court of (same) 11 January, year as below [A.D. 1391-2].

William Thory, 'Bocher,' put himself in mercy against   Mercy ij^d
John Raper of a plea of debt.

Agnes Taunt surrendered 2½ acres in Wynthorp to the use   Entry xij^d
of John Taunt, to hold in bondage &c., during the whole life of
the said Agnes &c.[1]

Alan Thory surrendered one place of pasture in Ingoldmels,   Entry iij*
at Rumforhadik, to the use of William Thory, to hold &c.

Sum v* vj^d.

Court of (same) held on Wednesday next before the Purification, year as below [31 January A.D. 1391-2].

---

[1] Exors. of John Dodik sen^r. recover debts.

Exchange xij^d Simon Cobbe and Agnes his wife surrendered all their right in lands and tenements, which fell to the same Agnes by the law of England after the death of John Dodik, late her husband, to the use of John, her son, in exchange for iij acres in Ardelthorp, called Ketilcroft, which the same John surrendered to the use of the said Simon and Agnes, to hold during the whole life of the said Agnes.

Sum xxj^d.

Court of (same) held on Thursday the Feast of S. Peter in Cathedra, year as above [22 February A.D. 1391-2].

Entry v^e John Ese surrendered 2½ acres with cottage in Ingoldmels to the use of John Pulayn, to hold &c.

Increase of rent xvj^d Entry v^e William Jonesson, a bond tenant of the lord, acquired ij acres of bond land in Ingoldmels of John Ese, and the said acres give to the lord of increase of rent xvj^d beyond the accustomed rent, viz. the acre viij^d, according to the custom of the manor, to hold &c.

Sum x^s iij^d.
Also of increased rent xvj^d.

Court of (same) held on Thursday next after the Feast of S. Gregory, year as below [14 March A.D. 1391-2].

Mercy x^d William Peticlerk, Richard Waytcroft, Walter Willoughs, Thomas Hubilton, John Pople have not come upon the inquisition between the parties.

Entry iij^s John Ferrour surrendered 1½ acres and 1 rood with a cottage in Ingoldmels to the use of John Everard, and Robert Smyth, to hold to them and their heirs after the death of John Wilson Walterson (sic), to hold according to the custom of the manor for ever.

Sum iiij^s ij^d.

Ingoldmeles. Court of the lord Duke of Lancaster held there 9 Feb. 16 Rich. II. [A.D. 1393-4].

Entry vj^s viij^d Alice ffoular of Skegnes in the presence of the grave and others of the homage, viz. John Polayn, William de Skegnes, William Godard, John Randson, Robert Hewson, William German, Walter Meriot, John Meriot, Ranulph Raper, William Johanson, Simon German, and William Gunny, surrendered xij acres of land and pasture, more or less, in Skegnes &c., and

the lord redelivered the whole of the said land to the said Alice,
to hold of the lord for life, (reversion) to John de Burgh, and
his heirs, to hold of the lord according to the custom of the
manor for ever &c.

Alice ffoular &c. surrendered ½ acre of pasture in Skegnes, | Entry vj^d
between land of William de Kyme on the south, and land
formerly Ralph Tomasson's on the north, to the use of John
Polayn, to hold to him and his heirs in bondage according to
the custom of the manor for ever &c.

Sum x^s xj^d.

Court of (same) held on Wednesday the Feast of S. Gregory
(12 March), year as above [12 March A.D. 1393-4].

Thomas Ward has not come upon the inquisition between Mercy iiij^d
William Petyclerk, and William White, therefore he is in
mercy.

Sum ij^s ij^d.

Court &c. held on Wednesday next before Palm Sunday,
year as above.

Thomas Marrays, who held of the lord on the day he died | Entry x^s
5 acres in Ardelthorp in a place called Metheland, and one rood,
of the right of Agnes his wife by the law of England, is dead.
and thereupon came Robert, son of the said Thomas and Agnes,·
and heir of the same Agnes, and asked to be admitted to his
inheritance, and he is admitted.

Sum xj^s iij^d.

[Heading on the back of the roll illegible.]

John Randson surrendered 1½ acres in Ardelthorp &c. to the   Entry xl^d
use of William de Dodík, to hold to him and his heirs according
to the custom of the manor for ever.

Sum x^s viij^d.

Court &c. held 8 May, year as below [A.D. 1394].

The presenters present that John de Modeland (and 5 others)
sold beer by discs, and not by sealed measure, therefore they
are in mercy.

Also that j marswyn coming upon the soil of the lord by   Wreck of
casting up was sold to John Polayn price xvj^d.   the sea
                                                     xvj^d

Mercy xx^d Also that John, the servant of Thomas de Ryg, drew blood
from Margaret wife of Alan Thory, therefore he is in mercy:
Mercy xx^d that John son of the same Thomas drew blood from the said
Mercy ij^s Margaret, &c.: also that the said Margaret and John (her) son
raised the hue upon the said John, and John, therefore &c.

Sum viij^s viij^d.

Court &c. held on Friday next after the Feast of S. Augustine, year as above [29 May A.D. 1394].
Mercy vj^d From John Baxter, a bond tenant of the lord, because he
demised land for a term of years vj^d.

Sum ij^s ix^d.

Ingoldmels. Court of Henry King of England of his manor
of Ingoldmels held there 5 November in the 1st year of the same
Henry after the conquest the 4th [A.D. 1399].
Demise Eudo Ka came into court, and with the licence of the court
xl^d demised to Thomas de Toynton one toft, and 2½ acres of land,
called Baxterland, in Ingoldmels, to hold &c. for the whole life
of the same Eudo, rendering to the same Eudo, or his attorney,
8^s of silver (power to distrain if rent in arrear, and if distraint
insufficient within 15 days to re-enter). Thomas shall bear all
charges &c.
Entry vj^s Simon Cobbe, who held of the lord 2 acres in Ardelthorp
for life, is dead, and thereupon comes William Cobbe (his)
brother, as next heir of blood, and asks to be admitted to his
inheritance, and is admitted &c.

Sum ix^s iiij^d.

Court held there &c. xxviij November, year as above [A.D.
1399].
Demise Richard Kyng and Mary his wife demised to William
vj^d German 2 acres in Skegnes, in a place called Beltplat, for a
certain sum of money for 3 years &c. Richard and Mary shall
bear all charges &c.

Sum viij^d.

Court held &c. 11th Dec., year as above [A.D. 1399].
The free jurors say on their oath that they have nothing
this day to present.
Mercy The bond jurors present that Margaret ffidkyn and (another)
ij^s viij^d baked bread, and brewed beer, and sold contrary to the assize.

also that Dionisius Kyng and (4 others) brewed and sold beer contrary to the assize, therefore &c.

Also that William Gryn, a bond tenant of the lord, fled for the death of Simon Cobbe, whom he feloniously slew, and therefore all his goods and chattels were seized into the hand of the lord, as forfeited, namely ij cows, price per head viij^s, xvj^s, hay, price vj^s viij^d, grain, and other utensils of the house, price xiij^s iiij^d, which chattels were sold to John Everard in full court by the steward for the said price, whereof the grave shall be charged. *Chattels forfeited xxxvj^s*

Also that Walter and William, sons of William de Thikthorp, bondmen of the lord, who used to pay to the lord yearly iij^d each for chevage, lately acquired certain lands and tenements in Ingoldmels to hold of the lord according to the custom of the manor to the same Walter and William and their heirs, therefore it is considered by the steward that now they be quit of chevage; also that John son of Thomas Smyth, John Smyth sen^r, and John son of William Gryn, bondmen of the lord, who used to pay to the lord for chevage yearly viz. iij^d each, are dead, therefore it shall cease &c. *Chevage exonerated*

Sum viij^s viij^d.
Also of forfeiture xxxvj^s.

Court held &c. on Saturday after the Feast of S. Hilary, year as below [17 January A.D. 1399-1400].

Alice daughter of Philip Baxter, a bond tenant [nativa] of the lord, has licence to marry Eudo de Wispyngton, a free man, and she gives for the licence xviij^d. *Merchet xviij^d*

Sum xx^d.

Court held &c. on Wednesday next after the Purification, year as below [4 February A.D. 1399-1400].

The presenters present that Thomas son of Alan Aldeat is of the age of xv years and more, and therefore is put in chevage &c. *New chevage iij^d*

Sum ij^d.
Also of new chevage iij^d.

pasture in Ardelthorp in the name of dower after the death of William Akewra, formerly her husband &c.

Demise
xij^d
John Cageok demised 3 acres in Ingoldmels for 5 years to Robert Henrison at rent of xx^s.

Demise
xij^d
Mary who was the wife of Henry Geffryson demised to Robert Henrison the third part of 4½ acres in Ingoldmels, which she holds in the name of dower, to have after the lapse of 5 years for the term of the life of the same Mary, rendering v^s yearly &c.

Entry
xviij^s
Simon Lamb, sen^r, died seised of vj acres in Ardelthorp, with a cottage &c., and upon this comes John, his son and heir, and asks to be admitted to his inheritance &c.

Sum xxij^s ij^d.

Court of the King of England Henry IV. held 24 April, year as above [A.D. 1400].

Entry xl^d
Alan Thory surrendered 2 acres in Ingoldmels, called Clerkesland &c., and the lord redelivered the said land to the same Alan, to hold of the lord according to the custom of the manor for life, and after (his) decease (it) shall remain to Walter Bunt and Joan his wife, and the heirs of their bodies, (and in default) to the right heirs of Alan for ever, to hold &c.

Entry viij^s
Agnes who was the wife of John de Dodik surrendered one messuage, and one place of pasture, and 3 selions of land in Ingoldmels &c., and the lord redelivered the said tenements to Agnes to hold for life, (remainder) to William her son for life, (remainder) to right heirs of Agnes.

Court &c. held xv May in the 1st year of the same Henry [A.D. 1400].

Entry viij^s
Robert Kigges in the presence of the steward and others of the homage surrendered one place of land in Ingoldmels, called Redeholm &c., abutting upon land of John Skypwyth towards the south &c., to the use of John Alanson and Agnes his wife, to hold to them and the heirs of their bodies according to the custom of the manor in bondage, (in default) to right heirs of the longer liver for ever, under the following condition, viz. that the said John and Agnes, their heirs or assigns, shall pay at Michaelmas to the said Robert, or his Exors, 20^s in the church of S. Peter of Ingoldmels, if they shall be duly demanded in the presence of six good and trustworthy men of

Ingoldmells, and at Easter (the same), and (at same feasts for 2 [1] years), and if (they) make default in the payment of the said sum in the form above for xv days after any of the said terms after they shall be requested in the above form then it shall be fully lawful to the said Robert to re-enter upon the said place of land, and seize, and hold it for ever according to the custom of the manor in bondage &c.

Court of Henry King of England &c. held 5 June in the 1st year of the same Henry [A.D. 1400].

It is ordered to attach John Ward to answer to John de   Attach-
Rochefort, chivaler, of a plea of debt.   ment

Richard Kyng and Mary his wife in their own proper   Judgment
person offered themselves against Walter Riddar and Isabel his wife, and Elizabeth, Alice, and Joan, daughters of John Polayn, of a plea of 1½ acres in Skegnes, which the same Richard and Alice Mary (sic) claim here in the lord's court, as the right of the same Mary against them &c., and they do not come, and are summoned. Judgment: Let the land be taken into the hand of the lord &c. And let the bailiff make known the day of the taking at the next court. And let them be summoned to be at the next court &c.

Sum ij^s.

Court held &c. xxvj June, year as above [A.D. 1400].

Sum x^d.

Court &c. held on Saturday next before the Feast of S. Mary Magdalene, year as above [17 July A.D. 1400].

Robert Stotevile and Mary his wife, Agnes formerly the   View
wife of William Gryn, and Matilda formerly the wife of William Derebarn, offered themselves against Robert Kigges of a plea of 1 messuage, and 10 acres in Ingoldmels, because they say that Simon Cook was seised in his demesne in bondage of the said (tenements) on the day he died, and, because he died without heir of his body, the demesne went back to Ralph Cook, brother and heir of the said Simon, and from Ralph it descended to Alice Cook, daughter and heir of the said Robert (sic), and from the said Alice to Mary, Alice (sic), and Matilda, daughters and heirs of Alice, and kinswomen and

[1] 6 payments in all.

heirs of the said Simon, and the said Robert comes, and
defends force, and injury &c., and asks a view, and it is
granted &c., and therefore it is ordered the bailiff that he
cause a view to be had &c.

Merchet xij^d Agnes Dodik, a bond tenant of the lord, has licence to
marry without the lordship.

Mercy vj^d William Polayn has not come to present, therefore &c.

Court &c. held on Saturday next after the Feast of S. Peter
ad Vincula, year as above [7 August A.D. 1400].

Entry ij^s Richard Kyng and Mary his wife in their proper persons
offered themselves against Walter Reder and Isabel his wife,
Elizabeth, and Beatrice (sic), daughters of John Polayn, of a plea
of 1½ acres in Skegnes, which the same Richard and Mary here
in the court of the lord claim as the right of Mary against
them &c., and they have not come, and at other times made
default in the court of the lord after being summoned &c., so
that then it was ordered the bailiffs that they take the said
land into the hand of the lord &c., and that they summon
them to be at the next court, and the bailiff now testifies the
day of taking, and they were summoned &c. Therefore it is
considered that the said Richard and Mary shall recover their
seisin thereof against them by default, and the said Walter
and Isabel, Elizabeth and Beatrice are in mercy.

Sum ij^s vj^d.

Court &c. held on Saturday next after the Feast of
S. Bartholomew, 1 Henry IV. [28 August A.D. 1400].

Mercy iiij^d John de Gunby in mercy for default, and it is ordered to
distrain him to answer to John Couper of a plea of debt.

Entry xij^d Robert Halgarth surrenders one acre in Ardelthorp to the
use of Alan Jakson, to hold &c.

Entry v^s Robert atte fflete surrenders the reversion of 4 acres in
Ardelthorp, and Wynthorp, with one cottage, to the use of Alice
his daughter, and the heirs of her body, (in default) to the
right heirs of the same Robert for ever.

Entry xl^d Robert son of Alan Hawitson surrenders one place of
pasture, and j acre of land, to the use of John Kemp, to hold
according to the custom of the manor for ever.

Sum ix^s viij^d.

Court &c. held 4ᵗʰ Sept., year as above [A.D. 1400].

Alice widow of John Halden, who held x acres in Ingold- | Entry xxˢ
mels with one messuage for life of the gift of the said John,
is dead, and thereupon come John Kemp and Beatrice his
wife, daughter and heir of the said John, and ask to be admitted
to their inheritance, and are &c.

Court &c. held xxvj Sept., year as above [A.D. 1400].

Robert son of Alan Hawitson demised to John Kemp | Demise xijᵈ
2 acres in Ingoldmels for 10 years &c.

John atte Halgarth died seised of j acre pasture in Ardel- | Entry xviijᵈ
thorp, and upon this comes Robert atte Halgarth, as next heir
of blood, and asks to be admitted, and is &c.

Sum iijˢ ijᵈ.

Sum of all these Courts viijˡⁱ vijˢ xᵈ.

Ingoldmels. Great Court of Henry King of England of
his manor of Ingoldmels held at Skegnes on Thursday next
after the Feast of S. Luke the Evangelist in the 2ⁿᵈ year of the
same Henry IV. [23 October A.D. 1400].

The jurors present that Alan Lawys (and 7 others) brewed | Mercy iijˢ jᵈ
and sold beer contrary to the assize &c., and that William
Aunyman drew blood from John Lark, and that the same John
drew blood from the said Walter (sic), therefore &c.

William Clymson surrendered ij acres in Ardelthorp, and | Entry iiijˢ
the lord redelivered (them) to the said William and Loretta his
wife, to hold according to the custom of the manor for their
whole lives, after their decease remainder to Richard Walker
and Beatrice his wife, and their heirs legitimately begotten,
under the following condition, viz. that the said Richard and
Beatrice, or any one in their name, shall pay to the said William
and Loretta, or their assigns, at the Feast of S. Martin next at
Ardelthorp xlˢ, and at the Feast of S. Michael next xlˢ, and at
the Feast of S. Michael then next following xxˢ, and if they fail
in the said payment in part or in whole at any of the said terms
then it shall be fully lawful to the said Wᵐ and Loretta or their
assigns to re-enter on the said ij acres, to hold &c.

John son of William de Gunby demised to John Couper | Demise xijᵈ
3½ acres in Ardelthorp for 5 years &c.

John Couper demised two places of pasture in Ardelthorp | Demise iijˢ
to John Randson for 20 years.

Sum xxvˢ jᵈ.

Court &c. held on Saturday next after the Feast of the Apostles Simon and Jude, year as above [30 October A.D. 1400].

Mercy xxij^d
Henry Vavasour, Ralph Dawbenay, Robert Gascrik, the abbot of Louth Park, the prior of Bolyngton, John Gyne, the lord de la Souch.

Sum ijˢ vjᵈ.

Court held &c. on Saturday the Feast of S. Edmund the King, year as above [20 November A.D. 1400].

Entry xxᵉ
John Cook in the presence of the grave, and others of the homage, surrendered vij acres with j cottage in Ingoldmels to the use of Alan de Scalflet, William Thory, and William Dodik, to hold to them and their heirs according to the custom of the manor for ever.

Sum xxˢ iiijᵈ.

Court &c. held at Ingoldmels on Saturday after the Conception of the Blessed Mary, year as below [11 December A.D. 1400].

Entry xxiijᵉ
William Wythson surrendered x acres in Ingoldmels to the use of William de Hiltoft, to hold to him and his heirs according to the custom of the manor for ever.

Sum xxiijˢ iiijᵈ.

Court &c. held on Saturday next after the Feast of the Epiphany, year as below [8 January A.D. 1400–1].

Sum xvijᵈ.

Court held &c. on Saturday next after the Feast of the Conversion of S. Paul, year as above [29 January A.D. 1400–1].

Sum iijˢ jᵈ.

Court held &c. on Saturday next before the Feast of S.

Court held &c. on Saturday next before the Feast of the
Annunciation, year as above [19 March A.D. 1400–1].

William de Skegnes, a bond tenant of the lord, acquired of   New rent
Robert de Kelsay one place and iij selions of land, containing   iiij^d
ij acres in Ingoldmells, to have to him and his heirs according
to the custom of the manor for ever, and he gives the lord of
new rent yearly according to the custom of the manor iiij &c.

Sum ij^s vij^d.
Also of new rent iiij^d.

Court of Henry King of England of his manor of Ingoldmels
held there xj April in the 2nd year of the same Henry after
the conquest the 4th [A.D. 1401].

Alice daughter of John Polayn, a bondwoman of the lord,   Merchet
has licence to marry Robert de Lancaster &c.   ij^s

The presenters present that William Baxster drew blood
from Thomas de Croft &c., also that the same Thomas drew
blood from William B. &c.

Sum xv^s vj^d.

Court held &c. xxiiij April, year as above [A.D. 1401].

Richard Gryn, and Agnes, sister of the same Richard,   New rent
acquired of Robert Sleght of Wynthorp two places of pasture,   ij^s
lying together in Wynthorp, containing xij acres, lying between
land of the said Richard on the east, and land of William de
Gipthorp on the west, and abutting towards the south and
north upon land of the said Richard, to hold to the said Richard
and Agnes, and their heirs, of the lord according to the custom
of the manor for ever, and they give the lord yearly of new
rent according to the custom of the manor ij^s &c.

Sum xv^d.
Also of new rent ij^s.

Court held &c. viij day May, year as below [A.D. 1401].

Sum xv^d.

Court held &c. on Saturday next before the Feast of the
Holy Trinity, year as above [28 May A.D. 1401].

X^{iana} Polayn, a bondwoman of the lord, has licence to   Merchet
marry without the lordship &c.   vj^s viij^d

Entry v^a John Kemp surrendered ij acres in Ardelthorp to the use of Robert Coper, to hold to (him) and his heirs according to the custom of the manor for ever.

Sum xij^s ij^d.

Court of Henry King of England of his manor of Ingoldmels held there xviij June, 2 H. IV. [A.D. 1401].

Robert Stotevyle and Mary his wife, Agnes who was the wife of William Gryn, and Matilda who was the wife of William Derebarn in their proper persons demand against Robert Kigges one messuage, and x acres in Ingoldmels, of which Simon Cook, a bond tenant of the lord, kinsman of the said Mary, Agnes, and Matilda, whose heirs they are, was seised in bondage in his demesne as of fee according to the custom of the manor on the day he died, and wherein they say the said Simon, kinsman &c., was seised of the said tenements in his demesne as of fee and right according to the custom of the manor &c. in the time of peace in the time of the lord Edward late King of England, the grandfather of the lord King that now is, by taking therefrom explees &c., and from the same Simon, because he died without heir of himself, the right and fee according to the custom of the manor &c. descended to one Ralph, as brother and heir, and from the same Ralph the right and fee &c. according to the custom &c. descended to one Alice as daughter and heir &c., and from the same Alice the right and fee &c. according to the custom &c. descended to the said Mary, Agnes, and Matilda, who now together demand as daughters and heirs, of whom &c., and therein they produce suit &c., and the said Robert Kigges, by Alan Kigges, his attorney, came, and defended force, and injury &c., and therein he demands a view &c., let him have it &c. Therefore it is commanded the bailiff of this court that without delay he cause the said Robert Kigges to have a view of the said tenements, and a day is given to the said parties here at the next court.

Entry v^a John Cageok surrendered 2 acres pasture in Ingoldmels, called 'hodgekynland,' to the use of William Mereot, to hold &c.

The presenters present that Alan Dobson died seised of ij acres in Ingoldmels, and they say that John, his son and heir, is of the age of v years, and it is granted by the steward in full

Court &c. held ix July, year as above [A.D. 1401].

Alan Kigges, attorney of Robert K., tenant, against Robert Essoin
Stotevile and Mary his wife (and the rest), plaintiffs in a plea
of land, (is essoined) by William German, wherein a view.

The presenters present that Mary Baly died seised of iiij acres Entry xv⁻
in Ardelthorp, and upon this came Beatrice and Amicia, daughters
and heirs of the same Mary, and ask to be admitted to their
inheritance, and are admitted &c.

Also that Thomas de Boyland died seised of ix acres, called Entry
Toretland, and that Beatrice (his) daughter is the next heir of xiij⁻ iiij⁴
blood, and she is admitted, and it is granted by the steward in
full court that Alice, (her) mother, have (her) custody &c.

Sum xxviij⁻ iiij⁴.

Court of &c. held xxx July, 2 H. IV. [A D. 1401].

The presenters present that Alice de Lym, a bond tenant of Demise ij⁻
the lord, in the presence of the grave, and others of the homage,
surrendered 6½ acres in Ingoldmels to the use of William Thory,
and William de Sibcey, to hold &c. for x years, (remainder) to Entry x⁻
right heirs of Alice, and upon this came Matilda who was the
wife of John Pople, as next heir of blood, and asks to be
admitted, and makes fine to the lord for the said lands, to have
them after the end of the said x years.

Alice daughter of John Pilat remised &c., and entirely for Entry vj⁴
herself and her heirs for ever quitclaimed to William de Skegnes,
his heirs and assigns, the whole right, and claim, which she had,
has, or in any manner could have in 2½ acres in Ingoldmels &c.

Sum xij⁻ vj⁴.

Court &c. xix day August, year as below [A.D. 1401].

Robert Thory surrendered 3 acres of land in Ardelthorp to Entry viij⁻
the use of William Mereot &c.

John Couper surrendered 2 acres of pasture in Ardelthorp Entry vij⁻
to the use of John Kemp &c.

Sum xv⁻ ix⁴.

Entry xlij⁕   Robert Kigges surrendered xxj acres in Ingoldmels to the use of Alan Kigges &c.

Entry xijᵈ   William ffouler surrendered j acre of pasture in Skegnes to the use of Alan German &c.

Sum iij^li xiiij⁕ ij^d.
Sum total of these courts xiij^li j^d.

Great Court of Henry King of England of his manor of Ingoldmels held there on Saturday next after the Feast of Dionisius, 4 H. IV. [14 October A.D. 1402].

The jurors upon the free inquisition for the king say upon their oath that this day they have nothing to present.

Mercy iij⁕   The jurors upon the native inquisition for the king present that Ranulph Bug (and another) baked bread, and sold it contrary to the assize &c., that John Kemp (and 8 others) brewed beer, and sold it contrary &c., also that Margaret daughter of Robert White, a bondwoman of the lord, ' alopata est cum Joħe de Westeby,' therefore she is in mercy and gives the lord for leyrwit.

Election of grave   Also they elect Robert Schaft to serve the lord king this year faithfully in the office of grave.

Sum xv⁕ j^d.

Court &c. held on Thursday next before the Feast of the Apostles Simon and Jude, year as above [26 October A.D. 1402].

Inquisition   It is ordered that an inquisition come between Robert Stotevile and Mary his wife and (her sisters), plaintiffs, and Alan Kigges, tenant of a plea of land.

Sum vj^d.

Court &c. held on Thursday the Feast of S. Edmund, year as above [16 November A.D. 1402].

Demise vj⁕   William Thory and William de Sibcey demised to John Everard 6½ acres in Ardelthorp and Ingoldmels, which they lately had of the demise of Alice de Lym, for 9 years &c.

Demise ij⁕   Alan Kyggys demised to William de Westmels 5 acres of pasture with ' le marsche.' lying in Skegnes, for 10 years &c.

in Ingoldmels, and the lord delivered the (same) to the said John, and Margaret his wife, and the heirs of the same John, to hold of the lord according to the custom of the manor for ever &c.

Sum xvj^s iiij^d.

Court &c. held on Thursday next before the Feast of the Conception of the Blessed Virgin Mary, year as above [7 December A.D. 1402].

John Cardyvax surrendered the third part of 1 messuage, *Entry xl^d* in which (he) dwells, and one place of pasture in Ardelthorp called Estcroft : and the lord redelivered the said tenements to the said John and Agnes his wife, and (his) heirs and assigns &c.

John Everard surrendered 1 messuage and 1½ acres in *Entry vij^s* Ardelthorp to the use of Philip Stotevile, and Margaret his wife, and the heirs and assigns of Philip &c.

John Everard surrendered 3½ acres in Ardelthorp to the use *Entry viij^s* of Philip Stotevile &c.

Sum xviij^s vj^d.

Court &c. held at Skegnes xxviij January [A.D. 1402–3].
Sum viij^d.

Court &c. held on Thursday next after the Feast of the Purification, year as below [8 February A.D. 1402–3].

Alan Kyggys surrendered 1 messuage, and 10 acres, lying *Entry xx^s* together in Ingoldmels, and the lord redelivered the same to the said Alan and Matilda his wife, to hold to them, and the heirs of Alan, according to the custom of the manor for ever.

Sum xx^s vj^d.

Court &c. held on Wednesday next after the Feast of S. Gregory, year as below [14 March A.D. 1402–3].

John Webster complains of Agnes Gryn of a plea of trespass, *Mercy ij^d* and therein he complains that the said Agnes broke the close of the same John at Ingoldmels, and consumed, and trod down his herbage with certain beasts, viz. calves and sheep, to the damage of the same John xx^d, and the said Agnes comes, and acknowledges that this was done, as the said John alleges against her, therefore it is considered that the said John recover the said xx^d against the said Agnes, and that (she) be in mercy, and it is ordered to levy &c.

Demise xij^d Mary Kyng demised to Robert Barber 2 acres of pasture in Skegnes for 5 years &c.

Entry iij^s iiij^d John son of William de Gunby and Alice his wife surrendered 1 messuage and 7½ acres in Ardelthorp &c. to the use of Alan Gryn, to have to (him) and his heirs according to the custom of the manor in bondage, after a term of 17 years, which John Kemp and John Randson hold &c., under the following condition, viz. that, if the said John and Alice or their heirs, or any one in their name shall pay to the said Alan or his Ex^{ors} at the Feast of S. Hilary next after the present date at Ardelthorp 20^{li} of silver, that then the said surrender of the said tenements shall be of no avail, otherwise the said surrender shall remain in its strength and virtue.

Court &c. held on Wednesday next after the Annunciation, year as below [28 March A.D. 1403].

Entry iij^{li} William Withson surrendered 2 messuages, and xxx acres and 3 roods in Ingoldmels and Ardelthorp to the use of William de Hiltoft, Richard Gryn, and William Thory, to have &c.

Demise xij^d John de Sibcey, chaplain, William de Sibcey and John Everard demised for xix years . . . , called Toynton place, for a certain sum of money in hand paid.

New rent xij^d ob. Robert atte Halgarth acquired of Robert Marrays, William Buttercake, and John de Sibcey, chaplain, 1 place of meadow, called Alaincroft, containing 6½ acres and 7½ perches, in Ardelthorp, between land of the Lord de Wilughby on the south, and land formerly of William atte Enges on the north, to have &c. to (him), his heirs, and assigns, of the lord according to the custom of the manor for ever.

Entry xij^s iiij^d [1] Alan Gryn surrendered 1 messuage and 7½ acres in Ardelthorp &c. to the use of John Kemp, to have &c., after the term of 17 years from Michaelmas next &c., under the following condition, that, if the said Alan, or his heirs, or any one in their name, pay, or cause to be paid to the said John or his assigns at the Feast of S. Hilary next at Ardelthorp xx^{li} of silver, that then the said surrender shall be of no avail, but otherwise (it) shall remain in strength and virtue.

Sum xxiiij^s viij^d.
Also of new rent xij^d ob.

[1] He hands on his security for 20l. to John Kemp.

Great Court with View of Frankpledge of the lord King Henry of his Duchy of Lancaster held at Ingoldmels on the Saturday next before the Feast of S. Luke the Evangelist in the 5th year of the same Henry after the conquest the 4th [13 October A.D. 1403].

The jurors present that Elizabeth Yngrayfe baked bread, and sold it contrary to the assize: also that John Kemp (and 6 others) brewed, and sold beer contrary to the assize, therefore &c.: also that Matilda Wigtoft is a tippler of beer, and sold contrary to &c.

Mercy ij^s x^d

Also they elect Walter Rydder to the office of grave, and he is sworn.

Election of grave

Sum xiij^s iiij^d.

Court of (same) held on Wednesday next after the Feast of S. Luke, year as above [24 October A.D. 1403].

It is found by the inquisition that Alan Kyggys broke an agreement with Gilbert Lamb to the damage of vj^s viij^d, therefore it is considered that the same Gilbert shall recover the said vj^s viij^d, and the said Alan is in mercy, and it is ordered to levy &c.

ercy ij^d

From Robert Malkynson for rescue made against the bailiff of the lord while doing his office &c.

Mercy vj^d

Sum xx^d.

Court of (same) held on Wednesday next after the Feast of S. Martin in winter, year as above [14 November A.D. 1403].

Mary Kyng, who held 1 messuage and xx acres in Skegnes, is dead, and upon this comes William son and heir of the said Mary and asks to be admitted to his inheritance, and he is admitted.

Entry xl^s

Sum vij^s ij^d.

Court of (same) held on Wednesday next before the Feast of S. Nicholas, year as above [5 December A.D. 1403].

[1] Robert Stotevile and Mary his wife (and her sisters), plaintiffs, and Robert Huson and Beatrice his wife have a day at the next court through the default of jurors of a plea of land.

Respite

Sum vj^d.

[1] Also they and W^m son of Robert Meriot.

Court held &c. on Wednesday the Feast of S. Stephen, year as above [26 December A.D. 1403].

Entry iij*   William Howetson surrendered 1 acre and 3 roods &c., and the lord redelivered the said land to the said W^m, to hold of the lord according to the custom of the manor for (his) whole life, and after his death (remainder) to Robert Huson and Beatrice his wife and their heirs &c.

Sum iiij* iiij^d.

Court &c. held on Wednesday after   .[1]

New rent   William Thory, a bond tenant of the lord, acquired ½ acre
j^d   with edifices in Waynflet, to hold to (him) and his heirs of the lord according to the custom of the manor for ever, and he gives of new rent.

Sum vj^d.
And of new rent j^d.

Court &c. held on Wednesday next after the Feast of the Purification, year as below [6 February A.D. 1403–4].

Demise   John Everard came into court, and granted to John de
xij^d   Modeland an annual rent of xxviij*, to be received yearly from viij acres in Ingoldmels &c., to have for 6 years, and if the said rent be in arrear &c., it shall be fully lawful for the said John Everard (sic) his heirs or assigns to distrain on the said land, and carry off the distraints, and retain them, until the said rent and arrears be fully satisfied.

Sum xx^d.

Court &c. held on Wednesday next after the Feast of S. Matthias, year as below [27 February A.D. 1403–4].

Sum xvj^d.

Court &c. held on Thursday next before Palm Sunday, year as below [20 March A.D. 1403–4].

Entry ij*   Ranulph Withson, chaplain, came into court and with the licence of the court remised, and quitclaimed to William Buttercake and Joan his wife, their heirs and assigns, the whole rights he had &c. in all those lands which were John Wythson's (his) brother, in Ingoldmels and Ardelthorp &c.

Sum ij* iiij^d.

---

    [1] Illegible.

Court &c. held on Thursday x April, year as below [A.D. 1404].

William son of John Alanson surrendered one place of land *Entry iiij*ˢ* and pasture in Ardelthorp, called 'le parke,' with one 'gaterowme,' containing ij acres &c., to the use of Alan Jakson and Juliana his wife, and the heirs of the same Alan &c.

Sum iiij^s vj^d.

Great Court of (same) held xix April, 5 H. IV. [A.D. 1404].

Robert Schaft and Matilda his wife surrendered 2 acres *Entry v*ˢ* pasture in Ardelthorp to the use of Thomas Ward, William Thory, and Wm Godard, to have &c.

The inquisition for the lord, viz. Richard Gryn, William *Mercy* Thory, William Godard, Alan de Schalflet, Robert Huson, *iij*ˢ *vij*ᵈ* Robert atte Halgarth, William de Skegnes, William Wythson, John Kemp, William Poleyne, William German, and Simon German, presents that Alice Plant of Skegnes took, and carried away thorns from 'les meles' without licence &c. : also that John Westmels of Skegnes, and Nicholas, formerly the servant of John Everard, took, and carried away thorns from the said 'meles' without licence, therefore &c. : also that a certain dog of William atte Mylne of Skegnes killed rabbits in the warren of the lord at 'les meles,' therefore &c. : also that John de Burgh, Walter de Sutton of Skegnes brewed and sold beer contrary to the assize &c. : also that whereas one acre of land called Cattysacre, which lately used to render to the lord yearly iij^s, is now devastated by the sea, so that no profit can be taken to the lord, therefore they say that discharge shall be made thereof in the account of the grave, until &c.

Sum viij^s vij^d.

Court of Ingoldmels &c. held on Thursday the Feast of the Apostles Philip and James, year as above [1 May A.D. 1404].

The presenters present that a certain dike in 'les meles' of *Mercy iij*ᵈ* Skegnes, called Wardyke, lying between 'le laa' and land of Margaret ffydkyn, is now defective in want of repair, which said dike Alan Kygs, as often as is necessary, of right ought to clean, and nevertheless he has not repaired it, therefore the said Alan is in mercy, and it is commanded that it be repaired on this side of the next court under the pain of vj^s viij^d.

Sum ix^d.

P

Court of Ingoldmels &c. held on Wednesday next before the
Feast of Corpus Christi, year as above [28 May A.D. 1404].

Mercy iij^s   The presenters present that Agnes daughter of Wm Kemp,
a bondwoman of the lord, ' alopata est ' &c. : also that Beatrice
daughter of Alan Godard, a bondwoman of the lord, ' alopata
est' with John Ward, chaplain, therefore &c.: also that (3
persons) cut synes in ' les meles,' and carried them away to the
damage of the lord king and the whole community, therefore &c.

Merchet   Mary daughter of John Kemp, a bondwoman of the lord, has
xviij^d   licence to marry &c.

                                         Sum xxxix^s iiij^d.

In tergo   Court of the lord King &c. held on Wednesday next after
the Feast of S. Barnabas [18 June A.D. 1404].

                                         Sum x^s.

Court of (same) held on Wednesday next after the Feast of
the Translation of S. Thomas the Martyr, 5 H. IV. [9 July
A.D. 1404].

Entry xij^d   William Buttirkake and Joan his wife &c. granted to Ranulph
Wythson, chaplain, for the term of his life, a certain annual rent
of liij^s iiij^d of silver to be taken from all the lands, and tenements, which were John Wythson's, father of the said Joan, in
Ardelthorp &c. (power to distrain).

Demise   John Kemp and Beatrice his wife granted to Robert Prior,
xij^d   chaplain, William Godard, and William Buttercake an annual
rent of lxvj^s viij^d, to be received yearly from all their lands in
the vill of Ardelthorp &c., to hold for v years &c. (power to
distrain).

                                         Sum ij^s.

Court of (same) held on Wednesday next after the Feast of
S. James, year as above [30 July A.D. 1404].

Entry   Walter son of Thomas Smyth surrendered 4½ acres in Ingold-
vj^s viij^d   mels to the use of Alan his son, to hold for (his) life, (remainder)
to right heirs of Walter for ever, to hold according to the custom
of the manor.

Entry x^s   (The same) surrendered the moiety of 1 messuage and of 7½
acres in Ingoldmels to the use of William his son, to hold to
(him) and his heirs &c.

Entry xl^d   (The same) surrendered the (other) moiety &c., and the lord redelivered it to Alice (his) wife to hold for life, (remainder) to right heirs of the said William, under the following condition, that, if the said Alice shall take a husband, and the said husband and Alice, and the said W^m son of Walter, or the heirs of the said W^m are not able to agree, or the said Alice willingly departs from the said moiety of the said messuage, and has her abode elsewhere, then the status of the said Alice, and the said moiety of the said messuage shall cease for ever, and then it shall be fully allowed to the said W^m and his heirs to enter upon the said moiety of the said messuage, and hold it according to the custom of the manor for ever.

Agnes Chapman, formerly the wife of John Dodyke, sur- rendered 1½ acres pasture in Ingoldmels &c. to the use of William son of Simon Cobb and Beatrice his wife, to have &c., after the term in which Robert Coper has an estate, as appears by the rolls of the court, to (them) and the heirs of the same William in bondage according to the custom of the manor for ever.

Entry iiij^s vj^d

Sum xxiiij^s viij^d.

Court of (same) held on Wednesday next after the Assumption, year as above [20 August A.D. 1404].

John Lytster surrendered 1 messuage, and x acres pasture in Ardelthorp, to the use of Robert and Richard Gryn &c.

Entry xx^s

Sum xxj^s.

Court of (same) held on Wednesday next after the Feast of the Nativity of the Blessed Mary the Virgin, year as below [10 September A.D. 1404].

Agnes daughter of Simon Wythson, a bondwoman of the lord, has licence to marry Robert Magnus.

In tergo

Merchet xl^d

Sum iij^s vj^d.

Ingoldmels. Court of the lord King Henry IV. of his Duchy of Lancaster held there xxij October in the vij^th year of the same King [A.D. 1405].

The free [tenants] present that a certain bridge called Whelebryg is in ruins in default of repair, which same bridge the prior of Bolyngton of right ought to repair, and mend, as often as necessary, and nevertheless he has not repaired it, to

P 2

the grave damage &c., and it is ordered that it be mended this side of the next leet under the penalty of xl^d.

The bond tenants present that John Skalflet drew blood from John Hyne, therefore &c., also that John Gryn raised the hue upon Alan Gryn unjustly &c., and they have respite concerning the taking of a hare until the next &c.

Election
of grave
John de Dodyk is elected to the office of grave, and sworn.

Sum xix^s iiij^d.

Court of the lord King &c. held 3rd November, year as above [A.D. 1405].

Mercy ij^d
Robert Derry puts himself in mercy against Robert de Cracroft in a plea of debt.

Sum xxij^d.

Court of (same) held on Wednesday the Feast of S. Katherine the Virgin, year as above [25 November A.D. 1405].

Sum viij^d.

Court of (same) held on Wednesday next before Christmas Day [23 December A.D. 1405].

New
chevage ij^d
The presenters present that John Godard, jun^r, is of the age of xvij years, and more, therefore in chevage &c.

Sum v^d.
Also of new chevage ij^d.

Court of (same) held on Wednesday next after the Epiphany, 7 H. IV. [13 January A.D. 1405–6].

Fealty
Matilda formerly wife of William ffraunk of Burgh came into court, and acknowledged that she held of the lord ij acres of land in Burgh, which she had of the gift of John Magnus, by the rent of j^d, and she owes suit of court and does fealty.

Sum vj^d.

Court of the lord King &c. held on Wednesday after the Purification, year as above [3 February A.D. 1405–6].

Demise
viij^d
William Kyng came into court, and by licence of court demised to Wm Taylor of Skegnes 2 acres of pasture, called Beltplat, lying in the fields of Skegnes (for 4 years).

It was presented that Agnes Bryteson, who held of the lord Entry
xiiij^s j messuage and xj acres of land and marsh on the sea banks in bondage, granted and demised the said tenements to Wm Jerman and —— son of Gilbert Meryot for a term of xv years, to have after the death of the said Agnes, as appears by the rolls of court, the reversion thereof belonging to (her) right heirs, and now to this court come John Ingrayne, chaplain, and Wm de Wyum, as kinsmen and coheirs of the same Agnes, and ask to be admitted to their inheritance, and are &c.

Sum xv^s vj^d.

Court &c. held 2nd March, year as above [A.D. 1405–6].

Court &c. held xiij day April, year as above [A.D. 1406].

Alan de Scalflet came into court, and by licence of court Entry vj^d granted to John Daulynson a certain annual rent of v marks, to be received yearly from all his lands, and tenements in Ardelthorp and Ingoldmels for two years &c. (power to distrain).

Sum ij^s v^d.

Court of (same) held on Wednesday the Feast of S. Augustine, 7 Henry IV. [26 May A.D. 1406].

It is found by the inquisition that John Lamb broke the Mercy ij^d agreement made between him and John de fflete, to the damage of the same John att fflete 5^s 4^d, therefore it is considered by the court that the s^d John att fflete shall recover &c.

Sum viij^d.

Court of (same) held on Wednesday next after the Feast of S. Barnabas, year as above [16 June A.D. 1406].

[1] Ralph de Burton was summoned to answer to Thomas and Plea Robert att Well in a plea of debt, and wherefore (they) say that the said Ralph 15 July 4 Henry IV. borrowed of (them) xxxix^s, to be paid to (them) at Ingoldemels at the next Christmas, the said Ralph, though often asked for the said money, did not pay, but says he was never bound to pay it, and still denies it, whereby they say they have received damage to iord, Merchet
viij^d value of xx^s, and thereof they produce suit &c. And t^h Ralph comes, and defends force and injury &c., and Sum xvj^d. he does not owe (them) the said xxxix^s, nor

An inquest to come in 6 pleas of debt between

(they) allege against him, and of this he put himself on the country, and (they) likewise &c.[1]

Merchet
xl[d]
Alice, daughter of W[m] Cobbe, a bondwoman of the lord, has licence to marry Walter son of Alan Gelyngson.

Sum iij[s] iiij[d].

Court of (same) held on Wednesday the Feast of S. Margaret the Virgin, year as within [13 July A.D. 1406].

Mercy x[d]
John de Gunby, Dionisius Petyclerk, Robert Magnus, Robert Barbor, Alan Tothoth and Thomas Homylton have not come upon the inquisition between Thomas and Robert att Well, plaintiffs, and Ralph de Burton, defendant in vj plaints of debt, therefore each of them is in mercy, and it is ordered to distrain the said jurors to be at the next court between the said parties, as before they were summoned by the bailiff of the lord king &c., and upon this the said parties and the jurors have a day at the next court through default of the jurors . . . ., and it is ordered that there come viij against the next court.

Sum xiiij[d].

Court of the lord King Henry IV. of his Duchy of Lancaster held at Ingoldmels on Wednesday next after the Feast of S. Anne, 7 Henry IV. [28 July A.D. 1406].

Mercy ij[d]
It is found by the inquisition that Ralph de Burton owes to Thomas and Robert att Well xxxix[s] in a plea of debt, and the damages are taxed at xx[d], therefore it is considered that (they) recover the s[d] xxxix[s], and the said damages, and the said Ralph is in mercy, and it is ordered to levy &c.[2]

Sum xiiij[d].

Court of (same) held on Friday after the Feast of S. Bartholomew, year as above [27 August A.D. 1406].

Sum iiij[s].

[1] Plea 2, debt xxxix[s], money lent 16 July 4 H. IV. to be paid on Feast of .. Baptist. Plea 3, debt xxxix[s], lent 17 July to be paid on Circumcision.

Court &c. held on Friday next after the Feast of the Nativity of the Blessed Virgin Mary, year as above [10 September A.D. 1406].

Court of (same) held on Friday next after the Feast of S. Matthew, year as within [24 September A.D. 1406].

Simon Lawys came into court, and did fealty for all those lands and tenements, which he (holds) of the lord, of the right of Alice his wife, according to the custom of the manor.

John Lamb surrendered the 4th part of 1 rood in Ingoldmels to the use of Wm Groun, to hold to (him) and his heirs of the lord in bondage according to the custom of the manor for ever.   *Entry vjd*

Sum xxijd.

Sum total of these courts lxxvs iiijd.

Ingoldmels. Court of the lord King Henry IV. of his Duchy of Lancaster held there ix Oct. in the xijth year of the same king [A.D. 1410].[1]

John de Sybsay, chaplain, Wm de Sybsay, and John Everard came into court, and by the licence of the court demised to John de Walpole 2½ acres in Ardelthorp &c. (for 8 years).   *Demise viijd*

Isabel widow of John Brok &c. demised to Richard Gryn 3½ acres in Ardelthorp &c., to hold for 12 years from the day of the death of the sd Isabel.   *Demise xijd*

Sum ijs vjd.

names of the affeerers   Wm Buttercake ⎱ sworn.
Robert Godard ⎰

Court of (same) held at Ardelthorp on the Thursday next after the Feast of the Apostles Simon and Jude, year as above [30 October A.D. 1410].

Isabel daughter of Alan Aldyat, a bondwoman of the lord, has licence to marry John Kedyngton.   *Merchet viijd*

Sum xvjd.

---

[1] 2 oxen worth xlvjs viijd.

View of Frankpledge of (same) held viijth November in the 12th year of the same king [A.D. 1410].

Inquisition of free [tenants]			
Robert Marrays.	John Ayr.	John Hodge	
Richard Whaytecroft.	John Palmer.	John Geliotson	
William Buttercake.	Alan Kigges.	Gilbert Doket	sworn.
Robert Lancaster.	William Sybsay.	John Lowys	

They present that Robert att Myln, and Simon May entered the fee of the lord, viz. on iij acres of land, with one messuage situated thereupon, lying in Burgh, which lately were John Ayr's of Burgh, and have not done fealty, therefore it is ordered to

Distrain distrain them against the next (court) for their services to be done: also that John de Gunby, jun^r, Wm Bulhed, vicar of the church of Wynthorp, and Robert Raven of Wynthorp entered the fee of the lord, viz. on v acres of pasture, lying in Wynthorp in a place, called 'harp,' which formerly were Walter Wylus's, and have not done fealty, therefore &c.

Inquisition of bond tenants			
Richard Gryn.	Alan de Scalflet.	William Wythson	
William Thory.	William Skegnes.	John Meryot	
William Godard.	Robert Halgarth.	John Dodik	sworn.
Robert Heuson.	John Kemp.	John Couper, jun^r	

They present that Rosa ffidkyn is a tippler of bread, and sold contrary to the assize, also that Matilda de Wiktoft is a tippler of beer, and sold &c., therefore &c.: also that John ffisch this year, and last, was a common forestaller of fish from the sea within the lord's lordship, to the grave damage of the lord and his tenants, therefore he is in mercy.

Chevage exonerated Also that Wm Cat, a bondman of the lord, who used to render to the lord for his chevage iij^d yearly, lately acquired of Wm Thory, a bond tenant of the lord, one acre of land with a house situated thereupon with appurtenances in Skegnes, worth yearly ij^s, as they say on their oath, therefore it is considered by the steward that from now he be quit of chevage, as is according to the custom of the manor.

Election of grave Also they elect John Meriot, and John son of Simon Lawys to the office of grave for the choice of the lord, and (the latter) was sworn &c., and afterwards in the place of the said John by the licence of the lord, and consent of the homage, Thomas Norman, a bond tenant of the lord, was sworn to serve this year in the office of grave.

Walter Geliotson in the presence of John Gryn, a bond   Entry ijˢ
tenant of the lord, elected in the place of Thomas Norman, the
lord's grave, in the absence of the said Thomas, as is the custom
of the manor in the peril of death of any [nativi vel native
tenentis] bond tenant or tenant holding in bondage, and of others
of the homage, viz. (names), surrendered 1 acre of pasture in
Ardelthorp to the use of Matilda his wife, and Joan daughter of
the same Matilda, to have &c. to (them), and the heirs of Joan,
of the lord in bondage according to the custom of the manor
for ever.

Simon Galway in the presence of Thomas Norman, the lord's   Entry iiijˢ
grave and others of the homage, viz.[1] (names), surrendered
2½ acres with a cottage in Ardelthorp to the use of Robert att
Halgarth and Thomas Norman, to have &c.

John Lamb came into court, and released &c. all his right   Entry viijᵈ
&c. in one cottage in Ardelthorp, between the cottage of Simon
Smyth on the north, and land of the church of S. Nicholas of
Ardelthorp on the south, to the use of William de Manby, and
Beatrice his wife, and the heirs and assigns of the same Beatrice,
to hold of the lord according to the custom of the manor.

Sum xijˢ ixᵈ.

Court of (same) held xx Nov. year xij [A.D. 1410].

The presenters present that Roger Horblyng drew blood   Mercy xijᵈ
from Walter son of Richard de Austhorp, therefore &c.; also
that Walter son of Richard de Austhorp drew blood from
Roger H. &c.

Sum ijˢ.

Court of (same) held at Skegnes xj Dec., year as above
[A.D. 1410].

Alan Kemp demised to Joan Kellok of Hoggesthorp 3 acres   Demise
of pasture, with the houses thereupon, to hold &c. for 12 years   xijᵈ
&c., rendering to the lord the king, and his heirs, dukes of
Lancaster, the rent before usual and of right accustomed
(Alan to do the services).

Thomas Hamound came into court, and did fealty for all   Fealty
those lands and tenements, which he holds of the lord in
Ingoldmels of the right of Beatrice his wife.

[1] Wᵐ Buttercake one, who was a freeman.

The presenters present that Matilda de Wylus of Wynthorp came into court, and acknowledged that she held half an acre with the house situated thereupon in Wynthorp, which was formerly Gilbert Bacon's dwelling in Bardenay, and she renders to the lord yearly j^d at the Feast of S. Michael only, and owes suit, and did fealty.

Sum xvj^d.

Court of (same) held viijth Jan., year as above [A.D. 1410–1].

Merchet viij^d   Agnes daughter of Robert White, a bondwoman of the lord, has licence to marry Robert Gron.

The presenters present that W^m att Mylnes of Skegnes on the Vigil of the Nativity of S. John Baptist last, and divers other times, cut thorns on 'les meles' of Skegnes, and carried them off without licence, and the said W^m, being present in court, is accused of the said trespass, and says that he is not **Mercy xx^d** guilty &c., but he puts himself upon the grace of the lord, and gives the lord for the said trespass by the pledge of (2): also that Robert Coper (and 3 others) are common players at bones, and quoits, contrary to the proclamation of the court, therefore they are in mercy.

Seizure   Also that John de Ingoldmels, a bond tenant of the lord, alienated by his charter a messuage in Yherburch, with houses situated thereupon, to Thomas de Blithe without the licence of the lord, therefore it is ordered to seize &c., and afterwards the said messuage is seized into the hand of the lord the king, to hold to him and his heirs, dukes of Lancaster, for ever, and **Demise ij^s vj^d** he demises the said messuage to Thomas de Blythe by Thomas Norman (his) grave, and he gives the lord for the farm ij^s vj^d.

Sum v^s iiij^d.

Court of (same) held xxij Jan., year as within [A.D. 1410–1].

Demise   Isabel formerly wife of John Brok &c. demised to Richard tenant of the lord, acquired of John Everard 6½ acres with 1 cottage, called 'popilland' in Ingoldmels, and they say that, whensoever any bond tenant of this manor shall acquire any tenements or lands of the bondage of the lord, that the same tenements or lands after the first alienation of right ought to give to the lord according to the custom of the manor an increase of rent for all future times, as often as they shall be alienated by the licence of the court. And so the s^d 6½ acres .&c. give to the lord according to the custom of the manor iiij^s iiij^d, viz. viij^d the acre to be paid at the usual terms for ever. Increment of rent

Also that Alan Thory, a bond tenant of the lord, acquired of Wm de Modeland 11½ acres with one messuage in Ingoldmels, called Modelandhous, to hold to the same Alan and his heirs after the term of xx years, which same term is now ended, and the said 11½ acres &c. give to the lord according to the custom of the manor vij^s viij^d yearly of increment of rent. Increment of rent vij^s viij^d

Also that Wm de Cokhill carried away one log, lying in the sea, and put it to his own use, without the licence of the lord, and contrary to the custom of the manor, therefore he is in mercy. Mercy vj^s viij^d

[1] John Kemp and Thomas Norman surrendered the reversion of 1 messuage, and xx acres of land and pasture, with appurtenances, as they lie in the vill and fields of Ardelthorp, and the reversion of one small place of pasture &c., which same lands and tenements were formerly Ralph Thomasson's, and the reversion of one house, called 'nuchaumber,' built in the said messuage, which same reversion of the said house Ralph Thomasson formerly granted and surrendered in the court of Ingoldmels to the use of Matilda Hamound, to hold after the death of Joan formerly wife of the said Ralph according to the custom of the manor for the term of the life of the same Matilda, which same Joan holds all the other lands and tenements aforesaid for the term of (her) life of the grant and surrender of the s^d Ralph formerly her husband, which same reversions &c. John and Thomas lately had of the grant and surrender of John Dawlynson of Ardelthorp son of the said Ralph, to the use of Wm de Skegnes, to have &c. to him, his heirs and assigns, after the death of Joan formerly wife of Entry vj^s viij^d

---

[1] Both nativi.

Ralph Thomasson, Matilda Hamound, and Beatrice late the wife of John Dawlynson, to hold of the lord in bondage according to the custom of the manor for ever.

Sum xiij^s ix^d.

Also of increment of rent in ij parcels xij^s.

Court of (same) held at Skegnes vth March, year xij [A.D. 1410–1].

Respite   A day is given by the prayer of the parties between Wm Clymson of Addlethorpe, plaintiff, and Robert att Halgarth, tenant, of a plea of land, and (they) have a day at the next court to be held at Ingoldmel with the council of the same to answer peremptorily without further delay in the said plea.

The presenters present that an instrument called a 'wyndays' of a certain ship came upon the soil of the lord at Skegnes, value x^d, by the ejection of the sea on the xixth day of February last past, in the hand of Thomas Norman: also that a pinnace came upon the soil of the lord king at Skegnes by the ejection of the sea, value v^s viij^d, on the 1st day of March last past, in the hand of Thomas Norman, for which let him answer: also

Wreck of sea x^s x^d   that one log came upon the soil of the lord at Skegnes by the ejection of the sea, value xij^d, on the 5th day of February last past, in the hand of Thomas Norman, for which let him answer: also that a certain fish, called 'marswyne,'[1] value iij^s iiij^d, came upon the soil of the lord by the ejection of the sea at Skegnes on the 1st day of February last past, in the hand of Thomas Norman, for which let him answer, and for so much more as he shall be able to raise to the use of the lord the king.[2]

Election of keepers of the banks of the sea   John de Burgh and Robert Barburgh were elected, and sworn, to be in the office of keepers of the banks of the sea of Skegnes by the said inquisition, and it is commanded the said John and Robert by the steward in the court that they well and diligently guard, and cause to be repaired all defects of the banks of the sea of Skegnes according to the custom before due

Pain   and of right used under the pain of xx^{li}, and that they compel all others within the lordship to help them to distrain for the repair of the said banks in the places defective, as is of custom, viz. each for his own portion, as it happens, and is ordained by the said township under the said penalty &c.

Sum xxij^d.

Of wreck of the sea x^s x^d.

[1] ? Porpoise.

[2] Names (given) of those jurors who appraised the said wreck.

Court of (same) held xxiiij[th] March, year xij [A.D. 1410–1].

Entry xij[a]

W[m] de Orby surrendered his whole right in 1 acre of pasture in Ingoldmels &c., which Matilda de Orby holds in the name of dower for the term of her life, and the lord redelivered (it) to (him), to hold &c. for life after the death of Matilda &c., and after the death of the said William the same William wills and grants that (it) remain to William (his) son, to hold for life &c., and after the decease of the same W[m] son of the said W[m] to the right heirs of the said W[m] de Orby, to hold of the lord according to the custom of the manor for ever.

Sum xvj[d].

Court of (same) held xvj[th] April, year as above [A.D. 1411].[1]

as yet of the court as below.

Fealty

W[m] Buttercake of Addlethorpe, Dominus John de Sybsay chaplain, and Alan att How of Wynthorp came into court, and acknowledged that they held of the lord one messuage, as it lies in Ingoldmells, and lies on the east side of the church of S. Peter of Ingoldmells, and xij acres of pasture, to hold to (them), their heirs and assigns, by the services therefore due and of right accustomed, and they did fealty, by a certain charter shown here in court, of which the date is at Ingoldmels on the Monday next before the Feast of the Annunciation, xij H. IV.

Sum xiiij[d].

View of Frankpledge with great Court of (same) held xxij April, year as below [A.D. 1411].

Mercy
iiij[s] ij[d]

The inquisition[2] of bond tenants presents (4 persons for breaking the assize of bread, and 11 for assize of beer, 1 tippler for selling contrary to the assize of beer, and 3 persons for not coming).

New
chevage
ij[d]

Also they present that John son of John Kemp, a bondman of the lord, is of the age of xv years and more, therefore he is put in chevage, and he gives to the lord ij[d].

Discharge
of chevage

Also that Robert Aldyat, a bondman of the lord, who used to render to the lord yearly iij[d] for his chevage, is dead, therefore let there be discharge of the said chevage: also that

Richard Gryn (a native) essoined ... Richard Whartcroft a freeman

Fines for
trespass
xviij^d

W^m att Mylnes (and 4 others) divers times this year cut the
thorns, and sines, in the 'meles' of Skegnes, to the grave
damage of the lord the king, and in lesion of his liberty, (they)
came here into court before the steward, and each of them for
himself put himself upon the grace of the lord by the pledge
of (4).

Leyrwyte
vj^s viij^d

Also that Elena daughter of Robert Godard, a bondwoman
of the lord, ' alopata est cum Johanne de Candilesby capellano,'
and the said John gives to the lord of fine ' pro alopatione pre-
dicta' by the pledge of John Ward, vicar of the church of
Mumby (and two others).

Seizure

Also that John Hobson of ffriskenay, otherwise called John
Marays, a bond tenant of the lord, acquired of Robert Gardyn
one half acre of pasture, with a house situated thereupon, in
ffriskenay, by a certain charter, and has not come to the court
to show the said charter, and do service, as is the custom of the
manor, therefore it is ordered to seize the said half acre &c.

The inquisition [1] of free [tenants] says and affirms all the
presentments above are true, and that they have nothing else to
present.

Sum xx^s.
Also of new chevage ij^d.

Court of (same) held on Thursday next after the Feast of
the Apostles Philip and James, year xij [7 May A.D. 1411].[2]

New rent
j^d ob.

The presenters present that Wm Godard and John att fflete,
bond tenants of the lord of this manor, acquired of Matilda who
was the wife of Thomas Wyloughs of Wynthorp one messuage,
with the edifices built thereupon, containing half an acre, and
one perch of pasture with appurtenances, in which the said
Matilda was enfeoffed jointly with Thomas de Wylloughs, her
husband, of the gift and feoffment of Gilbert Bacon, which
same messuage lies in Wynthorp next the common way which
leads to Whelebryg, to have and to hold the s^d messuage and
the said perch &c. to the s^d W^m and John, their heirs and
assigns, of the lord according to the custom of the manor, and
the said tenements were seized by the grave into the hand of

[1] 16 names given. Robert Magnus, Simon May, William de Caleflet, Ralph
de Burton, Robert Barburgh, John de Burgh, John Palmer, are fresh names.
[2] 6 sheep worth x^s.
1 horse „ xj^s.

the lord, and upon this came the said W^m and John, and made fine with the steward for the said tenements, and they give to the lord of new rent according to the custom of the manor 1^d ob.

Sum xviij^d.
Also of new rent j^d ob.

Court of (same) held xxviij^th May, year as above [A.D. 1411].
Isabel daughter of John Pullayn, a bondwoman of the lord, has licence to marry John Moryell, a freeman.   Merchet ij^s

Sum iiij^s ij^d.

Court of (same) held xviij^th June, year xij [A.D. 1411].

Sum xvij^d.

Court of (same) held iij^rd July, year as above [A.D. 1411].[1]
The presenters present that Robert Gryn, a bond tenant of the lord, died seised in one messuage, lix acres, and j rood of land, and pasture, in Ingoldmells, and they say that Richard, his son, is his next heir of blood, and has not come &c. Therefore it is ordered to seize the s^d lands &c. into the hand of the lord &c.   Seizure

Sum ij^s vj^d.

Court of (same) held at Skegnes vij^th August, year xij [A.D. 1411].[2]
Robert Gryn, a bond tenant of the lord, who held &c., died, as was presented by xij jurors in the preceding court, and now to this court comes Richard son of the said Robert, and asks to be admitted to his inheritance, as next heir of blood, and he is admitted, to have &c. to (him) and his heirs of the lord in bondage according to the custom of the manor for ever.   Entry x marks

Sum vj^li xiij^s x^d.

Court of (same) held xx August, year as above [A.D. 1411].
Wm Clymson of Addlethorpe, plaintiff, does not prosecute against Robert att Halgarth tenant of a plea of land, therefore he is in mercy.   Mercy ij^d

---

[1] Ralph de Burton attached by 9 horses worth 9^li in a plea of debt. 20 sheep worth ij marks.

[2] Dionisius Peticlerk attached by 3 trees worth 5^s.

Complaint   Robert Stutvile and Mary his wife, Matilda Derebarn, and
Agnes who was the wife of Wm Gryn complain of Robert
Hughson and Beatrice his wife of a plea of land, pledges to
prosecute (2), and they make protestation to sue in the nature of a
Summons   writ of consanguinity, and it is ordered to summon the s^d Robert
Hughson and Beatrice to be here at the next court to answer
(them) in the aforesaid plea.

Complaint   Wm Clymson complains of Robert att Halgarth in a plea of
land, pledges to prosecute (2).

Plea   Thomas Lokland by his attorney, John att ffleet, complains
against Alice Carter of Wynthorp in a plea of debt &c., and
therein he complains that whereas Robert Carter husband of the s^d
Alice on the Feast of S. Michael, x. H. IV., at Ingoldmels bought
a certain horse of the said Thomas for xxx^s, which same xxx^s
he was to pay to the same Thomas on Ascension Day following, on
which day the s^d Robert, although he was often asked, did not
pay the said sum, nor has he yet paid it, wherefore the s^d Thomas
Lokland after the death of the s^d Robert Carter at Ingoldmels
on the Feast of the Ascension next following asked the s^d Alice
Carter as wife of the s^d Robert to pay the said sum, which same
Alice in the year day and place aforesaid became debtor to the
s^d Thomas of the said debt, and asked a day for paying the said
sum at Ingoldmels on the feast aforesaid until the Feast of
S. Mary Magdalen next following, and had the day as she
asked, on which day the s^d Alice, although she was often asked,
did not pay the said debt, nor has she paid it yet, to the damage
of the said Thomas x^s, and thereof he produces suit.   And the
s^d Alice, being present in court, comes and defends force, and
injury &c., and protests, saying that she does not acknowledge
any such debt in the manner in which the same Thomas by his
attorney alleges against her, but she says that the s^d Thomas
ought not to have the said action against her, because she says
that the s^d Thomas does not show against her any special fact,
nor any record, by which she ought to be bound for the said
debt, and therefore she begs judgment whether the s^d Thomas
ought to have any action against her because of the s^d debt, and
the s^d Thomas likewise for that the s^d Alice does not contradict
the material (facts) alleged against her by the said Thomas, and
he asks judgment according to the custom of the court, and
damages &c.

Sum v^s vj^d.

Court of (same) held x^th September, year xij [A.D. 1411].

As yet as at other times it is ordered to summon Robert Summons
Hughson and Beatrice his wife tenants upon land by ij or iij
witnesses to answer to Robert Stutvile (and the others) pl^fs of a
plea of land.[1]

Thomas Lokland by his attorney John att fflete, plaintiff, Judgment
and Alice Carter of Wynthorp, def^t of a plea of debt, have a day
at the next court to be held &c. to hear judgment &c.

Wm Pelson, chaplain, Robert Ravyn, and John Gunby came Fealty
into the court held at Waynflet xiiij July 12 H. IV. before
Robert Waterton, chief steward of the duchy of Lancaster in
these parts, saying that lately certain lands and tenements in
Wynthorp were seized into the hands of the lord after the death
of Richard Ynglysch, because of the minority of his heir, by the
ministers of the said duchy, pretending that the same Richard
died seised thereof, and held them of the aforesaid duchy by
knight service &c., and they say that the said Richard never
was seised of the said lands &c., except jointly with the same
W^m, Robert, and John, and so he died &c., and this they proffer
to verify by their sealed charters, or otherwise, as the court shall
consider &c., praying the delivery of the s^d lands &c. out of the
hands of the lord, as the law requires &c., upon which the said
charters were examined in full court by the said chief steward,
and others of the council of the said duchy, and were approved
by witnesses and trustworthy persons of the law. It was found
that the s^d Richard never was seised of the s^d lands &c., except
jointly with the same W^m, Robert, and John, therefore it was
considered by the s^d chief steward in court that the hands of the
lord shall be entirely removed from the said seizure. And the
s^d W^m, Robert, and John were fully restored to all the lands,
and tenements, which were seized for the said cause, together
with the issues of the s^d lands &c. from the time of the s^d seizure
&c., and they did fealty.

Sum ij^s iij^d.

Ingoldmels. Court of the lord King Henry V of his Duchy
of Lancaster held at Skegnes on the Wednesday next after the
Feast of the Conception in the 1st year of the same King
[13 December A.D. 1413].

[1] So also in 2 other pleas of land.

Q

Plea

Robert att Halgarth complains of Thomas de Bardenay of a plea of trespass, pledge to prosecute the bailiff, and wherefore he complains that the same Thomas on the Thursday next after the Feast of All Saints 14 H. IV. made a hole with a spade in the common way of Ingoldmels at Halfcroft, to the injury of the said Robert ijˢ, and thereof he produces suit &c., and the sᵈ Thomas being present in court defends force, and injury &c., and says that he is not guilty of the sᵈ trespass, and this he asks may be inquired by the country, and the plaintiff likewise, therefore it is ordered the bailiff to summon xij lawful men against the next court.

Sum xᵈ.

Court of (same) held 24 Jan., year as above [A.D. 1413–4].

Sum iiijˢ ijᵈ.

Court of (same) held on Wednesday next after the Purification, year as within [7 February A.D. 1413–4].

Sum xlᵈ.

Court of (same) held on Wednesday in the 1ˢᵗ week of Lent, year as within [28 February A.D. 1413–4].

Entry
ijˢ vjᵈ

Whereas John Lamb holds for his life 5 acres of pasture with a cottage in Ingoldmels, the reversion thereof belonging to Robert Slyghhede and Wᵐ German, now in the present court comes the sᵈ Wᵐ, and surrenders all his right to the sᵈ Robert, and further he released, and quitclaimed the whole of his right and claim in the same, to have &c. after the death of the sᵈ John to the sᵈ Robert, and his heirs, of the lord in bondage according to the custom of the manor for ever.

Plea

Robert Bayly of Burgh complains of John Stevenson of Burgh of a plea of debt, pledge to prosecute the bailiff, and wherefore he complains that he owes him vjˢ vjᵈ for a cow, which he bought of him at Burgh on Thursday next after Michaelmas last, and which same vjˢ vjᵈ he should have paid to him at Burgh on S. Luke's day next following, and he did not pay, but detained, and still unjustly detains (the money), to the damage of the same Robert xlᵈ, and thereof he produces him above, and this he asks may be inquired by the country, and the plaintiff likewise, therefore it is ordered the bailiff to summon xij lawful men against the next &c.

It is found by the inquisition that Wᵐ de Skegnes owes   Mercy ijᵈ
Agnes Gryn as the pledge of John Kemp xxxixˢ xjᵈob.q., therefore it is considered that the sᵈ Agnes recover &c., and Wᵐ is in mercy, and it is ordered to levy &c.[1]

Robert Hughson, who held of the lord j messuage and   Entry
32½ acres in Ingoldmells, is dead,[2] and upon this comes   lxxiijˢ iiijᵈ
Thomas (his) son and heir, and asks to be admitted to his inheritance as next heir of blood, and he is admitted.

Sum lxxviijˢ.

View of Frankpledge held xviijᵗʰ April, 2 H. V. [A.D. 1414].

Richard Gryn.	Thomas Norman.	William de Scalflet	Inquisition of bond tenants
William Godard.	William Poleyn.	John de fflete	
William Thory.	Robert att Hallgarth.	William German	SWORD.
William de Skegnes.	John Guny.	Alan Aldiat	
		Ranulph Raper	

They present that Richard de Whetecroft of Burgh held of the lord on the day he died, in his demesne as of fee, one place of pasture, containing 8 acres, called Nolumland, and that the sᵈ pasture is worth yearly beyond reprises xlˢ, being so demised by the steward this year to Walter Goshauke of Orby, but by what services they know not, and they say that the sᵈ Richard   Fealty
died on Friday in the 2ⁿᵈ week of Lent last, and that John, son of Wᵐ Whetecroft, brother of the sᵈ Richard, is his next heir, and of the age of xij years and more, therefore it is ordered to seize the sᵈ 8 acres into the hands of the lord &c., so that an account may be made to the lord the king of the issues of the sᵈ pasture until the full age of the sᵈ heir, and they say that the sᵈ Richard held no other lands &c. on the day he died of the said lord the king as of his duchy of Lancaster, except jointly with Thomas Marays, and Wᵐ Buttircake of Ingoldmels according to the form of a charter to them made &c.

---

[1] An exactly similar entry follows.
[2] Diem clausit extremum.

Q 2

Inquisi-tion of free [tenants]	Robert Marays.	John Stevenson.	William de Sybsay
	William de Caleflet.	John Alanson.	Thomas Jakson
	Walter at Westende.	Alan Jakson Howytson.	Philip Stotevyle
	John Helwys.	John Hodge.	Thomas Hamound
			William Trow

sworn.

Mercy ix^d   They say and affirm that all things above presented are true, and besides they present that the lord de la Warr, Dionisius Peticlerk, and Matilda de Cromwell ought to come, and have not &c.

Sum v^s v^d.

Court of (same) held on the Wednesday next after the Feast of the Invention of the Holy Cross, year as above [9 May A.D. 1414].

Fealty   The presenters present that Thomas de Whetecroft son of Richard de Whetecroft of Burgh entered upon the fee of the lord in certain lands and tenements in Burgh of the grant &c. of Wm Buttercake of Ingoldmels, therefore it is ordered to distrain the s^d Thomas to do the services to the lord &c. And thereupon in the same court came the said Thomas, and acknowledged that he held of the lord one messuage and xxviij acres in Burgh, which (he) had of the grant of the s^d William Buttercake, together with other tenements in the vills of Wynthorp, and ffriskenay, and in the s^d vill of Burgh, by the name of all those lands, and tenements, rents, and services &c. in the vills of Burgh, Wynthorp, and ffriskenay, which the s^d Wm Buttercake had with other tenements, together with the s^d Richard de Whetecroft, and Thomas Marays of Ingoldmels jointly of the gift &c. of John de Hagh, John de Gunby, and Simon de Stalyngburgh of Thorp, in the s^d vills, which formerly were Wm de Whetecroft's of Burgh, father of the s^d Richard, to have &c. to the s^d Thomas de Whetecroft, his heirs and assigns, of the chief lords of that fee by the services therefore due and of right accustomed for ever, and he showed the charter thereof, of which the date was at Burgh vjth May 2 H. V., and upon this he was admitted in the same court, and did fealty &c.

says that when they were together at Ingoldmels within the lordship of the duchy of Lancaster, Easter 1 H. V., there they accounted for divers things between them had, and so they settled the account, and so the said John was in the debt of the s^d Alan xx^s. as the same Alan demanded above &c., and the s^d John, being present in court, admits that he owes the s^d debt of xx^s, therefore it is considered that the s^d Alan recover the s^d xx^s, and the damages are condoned, and the s^d John is in mercy, and it is ordered to levy &c.   Mercy ij^d

The presenters present that Wm Tappard has j pig digging   Mercy ij^d
in le Scalflet, this turn, to the injury of the lord and his tenants, therefore &c.

Sum xiiij^d.

Court of (same) held xxx^th May, year as above [A.D. 1414].
John Byrk demands against John Stevenson viij^s for 8 stone   Plea
of cheese, which he bought of him at Burgh, 4 July 8 H. IV., which same 8^s he should have paid him at Burgh on the 4th August following, and did not pay, but detained and still unjustly detains, to the damage of the s^d John B. ij^s &c. (John defends &c., and says he owes no money), therefore it is ordered the bailiff to summon xij lawful men &c.

William Thory complains of Simon Helsay of a plea of trespass, for that, whereas on the Feast of S. Nicholas 5 years since W^m and Simon were together at Ingoldmels, together with Richard Gryn, Wm Godard, Robert Hughson, Wm de Skegnes, Wm German, Simon German, and Gilbert Lamb, jurors to divide xv acres of land and pasture in Ingoldmels, called Dowss-overland, which same jurors were agreed as follows, viz. that the s^d Wm Thory should have the half part of the said 15 acres, viz. 7½, and the s^d Simon Helsay the other half &c., to them and their heirs according to the custom of the manor, under the condition that the s^d W^m should pay the rent, customs, and dues for his portion, and the s^d Simon the (same) for his, and so they were fully agreed in the presence of Wm Hiltoft, then locum tenens of John Rocheford, steward of the duchy of Lancaster, of Thomas Norman the grave, and of John Everard the bailiff, and afterwards on the Feast of S. Botulph following the s^d Simon refused to pay the s^d rent, and so each year on the Feasts of S. Botulph and S. Michael the s^d William was distrained, and gravely vexed for 3^d, which the s^d Simon of right ought to have paid, to the damage &c., therefore it is considered that the s^d W^m recover the 3^d, and for damages 3^d.

Sum xiiij^d.

Court of (same) held xx . .

Wreck   The presenters present that a certain fish, called a marswyne [porpoise], came up upon the soil of the lord at Ingoldmels by the ejection of the sea on the Friday next before the Feast of the Holy Trinity last past, which said fish was appraised by the tenants of the lord the king of his duchy of Lancaster in the presence of the grave at vj^s viij^d, and that on the same day one Thomas de Akewra took, and removed the s^d fish out of the fee of the lord, to the great prejudice of the s^d lord the king, and the lesion of his liberty, therefore he is in mercy, or let a writ be issued.

Demise vj^d   Robert Schaft &c. demised to Thomas Norman 2½ acres in Ingoldmels for 4 years &c.

Entry iiij^d   John Lamb surrendered one acre in Ingoldmels to the use of John Mylner, to have during the life of the s^d John Lamb &c.

As yet the presenters present that John att Munkys, chaplain, continually this year kept 2 dogs, and still keeps them, which said dogs divers times this year have taken, and killed hares, and rabbits, on ' les meles ' of Skegnes, to the grave damage and prejudice of the lord the king, therefore let a writ be made.

Sum ij^s.

Court of (same) held on Wednesday next after the Feast of the Translation of S. Thomas the Martyr, year as below [11 July A.D. 1414].

Fealty   Wm Buttercake of Ardelthorp, and John Couper of Ingoldmels came into court, and acknowledged that they held of the lord the king ij places of land in Ardelthorp, of which one is called ' Kylnhoustoft,' and the other ' Magplatt,' to have &c. to (them), their heirs and assigns, of the chief lord of that fee by the services therefore due and of right accustomed, and they showed their charter in court, of which the date is at Ardelthorp on the Lord's day next after the Feast of All Saints, 14 H. IV., and they did fealty.

From Alice daughter of John Randson for licence to marry   Merchet ij
without the lordship &c.

John de Sybsay chaplain, Wm de Sybsey, and John Everard   Entry ij
&c. surrendered 2 acres in Addlethorpe &c. to the use of John
de More &c.

And now at this court came Mary de Skalfflet, who
makes protestation to sue forth her plaint against W^m
Skekeneys, the tenant before named, in the nature of a plea of
a formedon [form of a gift] in remainder, and demands that the
tenant, before named, be called to answer to her, and upon this
she demands that the bailiff be examined to answer what he has
done in the said plea, and in what manner he summoned the
tenant, who says upon his oath &c. that he alone, and personally, summoned him to answer to the plaintiff, and because the
court nevertheless considered that the tenant was not summoned
upon the land, nor by a summons, but personally, therefore now
at this court nothing is exacted, but it is ordered the bailiff to
summon the tenant by two good and lawful summonses against
the next court, which shall be held on the Thursday next after
the Feast of S. Anne mother of the Virgin at Ingoldmels.

Sum v^s.

Court of (same) held on Thursday next after the Feast of
S. Peter ad Vincula in the 2nd year of the same King [2 August
A.D. 1414].

Robert Purk complains of John Helwys of a plea of trespass,   Plea
pledge to prosecute the bailiff, for that on the Thursday next
before Michaelmas day 1 H. V. the same John trod down, and
destroyed three acres of land, sown with barley and oats, with
his cattle, viz. with 2 oxen, 2 stirks, and 40 sheep, to the
damage of the s^d Robert xx^s, and thereof he produces suit &c.,
and the said John, being present in court, comes, and defends
force, and injury &c., and says that he is not guilty [1] &c.

Mary de Skalflet complains of Wm de Skegnes, sen^r, of a   Plea
plea of land, and makes protestation to sue forth her said plea
in the nature of formedon in remainder, and demands in her
proper person that the s^d W^m be summoned against the next
court according to what the law demands, and finds pledges to
prosecute (2), therefore it is commanded the bailiff that he

----

[1] 12 to be summoned.

summon by good summoners against the next court &c., and
have there then the names of the summoners &c.

Sum xviij^d.

Court of (same) held on Thursday the Vigil of S. Bartholomew, year as above [23 August A.D. 1414].

Merchet xij^d   Agnes daughter of Alan Gryn, a bondwoman of the lord, has
licence to marry Wm Bond of Wynthorp outside the lordship.

Demise   Thomas Hamound and Beatrice his wife surrender ix acres
of pasture in Ingoldmels with one messuage¹ &c., for a certain
portion of money, to the use of John Lawys, to have from
Christmas next to the end of 4 years, and if it happen that the
said ix acres with messuage shall be lost by the flow of the sea,
or in any other manner, so that the s^d John Lawys shall not
be able to enjoy (the same) during the said term, and if by
chance it happen that the s^d John Lawys, his heirs or executors,
shall be prevented from any way peaceably holding the said ix
acres &c., then the s^d Thomas and Beatrice will, and grant, that
the s^d Thomas, his heirs and executors, shall have, and retain
the said ix acres &c. for the term of ij years next following
after the term of the s^d iiij years, and the s^d Thomas and Beatrice,
their heirs or executors, shall support all charges and services
before due and accustomed.

Sum viij^s.

Court of (same) held on Thursday next before the Feast of
the Exaltation of the Holy Cross [13 September A.D. 1414].

Merchet viij^d   Alice daughter of Robert White, a bondwoman of the lord,
has licence to marry Thomas West of Andirby.

Respite   A day is given between Mary de Scalflet, plaintiff, and W^m
de Skegnes sen^r, tenant, until the next court in the same state
as now of a plea of land.

Entry   John son of John Dodyk of Addlethorpe, a bond tenant of s^d John Dodyk, the father, to hold of the lord in bondage according to the custom of the manor for (her) whole life, the reversion &c. belonging to the s^d John, brother of Joan, to have &c. the s^d reversion, when it shall happen, to (him) and his heirs of the lord &c.

Gilbert Dokytt surrenders ij acres pasture in Ingoldmels to the use of John son of Robert Smyth, to have &c. to him, and his heirs, after a term of x years next following, of the lord in bondage according to the custom of the manor, doing all charges and services before due and accustomed.   Entry ij^a

Sum vj^s iiij^d.

Total ix^{li} ix^s vij^d.

Court of (same) held on Thursday next after the Feast of S. Peter ad Vincula, year 2nd [2 August A.D. 1414].

Mary de Scalflet complains of Wm de Skegnes, sen^r, (as above except that date of the court is given, viz. Thursday the Vigil of St. Bartholomew).   Complaint

On which day it was testified by the bailiff that Wm de Skegnes, sen^r, was summoned, as regards land, which Mary de Scalflet demands against (him) by (2), on which day (he) the tenant &c. was essoined by &c., upon which essoin being adjudged, and sworn, a day is given to the parties at the next court to be held on the Thursday before the Exaltation of the Holy Cross.

On which day appeared as well the plaintiff, as the tenant, to whom it was commanded by rule of the court that the pl^t demonstrate her complaint which she has against the tenant, which complaint having been heard, and the defence made, the record is written in these words: Mary de Scalflet demands against Wm Skegnes, sen^r, one messuage, 8½ acres of bond land in Ingoldmells, because she says that Alan Poleyn, and Joan, formerly daughter of Alan Est, kinswoman of the s^d Mary, whose heir she is, were seised in their demesne in bondage of the s^d (tenements) on the day they died, as of fee tail, to them and the heirs of their bodies lawfully begotten, and, if it happen that they die without (such) heirs, then the said messuage, with appurtenances, to remain to the right heirs of the said Alan for ever. And because the s^d Alan and Joan died without (such) heirs comes one Mary de Scalflet, now the plaintiff, as kinswoman and next heir of Alan, viz. daughter of Walter Poleyn, brother of Alan Poleyn, nephew of Alan Poleyn aforenamed, to whom the messuage with appurtenances remains, and says that the s^d W^m unjustly deforced her of the messuage with 8½ acres.

Which plea having been made the tenant demanded a view, therefore it is ordered the bailiff that he cause him to have a view against the next court to be held at Ingoldmels on Thursday after Michaelmas. On which day it was testified by the bailiff that he caused Wm de Skegnes to have a view by (2) of the land, which Mary de Scalflet demands against him, on which day the s^d W^m, the tenant &c., is essoined by John Randson of the view, and so through the essoin a day is given to the parties until the next court to be held on the Thursday next after the Feast of the Apostles Simon and Jude.[1]

Ingoldmels. Michaelmas View of the lord Henry Archbishop of Canterbury and his fellows feoffees of the lord King Henry son of King Henry of his Duchy of Lancaster held at Skegnes on the Wednesday next after the Feast of S. Dionisius (Oct. 9) in the 6th year of the same King [12 October A.D. 1418].

Inquisition[2] of free [tenants] (names given).

Inquisition of bond tenants (names given).

Mercy v^s x^d

Who[3] present that Robert Barbour and John Westyby forestalled herrings at Skegnes, so that the neighbours of the country adjacent were not able to buy except through them, therefore &c.: also that Robert Mawnus of Burgh, and others their neighbours threatened presenters of the manor of Ingoldmels, viz. William Pullayn and others, so that they did not dare to present defaults there, therefore they are in mercy.

Mercy iiij^s x^d

The inquisition of free tenants, being sworn, present, and affirm all the above presentments, and say that John Burgh of Skegnes, one of the presenters, ought to come to present, and has not &c.: also that the feoffees of Robert Marys, Dionisius Petyclerk, (and 16 others), also that the tenants of the lands of Henry Vavasour, of Ralph Dawbenay, of Robert Gaskryk, of Robert Salfletby, of the lord de la Souche ought to come, and have not, therefore &c.

Mercy iiij^d

The tasters of beer present that (2 persons) would not send to have their beer tasted, therefore &c.

[1] There appears to have been another piece of parchment fastened to this, but now lost.

[2] Fresh names. *Liberi.* Thomas Watecroft. John Smythe. Robert Barbour. Simon May, Alan Kygs, John F·
Natini T·

Alice relict of Robert Whyte surrendered 1 messuage, 6½   Fine ij*
acres, which she had of the gift of the s[d] Robert for her life, to
the use of Simon (their) son, and the lord granted the (same) to
Simon, to hold &c. for the life of the s[d] Alice, rendering therefore yearly to (her) xx[s] &c. (power to distrain).

Simon Helyssay was elected to the office of grave &c. : John   Election
Orby and W[m] Smyth to taste beer, and sworn.   of
                                                           ministers
Sum xiij[s] ij[d].

Court held at Ingoldmels on Wednesday next after the Feast
of All Saints, year as above [2 November A.D. 1418].[1]

W[m] Skalflete, John his brother, and Walter Cardewax, executors of the will of Alan Skalflete and of Mary his wife, complain of Richard Grynne, Thomas Norman, and Simon Thomlynson of a plea of debt.
Sum ij[s] iiij[d].

Court held at Ingoldmels on Wednesday the Feast of S.
Clement the Pope, year as above [23 November A.D. 1418].

Simon Newcome, chaplain of Mumby, executor of the will of   The law
Simon Newcome, complains of John Skendylby of Grymysby of
2 pleas of debt, pledge to prosecute the bailiff, and in one plaint
he demands xxx[s], which he owes him as of the debt of the said
Simon, which he ought to have paid him &c., and did not pay,
but unjustly detained, and as yet detains, to the damage of xij[d],
and the s[d] John, being present in court in his proper person,
says that he owes him nothing, and this he offers to verify by
his law, and he found John Orby and Simon Hellyssay, pledges
to do his law, and he has a day on Wednesday next before the
Feast of the Conception next 12 handed.
Sum ij[s].

Court held at Skegnes on Wednesday next after the Conception &c., year as below [14 December A.D. 1418].

John Grayfe of Hoggesthorp demands against John Burgh   Mercy ij[d]
of Skegnes xj[s] viij[d] for cheese sold him, and it is testified by xij
jurors that the s[d] John Burgh owes him the said money &c.

Simon Newcome, chaplain, plaintiff, v. John Skendylby,
defendant, of Grymysby, proffers essoin by John Couper, and

<hr/>

[1] Mare and foal worth 13[s] 4[d].

the s⁰ John Skendylby alleged that the s⁰ essoin would not lie because the s⁰ Simon the plᶠ was seen in court &c., and so it is testified by the court that the s⁰ Simon is not present, therefore the s⁰ plᶠ is in mercy and the defᵗ is without a day.

Sum iijˢ iiijᵈ.

Court held at Ingoldmels on Wednesday next after Christmas, year as within [28 December A.D. 1418].

John Burgh of Skegnes complains of John Grayfe of Hoggesthorp of a plea of broken agreement, wherein he complains that the said John Grayfe sold to him cl pounds of cheese under this condition that it should be good, and it was not, to the damage of the s⁰ plᶠ cˢ, and the s⁰ defᵗ says that he did not *Venire fac* sell to him under the said condition &c., and he demands that this be inquired, and the plᶠ likewise, so it is ordered the bailiff that he cause xij to come.

Fine viijˢ John Palmer surrenders 1 messuage, 7½ acres in Ardelthorp to the use of Wᵐ Skegnes, Wᵐ German, John Dofdyke, and Robert Slyhed, and the lord granted (them) to (the same) &c.

Sum xijˢ.

Court held at Ingoldmels on Wednesday after the Feast of S. Hilary, vj H. V. [18 January A.D. 1418-9].

Marriage Idonea daughter of Simon Bayly of Wytherne, by her *xxᵈ* attorney Thomas Norman, comes into court, and asks licence to marry John Smythe, and she gives the lord for the licence &c.

Sum vˢ.

Court held at Ingoldmells on Wednesday 1ˢᵗ March 6 H. V. [A.D. 1418-9].

Fine Alan Kemp of Ingoldmells, a bond tenant of the lord, de-*vjˢ viijᵈ* mised, and to farm let to John Asche and Simon Tewar of Spyllysby ij places of pasture in the parish of Wylughby, containing ix acres &c. (for 14 years).

Sum xˢ.

Court held at Skegnes on Wednesday in the 3ʳᵈ week of Lent, year as above [22 March A.D. 1418-9].[1]

Court held at Ingoldmells on Wednesday 5ᵗʰ April 7 H. V. [A.D. 1419].

Sum ij˙ viij^d.

Court held at Burgh on Thursday in Easter Week, 7 H. V. [20 April A.D. 1419].

Sum iij˙ x^d.

Easter View of the lord the King held at Burgh on the Saturday next after the Feast of S. George, 7 H. V. [26 April A.D. 1419].

Great jury of free [tenants].

Jury of bond tenants.

The free tenants present that John Burgh of Skegnes, and (2 others) brewed and sold contrary to the assise. *Mercy xxiij^d*

The bond tenants present that, as to ij acres j rood, with a messuage, of which they are charged by the steward, and by the assent of Wᵐ German and Wᵐ Manby, in whose hands the sᵈ ij acres &c. are, which &c. John Lamb recovered by default against Alan Aldyad, that Wᵐ German have thereof iij roods with the messuage, and that Wᵐ Manby have thereof j acre and a half &c. *Partition*

Also that Matilda Franke of Burgh died seised of ij acres of free pasture in Burgh, which are held of the lord by suit of court and jᵈ rent, therefore it is ordered to seize it, saving the right to every one. *Seizure*

Also that Joan Dofdyke, who held of the lord 1 messuage, ix acres of bond land and pasture, is dead, and that Thomas son of Robert Schaft of Candelsby, Matilda daughter of Wᵐ Dofdyke, and Agnes daughter of the same Wᵐ Dofdyke, wife of Wᵐ Stokman of Little Steypng, are the next heirs, to have the sᵈ land, and it is ordered to seize it, saving the right of every one. *Seizure*

Also that Robert Ulryke of Hellysay in the parish of Mumby came at Ingoldmels about the Feast of the Purification, and there took and carried away j [ruthyr] rudder, worth xij^d, coming up of wreck of the sea, without licence. Also that Joan wife of Simon Humfray, Alice daughter of Thomas Chelys, the servants of Wᵐ de Welle, cut the sines on the meles contrary to the custom of the manor. *Mercy iiij^d* *Mercy vj^d*

Also that a certain common way at the east end of Lerthorp-gate is defective, and ought and used to be repaired by the *Mercy ij˙*

township of Burgh, who have their way there, therefore (the township) is in mercy, and nevertheless it is ordered that it be amended against the next court under the penalty of x⁴.

Sum vij⁵ v⁴.

Court held at Ingoldmells on Wednesday next before the Ascension, year as above [24 May A.D. 1419].

Mercy ij⁴ Alan Lowys of Ingoldmells complains of John Couper of Ingoldmells of a plea of debt, wherein he complains that whereas the s⁴ John became pledge, and undertook to pay to the s⁴ Alan vij⁵ iiij⁴ for Robert Pratt of Burgh &c., and he has not paid, to the damage of the s⁴ plꝰ xij⁴, and thereof &c., and the s⁴ John, being present in court, was not able to deny, therefore it was considered by the court that he recover the debt, and the s⁴ John is in mercy.

Fine ij⁵ John Couper of Ingoldmells demised &c. to John Carter of Wynthorp 2 acres of arable land in Addlethorpe (for 3 years) &c.

Sum iiij⁵ ij⁴.

Court held at Burgh on Wednesday in the week of Pentecost, 7 H. V. [7 June A.D. 1419].

As yet of the court held at Burgh &c.[1]

Matilda Rabyn, John Rabyn, and Wᵐ Rabyn of Wynthorp, executors of the will of Robert Rabyn of Wynthorp, by their attorney John at fflete, offered themselves against John prior of Bolyngton in a plea of ij debts, and demand &c.

Mercy ij⁴ Which said John the abovesaid prior came into court &c., and says that he owes him nothing &c., and this he is prepared to verify with his xij^th hand, viz. John prior of Catle [Catteley], Domꝰ Stephen Cellarer of Bolyngton, Richard Brygge vicar of Burgh, Dionisius Petyclerk of the same place, Robert Cawton, Robert Mawnus, John Thorelande, Wᵐ Caleflete, Thomas Watecroft, John Helwys of Burgh, John Alanson of Burgh, and John Bayly of Bolyngton, and so the said John prior of Bolyngton goes away quit, and the s⁴ plꝰ is in mercy for an unjust claim.

Mercy ij⁴ It is found by the inquisition, upon which Wᵐ Skalflete.

[1] 20 sheep worth xx⁵.

John Skalflete, and Walter Cardevax, ex^{ors} of the will of Alan Skalflete, pl^{fs}, and Richard Grynne, Thomas Norman, and Simon Thomlynson, ex^{ors} of the will of Wm Thory of Halton, def^{ts}, put themselves in a plea of debt, that the s^d pl^{fs} shall recover against the said def^{ts} xxxvj^s viij^d, and iij^s iiij^d for damages, and def^{ts} are in mercy.[1]

Thomas Marays son of Robert Marays of Ingoldmells, and Wm Sybsay of Ingoldmells came into court, and claim to hold of the lord j messuage, xij acres of land and pasture in Ingoldmells, of the gift and feoffment of John Sybsay, chaplain, and Wm Botyrkake, as in a certain charter &c. is more fully contained, of which the date was at Ingoldmels, 1 June 7 H. V., and they did fealty.   *Fealty*

Sum iij^s ij^d.

Court held at Burgh on Wednesday next after the Feast of the Apostles Peter and Paul, year as above [5 July A.D. 1419].[2]

John Burgh of Skegnes surrendered all the lands &c.,   *Fine* which he has on the present day in the vills of Skegnes,   *xiij^s iiij^d* Waynflete, and Wynthorp &c., and the lord grants (them) to the s^d John for (his) life, to hold according to the custom of the manor, and after (his) death to Simon (his) son, and his heirs, to hold &c. according to the custom of the manor for ever &c.

The presenters of the manor present that, whereas Robert   *Fine iiij^d* Marays of Ingoldmells was seised of 1 messuage, and 29 acres, 3 roods of land and pasture in Ingoldmells and Wynthorp, called Lamberdland, and by the licence of the court demised (the same) to Wm Botyrkake and Wm Skegnes for the term of 4 years, and after the term &c. to remain to the right heirs of the same Robert, to hold &c., and that the s^d term was completed at Christmas last. And Thomas, son and heir of the s^d Robert, comes into court, and asks to be admitted, and is admitted, to hold according to the custom of the manor.

Wm Skegnes of Ingoldmells, and Robert German, and John   *Fine v^s*

Plaint   John Rotheram of Boston and Alice his wife complain of Wm German of Ingoldmels of a plea of land, and make protestation to sue forth their plaint in the nature of a plaint for entry at a term which has passed, and they find pledges (2), and they ask that the s^d Wm German be summoned, as the custom of this court demands and requires, to the next court, and this by a good summons.

Sum vj^{li} ij^s x^d.

Court held at Ingoldmels on Wednesday next before the Feast of S. Mary Magdalen, year as above [19 July A.D. 1419].

Fine xl^d   Richard Grynne &c. demised to Robert Slyhed, and Wm German, 5 acres of pasture with a messuage in Ingoldmels (for 10 years) &c. And the s^d Richard shall do all the charges and services incumbent on the s^d land &c. during the s^d term, except the cleaning and repair of dikes, and a certain burden of right usual in a certain place called Sandryg, as often as it shall be necessary, which same burdens the s^d Robert and W^m during the s^d term shall support.

Mercy ij^d   The tasters of beer present that the wife of Robert Herryson refused to sell her beer to be tasted by the same &c., and is not willing to expose the sign called Alestake, therefore &c.

Sum vj^s vj^d.

Court held at Ingoldmels on Wednesday before the Feast of S. Lawrence, year as above [9 August A.D. 1419].

Mercy ij^d   Wm Skalflete complains of Wm Godard of a plea of debt, and demands iiij^s &c., and the s^d W^m, being present in court, is not able to deny, therefore it is considered by the court that the s^d pl^f recover &c.

Fine xij^d   Wm Stutvyle &c. surrendered ½ rood in Ingoldmels to the use of John Helwys of Burgh, Robert Slyhed of Ingoldmels, and John Smythe of Ingoldmels &c.

Fine viij^d

Amicia wife of Robert Tymson of Spyllysby complains of Attach-
John Skalflete of Ingoldmels of a plea of debt. ment

John Skendylby of Grymysby is in mercy for default Mercy ij^d
against John Alanson of Burgh of a plea of debt.

Sum iij^s.

Court held at Ingoldmels on Wednesday next before the
Feast of S. Matthew the Apostle, year as below [27 September
A.D. 1419].

John Skalflete of Ingoldmels is in mercy for default v. Mercy ij^d
Amicia wife of Robert Tymson of Spyllysby of a plea of debt.

Sum iij^s ij^d.

Sum of all these Halmotes ix^{li} xij^s ix^d.

Also of fines for release of suit of court xxxvj^s.

Court held at Ingoldmels on Wednesday next after the
Feast of Corpus Christi, 8 Henry V. [12 June A.D. 1420].[1]

Wm Godarde of Ingoldmels comes into court and asks licence Marriage
to marry Margaret his daughter to Robert Barbour of Burgh, xviij^d
and gives &c.

The presenters of the manor present that Thomas Toppyng Mercy ij^d
of Burgh, smyth, unjustly defamed the officers of the lord the
king at Skegnes, saying that they held there a false measure to
the deception of the people, therefore he is in mercy.

Sum iij^s iiij^d.

Court held at Ingoldmels on Wednesday next after the
Feast of the Apostles Peter and Paul, year as above [3 July
A.D. 1420].

Margaret daughter of Robert Whyte of Ingoldmels, a bond- Marriage
woman of the lord, asks licence to marry John Selby of xviij^d
Markeby &c.

Sum iij^s ij^d.

Court held at Skegnes on Wednesday next after th

rendered 1 acre viij perches of arable land in Ingoldmels &c., and the lord granted the s^d land to (her) for life &c., and after (her) death to John Dofdyke, son of the s^d John Dofdyke and Agnes, his heirs and assigns, to hold &c.

Sum iij^s iiij^d.

Court held at Skegnes on Wednesday next after the Feast of the Assumption, year as within [21 August A.D. 1420].

Sum xvj^d.

Court held at Ingoldmels on Wednesday next before the Feast of the Nativity of S. Mary, year as within [4 September A.D. 1420].

Sum xij^d.

Court held at Ingoldmels on Wednesday next before the Feast of S. Michael the Archangel, year as below [25 September A.D. 1420].

Mercy iiij^d — Wm Watkynson and Robert, presenters of the manor, have not come to present divers defaults, therefore &c.

Sum xxij^d.

Sum of all these courts xj^{li} xx^d.
Item of fines for suit xlvj^s iiij^d.
Item of new rent xxij^d.

Ingoldmels. Court held there on Wednesday next after the Feast of the Assumption, 9 Henry V. [20 August A.D. 1421].

Fealty — Simon May of Burgh, John Robertson, smyth of Ingoldmels, John Wynthorp, and Wm Hamond of Skegnes, chaplain, come into court, and claim to hold of the lord certain lands, and tenements, of the gift and feoffment of Alan Kygg of Ingoldmels, as in a certain charter is more fully contained, of which the date is 20 June, 9 Henry V., and they did fealty.

Marriage xviij^d — Isabel daughter of Alan Aldyad, a bond tenant of the lord, comes into court and asks licence to marry Wm Watkynson of Ingoldmels &c.

Sum ij^s.

Court held at Skegnes on Wednesday next after the Nativity of S. Mary, year as above [10 September A.D. 1421].

Sum x^d.

Court held at Skegnes on Wednesday next before the Feast of S. Michael, year as above [24 September A.D. 1421].

Robert Ose of Ingoldmels comes into court, and claims to hold of the lord in bondage 1½ acres &c., which descended to him by right of inheritance after the death of Richard Ose (his) brother, and he is admitted &c.

Fine iij⁵ iiij⁴

The presenters of the manor present that Wᵐ Godard of Ingoldmels, a bond tenant of the lord, who held of the lord on the day he died 69½ acres in Ingoldmels, and 5 acres, called Bugland, in Ingoldmels, and the reversion of a certain place of land called Toyntonland after the death of Stephen Toynton, chaplain, and Isabel mother of the sᵈ Stephen, [is dead], and that John (his) son is his next heir, who comes into court and asks to be admitted &c., and he does not give more now of fine than x marks because 5 acres are inundated by the sea, and 20 acres are let for certain years.

Fine lxvj⁵ viij⁴

Also that Wᵐ son of Alan Croft surrendered his whole right &c. in 1½ acres.

Fine viij⁴

Also that Alice wife of Simon Lowys in presence of xij of the homage surrendered the reversion of 3 acres, with a cottage, after the death of the sᵈ Simon Lowys, and the lord grants (it) to Robert Jakson, and Robert Gunny &c.

Fine iij⁵ iiij⁴

Also that Wᵐ son of Alan Croft in the presence of xij of the homage surrendered the reversion of 7½ acres after the term of vj years to the use of Robert Cowton of Burgh after the death of Wᵐ Dodyke, which term John Dodyke and John Hogge have of the grant of the lord, and of the said Wᵐ Dodyke &c. And the lord grants the sᵈ reversion to the sᵈ Robert Cowton &c.

Fine ij⁵

Sum lxxj⁵.

Sum total of these courts xvj¹¹ xvij⁴.

Ingoldmels. View of the lord Henry Archbishop of Canterbury and his fellows, feoffees of the lord King Henry V. of his Duchy of Lancaster, held at Burgh on Saturday next after the Feast of S. Dionisius in the 9ᵗʰ year of the same King [11 October A.D. 1421].

Ingoldmels. Wm Sybsay of same. Robert at Hall of Burgh. John Burton of Wynthorp. John Wynthorp of Wynthorp. Wm Stutvyle of Orby.

Inquisi-
tion of
bond
tenants

Richard Grynne of Ingoldmels. Thomas Norman of Ingoldmels. Robert Jakson of Ingoldmels. Wm Skegnes of same. Thomas Hewson of same. Wm Skalflete of same. Wm Pullayn of Burgh. Robert German of Ingoldmels. Wm Gyllyotson of same. Robert Hallegarthe of Ingoldmels. John Kemp of same. Simon White of same.

The bond tenants present that John Westmels of Skegnes brewed and sold contrary to the assize.

Office

Also Wm Thory was elected to the office of grave &c.

Mercy
iiij^s viij^d

The free tenants present, and say that they have nothing else to present than the s^d bond tenants have presented, but they say that Henry Johnson of Thorp, Thomas Taylor of Aswardby, tenants of the lands of Henry Vavaser, of Ralph Dawbenay, of Robert Salfletby, of Robert Gaskrike, and the prior of Bolyngton ought to come &c.

Fine xl^s

The presenters of the manor presented that Wm Wythson, a bond tenant of the lord, who held of the lord in Ingoldmels 1 messuage xxxv acres, is dead, but whether he died seised, or not, they do not know. And afterwards came Richard Grynne and others, and claimed part of the s^d tenements for a term of years by the licence of the court, and called to warrant the rolls of the court, and had a day to show &c., and into the present court come Robert Maunus, and Agnes his wife, daughter and heir of the s^d W^m, and ask that they be admitted &c., and are &c. to (them) and the heirs of Agnes, saving always the right and term of Richd Grynne &c.

Sum xlvj^s vj^d beyond the fines as by schedule annexed.

Court held at Ingoldmels on Wednesday after the Feast of All Saints, year as above [5 November A.D. 1421].

Wm Kyng of Skegnes offered himself against John Maryot of Ingoldmels in a plea of trespass &c., and therein he complains that the said John with his cattle divers times this year violated, and destroyed the meadow of the s^d W^m, to (his) damage x^s &c., and the s^d John, being present in court, defended the said trespass against him and his suit, and says that in nothing is he guilty &c., and he demands that this be inquired, and the plᶠ likewise, therefore let an inquisition &c.

Thomas son of Robert Schaft of Candelsby surrenders 9 acres in Ingoldmels, wʰ descended to him by right of inheritance after the death of Matilda, daughter of Wᵐ Dodyke, and mother of the same Thomas, to the use of Wᵐ Botyrkake and John son of Richard Grynne (for 4 years).

Fine xlᵈ

Sum vˢ xᵈ.

Court held at Ingoldmels on Wednesday next after the Feast of S. Katherine the Virgin, year as within [26 November A.D. 1421].

John Randson surrenders ix acres land and pasture, lying in the north field of Burgh &c., and the lord grants (them) to John Dodyke, Robert Grynne son of Alan Grynne, and John Randson, junʳ, son of the sᵈ John R., senʳ, their heirs &c.[1]

Fine vjˢ viijᵈ

Sum ixˢ.

Court held at Ingoldmels on Wednesday after the Feast of S. Lucy the Virgin, year as below [17 December A.D. 1421].

The presenters of the manor present one boat, coming up of wreck of the sea upon the soil of the lord at Skegnes, and upon this comes John Stalyngburgh of Hornyssebecke, and claims the sᵈ boat &c., and it is delivered to (him), and he gives the lord for groundage &c.

Ground-age ijˢ vjᵈ

As yet of the court. Wᵐ Cobbe of Skegnes, junʳ, by licence of the lord demises &c. to John Smythe 1½ acres in Ingoldmels (for xj years) &c.

Sum iiijˢ vjᵈ.

Court held at Burgh on Wednesday next after the Epiphany, 9 H. V. [7 January A.D. 1421–2].

Sum ijˢ viijᵈ.

Court held at Burgh on Wednesday next before the Purification, year as above [28 January A.D. 1421–2].[2]

Agnes Lockyn of Wynthorp, executrix of the will of John

Plaint

---

[1] Considered by the court that Alan Kygs recover xxvjˢ viijᵈ.
[2] 20 sheep worth 40ˢ.

Lockyn, complains of Walter Tutte of the same in a plea of detention, pledge &c.

Sum ij^s iiij^d.

Court held at Ingoldmels on Wednesday in the 3rd week of Lent, year as above [17 March A.D. 1421-2].

Mercy ij^d Walter Tutte of Wynthorp put himself in mercy against Agnes Locking in a plea of debt.

Wm Thory of Ingoldmels, pl^f, offered himself against John Cokke of a plea of broken agreement, wherein he complains that whereas (they) were agreed in all manner of trespasses between them moved &c. by the arbitration of Thomas Rygge of Welton, and Richard Grynne of Ingoldmels, afterwards contrary to the same agreement the s^d John Cokke prosecuted the s^d W^m by a writ, to (his) damage xx^s, and thereof &c., and the s^d John Cokke **Venire fac** &c. says that in nothing is he guilty &c., and this he puts upon the country to inquire &c., wherefore an inquisition.

Fine vj^s viij^d John Burgh of Skegnes and Simon his son surrender 2 acres in Skegnes to the use of Wm Kyng of Skegnes &c.

Fine ij^s (The same) surrender 2 acres pasture in Skegnes, called Ingrenes, on the north of the kyrkegarth of Skegnes, to the use of John Watlade in exchange for 2 acres (for ix years) &c. It is found by the inquisition, upon which Wm Wyhum, pl^f, and Elizabeth Pullayn, def^t of a plea of trespass, put themselves, that the s^d Elizabeth unjustly drove his beasts out of the pasture of the s^d W^m, for that the s^d W^m was always prepared to pay the rent due for the same pasture, therefore the same Elizabeth is in mercy.

Fine xiij^s iiij^d Simon Burgh &c. surrenders [1] all his lands &c. in Skegnes and Wynthorp with all appurtenances, and reversions &c. to the use of Wm Hamond, chaplain of Skegnes, and John Sybsay, chaplain of Ingoldmels, and John Smyth, to do and perform the will of the same Simon &c.

Fine xl^d John Couper &c. surrenders 1½ acres of pasture on the north part of the West Church of Ingoldmels to the use of John Kemp in exchange for 1½ acres of arable &c.[2]

Sum xxx^s x^d.

[1] xj acres land and pasture in Skegnes and vij acres pasture in Wynthorp.

[2] Provision that if lands granted to John Kemp and wife be distrained upon for any debt of John Couper or for rent they may distrain upon all his lands in Ingoldmels.

John Kemp surrenders 1½^a arable to use of John Couper in exchange.

Court held at Ingoldmels on Wednesday before Easter, 10 H. V. [8 April A.D. 1422].[1]

John Marchal of Ingoldmels complains of John Pyper of Burgh of a plea of debt &c., and he demands xxij^d, which he owes him for j horse &c.   *Venire fac*

Robert Jakson, and Robert Coper surrender 5 perches of arable in Ingoldmels to the use of Alan Kemp and Alice his wife, and the lord grants (them) to (them) for a term of x years, to carry out the last will of John Julotson, late the husband of the same Alice, which is this, that all the debts of the same John be well and faithfully paid, and well and faithfully to fulfil this (they) found pledges &c.   *Fine* xviij^d

It is found by the inquisition, upon which Wm Thory, plaintiff, and John Cokke, defendant, put themselves, that the s^d pl^f shall recover from the s^d John xiij^s iiij^d for damages &c., and the def^t is in mercy.   *Mercy* ij^d

Sum vij^s x^d.

View of Frankpledge held at Skegnes on Monday next before the Feast of the Apostles Philip and James, 10 H. V. [27 April A.D. 1422].

Inquisition of free [tenants].

Inquisition of bond tenants.

Robert at Hadyke, and Robert Gunny surrender iij acres pasture with cottage in Ingoldmels to the use of John Mariot, John Smyth, and Simon Whyte &c.   *Fine* v^s

John Godarde gives to the lord lxvj^s viij^d for the remainder of the fine of his land after the death of Wm Godarde his father &c.   *Fine* lxvj^s viij^d

Thomas Alanson surrenders 1 acre pasture in Ingoldmels to the use of Mary daughter of Thomas Rafson of Asfordby (for life, remainder to Thomas Alanson and his heirs).   *Fine* xx^d

Ranulph Raper &c. took of the lord x perches of pasture called 'le fflete' in Ingoldmels &c., to hold according to the custom of the manor of the lord, to (him) and his heirs and assigns for ever.   *Fine* vj^d

John Couper surrenders j acre 3 roods pasture in Ingoldmels &c. to the use of Thomas Norman, and John at fflete &c.   *Fine* iiij^s

John Everarde of Ingoldmels, yoman, outlawed at the suit   *Fine* vj^s viij^d

---

[1] Cow worth 8^s.

of Thomas Hobarde, citizen of London, and Wm Hobarde of Donyngton, gives to the lord of fine for having his goods &c., by the pledge of (2).

Mercy xxij^d

The bond tenants present (7 cases of breaking assizes of bread and beer).

Mercy iij^d

The free tenants present that Thomas Watecroft of Burgh drew blood from Walter Dawson &c.

Also the bond tenants present that Joan wife of Wm Dodyke, who held for life of the grant of the s^d W^m by licence of court ij acres iij roods of land, is dead, and that Thomas son of Robert Schaft of Candelsby as of the right of Matilda his mother, and Agnes wife of Wm Stokman of Little Stepyng are

Fine xl^d

the next heirs to have the s^d land, which same Thomas for his part &c. made fine as appears by the court rolls of last year, and Wm Stokman, as of the right of Agnes his wife, comes into court and asks to be admitted to the other part, and is &c.

Offices

Thomas Hewson and Wm Sybsay are elected to the office of constables, and sworn.

Also the bond tenants present that Wm Skalflete of Ingoldmels in the presence of Wm Thory, the grave, and others of the homage, viz. (12), surrendered his messuage, with all the lands &c., which he has in Ingoldmels and Mumby, containing 22½ acres, and the reversion of 9½ acres after a term of 6 years (to Thomas Norman and Simon Smyth): and the lord granted (the same) to Beatrice late (his) wife from the date of his death for the term of 12 years to carry out (his) last will, which is this, that Joan and Mary (his) daughters shall have from the s^d tenements within the s^d term of 12 years xx^{li} of good and usual English money for their marriage, viz. to each of them x^{li}; and that after the end of the above term then the said Beatrice shall well and faithfully have her dower in all the s^d lands &c., and that immediately upon the elapse of the above term Simon, and Thomas, sons of the s^d Wm Skalflete, shall have all the places of land underwritten, containing 16 acres 20 perches, viz. Scrynenland 2 acres, Chesterland 4 acres, Tappyngland 3½ acres, Pulinstoft 2 acres, Henryplatmagson 1 acre 1 rood, Hareward-toft 2 acres, ffletes 1 acre 1 rood lying next the dwelling house of Alan Kygs, to have &c. to (them), and the heirs of their bodies lawfully begotten, of the lords of this manor according to the custom of the manor for ever, saving to the s^d Beatrice, their mother, her dower in all the s^d

places of land for the term of her life, and, if it shall happen
that either of them die without (such) heir, that then all
the s^d places &c. shall wholly remain to the other surviving,
and to the heirs of his body &c., and if it happen further that
the survivor die without (such) heir, that all the s^d places of
land shall remain to the right heirs of the s^d Wm Skalflete, to
hold &c.

Fine
xxvj^s viij^d

As yet of the Easter View.

Also they present that the feoffees of Simon Sawer of Thorp,
Henry Johnson of the same, John Pullayn, the tenants of the
lands of Henry Vavaser, (and 11 others) ought to come &c.

Mercy xl^d

Sum v^ll xiij^s vij^d.

Court held at Ingoldmels Tuesday 12th May, 10 H. V.
[A.D. 1422].

Robert Herry came into court, and put himself upon the
grace of the lord, for that, after John Helwys, late grave at
Ingoldmels, arrested his beasts upon the 'lez' [leys] of Skegnes
for rent of the same in arrear, the s^d Robert without licence
freed those beasts, and he gives of fine for the trespass.

Mercy iij^d

Sum iiij^s j^d.

Court held at Ingoldmels on Tuesday in the week of Pentecost, year as above [2 June A.D. 1422].

Wm Botyrkake of Ingoldmels, John Godarde, Thomas
Norman, and Simon Walpole, wardens of the West Church of
Ingoldmels, complain of John Skalflete of a plea of debt &c.

Summons

Sum ij^s.

Court held at Ingoldmels on Thursday next after the Feast
of S. Botulph, year as above [25 June A.D. 1422].

John Dodyke of Ingoldmels offered himself against Beatrice
late the wife of Wm Skalflete, wherein he complains that (she)
did not make the fence between the tenements of the s^d John
and (her own), but in default of repair the beasts of the s^d John
strayed out of his pasture, to (his) damage ½ mark, and therein
&c., and the s^d Beatrice, being present in court, says that in
nothing is she guilty, and she demands that this be inquired,
and the pl^f likewise &c.

Venire fac

Magota wife of Simon Thomlynson of Ingoldmels, being diligently examined in the presence of Thomas Halle, clerk of the courts, Wm Thory the grave, and others of the homage &c., surrenders the reversion of 2½ acres pasture in Wynthorp, 1 acre 1 rood of pasture in Ingoldmels, after the death of the s^d Simon Thomlynson to the use of Thomas Norman, and John Smyth &c.

Fine viij^s

Sum ix^s x^d.

Court held at Ingoldmels on Thursday next before the Feast of S. Mary Magdalen, 10 H. V. [23 July A.D. 1422].

Wm Wyhum complains of Elizabeth daughter of John Pullayn of a plea of trespass &c., and therein he complains that on 6th April 10 H. V. (she) came unto (his) tenements in Ingoldmels, and there took one horse of (his), and unjustly without cause drove it away, and detained it &c., to (his) damage xl^s, and therein &c., and the s^d Elizabeth by her attorney, John Muriel of Bratoft, comes, and defends injury, and admits the taking of the s^d horse &c., and says that she took the s^d horse for vij^s vj^d of rent of assize of the same tenement being in arrear at the term of S. Botulph last &c., and so in nothing is she guilty, and the s^d Wm Wyhum says that he was always, and is prepared to pay the rent due and of old usual, and says that (she) desires more rent for the s^d tenements than of right she ought to receive, and this he is prepared to verify by the country, and the s^d Elizabeth by her attorney says that she does not claim more rent than the same Elizabeth and her predecessors, viz. John Polayn and other bond tenants of this manor, had, and were in possession of &c., by the hand of the s^d W^m

Venire fac Wyhum, and she demands that this be inquired, and the pl^f likewise &c.

John at fflete offered himself against the abovesaid Elizabeth Pullayn in a plea of trespass, and therein he complains that (she) came to a certain place of land of the same John at Ingoldmels, called les fforthyngrygges, and there took, and unjustly drove away one bay (horse), worth xiij^s iiij^d, of the s^d John, to (his) damage ij^s, and (she) by her attorney defends &c., and says that she took the s^d horse for ix^d of rent of assize of the same land, and of a parcel of pasture, called les hylles &c., and so in nothing is guilty, and says that (she) and her predecessors, viz. John Pullayn and other bond tenants of the lord, were in possession of the s⁴ rent, and payment, by the hand of the s⁴ John, and the lord was seised of the s⁴ John Pullayn, his bond tenant, and this &c., and the s⁴ John at fflete says that they never were in possession &c., but by oppression and coercion, and he demands that this be inquired by the country &c. Venire fac

John Couper surrenders 1½ acres in Ingoldmels &c. to the use of John Kemp &c., and the s⁴ John Couper and his heirs undertake to pay vjˢ by the year, which rent Amicia daughter of Robert Skalflete shall receive yearly from the s⁴ lands for the term of her life, and if the s⁴ rent of vjˢ be in arrear &c., so that the s⁴ Amicia distrain on the s⁴ land, then the s⁴ John Couper by the licence of the lord grants that it shall be allowed to the s⁴ John Kemp, his heirs and assigns, to distrain on all the lands of the s⁴ John Couper within this lordship for the s⁴ rent and damages &c. Fine iiijˢ

Robert Ose surrendered 1½ acres of arable land &c. to the use of John at fflete &c. Fine iiijˢ

Alan Grynne, a bond tenant of the lord, comes into court and asks licence to marry Matilda his daughter to Henry Taylor of London.[1] Marriage xl⁴

As yet of the court.

John Monkys of Wynthorp, chaplain, by his attorney complains of John Burgh of Skegnes of a plea of broken agreement, for that the s⁴ John Burgh demised to him a certain pasture at Wynthorp from the Purification last until the same feast next following under the condition that the s⁴ John Burgh shall warrant the s⁴ pasture &c., and so in default of the s⁴ John Burgh the beasts of the plᶠ were driven off, to (his) damage xlˢ, and the s⁴ John Burgh being present in court says that in nothing is he guilty &c., and demands that this be inquired by the country, and the plᶠ likewise, therefore &c. Venire fac

Sum xiijˢ x⁴.

Court held at Ingoldmels on Thursday next before the Feast of S. Lawrence, 10 H. V. [6 August A.D. 1422].

Wᵐ Taylor of Skegnes came into court, and acknowledged that he held of the lord 11 acres pasture in Skegnes of the gift Fealty

John Jaknefe of Wynthorp complains of Walter Tutte of Wynthorp, and demands xviij^d, which he owes him for a sheep

Venire fac sold to him &c.

Wm German complains of Joan Tant of a plea, and demands xiiij^d for his labour in going to harrow &c.

Fine iij^s John Couper surrenders 1 acre pasture in Ingoldmels to the use of John Holand and Alice his wife &c.

Court held at Ingoldmels on Wednesday before the Feast of S. Bartholomew, year as above [19 August A.D. 1422].

Wm Maryot complains of Alan Kygs of a plea of trespass, and therein he complains that, whereas he and his predecessors of right had, and without impediment peacefully continued &c. a way on the east side of the messuage of the s^d Alan unto a certain pasture of the s^d W^m at Ingoldmels &c., until the s^d Alan obstructed the s^d way with a fence and wall, to the damage of the s^d W^m xl^s. And the s^d Alan, being present in court, defends injury against him and his suit, and says that the s^d W^m never had any way in the time of the s^d Alan and his predecessors, as &c., nor had he of right any way on the lands and tenements of the s^d Alan, as the s^d W^m alleges against him, and this he is

Venire fac prepared to verify by the country &c.

Sum ij^s iiij^d.

Court held at Ingoldmels on Thursday after the Exaltation of the Holy Cross, 10 H. V. [17 December A.D. 1422].

Walter Tutte complains of John Jaknefe of a plea of trespass &c., therein he complains that the s^d John with a certain calf continually this year depastured, and violated his pasture at Wynthorp, to (his) damage v^s &c., and the s^d John &c. defends &c., and the bailiff is ordered to cause xij good and lawful

Venire fac men to come, by whom the truth of the matter may be better known.

Venire fac The same Walter Tutte complains of the same John Jaknefe of a plea of debt, and demands xj^d for hay sold to him &c.

Mercy ij^d It is found by the inquisition, upon which John Jaknefe and Walter Tutte put themselves, that the s^d John recover by his plea against the s^d Walter xviij^d, and ij^d for damages, and nevertheless Walter is in mercy.

Mercy ij^d It is found by the inquisition, that John Monkys, chaplain, recover nothing by his plea against John Burgh, but be in mercy for his unjust plaint.

Idonea daughter of John Kemp of Ingoldmels, a bond tenant of the lord, comes into court, and asks a licence to marry Thomas son of Robert Schaft of Candelsby.

Marriage ij

Mary daughter of the s⁴ John Kemp asks a licence to marry John Pose of Hoggysthorp.

Marriage xl⁴

Sum vij˙ iiij⁴.

Sum total of these courts xiij¹¹ vij˙ x⁴.

Item of fines for suit of court

as by schedule annexed xxxix˙ x⁴.

Fines for suit of court released this year, 10 Henry V. [A.D. 1422].

¹ From Alice Skypwyth ij˙, from Thomas Marays vij⁴, from feoffees of Thomas Rygge vj⁴, from Thomas Ruston vj⁴, from feoffees of Matilda Cromwell xij , from Agnes Hyltoft iiij⁴, from feoffees of John Gunby vj⁴, from Elizabeth Pullayn iiij⁴, from Alan Thory vj , from feoffees of Wᵐ Gypthorp esqʳ xij⁴, from tenants of land of (same) xl⁴.

Sum xxxiiij˙ vj⁴.

Foreign fines.

From the abbot of Louth Park xij⁴, from Robert Tyrwyth xij⁴, from tenants of lands of the lord de la Souche xl⁴.

Sum v˙ iiij⁴.

Sum total of fines xxxix˙ x⁴.

² Fines for suit of court released xiij Edward IV. [A.D. 1473].

From tenants of lands late Robert Rigg's vj⁴, from (same) late Simon Ruston's iiij⁴, from heirs of Dionisius Peticlerk iiij⁴, from Wᵐ Babyngton xij⁴, from Thomas Gipthorp iiij⁴, from feoffees of Robert Whetecroft iiij⁴, from Thomas Tottoth iiij⁴, from the Lord de Kyme for tenements late Gilbert Cokeryngton's iiij⁴, from Wᵐ Gunby iiij⁴, from Alice Massyngberd iiij⁴, from Wᵐ son of John Thory iiij⁴.

¹ 80 persons pay.   ² 58 tenants in all.

Foreign.

From heirs of Henry Vavasor xl^d, from the Master of the College of Tatsall xij^d, from the prior of Bolyngton xij^d.

xxv^s ij^d.

Court of the lord Henry Archbishop of Canterbury and his fellow feoffees of the lord King Henry V. of his Duchy of Lancaster held at Ingoldmels on the Thursday next after the Feast of All Saints in the 1st year of the reign of King Henry VI. [5 November A.D. 1422].

Judgment   Thomas Hewson of Ingoldmels demands v. John Couper, jun^r, xiij^s iiij^d, which he owes to him &c., and ought to have paid him &c. and has not paid, but unjustly detained, and still detains to the damage of the s^d plaintiff xl^d, and thereof he produces suit : and the s^d John Couper, being present in court in his proper person, admitted the debt, therefore it is considered **Mercy ij^d** by the court that the s^d plaintiff recover the s^d xiij^s iiij^d, but the damages are condoned by the officer of the court, and the s^d John is in mercy.

Sum x^d.

View of Frankpledge held at Skegnes on the Tuesday the Morrow of S. Hugh the Bishop, 1 Henry VI. [18 November A.D. 1422].

Inquisition of free tenants   John Moryel of Braytoft.   John Burton of Wynthorp. William Stutvyle of Ingoldmells.   Wm Butyrkake of Ingoldmels.   Wm Sybsay of Ingoldmels.   John Barleburgh of Skegnes.   Robert Magnus of Burgh.   Robert Slyhed of Ingoldmels. Simon May of Burgh.   Alan Kygs of Ingoldmels.   John Hogg of Ingoldmels.   Wm Wyhum of Ingoldmels.

Inquisition of bond tenants   Richard Grynne of Ingoldmels.   Wm Skegnes of Ingoldmels. Robert Hallegarth of Ingoldmels.   John Godarde of Ingoldmels. John Dodyke of Ingoldmels.   John at fflete of Ingoldmels.   Wm Pullayn of Burgh.   John Kemp of Ingoldmels.   John Maryot of Ingoldmels.   Robert German of Ingoldmels.   Thomas Hewson of Ingoldmels.   Wm Robertson Maryot of Ingoldmels.

Fealty   John Maysterson of Netylton came into court, and acknowledged that he held of the lords certain lands and tenements in Dunham by suit of court, and he did fealty : and he made fine for respite of suit of court until Michae̲l   next, and gives of fine xx^d, and not more, because the tenants of the land of Robert Blyton hold the moiety of the tenements late Robert Gaskeryke's, and the abbot of Kyrkestede the residue, whom it is ordered to distrain for fealty and other services.

Also John Harpyswelle of Toftnewton came into court, and acknowledged that he held of the lords certain lands and tenements in Toftnewton, formerly Robert Salfletby's, and he did fealty &c. (fine xx^d for respite of suit).

The tasters of beer present that Elizabeth Ingrayne refused Mercy ij^d to send for them to taste her beer, therefore &c.

The bond tenants present that Elizabeth Ingrayne baked Mercy xx^d bread and sold it contrary to the assize, therefore &c.

Also that a certain sewer at Burgh called Chalunettyngs is Mercy vj^d defective, and not repaired, and ought to be repaired by Richard Brygge, vicar of Burgh, therefore he is in mercy : and it is ordered that it be mended against the next court under the penalty of xl^d.

Also they elect Wm Kyng of Skegnes to the office of grave Election of officers this year, and he is sworn : also Wm Toke and John Skalflete to the office of tasting beer, and they are sworn.

The free tenants present, and affirm all the above presentments Mercy viij^d as true, and further they present that the tenants of the land of Henry Vavaser, and the prior of Bolyngton ought to come &c.

Beatrice, late wife of John Kemp of Ingoldmels, &c. surrendered 1 messuage 6½ acres in Ingoldmels to the use of Robert Grynne, Thomas Westhend, and John Randson, jun^r, after the death of the s^d John Kemp : and the lords granted to (them) this reversion &c. for xl years to fulfil the last will of the s^d Beatrice, and after the term &c. (the lands) shall fully remain to the right heirs of the s^d Beatrice to hold of the lords of the Entry x^s manor according to the custom of the manor for ever &c.

John son of Wm Modland, a bond tenant of the lord, came Fine v^s into court, and surrendered 3 acres with a cottage in Ingoldmels &c. to the use of Alan Kygs, Robert Slyhed, and John Smyth &c.

The presenters of the manor present that Beatrice, late the wife Fine xl^d of John Kempe, &c. surrendered 2 acres in Ingoldmels to the use of John Randson jun^r, and Alice his wife, daughter of the s^d Beatrice, after the death of the s^d John Kempe (reversion if Alice died without heirs of her body to right heirs of Beatrice).

Also that Thomas Norman surrendered 2 acres in Ingoldmels, Fine xij^d of which 1 acre lies in the waste land at Cokhyl, to the use of

Robert Jakson, Robert Gunny, Robert German, and Wm Smyth of Kyrkeby &c., and they give of fine xij^d, and not more because it is wasted by the sea.

Sum xj^s iiij^d.

Court held at Ingoldmels on Tuesday next after the Feast of S. Thomas the Apostle, year as above [22 December A.D. 1422].

Fine xij^d   John Couper, jun^r, surrenders 1 selion of arable land, lying in a certain place called Southcroft, containing by estimation 1½ roods, to the use of John Dodyke (and 2 others) &c.

John Couper, jun^r, by licence of the lords remised &c. to Alan Thory, son and heir of Wm Thory, his whole right &c. in an annual rent of iij^d, which &c. the s^d John Couper was **Fine for release viij^d** accustomed yearly to receive of a certain place of pasture in Wynthorp, called Dowsonplat &c.

Sum ij^s vj^d.

Court held at Ingoldmels on the Wednesday next after the Assumption, 1 Henry VI. [18 August A.D. 1423].[1]

Sum xxij^d.

Court held at Ingoldmels on the Wednesday next after the Exaltation of the Holy Cross, 2 Henry VI. [15 September A.D. 1423].

Complaint   Robert Ose, plaintiff, offered himself against John Skalflete, def^t of a plea of trespass, for that in this year he put a dead horse in a certain several dike of the s^d plaintiff at Ingoldmels, so that the s^d complainant was not able, because of the corruption of the s horse, to occupy his pasture there &c., to (his) damage vj^s viij^d, and thereof he produces suit, and the s^d Robert Ose (sic), being present in court in his own proper person, says that in nothing is he guilty &c., and he demands that this be **Venire fac** inquired by the country, and the plaintiff likewise, therefore the bailiff is ordered to cause xij to come of the next neighbourhood, and the same day it is found by the inquisition that the s^d John Skalflete is guilty to the s^d Robert to the value of xiiij^d, therefore it is considered by the court that the s^d Robert

---

[1] Three cows worth xx^s.

recover the s^d xiiij^d for damages, and nevertheless the def^t is in   Mercy ij^d
mercy.

Sum xviij^d.

Court held at Ingoldmels on the Tuesday next before the
Feast of S. Michael, 2 H. VI. [28 September A.D. 1423.]

Sum xvj^d.

Sum of all courts this year beyond fines for suit xij^ll x^s ij^d.
Also of fines xliij^s viij^d.

Ingoldmels.   View of Frankpledge with Great Court of the
lord Henry Archbishop of Canterbury and his fellows, feoffees
of the lord King Henry V. of his Duchy of Lancaster, held at
Skegnes on Saturday next after the Feast of S. Luke the
Evangelist, 2 Henry VI. [23 October A.D. 1423].

Inquisition of free tenants.

Inquisition of bond tenants.

The first inquisition presents that John Whatecroft, son of
Wm Whatecroft of Burgh, who came in the present court and
demanded certain lands and tenements that were in the hands
of the lord because of the minority of the s^d John, now they
say that the s^d John was of the age of 22 years at Easter last:
and the second inquisition comes, and presents the same. Also
the 2nd inquisition presents that Simon Peron of Hoggesthorp
entered the fee of the lord at Ingoldmels of the gift and feoffment of Richard ffoghler of Toynton, therefore it is ordered to   Distraint
distrain for fealty, and other services.

Also that the farmer of the meles at Skegnes, viz. Robert   Mercy ij^d
Barleburgh, made great destruction and waste in the meles
aforesaid against the form of his taking, as in cutting thorns
and sines growing there, and digging holes, to the grave damage
of the lords and the tenants there, therefore &c.

Thomas Cumburworth knt., Wm Magnus of Hamby, Richard   Fealty
Gunby of Gunby, and Thomas Halle of Candelsby came into
court, and did fealty to the lords for certain lands and tenements,
which they have in Ingoldmels of the gift &c. of John Gunby of
Gunby &c.

Sum ij^s viij^d.

Court held at Ingoldmels on the Monday next before the
S

Feast of S. Hugh, Bishop of Lincoln, year as above [15 November A.D. 1423].

Judgment Elizabeth Pullayn, and Joan Pullayn complain of Robert Jakson, and Wm Smyth, ex^ors of the will of Thomas Norman of Ingoldmels, of a plea of debt &c., and by their attorney, John Moryel of Braytoft, they demand xlij^s, which they owe for the s^d Thomas Norman &c., and the s^d Robert, and W^m in their proper persons here in court are not able to deny, therefore it is **Mercy ij^d** considered by the court that the s^d plaintiff recover the debt &c.

(The same ex^ors) complain of John Couper, jun^r, of a plea of debt, and demand xlij^s, which he owes to them as of the debt of the s^d Thomas Norman, and the s^d John &c. defends &c., and says that he does not owe them except xxij^s, and this he demands may be inquired by the country, and afterwards by the oath of the same John Couper it is found that he does not owe **Mercy ij^d** them except xxij^s &c., and the s^d John is in mercy for an unjust detention.

Sum xiv^d.

Court held at Ingoldmels on Tuesday next before the Feast of S. Thomas the Apostle, year as above [14 December A.D. 1423].

Sum x^d.

Court held at Burgh on the Monday next before the Epiphany, year ij [3 January A.D. 1423–4].

Sum x^d.

Court held at Skegnes on the Wednesday next before the Purification, year as above [26 January A.D. 1423–4].

Sum vij^d.

Court held at Ingoldmels on the Wednesday next before the Feast of S. Valentine, year as above [9 February A.D. 1423–4].

Attach John Asche and Simon Tewar of Spyllesby complain of John Stevynson of Burgh of a plea of broken agreement, pledge to prosecute the bailiff, who was summoned, and has not come; therefore it is ordered that he be attached.

Respite The plaint between Robert German of Ingoldmels, plaintiff, and Alice late the wife of Wm German, defendant, of a plea of trespass, is respited until the coming of the steward.

The presenters of the manor present that Margaret late the wife of Alan Thory of Ingoldmels, who held of the lord for the term of her life v acres in Ingoldmels, is dead : and that the s^d v acres by right of inheritance ought to descend to Wm Thory, son of the s^d Alan and Margaret his wife ; and the s^d W^m comes in the present court and asks to be admitted to the s^d land to hold of the lords in bondage according to the custom of the manor for ever &c. As yet a day is given to Wm Couper of Burgh, plaintiff, and W^m at Welle of Ingoldmels, defendant, of a plea of broken agreement &c., and afterwards comes the bailiff of Orby, and demands the delivery of the s^d plea into the lordship there, because the s^d W^m at Welle is a bondman of the lordship there &c., and it is delivered.

Fine x^s
Delivery

Sum x^s x^d.

Court held at Burgh on the Saturday the 5th March, 2 Henry VI. [A.D. 1423–4].

John Asshe and Simon Tewar of Spyllesby, plaintiffs, and John Stevynson of Burgh, defendant &c., by licence are agreed, and the defendant puts himself &c.

Mercy ij^d

Sum x^d.

Court held on Wednesday next after the Annunciation, 2 Henry VI. [29 March A.D. 1424].

Wm Derebarne, one of the presenters of the manor, has not come to present, therefore &c.

Mercy ij^d

Sum ij^s vj^d.

Court held at Ingoldmels on Wednesday next before Easter, year as above [19 April A.D. 1424].

John Kempe surrenders 5 acres in Ingoldmels &c., and the lords grant them to (him), and Agnes late the wife of Walter Gosehawke, and (their) heirs lawfully begotten (remainder in default to heirs of John).

Fine
xiij^s iiij^d

The presenters of the manor present that Thomas Taylor of Aswardby, a bond tenant of the lords, holds without licence of the court one rood of bond pasture in Ingoldmels of the value of ij^s iiij^d yearly, and has so held it through xiiij years past &c., therefore it is ordered to seize the s^d land into the hands of the lords for the s^d cause ; and afterwards the s^d Thomas Taylor

s 2

comes, and puts himself on the grace of the lords, and gives
for the s^d concealment, and to have the s^d rood to him and his
heirs to hold according to the custom of the manor for ever,
xiij^s iiij^d.

Fine xiij^s iiij^d

Mercy ix^d

Also they present that Robert Ose, and Ranulph Hewetson,
and others unknown, refused to sell barley and other things
coming into the port at Skegnes by the ' bussell ' of the lords
there, where of right and ancient custom it is ordained that no
one ought to sell anything coming into the s^d port except by the
' bussell ' of the lords there, therefore they are in mercy.

Sum xxviij^s ix^d.

Easter View with Great Court of &c. held at Skegnes on
Monday, 15th May, 2 Henry VI. [A.D. 1424].

Inquisition of free tenants.

Inquisition of bond tenants.

Fine j^s viij^d

Elizabeth Pullayn, daughter of John Pullayn, a bond tenant
of the lord, surrenders the whole of her part, viz. xj^s ij^d of a rent
of assize, parcel of a rent called Newcomerent of certain tene-
ments in Ingoldmels, to the use of Joan (her) sister, to have &c.
to (her), her heirs and assigns, to hold of the lords of this
manor according to the custom of the manor for ever &c.

The inquisition of bond tenants presents that Wm Otham,
bailiff of the wapentake of Candelshowe, came at Ingoldmels
xiiijth day of May last past and there assaulted Beatrice wife of
John Orby . . . , therefore the same W^m is in mercy.

Also the inquisition of bond tenants presents that the vicar
of Burgh has not mended a certain sewer next Chalunettyng at
Burgh, as was directed at the last view under the penalty of
iiij^d, therefore it is ordered to levy, and nevertheless it is ordered
that he mend it against the next court under a penalty of iiij^s.

Also they say that John Denys, who held of the lord in
bondage at Welton j toft with a house thereupon, lying in
Botheby in the parish of Welton, and j garden called Downegarth,
and j garden between the toft of the Lord de Wylughby on the
west and the toft of Wm Costall on the east, with other
lands, is dead, and that Thomas son of the same John is his next
heir and of the age of 8 years, therefore it is ordered to seize the
s^d lands &c.

Robert Cowton of Burgh surrenders the reversion of

7½ acres pasture, which he lately had of the grant of W^m son of Alan Croft, as is testified in the court held at Skegnes on the Wednesday next before Michaelmas, ix. Henry V., to the use of John More, miller, and the lords grant &c.

The same Robert Cowton surrenders the reversion of 1½ acres, which the s^d Wm Croft granted (8 Henry V.) to the s^d Robert Cowton, if it shall happen to descend to the s^d W^m, and the s^d John More gives of fine viij^d.   *Fine viij^d*

Alice widow of John Gunne, a bondwoman of the lords, comes into court, and asks a licence to marry Wm Cooke of Ingoldmels, a freeman, and gives for the licence.   *Marriage xl^d*

Also Margaret daughter of Alan Kemp, a bond tenant of the lords, asks a licence to marry John Dobson of Ingoldmels &c.   *Marriage xviij^d*

Also Alice daughter of John at ffete, a bondwoman of the lords, asks licence to marry John Lowlyn of Sutton, a freeman &c.   *Marriage vj^s viij^d*

Richard Grynne surrenders his estate in 1 messuage, and xxxv acres of bond land in Ingoldmels, late Wm Wythson's, to the use of Agnes, the sister of the same Wm Wythson, wife of Robert Magnus of Burgh, and the heirs of the same Agnes of her body lawfully begotten.

Agnes daughter of Wm Thicthorp of the West Parish of Ingoldmels, in the presence of Wm Skegnes, the Locum of the grave, and others of the homage, surrenders 1 acre of arable land, lying in Southcroft, to the use of Wm Gyliot, and Wm Trowe, to perform the last will of the s^d Agnes, which is this, that the s^d acre shall be sold by the s^d feoffees, and the money for it received be expended in the best way they can see for the soul of the s^d Agnes and for the souls of her ancestors &c.   *Fine iij^s*

Alice Skypwythe, the feoffees of Wm Gypthorp knt., of Wm Westyby, John German, the tenants of lands of Henry Vavaser, of Ralph Dawbenay, John Hyppyswelle, John Maysterson, the prior of Bolyngton, the tenants of land of the Lord de la Souch ought to come, and have not &c.   *iiij^s vj^d*

Sum xxviij^s viij .

Court held at Ingoldmels on Wednesday next before the Ascension, year as below [31 May A.D. 1424].

Sum vj^d.

Court held at Ingoldmels on Tuesday next before the Feast of Corpus Christi, 2 Henry VI. [20 June A.D. 1424].[1]

---

[1] 1 cow worth xiij^s viij^d.

Plaint

Wm Smyre of Ingoldmels complains of Wm Cracroft of Hoggesthorp, administrator of the goods and chattels of John Cracroft, in a plea of debt, and he demands xx^s &c., to the damage of the s^d plaintiff ½ mark : and the s^d Wm Cracroft in his proper person defends force and injury, and says that he owes him nothing &c., and this he is prepared to verify by his law : and the s^d plaintiff, because the s^d defendant has not his

Day

law, or pledges for his law, demands judgment, and so a day is given to the parties at the next (court) to hear judgment.

Fines for suit of court released, Mich. 2 H. VI. [A.D. 1423].

¹ From Alan Thory vj^d.
From Richard Skalflete iiij^d.
From feoffees of Thomas Rygge xij^d.
From feoffees of John Ayer vj^d.
From Thomas Marays vj^d.
From feoffees of Dionisius Petyclerke vj^d.
From tenants of lands of the Lord de Kyme vj^d.

From Alice Skypwyth ij^s.
From Agnes Hyltoft iiij^d.
From Ralph Cromwell xij^d.
From John Baxter iiij^d.
From Wm Orby iiij^d.
From feoffees of Wm Gypthorp knt xl^d.
From feoffees of Wm Gypthorp esq^r xij^d.

² From Ralph Dawbenay ij^s.
From John Hyppyswelle xx^d.
From John Maysterson xx^d.
From feoffees of the Lord de la Souch xl^d.

From the abbot of Louth Park xij^d.
From the prior of Bolyngton xl^d.
From Robert Tyrwhytte xij^d.

Sum lij^s.

View of Frankpledge &c. held at Ingoldmels on Thursday next after the Feast of S. Luke the Evangelist, 8 Henry VI. [20 October A.D. 1429].

Inquisition of free tenants.
Inquisition of bond tenants.

Mercy vj^d

And because it is testified here in court that Walter Maryot, a bond tenant of the lords, dwells at Mumby outside this lordship without licence, therefore &c.: also that Robert at Hadyk,

¹ Eighty-three tenants.   ² These are the foreign tenants.

son of W^m at Hadyk, a bond tenant &c., dwells at Boston outside the lordship &c.: also that Katherine daughter of Wm Cobbe, a bond tenant of the lords, is put out at a business at Wynthorp without a licence, and dwells outside the lordship &c.: also that the s^d Katherine has been deflowered by Walter Smyth of Wynthorp, tailor, therefore let there be levied from the s^d Katherine &c.

Lethyr-whyte v^s iiij^d

Thomas Hewson, John Smyth, and Alan Jakson surrender 2 places of land and pasture in Ingoldmels, w^h they had of the grant of Robert Couper &c., to the use of Wm Smyth &c.

Fine vj^s viij^d

The jurors upon the 2nd inquisition present that John Westmels of Skegnes brewed, and sold contrary to the assize &c.

Mercy xiij^d

Also that Thomas Sutton esq^r, and John Boys esq^r on Tuesday the Feast of S. Luke the Evangelist 8 H. VI. at Staynton unjustly vexed the tenants of the lord the king of his duchy of Lancaster as of his manor of Ingoldmels, viz. John Godarde of Ingoldmels, Wm Pullayn of Burgh, John Maryot of Ingoldmels, Wm Skegnes of Ingoldmels, Thomas Akewraa of Ingoldmels, Wm Skegnes jun^r of Ingoldmels, Thomas Hewson, and others, bondmen [nativi] and tenants of the said lord the king, by taking horses and other animals &c. for toll, and this contrary to the liberties of the s^d duchy, and they detained them until they had j tunic and one pair of gloves in pledge &c., therefore let a writ be made.

Writ

Also that Robert Barleburgh, who held of the lords in Ingoldmels by the law of England, as of the right of Joan his wife, daughter of John Godarde, a bond tenant of the lords, 1 messuage and 8½ acres, is dead, and that Richard (their) son is the next heir &c. (he is admitted).

Fine xx^s

Also that Mary daughter of Robert Gunny &c.

Lether-whyte

Also John son of John Baxter of Welton, a bondman, put himself in chevage, and gives to the lords yearly.

Chevage iij^d

Also they present that John Richemond of Skegnes cut the sines, growing upon the meles at Skegnes, and took them to Newcastel, therefore &c.: also that Robert Bryghtsance of Barton injured the port at Skegnes by throwing into the s^d port mud, stones, and other ballast, to the injury and grave damage of the lords, therefore &c.: also that Wm Coke of York broke and pulled down the signals called 'les Bekyns,' placed in the port at Skegnes for causing clearness to those entering the said port, therefore &c.: also that John Lyndyssay

Mercy vij^d

Mercy xij^d

of York cut the sines growing on the meles at Skegnes without licence, and took them to York, therefore &c.

Mercy xij^d   Also that Robert at Mylne of Skegnes forestalled the herring nets at Skegnes, so that Robert Ose of Ingoldmels and other tenants of the lords there were not able to have victuals for the sustentation of their houses, therefore &c.

The great inquisition affirms all the things presented above &c.

Sum l^s j^d.

Court held at Ingoldmels on Wednesday next after the Feast of S. Leonard, year as above [9 November A.D. 1429].

Sum ij^s iiij^d.

Court held at Burgh 3rd Dec., 8 H. VI. [A.D. 1429].

Sum ij^s viij^d.

Court held at Burgh on Wednesday next before the Feast of S. Thomas the Apostle, year as above [14 December A.D. 1429].[1]

Fine iiij^s iiij^d   Thomas Hewson surrenders 1 acre of pasture, with half a cottage in Burgh, with appurtenances, and the common of Skalflete belonging to the same &c., to the use of John Pullayn &c.

Sum vj^s vj^d.

Court held at Ingoldmels xvjth Jan., year as above [A.D. 1429–30].

Fine iiij^s   Alan Thore of Ingoldmels asks licence to demise 4 acres in Ingoldmels &c. to Richard Grynne (for 8 years) &c.

Court held at Ingoldmels on Monday next after the Purification, year as above [6 February A.D. 1429–30].

Fine vj^s viij^d   John Brytte of Loundon, and Alice his wife, daughter of John Gunne, a bond tenant of the lords, in the presence of John Godard in the place of the grave, and others of the homage, viz. (12), and the s^d Alice having been diligently examined before the steward, surrendered 2 acres and the 6th part of ½ an acre, late her father's, to the use of John Lewlyn of Ingoldmels, his heirs and assigns, under the following condition (blank).

Fine vj^s viij^d   Also (they) surrender &c. 2 acres and the 6th part of ½ acre

[1] 6 sheep worth vj^s; 1 horse vj^s.

in Ingoldmels to the use of Matilda daughter of John Guny of
Ingoldmels, a bond tenant of the lords, her heirs and assigns.

Sum xvj^s ij^d.

Court held at Burgh on the last day of February, 8 H. VI.
[A.D. 1429–30].

Robert Grynne of Ingoldmels, executor of the will of Alan   Mercy ij^d
Grynne, complains of Wm Warde of a plea of debt, and demands
xxxvj^s, which he undertook to pay him for John Heryng &c.,
and the said Wm Warde, being present in court, is not able to
deny, therefore it is considered by the court that &c.[1]

Sum ij^s viij^d.

Court held at Ingoldmels xxth March, year as above [A.D.
1429–30].

Sum ij^s iiij^d.

Court held at Ingoldmels on Wednesday next before Easter,
year as above.

John Cokke of Ingoldmels, plaintiff, offered himself against
John Marschal of Ingoldmels of a plea of broken agreement, for
that the s^d John Marschal sold to the s^d plaintiff one alphabet,
in which the pledge was challenged, so that he could not warrant
to him &c., to his damage xij^d, and thereof &c.: and the s^d
defendant says that in nothing is he guilty &c., and this he puts   Venire fac
upon the country &c.

View of Frankpledge with Great Court held at Burgh on
Thursday 4th May, 8 Henry VI. [A.D. 1430].

Great Inquisition.

Inquisition of bond tenants.

Who being sworn on the inquisition of bond tenants also
present, that Matilda late the wife of Alan Kygs of Ingoldmels,
who held for life of the grant of the s^d Alan Kygs certain lands
&c. in Ingoldmels and Skegnes, viz. xxj acres in Ingoldmels,
xvj acres in Skegnes, the reversion thereof being granted by the
s^d Alan to Wm Skegnes of Ingoldmels, sen^r, Wm Thomlynson,
and Robert Ulry, is dead, and that the s^d reversion was
granted under the condition that they carry out the last will of   Order to
the s^d Alan, which is this &c.   seize

---

[1] 1 horse worth xvj^s.

Fine
vj˙ viij^d

Also that Alan Hewetson, who held 2 acres 1 rood of bond land in Ingoldmels, surrendered them in the presence of the grave, and others of the homage, to the use of Margaret his wife (for life, remainder to Robert son of the s^d Alan) &c.

Fine
vj˙ viij^c

Also that Wm Johnson, a bond tenant of the lord, in the presence of (same) surrendered ij acres of arable and bond land in Ingoldmels to the use of Margery his wife (for life, rem^d to 3 to carry out his will, which is this that they hold them until they receive xx^s to distribute in alms for the soul of the same Wm Thomlynson (sic) and the souls of all the faithful departed, rem^d to John son of s^d W^m and Margery and the lawful heirs of the same John) &c.

Fine x^s

Also that Matilda wife of Robert Hamond of Hoggysthorp holds for life 5 acres of bond land in Ingoldmels, the reversion belonging to John son of Wm Skalflete of Ingoldmels, which John gives &c.

Mercy ij^d

Marriage
ij^s

Chevage
iij^d

Marriage
ij^s

Fine xxx^s

Also that Richard son of Robert Skalflete, a bond tenant of the lords, dwells outside the lordship without licence &c.: also Isabel daughter of John Gunne of Ingoldmels gives for licence to marry John Lewlyn of Hoggysthorp: also that Robert son of John Godarde of Hoggysthorp, a bond man gives &c.: also Alice daughter of the s^d John Godarde asks licence to marry &c.: also that Margery late the wife of Robert Thore, a bond tenant of the lords, holds for a term of 24 years, this year being the 19th, 1 messuage, 12½ acres of bond land and pasture in Ingoldmels, of the grant and surrender of the s^d Robert Thore, the reversion belonging to W^m (their) son, who gives &c.

Also that the lords of this manor have been used to have xij^d yearly for the occupation of the herbage at Cokhil in Ingoldmels, and thereof the graves were burdened each year, and now they ask to be allowed the s^d xij^d, because they say that there is great and grave damage to the lords and their tenants there.[1]

Sum lix^s ij^d.

Court held xth May, 8 Henry VI.

Sum ij^s iiij^d.

[1] A torn entry states that it is necessary in no manner to cut, or destroy the aines, but let them grow, and hold the land, lest it be wasted by the flow of the sea.

Court held at Ingoldmels xxxth May, year as above [A.D. 1430].

Sum ij^s.

Court held at Ingoldmels on Friday next after the Feast of the New Solemnity of Corpus Christi, year as above [16 June A.D. 1430].

It is found by the inquisition that John Marschal is guilty   Mercy ij^d v. John Cokke as the s^d plaintiff alleged against him in a plea of broken agreement, to the damage of the said plaintiff iiij^d, therefore let him recover &c., and the defendant is in mercy.

Sum ij^s.

Court held at Ingoldmels vth July, year as above [A.D. 1430].

Joan Bunte complains of Wm Watkynson of Ingoldmels of a plea of trespass, wherein she complains that on the day and year &c. the s^d W^m with his dog killed, and devoured two ducks with their progeny, worth &c., to the damage of the same plaintiff xij^d, and thereof she produces suit, and the s^d W^m   Venire fac comes, and defends &c., and says that in nothing is he guilty,   xij and this he puts upon the country.

Juliana late the wife of John Burgh of Skegnes, in the presence of Robert German, locum of the grave, Thomas Hall, the clerk of the court, and others of the homage, released to John Smyth, Wm Rabyn, and Robert Waterlade of Wynthorp her   Fine ij^s whole right &c. in the 3rd part of vij acres pasture in Wynthorp, late John Burgh's her husband, which (she) was assigned by the court &c.

Also (she) granted with licence of the court to Wm Kyng of   Fine Skegnes the 3rd part of xj acres of bond-pasture in Skegnes &c.,   vj^s viij^d to hold for the term of the life of the same Juliana.

Sum xj^s iiij^d.

Court held at Ingoldmels on Wednesday next after the Feast of S. James, year as above [26 July A.D. 1430].

It is found by the inquisition that Wm Watkynson is guilty   Mercy ij^d v. Joan Bunte to the value of ij^d, therefore &c.

Sum iij^s iiij^d.

Court held at Skegnes xvith August, 8 Henry VI. [A.D. 1430].

Fine xx^s Wm Skegnes, Robert Ulry, and Wm Thomlynson came into court before the steward, and surrendered their whole estate and right &c. in 16 acres of bond land in Skegnes, w^h they lately had of the grant of Alan Kygs, to the use of John Westyrby of Skegnes &c., fine xx^s and not more because divers times the s^d land was submerged by flow and reflow of the sea.

Fine xl^s (The same) surrendered their right &c. in 21 acres in Ingoldmels to the use of John Grynne of Kyrkeby, John Helewys of Burgh, and Robert German of Ingoldmels &c. : fine xl^s, and not more because 5 acres lie in the c acres, and are submerged &c.

Distraint The presenters &c. present that Wm Rabyn of Wynthorp holds of the lords, as of the right of Agnes his wife, daughter of Richard Englessch, 5 acres of land by suit of court and other services, whom it is ordered to distrain for fealty &c.   Also that John Wyghtyfeld of Uttyrby holds 1 cottage, with a garden adjacent, of bond land in Yerburgh, formerly of John **Seize** Ingoldmels, a bond tenant of the lords, without the licence of the court, therefore it is ordered to seize &c. for the s^d cause.

Sum lxij^s.

Court held at Ingoldmels vth Sept., 9 Henry VI. [A.D. 1430].

Sum ij^s.

Court held at Ingoldmels on Tuesday next before Michaelmas, year as above [26 September A.D. 1430].

Fine v^s Robert Gunne, John Smyth, and Thomas Harefot surrender the reversion of 1 toft, containing 3 acres, in Ingoldmels, late Simon Dawson's, to the use of John Lewlyn after the death of Alice wife of Thomas Harefot, and Isabel late the wife of Robert Lamb.

Fine v^s Thomas Harefot and Alice his wife, formerly the wife of Gilbert Lamb &c., granted by licence of court to John Lewlyn one toft, containing iij acres, and their third part, which they had of all the lands &c. of Gilbert Lamb, formerly Alice's husband, to hold &c. for the life of the s^d Alice, doing to the lords the services before due and accustomed, and rendering to the s^d Alice yearly &c. xiiij^s &c. (power to distrain if rent in arrear).

Robert Gunne (and the 2 others) surrender 1 acre and 1 rood **Fine ij˙** of bond land in Ingoldmels &c. to John Smyth, to hold after the death of Isabel, late the wife of Robert Lamb &c.

John Lewlyn and Isabel his wife, late the wife of Robert **Fine ij˙** Lamb, grant to John Smyth 1 acre 1 rood of bond land, which Isabel holds for life, of the grant of her late husband (John S. is to pay to Isabel yearly iij˙ iiij^d).

Sum xvj˙ x^d.
Sum of xvj courts and ij views xij^{li} ix˙.

Fines for suit of court released Mich. 10 H. VI. [A.D. 1431].

From Robert Umferavyle knt vj^d. (86 tenants.)
— Wm Grynne of Halton   iiij^d.
— Hamo de Sutton   xl^d.

Total xxxv˙ vj^d.

Foreign fines for (same) (5)
From John Blaunch iiij^d.

Sum vij˙ iiij^d.

Total xlij˙ x^d.

Court of the lord Henry Archbishop &c., feoffees of Henry V., held at Ingoldmels on Wednesday next before the Feast of S. Luke the Evangelist, 11 H. VI. [17 October A.D. 1432].

Sum xx^d.

View of Frankpledge with Great Court of (same) held at Skegnes on Monday next after the (same) feast, year as above [22 October A.D. 1432].

Great Inquisition.

Inquisition of bond tenants.

Which said jurors present that Wm Growne makes an unjust **Mercy ij^d** way within the close of Alan Thore at Ingoldmels at night against the will of the s^d Alan, therefore &c.

Also that John Sutton of . . . in the c° of Linc., gentylman, and John Boyes of Welyngham in the s^d c°, gentylman, on the Saturday the Feast of S. Luke 11 Henry VI. at Staynton in the s^d c°, unjustly took toll of Wm Pullayn of Burgh, and John Godard of Ingoldmels, bond tenants of the lord the king of his duchy of Lancaster, against the liberties of the s^d duchy, and to the prejudice of the s king, and the grave damage of

Writ   the s^d W^m and John, bond tenants, therefore let a writ be made against the s^d Thomas Sutton and John Boyes.

Fine
iij· iiij^d   Agnes, late wife of Robert Ose, in her pure widowhood, surrenders her right in the 3rd part of 1 acre, and 3 roods, which she had in the name of dower, to the use of John Orby and Roger Grynne &c.

Fine v·   John Orby, and Roger Grynne, bond tenants of the lords, surrender to the use of John son of Wm Grynne, a bond tenant, 1 acre, 3 roods of bond land in Ingoldmels, which they lately had of the grant by licence of the court of Robert Ose &c.

The great inquisition affirms all the above presentments, and has nothing further to present this day.

Sum x· vij^d.

Court held at Ingoldmels on Wednesday next after the Feast of All Saints, year as above [5 November A.D. 1432].

Fine xl^d   W^m son of John Julotson comes into court, and claims to hold of the lords 1 acre and 1 rood of bond land, which Robert Jakson and Robert Coper held for the term of 14 years now ended of the grant of John Julotson, the reversion thereof belonging to the s^d W^m and the heirs of his body lawfully begotten by the form of the grant &c., W^m is admitted &c.

Fine v·   Wm Smyth and Joan his wife &c. surrendered 1½ acres, called 'le harpe,' to the use of Wm Thore &c.

Fine xl^d   Wm Stokman of Halton and Agnes his wife surrendered 1 acre 1 rood in Ingoldmels to the use of Richard Grynne &c.

Sum xiij· ij^d.

Court held at Ingoldmels on Wednesday next before the Feast of S. Andrew the Apostle, 11 Henry VI. [26 November A.D. 1432].

John Cokke offered himself v. John Lewlyn of a plea of debt, and demands xiij· iiij^d which he owes him for wool sold him &c.: and the defendant defends, and says he owes him nothing, and this he puts upon the country, and the plaintiff likewise: The same John Cokke demands v. the same John

Venire fac Lewlyn in the above form xiij· iiij^d, and the defendant denies.[1]

Elizabeth Pullayn of Askeby next Partenay, Joan Pullayn

surrendered the reversion of 3 acres, and half one rood of pasture, parcel of the same pasture in Ingoldmels, containing 5 acres, which ought to descend by right of inheritance to the s⁴ Elizabeth Pullayn, Joan Pullayn, Isabel Pullayn, wife of John Moryel, and the heirs of Alice Pullayn, formerly the wife of Henry Dyconson, the daughters of John Pullayn, and remain after the death of Alice late the wife of Wᵐ Cooke, to the use of Robert Grynne &c.   Fine xˢ

Sum xˢ viijᵈ.

Court held at Burgh on Wednesday next before the Feast of S. Lucy the Virgin, 11 Henry VI. [10 December A.D. 1432].

Sum ijˢ iiijᵈ.

Court held at Burgh on Wednesday next after the Epiphany, year as above [7 January A.D. 1432-3].

Sum iiijᵈ.

Court held at Burgh xxviiᵗʰ Jan., year as above [A.D. 1432-3].

John Orby of Ingoldmels complains of Wᵐ Thore, John and William his sons, of a plea of trespass &c., wherein he complains that on the Lord's day &c. the s⁴ Wᵐ Thore with his sons assaulted the s⁴ John Orby at Ingoldmels, and ill-used, and beat the said John, and broke one of his arms &c., to the damage of the same plaintiff x marks, and thereof he produces suit; and the s⁴ Wᵐ comes, and defends &c., and says that in nothing is he guilty &c., and this he puts upon the country, Venire fac and the plaintiff likewise, therefore &c.

John Lewlyn came in the court, and acknowledged that he Judgment owes John Cooke iiijˡⁱ ijˢ, as the s⁴ John Cooke alleged against him in 6 plaints of debt: therefore it is considered by the court Mercy vjᵈ that the s⁴ John Cooke recover the debt, with damages, taxed by 4 of these jurors at ijˢ, and the s⁴ John Lewlyn is in mercy.

The presenters present that Agnes wife of Wᵐ Whyte raised the hue upon John Bunte justly, therefore (he) is in mercy: also that Wᵐ Thore, Wᵐ and John his sons, and John Pose of Hoggysthorp made an affray upon John Orby, therefore &c.

Court held on Wednesday next before the Feast of S. Nicholas the Bishop, 15 Henry VI. [5 December A.D. 1436].

Sum xviij^d.

Court held at Ingoldmels on Friday next after the Feast of the Nativity of our Lord, year as above [28 December A.D. 1436].

Wreck
x^s x^d

The presenters present 8 casks of beer coming up of wreck of the sea upon the soil and fee of the lords at Skegnes, whereof 1 with black soap of the price of vj^s viij^d in the custody of Roger Chapman of Ingoldmels, 1 cask of beer in the custody of Wm Baxter of Ingoldmels, also 1 of beer in the custody of Simon Andruson of Skegnes, also 1 in the custody of John Westerby, also 1 in the custody of John Richemond, also 2 in the custody of Robert Goye, also 1 empty cask in the church at Skegnes, the price of the 7 barrels 4^s 2^d, beyond the cost allowed to the finders.

Also they present one board of fir coming up of wreck of the sea, in the custody of Simon Andruson of Skegnes of the price of 4^d, also 1 small board of fir in the custody of John Westerby of the price of 1^d, also 3 Waynscottes coming of wreck as above, whereof 1 in the custody of Wm Kyng of Skegnes, 2 in the

Wreck
xiiij^d

custody of John Westerby of the same of the price of ix^d.

Sum xij^s ij^d.

Court held at Ingoldmels xvith Jan., year as above [A.D. 1436-7].

Marriage
xx^d

Agnes daughter of Wm Cobbe, a bond tenant of the lords, asks licence to marry Wm Johnson of Skegnes &c.

Sum ij^s.

Court held at Ingoldmels 5th Feb., 15 H. VI. [A.D. 1436-7].

Fine ij^s

Wm Watkynson and Isabel his wife &c., by licence of the court, granted to Roger Chapman 3 acres of land arable and bond in Ingoldmels, between land of Alice Skypwyth on the west and north and land of John Hyltoft on the east, to have for 12 years &c., W^m and Isabel shall support the services &c., and if any one distrain on the s^d 3 acres for any burden because of (their) default (he shall have them for 6 years more) &c.

Sum ij^s ij^d.

Court held at Ingoldmels on Wednesday next after the Feast of S. Matthias, year as above [27 February A.D. 1486–7].

John Grenne of Kyrkeby next Bolyngbroke surrendered   Fine ij˙
1 acre of bond land in Thorp next Waynflete, which he lately
had, with other lands, of the grant of Richard Grenne of
Ingoldmels (his) father, to the use of Robert Grene rector of
the church of ffrisby, and John Brese &c.

Sum (torn).

Court held at Burgh (torn).

The presenters present that Thomas Baker of Ingoldmels   Mercy iij^d
drew blood from Robert Mylner of Hoggysthorp, therefore &c.

Also that John Nichol of Anderby entered upon the fee of   Fealty
the lords in certain bond lands in Ingoldmels, as of the right
of Agnes his wife, late the wife of John Kemp, and (he) did
fealty.

Also that John Broune of Surflete holds &c., as of the right
of Joan formerly his wife, daughter of Alan Hallegarth, 1 acre,
1 rood of bond pasture at Ingoldmels by the law of England,
the reversion thereof belonging to the lords of this manor after
(his) death through default of issue of the same Joan, and she
a bastard.

Sum v˙.

Court held at Burgh 9th April, year as above [A.D. 1437].

Robert Jakson offered himself v. Thomas Whatecroft of   Mercy ij^d
Burgh of a plea of debt, and demands xiij˙ iiij^d, which he owes
him for wool sold him, which &c., to the damage of xx^d &c.,
and the s^d Thomas by his attorney, John Couper &c., defends
damages, but concedes the debt, therefore &c.

Wm Skegnes of Ingoldmels offered himself v. Thomas   Mercy ij^d
Whatecroft of a plea of debt, because he owes him and unjustly
detains xxxix˙ xj^d ob. q., which &c.; Thomas Whatecroft by his
attorney concedes the debt, therefore it is considered by the
court &c.

The presenters of the manor present 1 panel of a certain   Wreck i ˙
old ship coming on the soil and fee of the lords at Skegnes of
the price of ij^d in the hands of the grave.

Also that John Godard of Hoggysthorp, a bond tenant of the   Fine ˙
lords, who held of the lords on the day he died 3 acres of bond
land at Hoggysthorp, and 1½ acres in Ingoldmels, formerly free

T

land, now arrented by the lords according to the custom of the
manor &c., [is dead], and that Robert (his) son, of the age of xvj
years, is his next heir according to the custom of the manor, which
Robert comes into court, and asks to be admitted to his inheritance, and is admitted to hold of the lords the sᵈ tenements by
the rents, services, burdens, and customs of the sᵈ tenements
before due according to the custom of the manor, in bondage
for ever, and he gives for a fine.

Sum vˢ viijᵈ.

View of Frankpledge &c. held at Burgh 19ᵗʰ April, 15 Henry
VI. [A.D. 1437].

Great Inquisition.

Second Inquisition.

Fine xxˢ   John son of John Dodyke, a bond tenant of the lords, comes
into court, and demands one messuage called Buxhous, 7½ acres,
one place of pasture, containing 3 acres, called Ketylcroft, to
remain to him, and the heirs of his body lawfully begotten,
after the term of vj years now ended, according to the will of
John, his father &c.

Fine ijˢ   [1] Joan daughter of Wᵐ Cobbe asks to be admitted to 1 acre,
and 1 rood of pasture land, for life according to the will of the
sᵈ John Dodyke &c.

Fine xxˢ   Also (the jurors upon the 2ⁿ inquisition) present that Joan,
late the wife of John Randson, senʳ, who held of the lords by
right of inheritance 10½ acres of bond pasture, is dead &c., and
that John (their) son is their next heir &c.

The sᵈ jurors charged upon the tenour of a certain bill in a
letter of the lord Henry, Cardinal of England, one of the feoffees
of this manor, sent and enclosed to the steward of the duchy of
Lancaster, or his locum tenens, and sewn to this roll, say upon
their oath, that Wᵐ Sybsay of Ingoldmels and Thomas Marays
of the same by their charter granted to Thomas Whetecroft, John
Sybsay, Simon Newcome, and Wᵐ Wylokk, their heirs and
assigns, to the use and profit of Agnes Marays, all the lands &c.
in the sᵈ bill specified, to have &c. to (them) their heirs and
assigns for ever, by virtue of which gift and grant (they) were
seised thereof. And further they say that the sᵈ Thomas Marays
had no other estate or possession in the sᵈ lands, except jointly

---

[1] Elena daughter of same admitted to 1 acre of arable for life.

with the s^d Wm Sybsay : and therefore it is considered by the court that the s^d Thomas, John, Simon, and W^m shall be restored to their estate and possession aforesaid, the seisin of the officers of this lordship notwithstanding ; and that the hands of the lord and his officers be removed therefrom.

To ye hiegh and myghti prince and our ful g'cious Lord ye Cardinal of England cheffe feffe of the duche of Lancastre.

Bisechen mekely your pore tenantes and bedemen of ye said duche of Lancastre in the schire of Lincoln Thomas Whetecroft John Sibsey Simond Newecom and William Wylok your gode and g'cious Lordship to have in knowlach and to considre howe your said tenantes late token lawefull astate to the use and profit of one Augnes Mares of certayn landez and tenementez in Ingoldmels which be halden of ye said duche by ye gift and feoffement of one William Sibsey which had joynt estate in ye said landez and tenementez with one Thomas Mares whom God assoill. After whose dethe your officers gracious Lord of ye said duche there affermyng yat ye said Thomas Mares dyed sole seised where in trowth it is not so entered and put out your said pore tenantes agene ye trewe entent of ye feoffement foresaid. And so they wrongfully take and occupie ye p'fites of ye said landez and tenementez to your use g'cious Lord as they say. And on yat they waste and distroy ye howses bigged upon ye said tenementez. Please it to your gracious Lordship yat ye trowth of yis mater might be sufficiently and trewely enquered of and preved in yat cuntre in such wise as it may please beste your gracious Lordchip to purvey therfore yat trowthe of ye mater may be founden for ye said feoffees. And yat thay myght be restored by y^r said officers as right and concience will to thaire possession of ye said landez and tenementez with ye issues and profites taken by your officers yereof in ye mene tyme for Goddes love and in way of charite.

Right trousty and welbeloved. We grete yow wel with al oure hert and sende yow closed withinne thees a supplicacōn put unto us by Thomas Whetecroft John Sibsey Simon Newecom and William Wylok tenants of the duchie as ye may see by the saide supp^{on}. The which weel understande by yow. We wel and pray yow as wel in oure name as in the names of the remenant of the feffees of the saide duchie that ye administre unto the saide parties that compleyne suche justice and equite that they

have no cause resonnable to compleyne eftsones.   And God have
yow ever in his blessed keping.   Writen in Suthewerk the
vij day of March.

H, Cardinal of England.

To oure Right trusty and welbeloved oure Stuard of the
landes of the feffement of the Duchie of Lancastre withynne
Lincolnshire or to his locum tenens.

Mercy xvj⁴   The jurors upon the great inquisition present that Wᵐ
Whytyng of Braytoft, Alan Braytoftson of same, (and 2 others)
entered upon the fields of Burgh with their sheep, and occupied
the common there, where they have no common, therefore each
of them is in mercy, and nevertheless it is ordered &c. to
impound.

Mercy ij⁴   Also the bond jurors present that the mels at Skegnes are
gravely wasted by the destruction of [*i.e.* made by] the rabbits,
in the default of John Westerby, the farmer there.

Also they say that the 'bekyns' in the port at Skegnes are
not rightly placed, as of right they ought, by the farmer there.

Sum xlvij⁸ ij⁴.

Court held at Ingoldmels 1ˢᵗ May, 15 Henry VI. [A.D. 1437].
Fine xl⁴   The presenters present that Alice Gunne, in the presence of
the said presenters, granted, by licence of the court, to Walter
Pecher, and John Lewlyn 4 acres, and ⅓ʳᵈ of 1 acre, which (she)
holds, as of her third part of 1 messuage 12½ acres, called
Gunhous, after the death of John Gunne of Ingoldmels late her
husband, to have &c. for the term of (her) life.

Fine x⁸   Also that, whereas Thomas Schaft, who granted to John
Godard (and 2 others) 9 acres in Ingoldmels for a term of 5 years
after (his) death, to pay the debts of the sᵈ Thomas : remainder
to Alice (his) daughter : the sᵈ term was ended at Christmas
last, and Alice asks to be admitted &c.

Fine xxvj⁸ viij⁴   John Hyltoft, Robert Cracroft, Thomas Hewson, Roger
Chapman, John Couper and Thomas Halle of Candelsby, came
into court, and surrendered to the use of Richard Batyl of
Claxby, Wᵐ Colynson of Burgh, Wᵐ Brasse of Partenay, Wᵐ
Skegnes of Ingoldmels, and John Smyth of same, one pasture in
Wynthorp, called Sleyght layes, containing xviij acres, which
(they) lately had with other lands of the grant and surrender of

Richard Grynne, to have &c. to (them), their heirs and assigns, of the lords of this manor by the rents, services, burdens, and customs of the s^d tenements before due and accustomed according to the custom of this manor, in bondage for ever, and they give &c.

Sum xl^s iiij^d.

Court held at Skegnes 14th February, 20 Henry VI. [A.D. 1441-2].

The presenters present that William Trowe, who held[1] for life as of the right of Joan his wife, daughter of Wm Thykthorp, 1 acre in Ingoldmels in Southcroft, the reversion belonging to Thomas Gyllyot, son of Alan Gyllyot, son and heir of Wm Thykthorp, (is dead), which same Thomas asks to be admitted &c.   *Fine* xij^d

Sum iij^s iiij^d.

Court held at Skegnes vij^th March, year as above [A.D. 1441-2].

Also (the presenters) present that whereas John Hyltoft of Ingoldmels and his fellows, feoffees of Richard Grynne, held xij acres in Wynthorp for the term of 8 years (now) ended, by the will of the s^d Richd Grynne &c., the reversion belonging to Wm Grynne (his) son, and the heirs of his body, to hold &c. And the s^d W^m asks to be admitted &c.   *Fine* xxvj^s viij^d

Also that whereas the said feoffees held 14 acres in Burgh (in same way), the reversion belonging to John Grynne, son of Richd Grynne the younger for a term of xij years &c. (who admitted).   *Fine* x^s

Also that Wm Stere of Burgh made rescue upon John Polayn of Burgh, for that after the s^d John had arrested wood, and fagots, upon the soil of the same John at Burgh, for rent &c., the s^d W^m carried off the s^d wood, and fagots without licence, therefore he is in mercy.   *Mercy* ij^d

Sum xxxvij^s xj^d.

Court held at Burgh on the Wednesday before Easter, year as above [28 March A.D. 1442].

Sum x^d.

Court held at Burgh xviij^th April, year as above [A.D. 1442].

Sum xviij^d.

---

[1] By the law of England.

View of Frank Pledge with Great Court held at Skegnes 23rd April, 20 H. VI. [A.D. 1442].

Great Inquisition,[1]

Inquisition of bond tenants.

Fine xxᵈ   Wᵐ Cobbe of Ingoldmels surrenders 1½ acres of bond land in Ingoldmels &c. to the use of Roger Chapman, and John Smyth, to have &c.

Fine xxiijˢ iiijᵈ   Also the jurors upon the 2nd inquisition present, that Margery, late wife of John Dodyke, a bond tenant, had of the grant of the sᵈ John Dodyke 14 acres in Ingoldmels for the term of 10 years, (remainder) to Robert (his) son and heir &c., (who admitted).

Fine xlˢ   Also that Wᵐ Kyng of Skegnes, who held of the lords in bondage 22 acres, is dead, and Simon (his) son is the next heir, to hold to him, and the heirs of his body lawfully begotten, according to the will of the sᵈ Wᵐ Kyng, (who admitted).

Court held at Ingoldmels on Wednesday next before the Feast of Corpus Christi, 20 H. VI. [30 May A.D. 1442].

xiijˢ iiijᵈ   From Agnes Potter, as well because she does not hold any tenements of the lords, as because she dwells without the lordship without licence for 4 years.

Sum xvijˢ xᵈ.

Court held at Ingoldmels on Wednesday next before the Feast of the Nativity of S. John Baptist, year as above [20 June A.D. 1442].

Sum xijᵈ.

Court held at Ingoldmels xiᵗʰ July, 20 H. VI. [A.D. 1442].

Fine xlᵈ   Robert at Hadyke and Joan his wife surrender 3 acres of bond pasture in Ingoldmels : and the lords redelivered them to (them) for life, (remainder) to right heirs of Joan &c.

Marriage ijˢ   Katherine, daughter of John Randson the elder, asks licence to marry Robert Taylor of Huttoft.

Sum vjˢ ijᵈ.

---

[1] Robert Massyngberd of Burgh.
Thomas Whatecroft of same.
John Lewlyn of Sutton.
John Smyth of Ingoldmels.
Thomas Akewra of same.
Thomas Harefote of same.

Wᵐ Ward of Ingoldmels.
Robert Sybsay of same.
Thomas Jakson of Anderby.
Wᵐ Toke of Ingoldmels.
John Nevell of same.
Alan Runyar of same.

Court held at Burgh on Tuesday next before the Feast of
S. Lawrence, year as above [7 August A.D. 1442].

That Wm Skegnes of Ingoldmels, and Robert Grynne of   Memo-
same were appointed by the steward to superintend the repair   randum
of the 3rd part of a house in Ingoldmels, w^h Isabel late the
wife of Wm Watkynson has after the death of the s^d W^m &c.

Sum xij^d.

Court held at Ingoldmels 22nd August, year as above [A.D.
1442].

Wm West of Partenay complains of Richard Batyl of   Summons
Slotheby of vj pleas of debt &c.

Sum x^d.

Court held at Ingoldmels on Wednesday next after the
Feast of the Nativity of the Blessed Mary, 21 Henry VI. [12
September A.D. 1442].

Joan in the Wylughes, lately dwelling in Welton next Orby,   Fine viij^d
in the presence of Thomas Halle, the clerk of the courts, W^m
Thore, the grave, and others, according to the custom of the
manor, surrendered the moiety of 1 acre, and 9 perches in Ingoldmels: and the lords redelivered the s^d tenements to the s^d
Joan, her heirs and assigns &c.

Sum xviij^d.

Sum total of the 17 courts and 2 leets x^li xij^s iiij^d.

View of Frankpledge with Great Court of the lord King
Henry VI. held at Skegnes on the Tuesday next after the
Feast of the Apostles Simon and Jude in the 22nd year of the
same king [29 October A.D. 1443].

Inquisition of free tenants.[1]

Inquisition of bond tenants.

The jurors upon the 2nd inquisition present that the house   Mercy ij^d
of Richard ffyscher of Skendylby at Skegnes is in ruins, therefore &c.: and nevertheless it is ordered to seize the s^d house
into the hand of the lord, until &c.

Also they elect Robert Massyngberd to the office of grave   Officers
of the dikes this year.

---

[1] Among them are William Wylughby and William Grynne, both of Ingoldmells, and Robert Massyngberd of Burgh.

Mercy iiij⁴ The jurors upon the great inquisition present that a certain bridge at Wynthorp, called Welebrigge, is very defective for non-repair of the same, and it ought, and is accustomed to be repaired by the prior of Bolyngton, and he has not repaired it, therefore &c. ; and nevertheless it is ordered that it be repaired

Pain before the next View under the penalty of iij⁸ iiij⁴.

Mercy Also that Wᵐ Skypwyth knt., the feoffees of Wᵐ Gypthorp iij⁸ viiij⁴ of Thorp, Wᵐ Babyngton, John Edeward of Swaby, Wᵐ Tyr-whyt knt,, Henry Vavaser ¹ ought to come, and &c.

Chevage ² Wᵐ and Alan sons of Wᵐ Thore of Ingoldmels, John iij⁸ Amyson of Brynkhyl, are bond tenants of the lord, of which each gives for chevage &c.

> Sum v⁸ ij⁴.
> Also of chevage iij⁸.

Court held at Ingoldmels 13ᵗʰ Nov., year as above [A.D. 1443].

Mercy John Boston of Newarke for tenements in Dunham (and 9 ij⁸ ij⁴ others) ought to come &c.

> Sum ij⁸ iiij⁴.

Court held at Skegnes 4ᵗʰ Dec., year as above [A.D. 1443].

Wᵐ West, John Godard, Roger Chapman, and John Couper, bailiff, took of the lord the fishing at ' les Gotys ' in Ingoldmels, and upon ' les Sandys ' at Ingoldmels, and Skegnes, from Michaelmas next to the end of 10 years, rendering therefore yearly to the lord, his heirs or assigns, xiij⁸ iiij⁴.

> Sum ij⁸.

Court held at Ingoldmels on Wednesday next after the Feast of S. Hilary, year as above [15 January A.D. 1443-4].

> Sum xxij⁴.

Court held at Burgh on Wednesday after the Purification, year as above [5 February A.D. 1443-4].

> Sum xvj⁴.

Court held at Skegnes vijᵗʰ March, 22 H. VI. [A.D. 1443-4].

Fine viij⁴ John Couper &c. surrenders the moiety of 1 acre in Ingold-

---

¹ Eleven others.   ² Six others.

mels to the use of Robert Gunne and John Randson, which he
lately had, with other lands, of the surrender of Wᵐ Ravyn
of Wynthorp, and John Perisson of ffryskenay, formerly John
Pullayn's &c.

Sum ijˢ ijᵈ.

Court held at Skegnes 20ᵗʰ March, 22 H. VI. [A.D. 1443–4].

Sum xiiijᵈ.

Court held at Skegnes 8ᵗʰ April, year as above [A.D. 1444].

Sum xvjᵈ.

View of Frankpledge with Great Court of (same) 12ᵗʰ May,
22 H. VI. [A.D. 1444].
  Great Inquisition.
  Second Inquisition.
  The jurors upon the 2ⁿᵈ inquisition present that Wᵐ Nevel,   Mercy ijˢ
son of John Nevel, and Thomas son of Robert Jhoneson came
into the close of the sᵈ John Nevel at Ingoldmels in the month
of Decʳ last, and there took, and without licence carried off
1 ewe of Wᵐ Ladde of Mumby, therefore &c.
  Also that the prior of Bolyngton has not repaired a bridge   Pain
at Wynthorp, called Welebryg, as was ordered before this court iijˢ iiijᵈ
under a penalty of xlᵈ, therefore let the penalty be levied, and
nevertheless it is ordered that it be repaired before the next
View under a penalty of vjˢ viijᵈ.
  Also that the wife of Robert Jhoneson (and 2 others) refused   Mercy xᵈ
to allow the tasters of beer to come, and taste their beer, therefore &c.
  Also they present 1 empty pipe coming up of wreck of the   Wreck
sea upon the fee of the lord at Ingoldmels, worth 8ᵈ, in the   viijᵈ
custody of Wᵐ Thore.
  Also they present that Wᵐ Ravyn of Wynthorp, Thomas   Respited
Tothoth of same, (and 2 others) made a certain trench upon the to the
soil and fee of the lord at Jngoldmels, viz. between a certain common
gutter there, called Standum Gote, and Castelland Gote, with- council
out licence, to the grave damage of the lord, and his tenants,
as well of Ingoldmels as of Skegnes, and they hold the said
gutters open, so that the sea water comes, and flows on the
pasture of the lord, and his tenants aforesaid, because they

keep thus open the s^d gutter of Castelland Gote, therefore they are in mercy.

The jurors upon the great inquisition affirm all the above presentments, and further present that Agnes Hyltoft, late the wife of Wm Hyltoft, who held of the lord at Ingoldmels 7 acres **Fealty** of free land for the term of her life of the gift and feoffment of the s^d Wm Hiltoft, the reversion thereof belonging to John Hyltoft son of the s^d W^m and Agnes, (is dead), and the s^d tenements are held by knight service, suit of court, and the rent of 7½^d, and thereupon he did fealty.

Mercy iij^s iiij^d Also that Thomas Gysyl of Waynflete entered the warren of the lord at Skegnes, and there killed and carried off rabbits, therefore &c.

Ingoldmels. View of Frankpledge with court of the lord king Henry VII. of his manor aforesaid, parcel of his Duchy of Lancaster, held there 16th Oct. in the 8th year of the s^d king [A.D. 1492].

Great Inquisition.

John Massyngberde.	Robert Pelson.	John Hadike.
Robert Smyth.	John Westend.	John Nevile.
Robert Everard.	Robert Goshauk.	John Temper.
Robert Edlyngson.	John West.	Walter Chelys.

Second Inquisition.

Wm Skegneys.	Robert Cob.	Richard Thory.
John Randson.	Robert Scalflete.	Wm Skegneys.
Wm Thory.	Richard Grynne.	Thomas Jakson.
Robert Dodik.	Simon Cobbe.	Robert Godard.
Robert Thory.	Robert Thory jun^r.	Simon Thory,

Mercy vij^s j^d who say upon their oath that Simon Ruston, Thomas Rigge, Philip Kyme, Dionisius Peticlerk, John Babyngton knt., Thomas Gipthorp, Robert Tailboys knt., John ffoulestow, the Lady Wilughby, the Lady Joan Holand, Henry Vavasor knt., the abbot of Louth Park, John Gigor clerk, Katherine Bolles, Robert Cracroft [1] ought to come, and have not &c.

Mercy vj^d Also that Richard Pynder made trespass with his pigs in the meles, and John Gisell likewise, therefore &c.

Mercy xij^d Also that Beatrice Dodik, a bondwoman of the lord, has been deflowered by Henry Thory, therefore she is in mercy:

[1] And 25 others.

and nevertheless it is ordered to levy . . . from the s^d Beatrice for ' le lethirwhite.'

The great inquisition comes, and affirms all the above presentments, and further presents that Thomas Bonde unjustly occupied land of the lord.

To this court came Alice Raven, and asked to be admitted   Fine ij^s to the reversion of 2 acres in Ingoldmels &c.

Sum xj^s vij^d.

Court held 17th Oct., year as above [A.D. 1492].

Lady Agnes Skipwith, John Mares, Simon Ruston, Thomas   Fines for Whetcroft, Gilbert Cokeryngton, Thomas Gunby, Wm May,   suit Richard Grynne &c.   xj^s iiij^d

Sum xj^s iiij^d.

Court held 8th Nov., year as above [A.D. 1492].

The presenters present that Richard Caleflete, chaplain, who   Fine xx^s held of the lord according to the custom of the manor xiij acres in Burgh, is dead, and that Joan Caleflete and Margaret Cracroft are sisters of the s^d Rich^d, and his next heirs to the s^d tenements, therefore it is ordered to seize into the hands of the lord, until &c.: and upon this come the same Joan and Margaret, and ask to be admitted &c.: to whom the lord grants seisin thereof, to have to them, and their heirs and assigns, in bondage according to the custom of the manor for ever, by all rents, customs, and services, therefore before due &c. Also that, whereas Richard Grenne, who held of the lord all those lands, tenements, reversions, and services, and the reversion of ten^s for a term of life or of years, which lately were John Grenne's in Wrangle, ffriskeney, and Kirkeby next Bolyngbroke for the term of his life, except 2 crofts in Kirkeby, called Northcroft and Engecroft, is dead: and that Etheldrea, daughter and heir of Ralph Grynne, son of Richard Grynne, son of the s^d John Grynne, is the next heir &c.: which same Etheldrea, and Richard Skepper, her husband, came to the present court, and asked to be admitted to all the s^d lands &c., to whom the lord granted seisin, to have &c., to them and the   Fine x^{li} heirs of their bodies according to the custom of the manor, (in default remainder to) right heirs of the s^d Etheldrea according to the custom of the manor by all rents, customs, and services therefore before due &c.

Court held 30th Nov., year as above [A.D. 1492].

Fine iij[s]   [1] Robert Clay, vicar of ffriskeney, and John Randson, sen[r], surrender 3 acres in Ingoldmells Ardilthorp, parcel of the land of John Godard, to the use of Thomas Jakson, and upon this &c.

Fine
vj[s] viij[d]   The presenters present that John Godknap, who held of the lord by the law of England 7 acres in Ingoldmels, is dead: and that W[m] Godknap is son and next heir &c.

Sum xviij[s] viij[d].

Court held 21st Dec., year as above [A.D. 1492].

Sum xij[d].

Court held 3rd Jan., year as above [A.D. 1492–3].

Sum vj[d].

Court held 27th Jan., year as above [A.D. 1492–3].

Sum vj[d].

Court held 16th Feb., year as above [A.D. 1492–3].

Sum iiij[d].

Court held 16th March, year as above [A.D. 1492–3].

Will of
John
Mares   This is the last will of John Mares of Ingoldmels made there 7th April 7th year of the king: first I will that John Walton of Cumberworth, Robert Wadyngham rector of the church of S. Nicholas of Ingoldmels, Robert Goshauk, and W[m] Boston of the same, have and hold after my death for 2 years 1 messuage, and 30 acres, called Lambhous, in Ingoldmels Ardilthorp to the intent to maintain and provide for my boys, and for the expenses of my burial, and to pay the debts of me the s[d] John (remainder to my right heirs). These are the witnesses, W[m]
Fine lx[s]   Croft in the name of the grave, W[m] Skegneys, sen[r], Robert Thory, sen[r], W[m] Thory, Robert Thory, jun[r], and Robert Cob.

Sum lxj[s] ij[d].

View of Frankpledge with Court of the s[d] lord king held vj[th] May, year as above [A.D. 1493].
Great Inquisition.
Second Inquisition.

[1] Mention of Richard Quaderyng.

To this court came Wm Thory, son of John, and asked to be admitted to 15½ acres in Ingoldmells Ardilthorp, which John Bough lately held by the law of England by reason of issue begotten between him and Katherine his wife, and it is testified here in this court that the said William is the true heir according to the custom of the manor, because John and Katherine died without issue [surviving].[1]

Fine xiij^s iiij^d

Sum xxxvij^s ij^d.

Court held 17th May, year as above [A.D. 1493].

Sum vj^d.

Court held — June, in 8th year [A.D. 1493].

Sum viij^s.

Court held 29th July, year as above [A.D. 1493].

The presenters present that John Scalflete made trespass in keeping mares within the lordship contrary to the custom of the vill, therefore he is in mercy.

Mercy xij^d

Sum xvj^d.

Court held 18th August, year as below [A.D. 1493].

John Bartilmew of Leicester, attorney of Wm Mariot, surrenders 2 acres in Ingoldmels to the use of Simon Thory &c.

Fine iiij^s

Sum iiij^s ij^d.

Court held 12th Sept., 9 H. VII. [A.D. 1493].

To this court came Margaret Cracroft, late the wife of John Cracroft, and asked to be admitted to x acres of pasture in Ingoldmels and xiij acres of land in Burgh, which the same John assigned to her for the term of her life by his last will, made according to the custom of the manor: to whom the lord granted seisin thereof, to have to her, and her assigns, according to the custom of the manor by all rents, customs, and services therefrom before due &c.

Fine lx^s

Sum lx^s.

View of Frank Pledge with Great Michaelmas Court held on the last day of Sept. 9 Eliz. [A.D. 1567], in the name of John Tamworth, esq^r, farmer of the s^d manor, of the assignment of Wm Dodyngton, gent., who held of the assignment of Lady

Ingold-mells Aydel-thorp

---

[1] He is admitted.

parcel of the Duchy of Lancaster

Katherine Knolles, wife of Francis Knolles, knt., and of Prudence Deynton, to whom the lady the Queen by letters patent under the seal of her Duchy of Lancaster, 18th June, 8 ^h Eliz., demised the manor.

Great Inquisition

Francis Craycroft gent.
Robert Wolby.
Anthony Weselhed.
Robert Rutter jur'.
Thomas Newcome jur'.

(27 names)
17 sworn.

Inquisition of bond tenants

Thomas Backster sen^r jur'.   Anthony Oreby jur'.
Thomas Backster jun.   John Oreby jur'.
Henry Backster.   Thomas Oreby jur'.
Wm Backster jur'.   Wm Skegnes.
John Backster sen^r.   Richard Thory of Hotoft.
John Backster jun^r.

Information

To this court comes John Elryck, and gives the court to understand, that Richard Cock of Boston entered upon — acres of pasture in Wynthorp, which the s^d John Elryck affirms to be customary land, and parcel of this manor, and that Wm Elryck his father was seised in his demesne as of fee by copy of court roll according to the custom of the s^d manor, and died seised, and that Robert Elryck was his son, and next heir thereof, and was admitted &c., and died seised, and that one John Elryck was his son, and next heir, and entered, and sold the premises, as his free lands by the form of the common law of this kingdom, and not according to the custom of the s^d manor, and now the s^d Richard Cock comes to this court, and was not able to produce any evidence, w^h testified that the s^d lands were free, therefore let them be taken into the hands of the Queen, until &c., saving the right of every one, and further it is ordered the s^d Richard Cock that he permit John Elryck, and his assigns peacefully to occupy the s^d premises, until he produce evidence to prove his right in them, under the penalty of the forfeiture of x^{li}.

Surrender

Leonard Kyrckman and Gartrude his wife surrender 2 messuages 57½ acres in Ingoldmells Aydelthorp to the use of John Laund, who asks to be admitted, to whom the lady by her chief steward, John Dyon, grants seisin thereof, to have to him, his heirs and assigns for ever according to the custom &c. by the rents, burdens, customs, and services, therefore before due &c.

Fine cxv^s

At this court it is testified by the tenants that John Kyrck-man, one of the sons of John Kyrckman, deceased, is 21, and (he) asks to be admitted to a tenement called Spencer garth, and xv acres pasture, (and other lands). Fine
lxxviij^s

The aforesaid jurors come, and affirm that the testimony above is in all things true, and further they present Francis Craycroft to the office of grave: and further say that John Oresby, a customary tenant, was seised of 1 messuage and 26 acres 3 roods, and surrendered (them) to the use of Helen his wife, and John Stevenson, for 2 years after his death, to pay his debts, and funeral expenses, after which term to the use of Helen for xviij years, to educate their children, and pay them viij^{li} according to the tenour of his will, and the s^d jurors say that the s^d John died 8th August last, and that Robert Oresby is his son and heir, and is of the age of 2 years.

Thomas Thory of Boston surrenders 2 acres in Ingoldmells Aydelthorp to the use of Nicholas Thorp &c.

Who say upon their oath that John Lord Sheffeld, Wm Skypwyth knt., Richard Barty in right of the Lady Katherine Duchess of Suffolk his wife, Nicholas Thorp, the heirs of Wm Vavasour knt., Wm Craycrofte gent., the heirs of James Pack, Thomas ffuller esq^r for lands late Rygg's, the heirs of Thomas Greene, Wm Manby esq^r, John Kyme of Styckforth by right of his wife, John Langton jun^r, gent., by right of his wife, Edmund Wythypoll esq^r, Robert Craycroft, John Skypwyth, &c.[1] Verdict of
12 jurors

And that Thomas Pynder (and 6 others) are residents, and ought to come, and have not, therefore &c.

And that Margaret Dyckson, Ralph Baggot, (and 12 others) were summoned to be before the steward, assigned to execute the statute of labourers, and have made default, therefore &c.

And that 4 sheep, viz. 2 white wethers, one ewe, and one white hogg, of which 3, viz. 2 wethers and the hogg, came as estrays within this manor 1 May last, and the ewe came as estray 1 June last, (are) in the hand of John Hogland.

It is ordained by the court that John Hogland well and sufficiently repair the pound of the lady before S. Martin's day, under the penalty of the forfeiture of x^s: and that Thomas Thory repair &c. the pound at le Seadyk, and mend the dike there under the penalty of ij^s for each default. Pain

----

[1] Fifty-four in all.

[1] And that Richard Dyckson assaulted Robert Richardson, the pinder there, and rescued lx sheep, which Robert took as doing damage in the s[d] fee, and was taking to the pound, therefore &c. : and that the same Richard Dyckson permitted his pigs to upturn the pasture of his neighbours, therefore &c.

And now comes the jury of bond tenants and presents that W[m] Walpole is a trespasser in depasturing the gaytes with his beasts, therefore &c. : and that [2] Thomas Backster, a bond tenant of the lady, dwells without this lordship, viz. at Slothby, and gives of chevage &c. : and that Anthony [3] Oreby dwells within this lordship, and has issue, Bartholomew and John, sons, Alice and Mary, daughters : [4] W[m] Skegnes dwells at Strubby and has no issue : and Agnes Skegnes daughter of James Skegnes, a bond tenant, dwells without this fee, viz. at Bolingbrooke, viz. with John Mann esq[r], and is of age, therefore it is ordered the bailiff to bring the body of the s[d] Agnes to the use of the Queen.

*Present-
ments of
natives*

*Ingold-
mells cum
Aydel-
thorp*
Court of pleas of the lady the Queen and of 3 weeks to 3 weeks held 12th July, 10 Eliz., John Tamworth esq[r] being farmer of the s[d] manor [A.D. 1568].

*Ingold-
mells cum
Aydel-
thorp*
Court of pleas of the lady the Queen, and of 3 weeks to 3 weeks, held on Friday — August, 10 Eliz., John Tamworth esq[r] being farmer of the s[d] manor [A.D. 1568].

W[m] Skegnes, son of James Skegnes, a bond tenant of the lord, is sworn to declare by what ways, means, and manners Agnes ——, dwelling with John Mann esq[r], was abducted, by whom, and to what places, who says that the s[d] Agnes —— was taken from the service of the s[d] John Mann to the vill of Halton, and the s[d] William, knowing that the said Agnes was [at Halton], went to her, and questioned her why she fled from her s[d] master, who said that he (said) that if she did not marry

---

[1] A case of bloodshed, of fishing in the separate ponds of neighbours, of common trespassers depasturing the common ways with their beasts, and several persons keep mares against the custom of the manor. A case of breaking the assize of beer. Two tasters of beer and 2 constables elected.

[2] Four others.

[3] John Oreby has a son. John Skegnes has no issue. John Backster has 1 son 2 d[s].

[4] Four others.

Oliver his servant he w^d detain her in prison for as long as she lived.

Thomas Stutt complains of Thomas Holtby that he 11th July 9 Eliz. within the jurisdiction of this court, trying to deprive the said plaintiff of his good reputation and name, uttered these English words of the s^d plaintiff, viz. 'Thou art a theef, and a villayn, and a blood—' by which the plaintiff says he was damaged : and the defendant comes, and defends &c., and says he is not guilty, and of this he puts himself upon xij, and the plaintiff likewise, so &c. And afterwards at the next view held the jury of the great inquisition being charged therein by assent say that the s^d Thomas Holtby is guilty (fine for uttering scandalous words 16^s, and costs 2^s 6^d).

View of Frank Pledge with Great Michaelmas Court of the most illustrious Princess the lady Elizabeth by God's grace Queen of England France and Ireland, Defender of the faith &c., held there on Thursday the last day of Septr in the 10th year of her reign : John Tamworth esq^r, farmer of the s^d manor, John Dyon esq^r, chief steward [A.D. 1568].

Ingold-mells cum Aydyl-thorp

Richard Hyltoft esq^r	Thomas Thory jun^r jur'	*Inquisi-tion for the lady the Queen*[1]
John Launde	William Walpolle jur'	
Thomas Newcome jur'	William Hypwell jur'	
Anthony Orby jur'	Henry Backster jur'	*Inquisi-tion of bond tenants*
John Orby jur'	John Backster sen^r jur'	
Thomas Backster sen^r jur'	William Skegnes jur'	

Christopher Crofte complains of Robert Westorn of a plea of debt &c., the def^t admits the s^d debt (5^s 11^d), therefore it is granted by the court that he recover &c.   *Mercy iiij^d*

The bailiff testifies that he distrained Leonard Temper by 2 mares, so that he be at this court to answer to John Hareby in a plea of detention, and to Robert Rutter (and another) in pleas of debt, and (he) has not come, therefore it is granted by the court that (he) forfeit the said mares, if he has nothing to say why he was not able to appear, and afterwards he appeared, and they are remitted to him out of grace.   *Deposition of the ba..ilf*

The bailiff testifies that he took into the hands of the Queen 15 acres of customary meadow and pasture in Burgh-in-the-Marsh in the tenure of Robert Craycroft gent.,[2] and now come

---

[1] 19 names, 16 sworn.   [2] So also with 2 other tenements.

U

Robert Craycroft, and Anthony Mawer, and ask that the hands
of the Queen be removed from the tenements now in their
tenures, and produced in court their copies thereof, which the
Queen by the steward of the court allowed, and they asked that
the sd lands mt be delivered to them, together with the issues
from the time of seizure, and therefore it is ordered the bailiff
that he remove his hand therefrom &c.

Exoneration on showing evidence

At this court the jurors, viz. (names), were charged to inquire
concerning an easement of a way, which Thomas Stutt claimed
to have, appendant to his customary messuage in Ingoldmells,
who say, as after shall appear in this court.

Charles Totofte esqr, son and heir of Anthony Totofte, gives
for fine for common suit released.

And further at the court of 3 weeks to 3 weeks held
20 August 10 Eliz. (Elizabeth Owresby wife of Thomas Owresby
and widow of Simon Luddyngton was assigned her dower
4½ᵃ pasture in Wynthorp, in a certain pasture on the west part
of the close, called Sleyghte lease &c., to have for her life).

A day is given to the jurors of the great inquisition to return
their verdict upon the articles of the leet at the next court of
3 weeks to 3 to be held here under a penalty to each making
default of 5ˢ, and that meanwhile they assemble in the church
of the East Church of Ingoldmell on the 14th day of this month
under the sd penalty: and the same day is given to the jurors
of bond tenants to return their verdict under sd penalty.

Fine xvjˢ

Thomas Luddyngton, son and heir of Simon Luddyngton
&c., is admitted to 8 acres pasture in Ingoldmells.

Fine xxixˢ

Thomas Wyllerton and Agnes his wife, daughter and heir of
Wm Thory, took out of the hands of the lady 1 messuage,
7 acres 1 rood in Aydylthorp, which Wm Thory, father of Agnes,
held by copy of court roll according to the custom &c., to him
and his heirs, and which were forfeited because Agnes did not
come within a year and a day after the death of the sd Wm to
take the premises, to whom the Queen by her steward granted
seisin &c.[1]

The jurors of the native inquisition present that John

. . . Vavasour, George Portington gent. and Anthony Portington gent. for lands late Pack's, Thomas ffuller esq^r for lands late Rygg's, Leonard Irby esq^r, John Langton jun^r, gent., for land late Palmer by right of his wife, Wm Manby esq^r, John Kyme of Styckforth gent. for lands late Salter, Edmund Wythypole esq^r for lands in Momby are free tenants, and ought to come &c.: and that John Langton, jun^r, by right of his wife, the heirs of Thomas Greene, John Kyrckman, tenants by copy, ought to come &c.: and that Richard Thory, a bond tenant of the lady, dwelling at Hotoft, Thomas Backster jun^r, a bond tenant, John Backster jun^r dwelling at Ingoldmells on land of Peter Greenwyck, and Thomas Orby, a bond tenant, have made default at this day, therefore &c. Further they present that Thomas Holtby (and another) have trespassed in collecting rushes and 'syles' [? sines], growing upon the meales, therefore &c.

The jurors of the great inquisition come, and affirm all the above presentments, and further present that John Hogland (and another) are common trespassers in cutting 'cirpos Anglice seynes' in the meales, therefore &c.: also that Roger Bancrofte (and another) are common trespassers on the banks of the sea, called 'seadyks,' with their horses, to the grave damage of the neighbours &c.[1]

To this court come Thomas Stutt of the one part, and Nicholas Thorp and Thomas ffarro of the other, and because a controversy and strife was moved between (them) concerning an easement of a certain way, which the s^d Thomas claims to have appendant to his customary messuage in Ingoldmells unto the Queen's way, upon this the aforesaid tenants of the manor are charged to enquire of the s^d easement, and to present the certitude thereof: the said parties agreed together that the same Thomas has easement for his carriages with waggon only from his mansion house by the bank of the sea, Anglice 'the seadyke banck,' in and across a pasture close, called Kyme platts &c., to have, and to enjoy the s^d easement of way to him, his heirs and assigns, as appendant to his s^d messuage for ever, between the Feast of the Nativity of S. John Baptist, and the Feast of S. Michael yearly &c., and besides that the same Thomas shall repair at his own cost one 'le clowte' between him and the close in the tenure of Robert Hunter, and likewise shall repair

---

[1] Assize of beer and bread.

one 'le clowte' between ' Isball landes ' and the lands of Nicholas Thorp for ever.

And further the same jurors, viz. (names), say that Leonard Kyrckman, who holds by copy of court roll 8 acres in Aydylthorp, demised them to farm to &c., for a term of 4 years without a surrender &c., for which they are forfeited.

Court of pleas, and of 3 weeks to 3 of the Lady Elizabeth held 10th January in the 11th year of her reign [A.D. 1568-9].

Mercy iiij^d   Wm Skypwyth knt. by his attorney complains against William Walpolle of a plea of trespass &c. The same plaintiff says that the s^d def^t, 16th Sept. 10 Eliz., broke, and entered his close at Aydylthorp, within the jurisdiction of this court, and depastured &c. his herbage there with 100 sheep, continuing the trespass until the 18th of Sept., to the damage of the s^d plaintiff xxxix^s x^d, and therein he produces suit : the def^t comes, and defends force, and injury, and says that he is guilty of the trespass, but not to the damage aforesaid, and of this he .puts himself upon 12, and the s^d plaintiff likewise, therefore &c., and afterwards the damages of the s^d trespass are assessed at xiiij^s, and expenses xij^d.

Mercy iij^d   John Hypwell v. Wm Walpolle of a plea of trespass : says that he assaulted him at Ingoldmells Aydylthorp within the jurisdiction of this court, he being then constable of east Ingold-mells, and beat him &c. : the xij say that the defendant is guilty, and assess the damages at viij^s.

Fine xxj^s   Thomas Thory of Boston and Anna his wife surrender 10¼ acres in Ingoldmells to the use of Robert Bough.

Court of pleas &c. held 15th March, 11 Eliz. [A.D. 1568-9].

Robert Rutter v. Leonard Temper. The plaintiff says that, as grave, he ought to collect all rents, and profits of the manor, and in time of his office he took beasts of the defendant in the name of distraint for his rent, viz. xxij^d in arrear, and the defendant undertook to pay the s^d xxij^d with ij^d for expenses in taking the distraint, and has not paid to the damage of ij^s vj^d &c. The defendant says that he undertook to pay ij^s, and paid ij^s, and he does not wish to plead another plea, therefore for the insufficient plea the s^d plaintiff shall recover the said sum together with the costs.[1]

---

[1] John Hareby recovers xix^d v. Thomas Newcome for a levy on the inhabitants of the lordship of 1^d per acre to clean out the sewers, he being guardian of the dikes and sewers.

The bailiff is ordered to seize all the lands of Thomas Backster sen[r], a bond tenant of the lady, regardant to the s manor, and to answer to (her) for the issues therefrom under the penalty of xx[s], and afterwards (he) is ordered to remove his hands therefrom.

W[m] Stevenson entered on the soil of W[m] Halle, and made an affray, and drew blood &c.

And [they say] that Roger Bancrofte is a common trespasser on the sea bank, called 'le seadyk,' through the whole winter, to the grave damage of the tenants of this fee, and against the custom, therefore &c.

And further they say that Robert Rutter, and Thomas Farrow, tenants by custom of this manor, prosecuted divers customary tenants of this fee, viz. Thomas Stutt and John Hareby, guardians of the dikes, called Dykegraves, before W[m] Skypwyth knt., for matters touching the common sewers within the jurisdiction of this court, contrary to the liberties and franchise of this manor, therefore let consultation be had with the council of the lord.[1]

A pain is put upon all tenants and inhabitants of this fee that none &c. put or permit any horses, or other animals, or cattle, to pasture upon the banks of the sea, called the seadykes, nor keep any mares to pasture at large within this lordship and outside houses &c.

W[m] Skegnes, son and next heir of James S., admitted to 9½ acres in Ingoldmels.

Court of pleas &c. 2 May, 11 Eliz. [A.D. 1569].

W[m] Craycrofte gent. and Susan his wife surrender 1 messuage and 32 acres in Ingoldmells Aydylthorp, formerly Richard Craycrofte's esq[r], to the use of John Waddingham &c.

Rent
xxj[s] iiij[d]
Fine lxiiij[s]

At this court the jurors of the inquisition of bond tenants certify a true inventory of all the goods and chattels, which were in the custody of John Orby, a bond tenant of the lady to this manor regardant, while he lived, which goods &c. were appraised by Anthony Weselhed, Robert Rutter, Thomas Newcome, and James Crake, sworn to this: and upon this the s[d] goods &c. were permitted by the consent of the court to remain

---

[1] Thomas Skegnes of Skendleby died 8 years past seised of lands in ffyrsby held according to the custom of the manor, and no one has come to take them, and Richard Hyltoft esq[r] has taken the profits : the bailiff to seize.

in the custody of Elizabeth Orby, relict of the s^d deceased, at the will of the lady the Queen. A part of which inventory remains with the court, the other with the s^d Elizabeth.

Court of Pleas &c. 11th July, 11 Eliz. [A.D. 1569].

To this court came William Skegnes, as well in his own name as in that of Elizabeth Skegnes his sister, and produced into court letters patent of the Queen under the seal of her Duchy of Lancaster &c., by which the s^d Queen of her certain knowledge and mere motion manumitted and freed from all yoke of servitude the same W^m and Elizabeth, and their sequels, of which letters the tenour follows in these words (omitted).

To this court came Elizabeth Orby, relict of John Orby &c., and gives of fine for the administration of the goods (as per schedule) xl^s, and administration is granted &c. to her, and Robert Orby son of the s^d deceased.

Court of Pleas &c. 1 August, 11 Elizabeth [A.D. 1569].

[1] The jurors of the last court of pleas, and of 3 weeks to 3 weeks, who had a day to return the residue of their verdict upon the matters and articles &c., say that the custom of the s^d manor is, and from time immemorial has been, that it is not lawful for any tenant by the custom of this manor to implead or make complaint against any other person holding of the lady the Queen, within this manor or lordship, for any matter, or cause, arising within the lordship which could be determined in the court of the same manor, outside the court of the manor aforesaid, under the penalty of amercement, and that Robert Rutter, Nicholas Thorp, (and 4 others), tenants of the lady by custom of this manor, moved law suits and complaints against Thomas Stutt, a tenant of the lady, concerning matters which belong and pertain to the common sewers, or sea banks of this manor, and concerning matters

liberties of the s^d manor, and against the custom of the same manor.[1]

And further they say that a certain iron war engine or a chamber of a gonne, weighing six stone of iron, to the value of vj^s viij^d, was found within the s^d manor, as wreck of the sea, by John Weselhed, Francis Craycrofte gent., (and 2 others), and it is directed them to produce the s^d engine in court under pain of forfeiture of the moiety of the profit thereof.

Court of pleas &c. 22 August, 11 Eliz. [A.D. 1569].[2]

Court of pleas &c. 19th Sept., 11 Eliz. [A.D. 1569].

A pain is put upon all tenants of the s^d manor, that each of them this side of the next court of view assemble on Wednesday the Vigil of S. Michael next at Skegnes meales within the jurisdiction of this court, and inquire, who made waste and destruction of the brambles and thorns, growing at Skegnes meales, and also of the rabbits there, and certify at the next court their verdict thereof under the pain to each of them in default iij^s iiij^d.

View of Frank Pledge with Great Michaelmas Court of our lady Elizabeth by God's grace Queen of England France and Ireland by reason of her Duchy of Lancaster held 10 Oct. in the 20th year of her reign [A.D. 1578].

John Kyrkeman gent.	Great Inquisition
John Kyme gent.	
Anthony Weslehed.	
Thomas Newcome. (16).	

Laurence Baxter. John Baxster sen^r.

They say that Edmund Tothbye, (and another), made an affray upon Francis Ranson, therefore &c.

And that Thomas Motley trespassed in 'le sedyke,' therefore &c.[3]

Inquisition of bond tenants

Mercy xx^s

Mercy xij^d

---

[1] 2 persons fined x^s for cutting thorns on Skegnes meales to the damage and disinheritance of the lady.

[2] Valentine Browne esq^r for lands late Skalflett, a free tenant.

[3] I omit the conveyancing entries: the form is now 'to have &c. to him and his heirs and assigns for ever of the lady the Queen by the rod at the will of the s^d lady according to the custom of the manor by the ancient rents and services before therefrom due and of right accustomed.'

INDEX

Brock, Matilda, 80
— Walter, 14, 124
Broghton, John de, 159, 160, 161
Broune, Brun, Joan, 273
— John, 1, 273
— Thomas, 23
— Walter, 38
— William, 23
Browne, Valentine, 295 n.
Brunham. *See* Burnham
Brygge, Richard, 238, 255
Bryghtsance, Robert, 263
Bryteson, Agnes, 213
Brytte, Alice, 264
— John, 264
Budde, William, 103, 104
Bug, Bugge, Agnes, 24, 25
— Alan, 6, 7, 9, 19, 25, 79, 80, 105
— Beatrice, 140
— John, 163
— Matilda, 25
— Ralph, 167
— Ranulph, 157, 161, 171, 180, 204
— Robert, 5, 25, 99, 126, 128
— Roger, 116, 124, 126, 128
— Walter, 6, 10, 24, 25
— William, 80, 99, 111, 116, 121, 163
Bugland, 243
Bulhed, William, 216
Bullington, Bolington, the prior of, 36, 37, 44, 45, 46, 83, 84, 95, 96, 97, 106, 110, 113, 136, 147, 155, 156, 159, 160, 161, 190, 200, 211, 238, 244, 254, 255, 261, 262, 280, xvii
— Stephen, cellarer of, 238
Bungidayle, 128, 129
Bunt, Joan, 196, 267
— John, 271
— Walter, 196
Buntyng, John, 165
Burgh, 54, 78, 79, 91, 102, 121, 170, 182, 183, 212, 228, 237, 238, ix, x, xiv, xx
— Churchyard of St. Peter of, 14
— common of, 44, 45, 46
— fields of, 276
— north field of, 245
— presentment of, 34
— sewer at, 255
— vicar of, 255
— Alan de, 151
— Alice de, 2
— Bernard de, 1, 14, 24, 46
— Hugh, son of Roger de, 44
— John de, 190, 193, 209, 220, 222 n., 235, 236, 239, 251, 253, 267
— Juliana, 267
— Maria de, 151
— Matilda de, 37, 121
— Richard de, 83

Burgh, Sarah de, 46
— Simon de, 239
— Walter de, 150
— William de, 37, 42, 71, 107
Burnham, Brunham, Thomas de, 9, 16, 19, xx
Burtoft, John de, 130, 136, 171
— Peter de, 17, 77, 87
— William de, 124
Burton, John de, 163, 164, 171, 244, 254
— Ralph de, 111, 213, 214, 222 n., 223 n.
Bussell, the lord's, 260
Buttercake, Butyrkake, Joan, 208, 210
— William, 206, 208, 210, 215, 216, 217 n., 221, 227, 228, 230, 239, 243, 245, 249, 254
Buxhous, 274
Byrk, John, 229

Cadenay, Alice de, 52
— Robert de, 52
Cadyhorn, John, 124
— William, 22, 34, 44, 46, 70, 103, 104, xxi
Cadyhornbrig, 140
Cage, Margaret, 152
Cagoke, Cageok, John, 196, 202
— Thomas, 66
Calceby, Henry, vicar of 39
Caleflete, Caldeflet, Joan, 283
— John de, 152
— Richard, 283
— Robert de, 78, 124, 125, 127, xxi
— Walter de, 78, 86
— William de, 77, 78, 79, 81, 87, 124, 125, 127, 222 n., 228, 238, 251
· Calodes, Richard, 44
Camera, Norman de, xxii
Camilla, 32, 60
Candilesby, John de, 222
Candlesby, bailiff of, 57, 58, 61
— fee of, 136
Candleshoe, bailiff of, 260
Canterbury, Archbishop of, 254, 257
Cantilupe, Cauntelu, George de, xxiii
— Lady Joan de, 150, 153
— Milicent de, xxiii
— Nicholas de, 71, 86, 88, 89, 92, 95, 101, 108, 156, 163, 164, 174, 181, 186
— William de, 86, xxiii
Capeltoft, 159
Cardywax, Cardyvax, Cardinaus (? Cardiuaus), Agnes, 185, 205
— Joan, 134
— John, 134, 180, 186, 188, 205
— Walter, 235, 239
— William, 117, 144, 160, 169

Groun, Growne, William, 215, 269
Groundage, 245
Grymeslant, Robert de, 124
Gryn, Grynne, Grene, Greene, Agnes,
197, 201, 202, 205, 224, 227, 232
— Alan, 136, 206, 212, 232, 245, 265
— Alicia, xxx
— Etheldrea, 283
— John 181, 195, 212, 217, 245, 268,
270, 273, 277, 283, xxx
— Ralph, 283
— Richard, 201, 206, 209, 211, 215,
216, 218, 221 n., 223, 227, 229,
235, 239, 240, 244, 245, 254, 261,
264, 270, 273, 277, 282, 283, xxx
— Robert, 136, 184, 211, 223, 245,
255, 265, 271, 273, 279, xxix,
xxx
— Roger, 270
— Thomas, 287, 291
— Walter, 3, 5
— William, 5, 195, 197, 202, 224, 269,
270, 277
Grynnsland, Edmund de, 155
Guardianship, 141
Guldelsmere, ix
Gunby, Alice de, 206
— John de, 115, 129, 136, 163, 164,
168, 181, 190, 198, 199, 206, 214,
216, 225, 228, 253, 257
— Richard, 257
— Thomas, 283
— William de, 199, 206, 253
Gunhous, 276
Gunny, Gunne, Alan, 129, 131, 135
— Alice, 261, 264, 276
— Beatrice, 131
— Isabel, 266
— Joan, 131
— John, 135, 149, 154, 168, 169, 227,
261, 264, 265, 266, 276
— Mary, 263
— Matilda, 131, 265
— Ralph, 5
— Robert, 243, 247, 256, 263, 268,
269, 281
— Simon, 131
— Thomas, 131
— William, 6, 18, 28, 95, 100, 131,
133, 169, 192
Guy, Alan son of, 135
— John son of, 19, 24, 88, 121, 135,
161
— John son of John son of, 112, 149
— Juliana widow of John son of, 112
— Sibill d. of William son of, 71
— Simon son of, 144, 148
Gyliot, Gyllyot, Alan, 277
— Thomas, 277
— William, 261

Gyne, John, 200
Gysyl, Gisell, John, 282
— Thomas, 282

Hackthorn, 106, xxii, xxiv
Haco, William son of, xxii
Hadik, Hauedik, 12
Hadik, Hadyk, Hafdyk, Hafdick,
Hauedik, Agnes atte, 134
— Alan atte, 50, 74, 76, 86, 183
— Beatrice atte, 140
— Joan atte, 278
— John atte, 174, 191, 282
— Richard atte, 142, 164, 174
— Robert atte, 35, 48, 60, 61, 66, 99,
103, 136, 140, 142, 146, 247, 262,
278
— Roger atte, 134, 140
— William atte, 19, 33, 72, 263
Hagh, John de, 175, 228
Halberthorp, Richard son of Philip
de, 128, 129
Halcroft, 226
Halden, Haldan, Haldeyn, Alice, 199
— John, 147, 153, 199
— Roger, 16
Hale, John de, 110, 115, 129, xxvi
— Nicholas de, 108, 136, 144, 153,
156, 163, xxvi
— Simon de, xxvi
— William de, 174
Halfcroft, 226
Halgarth, Hallegarth, Alan atte, or
del, 44, 45, 64, 73, 107, 108, 136, 141,
142, 273
— Alice atte, 108, 126, 146
— Beatrice atte, 113
— Joan atte, 108, 115, 273
— John atte, 199
— Matilda atte, 74
— Ranulph atte, 50, 74
— Richard atte, 140
— Robert atte, 128, 146, 174, 198, 199,
206, 209, 216, 217, 218, 220, 224,
226, 227, 244, 254
— Sarah atte, 115
— Stephen atte, 23, 56
— Walter atte, 50, 69
— William atte, 23, 41, 56, 57, 73, 111,
113, 115, 126, 140, 141, 145, 147,
148, 154
Hall, court of the, 23
— Gilbert atte, 186
— Robert at, 244
— Thomas, 250, 257, 267, 276, 279
Halton, John son of Simon son of
Petronilla, 105, 109, 110, 130, xxi
— Robert, xxii
Hamon, R. fitz, x
Hamound, Beatrice, 217, 232

PRINTED BY
SPOTTISWOODE AND CO. LTD., NEW-STREET SQUARE
LONDON

Y

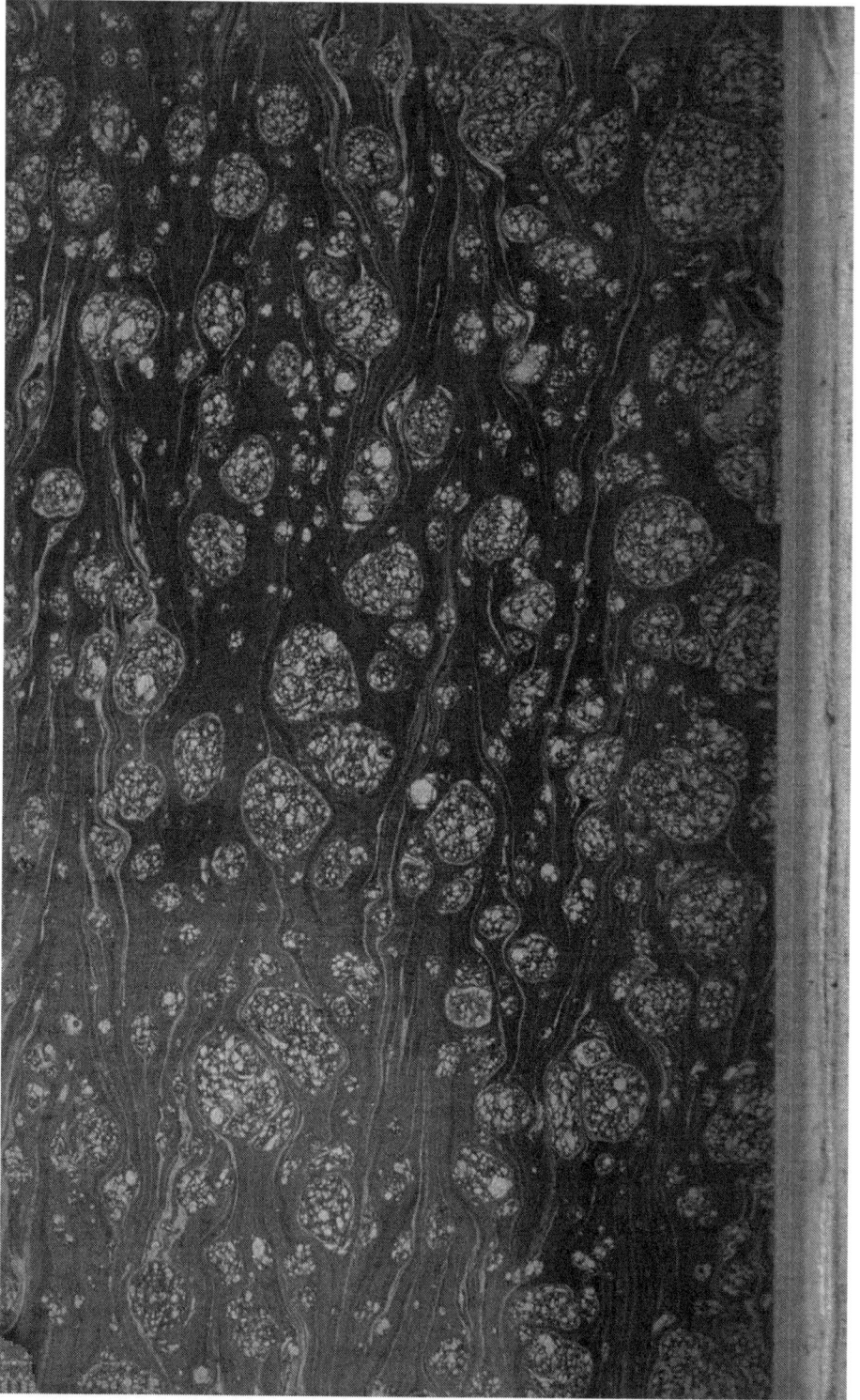

www.ingramcontent.com/pod-product-compliance
Ingram Content Group UK Ltd.
Pitfield, Milton Keynes, MK11 3LW, UK
UKHW021534240125

4287UKWH00046B/636